Jn.L. Mc Creight

HISTORY OF THE
HEBREW COMMONWEALTH

HISTORY OF THE HEBREW COMMONWEALTH

BY

ALBERT EDWARD BAILEY, A.M.

FORMERLY DIRECTOR OF RELIGIOUS EDUCATION IN WORCESTER ACADEMY
PROFESSOR OF FINE ARTS AND DEAN OF THE EVENING AND EXTENSION DIVISION,
BUTLER UNIVERSITY

AND

CHARLES FOSTER KENT, Ph.D., Litt.D.

LATE WOOLSEY PROFESSOR OF BIBLICAL LITERATURE IN YALE UNIVERSITY

REVISED AND ENLARGED EDITION

WITH MAPS AND ILLUSTRATIONS

CHARLES SCRIBNER'S SONS

NEW YORK   CHICAGO   BOSTON   ATLANTA
SAN FRANCISCO   DALLAS

of the University of Chicago, who as a representative of the Commission on Standardization of Bible Courses for Secondary Schools, has read the proofs of this volume and to the many scholars, authors, and publishers who have generously allowed the use of their photos and photographs in order to make it

PREFACE

No chapter in human history is more thrilling than that which records the long struggle of the Hebrews for independence, for a home, for power, for their religious and social ideals and for the perpetuation of their institutions. It begins with their grinding industrial enslavement by Egypt and ends with the heroic though vain effort to break the iron shackles of Rome. In the face of bitter opposition they developed the first democratic state known to history. Through centuries of foreign oppression and persecution they clung to their democratic ideals until at last the whole world is beginning to appreciate and appropriate them.

The aim in this volume is to present the facts that are essential to a clear understanding of the growth and meaning of these ideals and of the matchless literature that records them. The study of each period gathers about the personalities of prophets and patriots like Moses, David, Elijah, Amos, and Nehemiah, who not only represented their age but also largely guided its development. The rich contributions of geography and archæology have been freely drawn upon to make that ancient history vivid and real. For each chapter detailed suggestions are provided for the guidance of teachers of college, secondary school, and intermediate classes, inasmuch as the volume is intended for those who wish to work as well as for the general reader.

The authors are deeply indebted to Professor Ira M. Price

of the University of Chicago, who as a representative of the Commission on Standardization of Bible Courses for Secondary Schools has read the proofs of this volume, and to the many scholars, authors, and publishers who have generously offered the use of their plates and photographs in order to make it possible to produce a thoroughly equipped text-book.

CONTENTS

CONTENTS

ILLUSTRATIONS

ILLUSTRATIONS

MAPS

THE SURVIVING AUTHOR
DEDICATES THIS REVISED EDITION
TO HIS SON
CHARLES EDWARD BAILEY
WHO AT THE AGE OF TEN TRAVELLED
THROUGH THE BIBLE LANDS WITH HIS
FATHER AND ESTABLISHED A LIFELONG
ENTHUSIASM

WHO WAS WHO IN THE XVIII DYNASTY

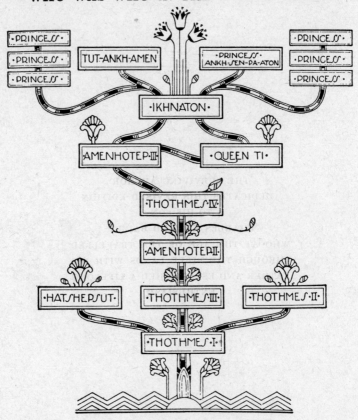

Fɪɢ. 22—THE EIGHTEENTH DYNASTY

The family "tree" began actually with Ahmose (1580–1557 B.C.) not here shown; but the first name of consequence to the Hebrews is Thothmes I (Thutmose), pharaoh from about 1535 B.C. With him the enslavement of the Hebrews begins (Exodus 1). His favorite daughter Hatshepsut (left) adopts the infant Moses. She and her two brothers, Thothmes III and II (centre and right) are involved in the family feud that engendered such hatreds (see Fig. 17). Thothmes III emerges as the great oppressor. His son, Amenhotep II, is the erratic pharaoh of the exodus. Thothmes IV is the unexpected pharaoh. With Amenhotep III and his queen, Ti, we see the beginnings of the humanizing policy that produced Ikhnaton, reformer and pacifist, because of whose relaxed grip on Asia Joshua was able to penetrate Palestine. The dynasty ends with the boy-pharaoh, Tut-ankh-amen, who married one of his seven half-sisters.

HISTORY OF THE
HEBREW COMMONWEALTH

I

THE WORLD IN WHICH THE HEBREWS LIVED

1. **Extent of the Hebrew World.** The boundaries of that part of the earth's surface in which the stirring drama of Hebrew history unfolded were not hard and fast. In the early periods the Hebrews were almost entirely ignorant of lands beyond Palestine; but as they came in contact with trading nations and with great world-powers their horizon widened until on the north it touched the Caucasus Mountains, on the east Ophir (probably the west coast of India), on the south Ethiopia (the Sudan), and on the west Tarshish (Spain). While these distant points were known to the Hebrews, their history was staged almost entirely upon a much smaller area. The real Hebrew world is the space between the Nile and the Mediterranean on the west, the mountains of Armenia on the north, the Tigris River and the Persian Gulf on the east, and on the south a line stretching across the desert from the Persian Gulf to the forks of the Red Sea. [See Map No. 1]. This area measures roughly 548,000 square miles, or about that of California, Utah, Montana, Oregon, and Washington. Within this area the Old Testament characters moved, and the empires that ruled the ancient world had their seats.

2. **Its Nature.** Not all of the Hebrew world was fit for habitation or even for temporary settlement. Across the whole southern half stretched the great Arabian desert, an arid sheet of rock with here and there areas of hard-packed gravel or drifting sand. These desert patches could support no life. On their borders the sterile wastes gave place to steppe lands that furnished food enough for roving tribes

1

though not for a settled people. If tribes wished a fixed
abode they had to seek richer regions on the northwest, the
coastal mountains and valleys of Syria and Palestine, where

FIG. 1—DESERT AND OASIS

This is a scene in the peninsula of Sinai. Of what is the desert in this picture
composed? Why should the mountains be so bare when there are palms
in the foreground? How many people do you estimate could live in this
oasis permanently? Compare this region with the Egyptian valley (Fig.
2) as to fertility, comfort in living, and the probability that its people
would develop arts, sciences, and literature. Which region would produce
the best warriors? Why? The hardier stock?

winds from the sea deposited their moisture, or on the
northeast, the rolling uplands of Mesopotamia or the alluvial
plains of the Tigris and Euphrates Rivers. Across the

barrier of the Red Sea to the west was another fertile river valley—Egypt, the gift of the Nile, earliest peopled and best protected. Thus the habitable Hebrew world was surprisingly small. Counting out perhaps a third of the total area as worthless desert and more than a half as steppe land, there is left barely 100,000 square miles—the area of Wyoming—capable of sustaining a fixed population and producing a surplus wealth. In fact, reckoning only the rich alluvial sections, the area is reduced to the Nile Valley, which from the Mediterranean to the Sudan is the size of Maryland (12,000 square miles), and the lower Tigris-Euphrates valley, the size of New Hampshire (9,000). It is easy to see, therefore, that while in the two early centres of civilization, Egypt and Babylonia, a livelihood could be gained on fairly easy terms, it meant a struggle in Syria and northern Mesopotamia, and in the rest of the Hebrew world it was a prize to be fought for and won by only the hardiest.

3. Its Peoples: Amorites, Hurrians, Sumerians. These varied lands have been the home and the melting-pot of a succession of races. First of all are the recently discovered aborigines. Whether the 50,000-year-old cave men of Galilee and Mt. Carmel left any descendants we are not sure; but beginning with the 20,000-year-old men of the Samaritan caves there is an unbroken succession to the early bronze culture found everywhere in Palestine. This aboriginal race is the one commonly called Amorites in the Bible. They were agricultural hill-dwellers who cultivated the valleys and later built their towns, like Gezer, Jerusalem, Megiddo, etc., over the caves in which their prehistoric ancestors lived and were buried.

Mingling with these Amorites came the Hurrians, perhaps an aboriginal highland race that stretched from Asia Minor to India and then invaded Mesopotamia and Syria. Their delicate pottery was found at Ur under the eight-foot stratum of silt left by the great Flood. The later Assyrians were Hurrian by race. From 2500 to 1500 B.C. the Hurrians

Fig. 2—NILE VALLEY

Egypt to the second cataract is a thousand miles long, but averages only ten
miles wide. What means of communication have the various parts of
the valley? What means for reaching the outside world? In the picture,
how many deserts do you discover? (Look beyond the river.) How
abrupt is the transition from the desert to the town? On what does the
fertility of such a country depend? What evidences do you see of dense
population? of large public works? So situated and so constituted, would
this land be likely to have produced an early civilization? Which country would tend to produce a more progressive race, Egypt, Babylonia, or
Assyria? Why? (See Figs. 1, 2, 5, 7, 8.)

colonized Palestine so thoroughly that Egyptian texts call
Palestine the "land of the Hurrians." Their culture was
taken over by the Hebrews and the Israelites when they
entered. The high head and prominent nose that charac-

FIG. 3—STEPPE LAND

This is fertile limestone soil. Why is there no more vegetation? During what time of year is this growth found? What do the inhabitants do the rest of the year? Steppe land might be called "step-lively" land; can you see why? What is a nomad, and why should nomads exist? What are the advantages of nomad life as contrasted with fixed life?

terize the Armenians and some types of modern Jew are derived from the Hurrian element in their stock.

The Sumerians came into Mesopotamia from the east or southeast after the Flood, took over the civilization of the Hurrians and became a great commercial people. Around 3500 B.C. they controlled all the trade routes in that part of the world. They never colonized or controlled Palestine, but disappeared about 2000 B.C.

4. **The Egyptians.** This race of prehistoric ancestry de-

veloped one of the earliest and most influential civilizations of the world. It dominated the coast of southwest Asia from earliest times till Egypt ceased to be an independent power. From Gebal (Byblos, near Beirut), her chief port in Syria, she so commanded the trade routes through all the north and east that by 2650 B.C. King Unas could call the Mediterranean "the lake of Pharaoh." Trading-posts were established inland at strategic points and along the caravan routes of Palestine and Syria. The Bible says little about this domination whether commercial or political, but wherever excavators dig in these countries they find Egyptian remains—scarabs, stelas of the Pharaohs and Egyptian temples built to local gods. As a dreaded power Egypt looms dimly behind all the literature of the Old Testament.

5. **Northern Invaders.** Of races that dominated Palestine from the north, the Bible mentions the Hittites. The term, political and geographical rather than racial, refers to a succession of races that ruled from eastern Asia Minor between 3000 B.C. and 1200 B.C. One of these races was certainly Hurrian, as were the Old Testament Hittites.

6. **Sea Peoples: Canaanites and Philistines.** Egypt had constantly to reckon with another commercial power almost as strong as her own—the Ægean or Minoan, centred in Crete. Before 4000 B.C. this energetic sea people had established trading colonies all up and down the Mediterranean coast. In southwest Palestine their port of entry was Beth-Eglaim (Tell el-Ajjul) four miles south of Gaza. Through their inland posts, Gerar, Beth Pelet, Gezer, Beersheba, Petra, etc., they controlled the rich grain fields of southern Palestine, the copper mines south of the Dead Sea and the Red Sea trade route to India. Farther north they took root at Askalon, Joppa, Dor, Akko, Tyre, Sidon, Megiddo, Taanach and Beth-shan. They were political and commercial masters over the aboriginal Amorites and the Hurrians. About 1450 a second wave of these traders arrived from Mycenæ in Greece, and for the next two hundred years

the country was flooded with "Mycenæan ware." Egypt saved its trade only by making alliance with them. In the Old Testament these sea peoples appear under various names: Caphtorim (Cretans); Perizzites (metal workers); Hivites (Achæans or proto-Greek); Girgashites (Teucrians from near

FIG. 4—AMORITES

Found on the pylon of the mortuary temple of Ramses II at Thebes, 1225 B.C. They represent Semitic races of various names from whom the Hebrews took the land of Palestine both east and west of the Jordan. What grade of intelligence is here indicated?

Troy). All these, who settled chiefly on the seaboard, are lumped together as Canaanites. In time they adopted the language of the country, which was Phœnician-Hebrew, and were ultimately absorbed into the people we call Israelites.

Still a third wave came from the west in the twelfth century before Christ, fragments of Ægean peoples driven from their homes by the ancestors of the Greeks who were pressing down from the Balkans. Ramses III saw them threaten the overthrow of Egyptian trade and so fought them all along the Syria-Palestine coast, 1190 to 1185 B.C., but the best he could do was to keep them out of the Delta. They settled most largely in the old Minoan ground of southwest Palestine, were amalgamated with their ancient compatriots there and finally gave their name to the whole of Palestine. The Israelites never wholly dislodged them. Anthropologists say that one-fourth of the present inhabitants of Palestine are of the Philistine type.

7. The Semites: Akkadians, Phœnicians. By the term
Semite we must understand not a race but many races that
adopted a Semitic language. Within this group are Babylonians, Assyrians, Phœnicians, Hebrews, Arameans, Arabs,

Fɪɢ. 5—BABYLONIA: EZRA'S TOMB

What sized river is here suggested? What does the absence of background
tell of the general character of the land? What does the nature of the bank
tell? What do the palms tell? If a river of this size in such a land
needed to be controlled, what arts and sciences would this necessity develop? In which of the regions pictured in this chapter would you
think civilization would soonest develop? Why? What barriers or
obstacles do you discover that would tend to isolate the inhabitants from
the rest of the world? How would isolation of a country affect its development?

and many lesser known peoples. We do not know whence
the first arrivals came; they just appear, first in northern
Mesopotamia. They became dominant there about 2600 B.C.
when Sargon of Agade wrested the leadership from the
Sumerians. The speech of these people written in the cuneiform character taken over from the Sumerians and called
Akkadian (from Akkad, or Agade), became the universal

language of business and diplomacy from the Ægean to the Indus. The language of the Amarna tablets written by Palestine kings to the Pharaoh of Egypt is Akkadian.

The word Phœnician is Greek for all the swarthy peoples along the east Mediterranean seaboard. The name properly

An Aramean.   A North   A Judean of
                 Aramean.   Shishak's Day.

Fig. 6—A GROUP OF SYRIANS OR ARAMEANS

Compare Fig. 9. What similarities of feature do you discover in these types? Is there any especially intellectual countenance? Are there any evidences of refinement or spirituality? Are any of the men strong-willed? Are any physical weaklings? Pick out specimens that are fit to be world conquerors. Any that would make religious fanatics. Imagine these men living in America to-day: what kinds of citizens would they become, and what would be their probable occupations?

applies to a part of the downward-moving, Semitic-speaking peoples that gave Sargon to Agade. Their language is now known from the Ras Shamra texts to have been the common language of Syria-Palestine from 2000 to 1400 B.C. This older Hebrew language with its culture was impressed on both the Canaanite traders and the Israelites who came in under Joshua.

8. **The Semites: Hebrews, Israelites, Jews, etc.** While these three terms are ordinarily used interchangeably, there is a technical difference. Hebrews are all the inhabitants of Palestine of whatever race who spoke the Phœnician-Canaanite-Hebrew tongue. In this group are the Habiru who first came to our attention in 1888 in the Amarna tablets. The Israelites are the special band that came in under Joshua,

became the political masters of the earlier Hebrew-Canaanite-Amorite inhabitants, took over their culture and ultimately formed the two kingdoms of Judah and Israel. The Jews

Copyright by Underwood and Underwood, N. Y.

FIG. 7—THE SYRIAN VALLEY

View northwest from Baalbek. How high are these Lebanon mountains? You are standing on a parallel range. Why would the long valley between probably be fertile? What evidences can you discover that it is? Would you prefer to live here or in Egypt, Babylonia, or Assyria? Why? Would a higher degree of civilization be possible here? Why? Which of the four regions would produce the hardier race? How do you account for the fact that there are more Syrians in the United States than Egyptians or Mesopotamians?

are the post-exilic, Hebrew- or Aramaic-speaking people, whether or not they had been in exile, who accepted the intensified and narrowed religion of Nehemiah and Ezra.

We know nothing of the origins of the Arameans as a race —if they are a race. We know only that the Aramean language appeared in Mesopotamia as early as 3000 B.C., that it spread over the entire Biblical world and that throughout the later period it supplanted classical Hebrew until Greek in turn supplanted it.

The Arabs, the youngest group of Semites, are a ruling aristocracy from the north who began to dominate the Hamitic culture of south Arabia about 1000 B.C. They took over the trade routes across the desert and figure largely in the markets of Palestine and Phœnicia as well as in the pages of the Prophets. Their day of glory began when Mohammed in the seventh century welded them into the greatest missionary force in history.

9. **The Rôle of the Coast Land.** The land where the Hebrews finally crystallized into a nation is a strip of mountain and fertile valley that lies along the eastern Mediterranean coast and extends inland for perhaps a hundred miles. Today it is divided into two parts: (1) the northern half, extending from Damascus and Beirut to Alexandretta and the Euphrates, and named Syria; (2) the southern half, reaching from the same dividing line to the desert and the Egyptian boundary, and called Palestine or the Holy Land.

This coast land has been often likened to a narrow bridge connecting the civilizations of Egypt and the Tigris-Euphrates valley. Certainly its history confirms the simile, for across it have gone the caravans and the armies of all the ancient empires, treading the oldest highway known to man. This bridge simile explains partly why the coast land never became the seat of a great empire: it was useful for crossing but not attractive as a home. Kings fought for it because its highroad controlled traffic and led to richer booty beyond. Thus it came to pass that over it from the north swept the armies of Sargon and Hammurabi—though they were halted on the frontier of Egypt—of Assyria during its period of greatness, of Babylon, Persia, Greece, and Rome. From the south, Egypt, during its days of power, burst through repeatedly—Ahmose, Thothmes III, and the other eighteenth-dynasty kings, Seti and Ramses of the nineteenth, and the occasional "smoking firebrands" of the dying empire. In later days the armies of the caliphs surged back and forth across it from Bagdad to Cairo;

Fig. 8—TIGRIS VALLEY AT NINEVEH

The hill in the distance is the south citadel of old Nineveh, now called the "Hill of Jonah."   What kind of building crowns the hill?   What had the prophet Jonah to do with this city?   (Jonah 3:1-3.)   What is the stream in the foreground?   Discover evidences of farming.   Why is the hill in the foreground not cultivated?   Is this region more or less fertile than Egypt, Babylonia, and Syria?

Napoleon and Ibrahim Pasha trod the bridge in pursuit of greater empires; and in the great World War, Germany and her Turkish ally first threw men across it to pierce Egypt, and then Britain countermarched from Egypt in order to join its other battalions coming up the ancient highroad of Mesopotamia to redeem for civilization all the ancient Semitic world.   It is one of the outstanding wonders of history that a people of a land so small, so divided, so poverty-stricken, so trampled upon, has nevertheless been able to stamp its genius upon the thought and life of the whole world.

10. **Our Heritage from the Hebrew World.** We owe to this small corner of the globe a larger debt than perhaps we imagine. First of all comes the Hebrew religion, which has

A North Aramean.   An Aramean Envoy About 2000 B.C.   An Aramean of Merom.

Fig. 9—A GROUP OF ARAMEANS
Compare Fig. 6 and see questions.

been one of the greatest moral forces in history. By-products of that religion are the Old Testament with its wealth of spiritual teaching and inspiration, and Christianity with its New Testament. From the Arabian desert also came the religion of Mohammed, which dominated the civilized world for a century and still controls the consciences of one-fifth of the human race.

We owe to the early peoples of this area the beginnings of many of our sciences and arts. In Babylonia, and contemporaneously in Egypt, arose the earliest cities, the earliest empires, with the arts of war on which empires were founded. There irrigation was first developed and the necessary implements of buckets, sweeps, and wheels were invented. In building we find there the arts of brick-making, arch construction, and decoration with sculpture, paint or enamel. Seal and gem cutting of the most delicate kind was practised. Medicine began in Babylon, or Egypt, or both, as did astronomy and mathematics. The Babylonians predicted eclipses, invented a calendar and passed on to us their system of reckoning time by the year, month, and week. We, as they, name our days after the gods associated with the heavenly bodies, and we still use their scheme of dividing the day into two periods of twelve hours each. From Phœnicia came our alphabet and the science of deep-sea navigation, while from Egypt came written speech, the use of metals, and the science of engineering.

But the chief claim of the Hebrew world to our regard lies in the fact that the ideals of democracy which to-day we regard as distinctively our American heritage first developed within this area. Though the great military despotisms of Egypt, Babylonia, Assyria, and Persia that flourished in these lands have caused people to think of autocracy and the East together, it is nevertheless true that under the iron heel of these very despotisms there grew and blossomed a tiny flower. It is the flower of human freedom, of the rights of man, of the possibility of self-determination, of the duty of brotherhood. Certain ancient kings of Babylon and Egypt were the first to express these ideals, but their teachings were vague and fell upon poor soil, and so they died and left no trace in human institutions. It was in the soil of the barren steppe lands that encircle Palestine and among the nomadic tribes of the wilderness that the seeds of democracy first took root. Among the Aramean tribes that under the leadership of Abraham and Jacob found a home in southern Palestine all property was held in common, each man had equal rights and responsibilities, and the chieftain was the servant of all. Whenever the independence of this liberty-loving group was endangered, each man rose to put down the despot. In time their ideals regarding the fundamental right of man and his duties to his fellows were expressed in definite laws, and all later democratic legislation is largely an unfolding of what is there set forth in principle.

II

THE REDISCOVERY OF THE HEBREW WORLD

11. **The Dust of Time.** A century ago the Bible was practically our only source of information about the Hebrews and the Hebrew world. The empires that once flourished in the East had fallen into decay; the ruins of their civilization had been covered by the sands of a neglected land or reduced to meaningless heaps by rain and flood; and the superstition of the half-civilized tribes that squatted among the wrecks of former temples and palaces made approach and study exceedingly difficult for European scholars. Historians were also hampered by the theory, once held by many, that it was irreverent to apply to the Bible the same literary and historical tests that were used with other historical records. The result was that knowledge of the backgrounds of the Bible was most meagre: Babylonia, Assyria, Persia, Egypt, and Asia Minor were totally unknown except for stray references in Greek and Roman literature; and we were ignorant regarding many periods of Hebrew history where the Bible was silent, and even when it spoke, its testimony was not understood. Today all this has been changed.

12. **The Rediscovery of the Bible.** During the last two generations the Bible has gained a new interest and meaning. Scholars have been at work reverently examining the ancient texts, and they have learned to interpret the testimony that each bears regarding its origin and date. Instead of one flat level of historic narrative they have discovered various layers of material coming from different ages and representing different grades of civilization and different

15

🦅	A
	Ả
	Ä
or \\	I
or ☙	U or W
	B
▫	P
	F
🐦 }	M
～～～ 𐀪 }	N
🐟 }	R and L
🏛	H
🔗	Ḥ
◉	KH
⬱ }	S
⬭	SH
⬭	K
◿	Ḳ
🔺	G
⌂,	T
⬱	TH
⬭	Ṭ
🦢	TCH or Ṣ (?)

types of thought. They have recognized among the oldest fragments certain folk-songs that perpetuate ancient deeds of daring, like the Sword Song of Lamech (Gen. 4^{23-24}), or the Song of the Well (Num. 21^{17-18}), or the conquest of early foes, like the Moab Victory Chant (Num. 21^{27-30}), or the Triumphal Ode of Deborah (Judg. 5). They have learned to interpret the characters of the patriarchs, partly as idealized portraits drawn by later prophets for the purpose of teaching religion, and partly as graphic summaries of the movements of tribes and nations—lenses through which we can view the distant march of peoples. This primitive way of writing history, so that it could be conveniently memorized and handed down, may be seen in such passages as Genesis 10, which lists the descendants of Noah. The sons of Ham are Cush (Ethiopia) and Mizraim (Egypt) and Put (the Libyans) and Canaan (Syria and Palestine). "And Canaan begat Sidon (the city of the Phœnicians), his first-born, and Heth (the Hittites)." This list is evidently not a family tree but a memory-device to indicate racial relations.

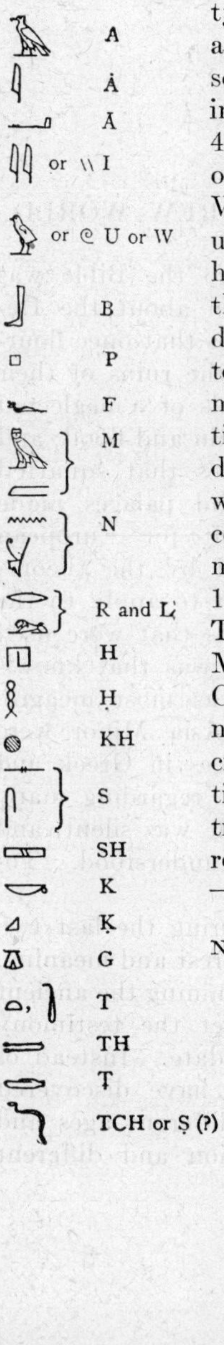

Fig. 10—THE HIEROGLYPHIC ALPHABET

Note the separate characters to denote three different sounds of A. Our letter O is usually expressed by the chicken (U or W). The two feathers (I) stand for the sound of *i* in *machine*, and therefore are the equivalent of our E. Our sound of *i* as in *ice* would probably be expressed by the signs for A I, namely the third and fourth in the column. W is the same as *oo* in *moon*. C would be expressed by S or K, depending on its sound. The Egyptians, like the Chinese, could not distinguish between L and R. Try writing a letter in the hieroglyphic characters.

New light is also shed on Hebrew history by the prophets. As long as they were thought to be lofty and inspired fortune-tellers, speaking in riddles of great events that would come to pass a century or a millennium hence, they were studied largely in the light of future history, in order that each prophecy might be attached to its definite fulfilment. The result was a complete misunderstanding of this portion of the Bible. Now we see that the prophets were not soothsayers but spiritual geniuses and statesmen who were inspired to interpret to the men of their own day God's nature and demands, and that when they predicted, their prediction was based upon the great moral laws of the universe. Accordingly the prophetic books have become for us veritable mines of information. We find revealed in them the political and social conditions of the age in which the prophet lived. We are able to observe the people's loyalty or disloyalty to their God and to observe the foreign influences that brought corruption in Israel's religion and morals, and led to slavery and exile. It is difficult to overestimate the gain that has come to our knowledge and insight with the discovery that the Bible is a great human document, throbbing with the life and the hopes of many generations.

13. **The Egyptian Records.** Up to the beginning of the nineteenth century Egypt was a sealed book. Its ancient language fell into disuse soon after Rome conquered it in the second century before Christ. The Arab conquest in the seventh Christian century cut it off from direct contact with Europe, and through misrule and neglect in the succeeding centuries practically all memory of it was lost. Its wonderful monuments fell into decay and were used as quarries for the building of mosques and houses. When Napoleon occupied Egypt in 1798 he took with him a group of scholars who made a thorough survey of the entire land, its monuments, its plant and animal forms. Their published results aroused the world's interest in that forgotten land. Napoleon's engineers, while digging the foundations of a

FIG. 11—THE ROSETTA STONE

A basalt tablet discovered 1799 at Rosetta. Upper register, hieroglyphic;
middle register, demotic; lower register, Greek. A reading-glass will
bring out the characters clearly. In the hieroglyphic notice the ovals
(cartouches) that contain the names of Ptolemy. The first step in the
translation of the hieroglyphic was the discovery that the king's name was
always so enclosed. The sounds of the characters in "Ptolemy" could
then be inferred from the Greek.

fort near the Rosetta mouth of the Nile, found by chance a stone bearing an inscription in three languages, the ancient sacred picture-writing (hieroglyphic), the common Egyptian script, and Greek. Champollion, a French scholar, began to study the Rosetta stone, and in 1822 announced that he could read the hieroglyphic language. He thus furnished the world with a key that could unlock the vast treasure-house of Egyptian history. Since his day scholars have laboriously copied and translated every inscription in Egypt, and through the enlightened interest of the later rulers of Egypt, learned societies have been allowed to dig for additional sources of knowledge. Each year adds to our information.

This romantic rediscovery of a forgotten world helps our understanding of Hebrew history. We have learned much of the fortunes of Palestine previous to the coming of the Hebrews. We know its civilization, its religion, its political relations with the great world-powers, and we can therefore account for some of the transformations seen in the Hebrews when they lived in this remarkable land. Many historic references in the Old Testament have been corroborated by the Egyptian inscriptions. Egyptian customs have explained certain Hebrew customs. We understand now the background of such thrilling narratives as the Joseph story. We see why Egypt exercised such a sinister influence on the little kingdom of Palestine; and latterly, through the unearthing of precious manuscripts, we have learned about the fortunes of a large section of the Jewish race that took refuge in Egypt at the time of the exile. As yet we have found no records of the Hebrew bondage and exodus—the experiences that loom so large in the Bible; but the sands of Egypt undoubtedly hold many secrets that some day will be revealed and will make clear to us this and many other chapters in Hebrew history that are now obscure.

14. **The Babylonian and Assyrian Records.** The Tigris-Euphrates valley suffered the same fate as Egypt: for cen-

turies it was forgotten and its language lost. In 1835 Henry Rawlinson, a young English officer attached to the Persian army, discovered in the Zagros Mountains a limestone cliff, called the Behistun rock, rising 1,700 feet from the plain, with a great inscription in three languages far up on its perpendicular face. He set himself the dangerous task of copying the whole inscription, and then for years he and other scholars worked to decipher the Median and the cuneiform on the basis of the third language, the Persian. Not until 1857, after twenty-two years of work, was the process complete. From that day to this translation has gone on, excavation has furnished historical inscriptions by the yard and rod, and clay tablets by the bushel; so that now we have a clearer understanding of the history, the literature, and the religion of the Tigris-Euphrates valley than we have of any other ancient civilizations except possibly those of Greece and Rome.

These achievements have had a more direct bearing on our knowledge of Bible history than have the results of Egyptian exploration, for during most of Old Testament times Egypt was in her decline, while Babylonia and Assyria were masters of the world. Moreover, Palestine, being Asiatic rather than African, was exposed constantly to influences from the East. Its population, as we have seen, was closely related to that of Babylonia, and the intercourse of trade made ideas the common property of both lands. When the literature of Babylonia came to light, therefore, the Old Testament acquired a new significance. We now know the sources from which the Hebrews derived their ideas of the universe and of ancient history (cf. Figs. 108 and 124), their knowledge of the arts, and their business and social customs; and we know the detailed history of those great monarchs who ruled so much of the world during the Old Testament period, from 1000 to 300 B.C., and who dominated and finally ruined the political life of Israel. So that, whereas the Bible gives us the inner history of the Hebrews and shows

FIG. 12—INSCRIPTION OF BEHISTUN

Behistun is on the main caravan route from Bagdad to Teheran, 65 miles west of the ancient Persian capital Ecbatana. This inscription of Darius is about 500 feet from the base of the cliff, just over a large spring at which every caravan and army that ever passed from Persia to Babylonia has drunk. Darius knew how to advertise! The figures represent Darius receiving the submission of certain rebels, who have ropes around their necks. Of the nine panels of text, the five to the right are Old Persian, the three to the left are cuneiform, of the language of Susa, while the one panel above these is Babylonian cuneiform. The last two are translations of the Persian. Find Darius, the chief rebel, and the protecting divinity, Ahura Mazda.

us their struggle for a faith and for national existence, the mounds of Mesopotamia give us the external view and enable us to see Israel the prey to the ambitions of great kings, one

Fig. 13—MOUND OF TELL HESY, POSSIBLY LACHISH

II Kings 14^{19}.   It lies in the foothills of Judea sixteen miles east of Gaza.   The excavators have cut down a third of the mound layer by layer, each layer representing a distinct settlement.   Eight cities, one above the other, were thus laid bare.   The lowest and oldest stratum contained Amorite pottery and bronze utensils, and is dated 1700 B.C.   City II is dated by Egyptian scarabs about 1500 B.C.   City III is dated by scarabs and a cuneiform tablet about 1400 B.C.   City IV, containing Phœnician pottery and the earliest iron, dates 1400–1000 B.C.   In City V and VI, Jewish ware prevailed.   In cities VII and VIII the red and black figured Greek pottery was common, suggesting the dates 550–350 B.C.   Absence of coins and other characteristic remains show that the site was deserted after 350 B.C.   Which of these cities fell prey to Joshua (Josh. 10$^{1\text{ff.}}$)?   Which was fortified by Rehoboam (II Chron. 11^9)?   Which was taken by Sennacherib (II Kings 18$^{13\text{-}16}$, Is. 36$^{1\text{-}2}$)?   For pictures of this siege, see Figs. 104, 105, 106.   Why should so much rubbish accumulate on the site?

among many petty states that intrigued and suffered in the losing game of world-dominion.

15. **The Land of Palestine.** Within the last century, Palestine also has been explored with a view to finding what contribution it can make to our knowledge of Bible times.   Unfortunately the Turkish Government did not look with favor upon such exploration, so that while geographers have mapped the surface with great thoroughness and have identified many of the places mentioned in the Bible, the

ruined mounds of many ancient cities that dot its surface
have hardly been touched. Nevertheless, to know the
topography of Palestine is a great gain, for we can now follow with considerable certainty the journeys of patriarchs
and heroes and kings, the march of armies, the movements
of tribes and races, and we can appreciate how the mountains and valleys of the land, its geology and geography and
rainfall, have had a determining influence in shaping Hebrew
history. Within the past generation or two, several mounds
have been thoroughly explored: old Keriath-Sepher in southwestern Palestine, where the remains of twelve cities of different periods were found on top of one another; Gezer, below whose later Jewish and Amorite remains were found the
caves of its prehistoric flint-men; Jericho, whose walls and
citadel show the defensive engineering of thirty-three centuries ago; and the tremendously important mounds of
Megiddo and Beth-shan are still in process of excavation
(1935). We are still woefully lacking in direct testimony
about the Old Testament period. The material for large
information undoubtedly exists, but it is all underground.
Now that the affairs of Palestine are in liberal hands, the
golden age of archæology seems to have arrived. We may at
any time expect startling additions to our knowledge of the
Hebrew people.

16. **Other Sources.** We are indebted to the Greek Herodotus for a few facts about the Hebrews, and to Arrian, the
contemporary chronicler of Alexander the Great; to the
Jewish writer Josephus, of the first century A.D., for the
beliefs of his day about his nation's history, and for his detailed account of the wars with Rome; to the Roman his-
torians for many facts that fall within the period of Roman
interest in the East, the first centuries before and after
Christ; and to the ruins of the Græco-Roman cities, particularly east of the Jordan, for a knowledge of the external features of their life. Then there are the scattered inscriptions, chiefly in Greek and Latin. which have come to light

from time to time; and coins by which we fill in the lists of kings or rulers. Other Hebrew writings besides those included in our Bible also contain historical data—the books of the Maccabees, Esdras, and Tobit; while from Ecclesiasticus the Wisdom of Solomon, the Psalms of Solomon, the Ascension of Isaiah, and the like, we glean many a hint as to the moral and religious ideals of the Jews in the centuries immediately preceding the Christian era. These varied records, and especially the Bible and the cuneiform literature of Babylonia and Assyria, furnish the data from which we may gain a clear and vivid idea of the life of the Hebrews during the twelve centuries that lie between their first entrance into Palestine and the final destruction of Jerusalem.

THE CRADLE OF DEMOCRACY

17. The Biblical Account of the Egyptian Sojourn. The history of the Hebrew nation begins with the bondage in Egypt, for the earlier stories in Genesis simply record the experiences of individuals and tribes. In the book of Exodus we find the Hebrews, some hundreds or perhaps thousands in number, occupying the land of Goshen in the eastern Delta and under the lash of the taskmaster building store cities for the reigning Pharaoh. They are multiplying rapidly. Pharaoh fears that unless something is done to check their growth they will some day get out of hand. He therefore orders that the taskmasters make their labor exceedingly hard and painful, and when this proves ineffective, that all male children be drowned at birth. One mother manages to conceal her child for a while, then places him in an ark of bulrushes among the river reeds. By chance Pharaoh's daughter comes there to bathe, discovers the baby, takes pity on him and has him brought up in the palace as her own son. In memory of his finding she calls him Moses. The Hebrew story-tellers, through similarity of sound, derive the name from the verb "to draw out," but Moses is probably the Hebrew form of the Egyptian word for child (*mos*).

When Moses was grown, he one day saw an Egyptian beating a Hebrew. Impelled by hot indignation, he killed the Egyptian. When the deed became known Moses escaped arrest by fleeing to the land of Midian on the east or north of the Red Sea. Here he married the daughter of the priest Jethro and for twenty years served his father-in-law as a

herdsman. But the memory of his people's wrongs burned
in his soul, until one day his duty flamed up before him as a
compelling vision of Jehovah in a burning bush, and he
heard a clear call to the seemingly impossible task of rousing

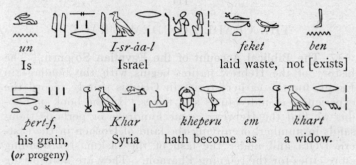

un	*I-sr-āa-l*	*feket*	*ben*
Is	Israel	laid waste,	not [exists]

pert-f,	*Khar*	*kheperu*	*em*	*khart*
his grain,	Syria	hath become	as	a widow.
(*or* progeny)				

FIG. 14—EARLIEST MENTION OF ISRAEL

The Egyptian text of two lines of Merneptah's stela (Fig. 21), a transliteration
and a translation. After the word *Israel*, note the figures of a man, a
woman, and three straight lines (a plural sign). These constitute a "determinative," and indicate the nature of the word just used: *i. e.*, the word
"Israel" denotes a man and a woman many times repeated! Notice the
play on words in the characters for *Syria* and *widow*.

the spirit of revolt and leading the horde of Hebrew slaves
out of their cruel bondage.

Moses was not disobedient to the heavenly vision, but
returned to his kindred and called them in the name of the
God of their fathers to follow him into the desert. He
repeatedly interviewed Pharaoh in person, and to the accom-
paniment of signs and wonders demanded the release of his
people that they might sacrifice to their God in the wilderness. The only result was an increase of burdens: the task-
masters made the Hebrews gather the necessary straw in
addition to making the bricks. But Moses encouraged the
people with Jehovah's promises, confounded Pharaoh's
magicians who tried to duplicate his supernatural signs, and
by bringing upon the land a series of ten fearful plagues,

the last of which was the death of every first-born of the Egyptians, finally frightened Pharaoh into releasing the Hebrews.

Hastily the clans were summoned, a sacrificial meal called

Find two men getting water in jars from a pool (see the lilies); two men mixing the mud; a carrier; a man making bricks in a mould; a man laying the bricks in rows; a man mending his hoe.

FIG. 15—BRICK–MAKING

Painted on a tomb at Thebes, Egypt.
Find two task-masters with sticks (Ex. 1¹¹; 5¹⁴): men carrying and depositing mud; two men carrying dried bricks with a yoke; one returning with empty yoke.

the Passover was eaten, and the flight began. Men, women, children, and many cattle poured eastward along the caravan road to the wilderness. Then avoiding the military wall and the fortresses that guarded the narrow frontier of the isthmus, they turned southward and halted for the night on the shore of the Bitter Lakes. Pharaoh in the

FIG. 16—BRICK OF RAMSES II

Made of unbaked Nile mud and chopped
straw, stamped with the prenomen of
Ramses II, *viz.*: User-maat-Ra-setep-
en-Ra ("Strong is the Truth of Ra,
the chosen one of Ra"). The size of
the brick is 15 x 7¾ x 4¼ inches. For
straw in bricks, see Ex. 5⁷. For the
process of brick-making, see Fig. 15.

meantime had repented
of his fears and sent after
the fugitives an army of
chariots and horsemen.
But Jehovah sent a
strong east wind all that
night, which blew the
shallow waters aside and
uncovered enough flats
to allow the Hebrews to
escape. The Egyptians
attempted in the morn-
ing to pursue, but the
returning waters en-
gulfed their army, while
the Hebrews advanced
safely to the open wil-
derness. This great de-
liverance is the first and
most significant incident
in their history.

18. **Confirmations of
the Biblical Account.** In
spite of the prominence
of the supernatural in
the later versions of the
story and the complete
silence of the Egyptian
records, there is no rea-
son to doubt the essen-
tial truth of the events
recorded. In the first
place, the Hebrews them-
selves never doubted it.
The providential phe-
nomena of the plagues

and the retiring sea made a tremendous impression upon their memories and forever linked their escape with the thought of the power of Jehovah, their new-found God. All through the Old Testament, in story and psalm and prophecy, the exodus constantly recurs as the outstanding fact at the beginning of their national life and the solid argument why they should remain faithful to Jehovah their deliverer. In the second place the story itself, while not minutely specific, shows with reasonable clearness a background corroborated by the Egyptian records.

19. Biblical Chronology and Egyptian.

While as yet the data afforded by archæological discoveries are not

Courtesy of the Metropolitan Museum, New York.

FIG. 17—STATUE OF HATSHEPSUT

This is the youthful and altogether feminine-looking queen who as princess, if the new chronology is correct, rescued and reared the infant Moses. The statue, which once adorned her unique mortuary temple at Thebes, was found smashed to bits and buried in rubbish. With infinite pains the fragments have been fitted together and the original beauty is again revealed. The wrecking was done by her brother and husband, Thutmose, pharaoh of the oppression. By this means he hoped to destroy the personality and the future existence of his rival.

conclusive, scholars are coming more and more to the opinion that the Old Testament chronology is substantially correct and that the events narrated in the book of Exodus can be equated fairly accurately with Egyptian history.* The

* See, however, Appendix V.

Biblical zero date for reckoning this period is the foundation
of the Temple at Jerusalem by Solomon, now almost conclu-
sively set at 967 B.C.   Since I Kings 6¹ places this event 490
years after the exodus, the latter event must be 1447 B.C.
Moses was born eighty years before the exodus (Ex. 7⁷); his
birth was therefore 1527 B.C.   If he was forty years old when
he fled to Midian (Acts 7²³) that incident occurred in 1487
B.C.   His forty-year residence in Midian (Acts 7³⁰) would
date his return 1447 B.C., the year of the exodus.

Now all these dates fall most interestingly into the scheme
of Egyptian chronology as set forth by Breasted in his History of Egypt.   The birth of Moses (1527 B.C.) falls in the
reign of Thutmose I who ruled more than thirty years from
before 1531 to 1501 B.C.   This Pharaoh must therefore be the
one who "knew not Joseph" and who issued the decree that
all the Hebrew men-children should be killed (Ex. 1¹⁶).   It
so happened that his heir to the Egyptian throne was famous
Hatshepsut, her father's favorite daughter.   It is not un-
likely therefore that she was the princess who found Moses,
reared him and educated him "in all the wisdom of the
Egyptians" (Acts 7²¹⁻²²).   Josephus says that this princess
was named Thermouthis.   This may well be a reminiscence
of the family name Thutmose.   Moses' own name is derived
from the Egyptian MS, part of this same family name.

In 1501 B.C. a son of Thutmose I superseded his father,
through a coup of the priests of Amon, and to make legiti-
mate his claim married his half-sister Hatshepsut—for the
throne actually descended through the females of the line.
This prince took the throne-name of Thutmose III.   But his
brilliant queen, by her own genius and the help of a court
clique, was able to get the whip hand and in spite of temporary interruptions to be absolute ruler for many years.
During this time she might easily have advanced the fortunes of her favorite Moses.   A late Jewish tradition recorded by Josephus makes Moses a general who repulsed an
Ethiopian invasion, marched to Meroe in the Sudan and

married an Ethiopian princess. The Bible also says that Moses had a Cushite (i.e., Ethiopian) wife (Num. 12¹). Egyptian records show that an invasion of Ethiopians was repulsed in the reign of Thutmose III.

About 1490 B.C. the great queen died and her brother-consort, Thutmose III, assumed full power. His hatred of his former partner was so great that he hacked out her name and figure from all her monuments. All the queen's favorites fled for their lives, among them, doubtless, Moses. His flight to Midian is said to be in 1487 B.C., not long after the queen's death.

20. **The Pharaohs of the Oppression and the Exodus.** The great Pharaoh of the Oppression is therefore Thutmose III whose reign began with his sister's in 1501 B.C. and ended fifty-four years later in 1447 B.C. The Bible says that he ruled "many days." He was one of the greatest of all the Pharaohs, a man of tireless energy, a great general, a great organizer, and a great administrator. He covered Egypt with superb monuments. Temples bearing his cartouches are extant in over thirty cities. We know also that he employed Semitic slaves for this work. A tomb-painting of the eigtheenth dynasty in the Theban cemetery shows Semites making bricks for the temple of Amon at Thebes. The inscription runs: "The taskmaster saith to the laborers, 'The stick is in my hand; be not idle.'" Moreover sunburned bricks have been found bearing the name of Thutmose III and made without straw. (cf. Ex. 1¹¹).

Thutmose III was the greatest of Egyptian conquerors, a genius like Alexander or Cæsar. He cowed Palestine by seventeen annual raids and laid the foundations of his empire so securely that by loot and tribute it was the richest in the world. Four generations of successors hardly sufficed to spend the wealth. The last flicker of its splendor one can see in the burial treasures of King Tutankhamen. We know of his operations in Palestine not only from his inscriptions at Karnak but from his two temples recently unearthed at

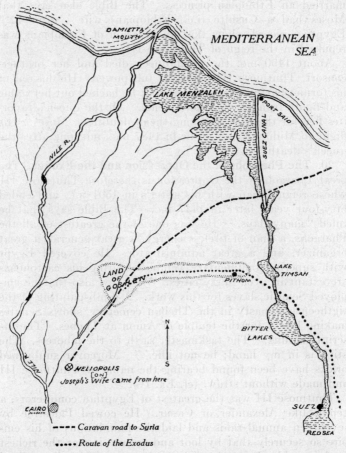

FIG. 18—MAP OF GOSHEN

Observe the peculiar shape of the land of Goshen, the long handle having been
    made possible by the waters of a canal dug in ancient times from the Nile
    to the Red sea.   Queen Hatasu's expedition to Punt sailed from Thebes by
    way of this canal.   Note also that the Bitter Lakes were formerly an exten-
    sion of the Red Sea.   The Hebrews crossed one of the connecting shallows.

Beth-shan in the Jordan valley. They date from after his decisive battle at Megiddo, May 15, 1479 B.C.

When Thutmose III died in 1447 B.C., Moses returned to Egypt to deliver his people. He found on the throne Amen-

FIG. 19—STORE CHAMBERS AT PITHOM

Part of a city affirmed by the Hebrew tradition to have been built by them. See Fig. 16 for a brick found here.

hotep II, a man whose character corresponds with that of the Biblical Pharaoh of the exodus. This king was a powerful brute, stronger than any of his contemporaries, and fond of the utmost cruelties to captives in war. Kings captured in his Syrian campaigns were hung head downward from the prow of his returning galleys, tortured all the way to Thebes, and slaughtered before Amen at last by the Pharaoh's own

hand. Amenhotep II now lies in his tomb in the Valley of
the Kings and the bow that none but he could bend is in
the Cairo museum. On the new chronology we are following, this Amenhotep II would be the Pharaoh before whom
Moses and Aaron stood and because of whose hardness of
heart the ten plagues were sent.

The Pharaoh who succeeded Amenhotep II was not his
firstborn. According to a folk-tale in circulation some centuries later and engraved on a granite monument still to be
seen between the paws of the Sphinx at Gizeh, the appointment of Thutmose IV to the throne was quite contrary to
expectation. If his father was indeed the Pharaoh of the
exodus, the oldest brother who would naturally have been
Pharaoh was a victim of the tenth plague !

During the reign of Thutmose IV (1420–1411 b.c.) and the
first part of the reign of Amenhotep III (1411–1375 b.c.) the
Hebrew tribes were in the Wilderness undergoing the hardships that were to transform them from a loosely organized
horde of slaves to a compact and hardy race under leadership. By the time they were ready to enter Palestine the
vigor of Egypt had temporarily spent itself there, and the
chaos that ensued made the penetration possible.

21. **The Land of Goshen.** We have been able probably
to locate the home of the Hebrews in Egypt. It is a long
funnel-shaped section of the eastern Delta, its apex formed
by the Wadi Tumilat that reaches eastward to the present
Suez Canal, and its base running north and south from the
modern Zagazig to Belbeis. The fresh-water canal that to-
day supplies Ismailia and Port Said runs along its northern
border, as does the present railway, and the old caravan road
to Syria crosses the western end. This section of Egypt is
the only one that satisfies the conditions of the Biblical
story. It was Ramses II who first irrigated, developed, and
colonized Goshen, which at the time of the coming of the
Hebrews was only grazing land. Both of the store cities,
Raanses and Pithom, lay within this territory. Two hundred years after the Hebrews had departed, Ramses II built

a royal residence and temples
here. No doubt that is the reason his name has been so persist-
ently associated with the Hebrew bondage.

22. **The True Significance of
the Bondage and Exodus.** It is
startling to realize that political
and industrial slavery was the
cradle of the first real democracy
and of the first religion that
taught loyalty to one God and
justice and consideration for all
men. The Hebrew nation began
in a revolt against inhuman treatment and that revolt took the
form of a general strike. The organizer and leader of that ancient
walk-out was one of the slaves
who by a fortunate circumstance
had been able to climb out of
slavery and get an education and
a world view of things. The people whom he led was from the
start democratic. It had no internal system of class government, except that it had inherited
from a distant nomadic past the
custom of each family's acting
through its oldest member. These
elders all willingly co-operated
with Moses in his plan of revolt.

Fig. 20—VICTORIOUS
HYMN OF MERNEPTAH

Containing the earliest-known
reference to Israel. *Cf.* Fig.
14. This stone was originally
used by Amenhotep III in his
mortuary temple at Thebes.
His inscription is still on the
other side. Why should Merneptah have used a second-
hand stone? The figures at
the top represent the god
Amon presenting a curved
sword to the king (repeated
bisymmetrically).

The bondage in Egypt accomplished this for the Hebrews:
it taught them to hate political and industrial tyranny of
every kind. The memory of their own experience enlisted
their sympathies ever afterward in behalf of all victims of
oppression. No other ancient people showed such tender

consideration for the slave, the resident alien, the widow, the orphan, and the hired laborer. Many of Israel's noblest philanthropic laws are reinforced by the comment, "Remember that you were a slave in the land of Egypt." Above all, this experience led the Hebrews to think of their deity as a god full of sympathy for the afflicted and dependent, and ever eager to champion their cause against cruel oppressors. It is this strong social element in Israel's early religion that distinguishes it from all other early faiths, and that led the Hebrew prophets of a later age to reject sacrifices and ceremonies as a means of pleasing God and to proclaim justice and mercy and love as the sole basis of his favor.

Fig. 21—THUTMOSE III, POSSIBLE PHARAOH OF THE OPPRESSION

IV

THE SCHOOL OF THE WILDERNESS

23. The Route to Mount Sinai. Moses evidently had no definite plans for his horde of runaways beyond getting them safely out of Egypt. He might have taken them in one of three ways: (1) The caravan road to Syria, which would have led them among the newly arrived pirates, the Philistines; (2) the road southward along the eastern shore of the Red Sea, which would have led them into the Egyptian garrisons stationed to guard the copper and turquoise mines at Dophkah; and (3) the road he had travelled twice before to the land of Midian, a route used to-day by the pilgrims from Cairo to Mecca. The last road would bring them most speedily beyond Egyptian authority. There is positively no evidence to decide which of the two latter routes he took. Our only authority for placing Mount Sinai where it is generally found on the maps is an ignorant monk of the fourth century A.D. In fact, if the data given in the Bible are carefully weighed, they point to the location of Sinai-Horeb somewhere in the land of Midian east of the Gulf of Akabah, or in the Mount Seir group north of that point. On the whole, it seems probable that the Israelites went straight to Elim (Elath) at the head of the Gulf of Akabah; they sought the mountain of Jehovah to the northeast in the vicinity of Mount Seir, made their attempt to enter Palestine by way of Kadesh Barnea and the South Country; lost their grip upon what little purpose they had and became nomads with Kadesh as their centre; and last of all, struck for the richer grazing-lands that overlooked

FIG. 23—MOUNT SINAI

This is one of the oldest mountains in the world. Its granite and porphyry
    mass reared itself from the primeval ocean and has come down unchanged
    through all the geologic epochs; though round its base the Red Sea once
    threw a girdle of coral, and to the north lie vast sheets of limestone laid
    down in the chalk age.   The Arabs call it Jebel Musa, or mountain of
    Moses.   It rises 7,915 feet above the sea.   It has been regarded as the
    Sinai of scripture only since the sixth century.   In the plain where the
    sheep are the Hebrews are said to have waited for the giving of the Law
    (Ex. 19²).   Note the character of the vegetation.
Within the circuit of the mountain tradition has located the Well of Moses
    (Ex. 2¹⁵⁻¹⁷), the revelation of Jehovah to Moses and the seventy elders of
    Israel (Ex. 24⁹), the cleft where Moses saw the glory of Jehovah (Ex. 33²²),
    and the cavern where Elijah concealed himself (I Kings 19⁹ff.).

the Jordan from the east.   (See Map No. 4.)   This itiner-
ary occupied "forty years," that is, about two generations.

   24. **The Covenant at Mount Sinai.** The most important
incident in this period took place around Sinai-Horeb.   It

is probable that in the one hundred and fifty years of their bondage knowledge of their primitive god had almost disappeared; and now the slaves found themselves beyond the protection of the Egyptian deities, without a definite faith in a god of their own. Moses, with clear insight into the needs of his people, made haste to lead them to the spot where Jehovah had showed himself to him, and there by means of a solemn blood rite caused the Hebrews to adopt Jehovah as their sole tribal god. A covenant was entered into by both parties, by which the tribe agreed to be faithful to Jehovah and his commands, and Jehovah agreed to be the special protector of the infant nation.

The people's duties in this contract were expressed in the form of ten words or short statements (the Decalogue)—doubtless so numbered in order to be easily remembered by the ten fingers. The oldest form of this law is probably found in Exodus 34, but the more familiar and infinitely greater Decalogue is that found in Exodus 20^{1-17}, which defines man's duties to God, to his parents, and to his fellow men.

In order to assure the tribes by a definite symbol that their God was ever with them, Moses built a wooden shrine called the ark, and had it carried on poles by the priests, as were the shrines in the Egyptian temples. He also made for it a tent surrounded by a forbidden area, again after the Egyptian style. This primitive sanctuary was regarded as the special home of Jehovah, to which Moses went to learn the divine will and before which Jehovah's oracles were interpreted to the people. When orders came for the tribes to march, the ark of Jehovah was carried before them. Jehovah was compelled to be a wandering deity because his people were nomads. Not till the Hebrews ceased to live in tents, in Solomon's time, did Jehovah have a fixed abode at Jerusalem. To us the symbol seems childish, but to the Hebrew the reminder that God was ever with them was an inspiration and a safeguard.

The events about Sinai had such vast significance for the future of Israel that the later biblical writers have surrounded them with the symbols of mystery and majesty:

Fɪɢ. 24—MONASTERY OF SAINT CATHARINE

It lies 5,014 feet above the sea, on the spot where the emperor Justinian built a fort in 530 A.D. to protect the hermits and pilgrims who came hither. Formerly the monastery is said to have contained as many as 4,000 inmates, but there are now not more than 30, mostly natives of Crete and Cyprus and professing the orthodox Greek faith. Find the entrance, the garden, the church tower. Moses' well is behind the church, and waters the garden. The Chapel of the Burning Bush, in the apse, marks the spot where Jehovah appeared to Moses (Ex. 3[1,2]). The monastery contains a famous library, in which in 1844 Tischendorff discovered the famous Codex Sinaiticus. A flight of 3,000 steps cut in the granite ascends from the monastery to the top of the mountain, through the dark cleft above to the right.

clouds and darkness, thunders, lightnings and earthquakes. The narratives that gather about Sinai prove that the Hebrews, in common with all primitive peoples, held the conviction that law is something greater than the individual and more sacred than the nation. Thus these ancient teachers dramatically and effectively taught that law and conscience are both divinely inspired.

25. **Canaan and the Wishful Eye.** Rumors of rich land to the north induced the tribes to transfer their base from the holy mountain to the oasis of Kadesh Barnea, which lies fifty miles south of Beersheba and seventy-five southwest of Hebron. Twelve spies were sent to see how desirable the country was. They reported a land "flowing with milk and honey," and they brought back huge clusters of grapes. There was a division of opinion regarding the wisdom of forcing an entrance. Caleb and Joshua, an enthusiastic minority, said, "Go up and take possession of the land!" but the majority wrung their hands as they recalled fenced cities and giant inhabitants in whose sight the Hebrews were as grasshoppers. This exhibition of cowardice was infectious. All the people turned back from the bold enterprise, and Moses was disgusted. Yet this result might have been predicted. What could a rabble of runaway slaves, without organization, equipment, or experience in war, have accomplished against a civilization that was centuries old and firmly intrenched! A new body and a new spirit must first be created.

26. **The Gifts of the Wilderness.** It is easy to follow the hardening processes that made this rabble fit to survive and to conquer their more powerful foes, for the books of Exodus and Numbers are filled with evidence. First there were hostile tribes, like the Amalekites and the men of Arad, who took toll of them. Scant rations followed by an oversupply of quails carried off more. There must have been many pestilences, induced by starvation and the hardships of desert marching, for Jehovah is said to have punished them repeatedly for their murmurings by slaying thousands of them. There were rebellions against the leadership of Moses, each of which was put down with blood-

FIG. 25—SCENE OF THE FIGHT WITH AMALEK

Find the oasis for the possession of which the fight occurred. The hill on which we stand may well have been the one where Hur and Aaron stayed up the hands of Moses (Ex. 17$^{11-12}$). Picture to yourself the difficulties a host of runaway slaves would have to sustain itself and fight off enemies in a country like this!

shed, and one encounter with poisonous snakes that took off many people. This was indeed a struggle for existence, in which the weaker tribesmen went down and a new generation arose that was hungry enough to attack any man, and

Fig. 26—BEDOUIN TENTS NEAR MOUNT SINAI

These dwellings differ in no essentials from those used by the Hebrews.   What animal yields hair of this hue?   Of what would the ropes be made?   What would be the shape of the tent-cloth if laid flat on the ground?   How is it held up?   Imagine the fate of books, pictures, bric-à-brac, pianos, and parlor furniture if housed thus!   What is the relation of civilization to fixed abodes and the possession of property?   What determines whether a nation is civilized?

hardy enough to beat him.   This new people was the product of the desert.   The Hebrews were now brothers in spirit
and body to all those Bedouin freebooters who down to our
own day have terrorized the borders of Palestine.   With
such an instrument Moses and Joshua could at last strike
successfully.

27. **The First Foothold in Palestine.**   Moving northward
on the east side of the great depression of the Arabah, the
tribes skirted less fertile Edom and Moab till they passed
the head valleys of the Arnon.   They were now 3,000 feet
above sea-level, on the borders of the Amorite country,
which is well watered during the winter and spring, and in
every way was suited to their needs.   There was pasture for
large droves of cattle, and opportunity for some agriculture.
Sihon ruled the southern portion, from the Arnon to the
Jabbok, with his capital at Heshbon.   Og ruled the northern
part, from the brook Jabbok well up toward Damascus, with
his stronghold at the marvellous underground city of Edrei.
Both these kings were conquered and slain by the Hebrew
tribesmen, and the huge iron bedstead of Og was preserved
for generations as a trophy.   The story of Balaam which is
introduced at this period suggests the natural terror with
which the inhabitants of the land regarded this invasion of
nomads, and the ineffective magic with which the king of
Moab tried to stop them.

We must not imagine that the conquest was completed
in one campaign.   The ancient narratives in the book of
Judges plainly indicate that there was a long period of fighting and squatting and shifting, and some permanent settling and intermarrying.   It may have taken fifty years for
the actual control of this east-Jordan land to pass from the
Amorites to the Hebrews.

28. **Moses the First Great Hebrew.**   The more we study
the personality of Moses the greater he seems.   Only a man
of heroic mould and dauntless faith would have dared to defy
the tyrant who ruled the world-empire of Egypt and to

lead a rabble of undisciplined slaves out into a trackless wilderness. Only a man of masterful powers of control could have maintained himself for two generations the acknowledged leader of these rebellious tribes. Only a man possessed of an iron will and a physical frame of steel could have stood the strain of wilderness life and in addition have carried the mental burden of his people's physical and spiritual needs. Yet these are the less surprising accomplishments of this wonderful man. The proof of his colossal genius lies rather in these things—that he was able so to organize the Hebrews that his authority after his death increased rather than diminished, and served to keep the state essentially democratic; that he attached the people to Jehovah by ceremonies so free from the debasing forms which surrounding nations used that they have survived to the present day; and that he established civil laws so wise that all future generations of Hebrews sought authority for their legislation by ascribing it to him.

But the ultimate greatness of Moses rests not so much in what he accomplished as in what he

Fig. 27—MOSES

By Michelangelo.

Designed for the decoration of the tomb of Pope Julius II and finished in 1545. It is now in the church of Saint Peter in Chains, Rome. It is one of the grandest figures ever carved. How has the sculptor indicated that Moses is the law-giver? How has he indicated his great age? his undimmed vigor? (Cf. Deut. 34⁷.) The horns were given to Moses on the basis of a passage in Exodus that was mistranslated in the Latin Vulgate.

Moses has just discovered that the Hebrews are worshipping the golden calf. How is this shown?

was. It is his spiritual quality, rare in any day but unaccountable in that primitive epoch, that made him one of the few commanding figures of all time; it is his courage, his devotion, his wisdom, his unwavering trust in Jehovah. He was the first great prophet not only in Hebrew history but in world history, speaking out of personal knowledge of God his convictions about the divine will for man. Through this work as spokesman of Jehovah, as prophet of the unseen, he confirmed—one might almost say created —in the Hebrew race their marked capacity for religion. His absolute faith in the ability of Jehovah to lead his people into a "large place" inspired others with that faith. And the prophets of a later age, in picturing the glories of their Messianic deliverer, could think of no higher praise for him than to cause Moses to say in prophecy: "Jehovah your God shall raise up for you a prophet like me." He was indeed like a lofty mountain peak, to which men toiling in the valleys afar off lift their eyes to find inspiration and blessing in its loftiness and purity and majesty.

THE HOME OF THE HEBREWS

29. The Eastern Shelf. When Moses surveyed the landscape from the top of Pisgah, he saw a land of exceeding beauty and diversity. His point of vantage was a rounded bastion of the lofty Moabite plateau, sculptured out by the winter streams that fell on both sides of it to the Jordan plain. Its summit was 2,643 feet above the sea, and it was one of a score of similar projections that guard the long edge of the east-Jordan battlements. Eastward behind this foremost line other summits rise somewhat higher, and between all the tops lie shallow valleys that roll away to a well-nigh limitless horizon. Near at hand, by the western edge, the swelling hills and vales are green with crops, but as the eye runs eastward toward Arabia it detects a rustier hue; until after twenty miles or so, when the winds from the sea have dropped all their moisture, the green of vegetation gives place entirely to the brown of the desert.

It is the lure of the green that has tempted the desert dwellers from long ago; and there is no natural barrier to check their advance. All the east-Jordan land is like a narrow beach on which the desert tribes have rolled and broken since history began. Its little strip of pasture is a veritable paradise in the eyes of men accustomed to roam long and far for a bare sustenance, and therefore it has always been debatable ground, first to be attacked and first surrendered. Only once in its long history has any civilized power been able to build and hold a bulwark against this human drift, and that was in the first and second centuries A.D., when Rome established the powerful cities of the Decapolis to protect the lines of her great roads. To-day we wonder at the ruins of Jerash (Fig. 140) and Amman (Fig. 141) and Gadara and Arbila with their beautiful columns and forums and enormous theatres, mute testimony to the

FIG. 28—MOUNT NEBO

You are looking south. Find the location of Mount Nebo on the map and then tell what lies off the picture to the right, and to the left. Nebo, or Pisgah, is merely the westernmost projection of the east-Jordan table-land, a sort of pulpit or observation platform. Who made the many paths that cross the picture?

power of that civilization that once undertook to civilize and rule the world. All that Rome stood for has vanished under the vandal hand of the Turk. Her roads have been quarried to furnish mill-stones, and in their stead one sees now only lone mile-stones and the countless trails made by unshod feet, the feet of men and sheep and goats and camels.

As this table-land runs northward it is cut into four sec-

tions by rivers that have worn deep canyons into the limestone. From south to north the rivers are as follows: (1)
the Arnon, falling into the Dead Sea midway its length; (2)
the Jabbok, flowing into the Jordan midway its course; (3)
the Yarmuk, emptying into
the Jordan just below the
Sea of Galilee. The four
sections of the plateau
have borne various names.
The southmost was for-
merly called, after the tribe
that lived there, Moab.
Now it is named after its
chief town, Kerak. Be-
tween the Arnon and the
Jabbok the land is some-
times called Moab, for the
Moabites once owned most
of it, and sometimes Am-
mon, after the old tribe of
that name. The name
Gilead is now usually ap-
plied to it and to the section next on the north.
The third section has al-

Fig. 29—IN THE DEAD SEA

Showing the great buoyancy of the water.
Shortly after this picture was taken
a wind capsized the man with the
umbrella and the sail got wet. On
drying the umbrella was so incrusted
with salt that it could not be shut
and had to be thrown away.

ways borne the geographical name Gilead, though in Christ's
day it went by its political name of Decapolis, because
of the ten cities of the Greeks that lay mostly within its
borders. The northmost section is Bashan, though the
large hollow around the sources of the Yarmuk is called
specifically the Hauran. In Moses' day the whole plateau
north of the Arnon was called the land of the Amorites, or
the kingdoms of Sihon and Og.

30. **The Great Trench.** At Moses' feet, sheer down from
Pisgah's watch-tower, the rugged wall of Moab dropped to
the Jordan valley and the Dead Sea. Some ten miles away,

yet seemingly not more than two, rose the valley's western wall, the adamantine cliffs that bear on their top the twisted wilderness of Judea. Between that western wall and the eastern one on which he stood, lay the most astonishing valley in the world—a vast ditch, a chasm, which extended far out of sight to the north, where snowy Mount Hermon sends its roots down into the plain, and the southern end of which Moses and his horde had but recently crossed at the head of the Gulf of Akabah. It is what the geologists call a "fault." Long ago when things were in the making, the earth cracked here. A huge slice fell downward, as the eastern plateau was thrust up, and along the crack oozed out streams of lava from below. One may to-day see their black dikes cropping out here and there, or ride over miles of stones that once showered out of old craters when Jehovah "rained fire and brimstone upon Sodom and Gomorrah," or bathe at many places in sulphur springs still hot with internal fires. But the astonishing feature of this great trench is its depth. It sinks to the sea-level far to the north by the Waters of Merom. At the Sea of Galilee it has fallen to 682 feet below the sea; on the Dead Sea shore below Nebo it has reached the depth of 1,292 feet, while the

FIG. 30—BAD LANDS OF THE JORDAN VALLEY

This is the old lake bed, now exposed by the shrinking of the waters. A little rain transforms the dusty ground into ooze the consistency of soft soap. Woe to the carriage that attempts a passage under such conditions. Harder strata form caps over this silt at places, and so protect it from being washed down. The result is a series of terraces all along the lower valley, taking the shape of *mesas*, as shown in the picture.

bottom is 1,308 feet lower still. From the top of Nebo to the lowest point of the rift, therefore, the distance is a perpendicular mile. If the ocean could be sluiced in here, the Dead Sea would expand to a length of 140 miles, and still be only a few rods wider than it is at present.

Indeed, long ago the lake did reach these dimensions. The rains of the glacial age once filled the valley to beyond the level of the sea, to old lines of beaches still visible on the hillsides. But as the rainfall slackened, rapid evaporation, due to the nearness of the desert, caused the lake to shrink. When human history began, the shrinking had nearly stopped; and now, with minor fluctuations, the lake hangs stationary just at the balancing point between the intake from the Jordan River and the outgo from evaporation—for there is no outlet for the great sink-hole except upward. Thus it comes about that six and a half million tons of water every day go up to heaven from the surface of this sea! What is left is so charged with the salts and minerals that have been washed in by the Jordan that four buckets of water when evaporated produce one bucket of solid matter. One cannot sink in the Dead Sea. (Fig. 29.)

Though from the heights of Nebo the Jordan valley is fair to look upon, it is a most uncomfortable stopping-place. The air is heavy. The winds sweep high above it from the western hills to the eastern, and the sun bakes down in the hollow until the air quivers as in a furnace. It is never cold there, and in the summer the temperature mounts to one hundred and twenty-five degrees and higher. The ground, too, has a sickly and ulcerous appearance in the region around Jericho, so filled with chemicals is it, though farther north it becomes more normal. If the old aqueducts of Roman times could be again used, or if the Jordan itself could be canalled off for irrigation, the wretched soil might be washed and redeemed and the whole plain blossom as the garden of the Lord. Some day this will be done. In the meantime, from the Sea of Galilee to the salt mountain be-

low the Dead Sea, the large part of this valley is only an unhealthy jungle in which the Arabs spread their black
tents when driven thither by the parching of the plateaus
above.

Historically this great rift was the most important factor
of Israel's environment. It has been a divider. Were it

Fig. 31—THE WATERSHED OF JUDEA

Near Beeroth, on the main road northward, thirteen miles from Jerusalem,
where the valleys of Ajalon and Michmash almost meet. What is this
land good for? Why should there be no trees? Why are there stone
walls?

not for this steep descent and ascent, for this salt sea, for
the debilitating climate of this old lake bottom, or, to put
it conversely, if the plateau of the east had rolled unbroken
to the summit of the western ridge, the Arabs would have
turned all Palestine into debatable ground; the Hebrew
democracy could never have arisen and flourished, civilization would not have gained a foothold, and the religion of
Israel that needed for its development a certain isolation
would never have blossomed in the prophets or fruited in

FIG. 32—MIZPAH

A typical Judean hill surmounted by a village. See how the level strata of limestone form giant steps to the very summit (2,953 feet). Look up the connection of King Asa with this hill (I Kings 15^{22}), Gedaliah (II Kings 25$^{23,\,25}$), and Judas Maccabæus (sec. 212). The crusaders thought that this was Shiloh and built a church here in 1157, which now does duty as a mosque over the tomb of Samuel. Was Samuel buried here (I Sam. 25^1)? The view from Mizpah extends from the Mediterranean to the mountains of Moab and from Hebron to Mount Gerizim.

Jesus. So a mere shudder of the old earth long ago changed the history and the destiny of the human race!

31. **The Central Roof.** When Moses looked westward across the chasm of the Jordan he saw a sky-line that was

nearly level, and higher than Nebo. Above the precipitous Judean cliffs the chalky hilltops climb slowly away until at an air-line distance of thirty miles they reach a long crest. North and south the ridge runs, its highest point opposite the centre of the Dead Sea, 3,737 feet; thence by Hebron 3,370, Bethlehem 2,690, Mizpah 2,835, Bethel 2,890. As the roof extends northward, the valleys that divide the hill-tops become broader, though the mountains themselves remain nearly as high—Sinjil, near Shiloh, 2,600, Gerizim 2900, Ebal 3,000. But just beyond Ebal the long ridge lowers its crest; it breaks into rounded hills. Then one spur, veering to the northeast, runs out to a point at Mount Gilboa, 1,600 feet high, and abruptly stops, while another and longer spur runs northwest in a chain of dimpling hills until it culminates in Mount Carmel, 1,800 feet high, thrusting itself boldly into the Mediterranean. The central range of Palestine has thus broken down completely.

The broad plain of Esdraelon now interposes, a wonderful triangle of verdure fifteen miles on a side. Beyond this again rise the splendid hills of Galilee, separated from each other by long finger-like valleys running up from the east and the west and almost touching each other. North of this diversified country the great central ridge rises again almost abruptly, with many cusps 2,000 feet high. Finally the magnificent range of the Lebanon Mountains dominates the sky-line on the north and passes beyond the limits of Palestine. Its first peak is 8,000 feet high, and its highest three above Beirut are over 10,000. Thus the whole of central Palestine is a mountain range, parallel with the Jordan valley and the seacoast, breaking down, however, into broad plains and valleys in Lower Galilee.

This central section, too, has strongly influenced Israel's history. The plains of Galilee and the valleys of Samaria, because they were crossed by the roads from everywhere, were the earliest to fall to the invader; and the people, exposed to every heathen religion that travelled these same roads, lost earliest their desert faith in Jehovah and their desert purity of life. The Hebrews who once lived here have almost vanished without leaving any appreciable impress upon the life of mankind. But Judah, high on her

FIG. 33—THE WILDERNESS OF JUDEA

On the road from Jerusalem to Jericho, looking southwest. Contrast these smooth hills with the rocky terraces on the west side of the watershed (*cf.* Fig. 32). The difference lies in the relative hardness of the rocks: on the west, limestone strata; on the east, chalk. The soil here is white. In the winter there is a scant vegetation on which countless flocks graze. In the summer the hills are parched brown.

central ridge, lying on the road to nowhere and isolated by her bulwark of mountains round about, kept the invaders at bay a century and a half after her sister kingdom had fallen, and developed her ideas of religion until they became narrow enough and intense enough and vital enough to survive even the destruction of the state. The mountains round about Jerusalem proved to be the everlasting arms beneath her faith.

32. **The Westward Meadows.** Moses could not see beyond the central range, and he was probably ignorant of

the fertile fields that stretched westward some sixteen miles to the sea. His people were destined not to possess this garden-ground for many generations; for the Philistines, soon to settle on the western shore, would exterminate the

FIG. 34—THE GARDENS OF JAFFA

Looking southwest. To the right of the city is the sea. The trees are date-palms, oranges, figs, and pomegranates. Their culture is made profitable by irrigation, the water being raised from wells by immense wheels with buckets on them. Modern Jewish colonists use the gasolene engine. Oranges are exported from Jaffa to the value of $1,250,000 a year—the most luscious oranges in the world, juicy, seedless, and measuring up to sixteen inches in circumference.

Canaanite lowlanders and in due time encounter the Hebrews who would cross the great rift from the east to conquer the Amorite highlanders. These two newcomers fought each other for generations to determine who should control the plain. In the end the Philistines won.

The plain is the most fertile part of Palestine. From Gaza on the south, where the desert ceases, the rolling fields

are golden with grain. Olives and palms flourish, and in
these days, by the aid of wells and irrigation, thousands of
boxes of the most luscious and the largest oranges of the
world are raised here. As the plain stretches northward it

Copyright by Underwood and Underwood, N. Y.

Fig. 35—SUMMIT OF MOUNT HERMON

The most conspicuous and the most beautiful mountain in Palestine, 9,166 feet
   high.   It is covered with snow most of the year.   The Bible gives evidence
   of the impress it made on the Hebrew imagination.   Look up Ps. 89¹²;
   133³; Song of Sol. 4⁸.   This is perhaps the "high mountain" of Matt. 17¹.

gradually narrows and ends in a long point where Mount
Carmel crowds it into the Mediterranean.   North of Carmel the coastal plain begins again with a wide sweep inland,
but soon narrows above Acre to the merest strip, which
widens a little opposite Tyre and Sidon.   This northern
coast plain was never held by the Hebrews, but was the
home of the Phœnician branch of the Canaanite family.
Thus the Phœnicians above and the Philistines below were responsible, in part at least, for the Hebrew aversion to the sea.

One other reason must be given why the Hebrews failed to take to the sea: the absence of harbors. Note on the map the long, unbroken curve of coast-line from Gaza to Mount Carmel. There is not a suggestion of an anchorage where a vessel could lie safe from the pounding of the winter gales. If shepherds and vine-dressers are to become sailors, the sea must come invitingly to the hills, as it did in Greece; or the mountains must crowd down to the shore and force an expanding people to take to ships—as they did in Phœnicia. So while Phœnician sails dotted every sea and Phœnician merchants squeezed profit out of the wares of all the world, the Hebrew stayed by his sheepfolds listening to the pipings for the flocks and hugging his religion to his breast, until war and persecution in the latter days scattered his children to the four corners of the earth.

To sum up: Palestine presented to the Hebrews four parallel zones running north and south: (1) The eastern table-land, (2) the Jordan valley, (3) the central highland, (4) the maritime plain. While all of these zones were possessed by the Hebrews, in part at least and for a longer or a shorter time, the central highland became their real home.

THE STRUGGLE FOR A HOME

33. Canaanite Palestine. The Hebrews may well have paused to reckon the cost before throwing themselves into the land of Canaan. To conquer an intrenched civilization is no holiday pastime, especially when the invaders have not much more than their own courage to rely upon. In the present case the Hebrews had no special skill in war, and while the accounts speak of destroying with the edge of the sword, it is probable that the only weapons used by the Israelites were flint knives, bows, arrows and spears with flint heads, clubs and stone hatchets—unless, indeed, they had captured something better from Sihon and Og. They had no machinery of assault nor chariots nor horses, nor did they know the use of metals. Not one of them had probably ever lived in a house or constructed a fortification.

The older inhabitants, on the contrary, were well advanced in the arts. They had cities, situated for the most part in advantageous sites and walled with stone. They had bronze weapons and tools of various kinds. They had stable governments, also, and many of their arts and institutions were those that make up what we call civilization. The odds certainly seemed to be with the defenders. In one respect, however, they were at a serious disadvantage: they had suffered severely under the conquests of Thutmose III whose persistent policy of devastation from 1479 B.C. had weakened their resistance. But now that the grip of Egypt was relaxing under Amenhotep III, they felt themselves helpless against the threat of invasion, as the whole mass of the Amarna tablets shows. Moreover, the rival kings of the

FIG. 36—PHILISTINE PRISONERS OF RAMSES III

Relief on the second pylon at Medinet Habu, Thebes.

Notice the peculiar head-dress made of feathers; likewise the hand-cuffs made of wood and suspended round the neck. Find a prisoner with elbows tied behind his back and one with arms tied over his head. Why the scant clothing (Is. 20$^{1-4}$, and sec. 123).

petty cities of Palestine had fallen apart; the stronger were preying upon the weaker. As a result they presented no united front to the enemy. Joshua and his warriors could conquer them piecemeal.

34. **A Canaanite City.** In order to appreciate part at least of Joshua's task, it may be well to take a look at a Canaanite city. The following description is condensed from Macalister, the excavator of Gezer (*A History of Civilization in Palestine*).

The ridge of rock is surmounted by a city about half a
mile in length, surrounded by a colossal wall which is broken
at intervals by shallow projecting towers. This wall stands
twenty or thirty feet above the ground and is about fourteen

FIG. 37—WALL AND RUINS OF JERICHO

Looking west to the mountains of Judea. The outer wall (right) is made of
fairly large round stones piled up without mortar, and slopes inward.
On top of this rose a wall of brick about eight feet thick. Behind this the
little houses of brick and stone were huddled. This is the Middle Bronze
city. Off the picture to the left was another strong wall defending the
citadel of the later town captured by Joshua. The whole city measured
only 1,200 feet from north to south, and about half that in width. It is
easy to see how Rahab's house might be built on the wall (Josh. 2[15]).

feet thick. The top is protected by a breast-high parapet
from behind which the defenders can throw down missiles
on a besieging army. In the wall facing us is a gate of the
city—a narrow entrance flanked by two massive towers
of brick. The entrance is closed with two great port-

cullises of wood dropped into the spaces between slabs
of stone. Passing through the gate, which is paved with
cobblestones polished smooth by footwear, we see narrow,
crooked, unclean streets. Our nostrils are assailed by the
stench of an airless, drainless, Oriental town. We see one-
story stone houses plastered with mud. The roofs are flat.
There is a courtyard around which the two or three rooms
are arranged. There is no furniture. Human beings and
animals herd together at night, the former separated from
the latter by being on a raised platform. Offensive insects
infest every corner. Melancholy dogs prowl about. Here
is a knot of children—particularly evil-looking morsels of
humanity, with distended paunches, the result of unre-
strained water-drinking. They all wear conspicuously some
kind of amulet to avert the dreaded "evil eye," and they
wear very little else.

Passing inward from the gate we soon come upon a house
like the rest, but larger. It is the home of the "king." In
the courtyard there is an opening in the rock which excites
our astonishment. It is the mouth of a huge tunnel that
sinks at an angle of about thirty degrees, some twelve feet
across and twenty high, with a flight of stairs cut along
the bottom of it. This shaft goes down to a spring which
by some means the wise ones were able to locate, still inside
the hill though beyond the circle of the walls. This is the
water-supply—useful always, but absolutely invaluable in
time of siege.

Wandering through the crooked lanes we find ourselves in
an open square in the highest part of the city. This is the
"high place," the centre of the city's religious life. Here the
top of the rocky ridge is exposed. In it they have cut an
altar with steps mounting on one side; there are curious cup-
shaped hollows in the surrounding rocky floor, for what
purpose we do not know; there is a stone with a large square
excavation in it, probably a laver; and there are half a dozen
standing pillars of stone from five to seven feet high, round

and with rounded top, the dwelling-places of the local deity
or Baal. (See also Fig. 112.)

Resuming our walk, we find a potter at work in his little
cell of a shop. He rotates the wheel with one hand and

Fig. 38—STONE PILLARS OF GEZER

Mr. Macalister, the excavator of Gezer, stands above. He has dug out this
row of standing stones, the first found in Palestine, and kept back the
rubbish with a wall of stones. This is the High Place of Gezer. These
stones were the symbols—if not the residence—of the Baal of Gezer. The
receptacle is probably for the blood of sacrifices. Under the pavement
of this sanctuary were clay jars containing the bodies of children, doubtless used in sacrifice. (I Kings 16³⁴.)

shapes his dish crudely with the other. Next door is a
worker in flint—for though bronze is now in use, the old
material is still used for rough work. Rock is quarried with
flint, wheat is reaped with a flint sickle, the skins of slaughtered animals are scraped with flint. So the tradesman
finds plenty of custom as he sits and splinters flakes off the
pebbles that are found in abundance in the chalky hills

around. Next is a carpenter and joiner, working with tools of bronze and bone. Then comes a weaver and next a goldsmith, who turns out from his moulds, by the gross, copies of earrings and amulets such as are worn in Egypt. He never thinks of striking out on an original line of his own. As we look, a quarrel breaks out between him and a customer over a false weight—for this man, like most dealers, keeps two sets of weights, a heavy one to use in buying goods and a light one to use in selling them!

So the busy life of the town goes on. Like all Orientals, the people pass their time in fear of the caprice of their deity or of their despot, but in spite of fears they seem fairly happy and contented. Most of them cultivate by day the vineyards and fields that lie about the foot of their hill, and return to their stuffy huts at night. They eat and drink, they marry and are given in marriage, they buy and sell, and they have no further anxieties until some wild tribe sweeps down on their fields from the desert, or some mighty king from Egypt or the north comes through on a raid. Then it is usually a choice between slavery and the sword.

35. **The Capture of Jericho.** A city just like the one described lay directly in the path of the Hebrew advance. It was a city of strategic importance, for it commanded the two fords of the Jordan to the east of it and three important trails that led up into the central highland—one southwest toward Hebron, one west to Jerusalem, and one northwest to Bethel. To leave it untaken would be to have all communication cut with their base on the Jordan. Joshua, the new commander, sent spies at once, who reported that the inhabitants were thoroughly frightened at the accounts that had come of the Hebrew conquest of Sihon and Og, and that there were those inside who could be counted upon to aid. Joshua therefore attacked in force, awed the inhabitants by mysterious and silent marches around the city, then stormed the town over walls thrown down by an earthquake. The scripture naturally ascribes the quake to Jehovah's direct act.

As it was the first prize taken, it was devoted to Jehovah; that is, it was completely burned; every piece of gold, silver, bronze, and iron was turned into the treasury of Jehovah, and all cattle and captives—male and female, young and old—were killed as a thank-offering to him. This wholesale slaughter was nothing new to the Israelites or to the conquered· all Semitic races used to honor their gods in this way.

35a. **The Testimony of Archæology.** Professor John Garstang made extensive excavations in Jericho in 1929–33, as a result of which these facts emerge:

Jericho was an old Canaanite city founded before 2000 B.C. At the time of its greatest prosperity, 1800–1600 B.C., it covered twelve acres—large as Palestine cities go. Overthrown about 1600 B.C., it was rebuilt in a smaller area, about six acres, and surrounded with two parallel walls of brick about fifteen feet apart and twenty-five to thirty feet high. The pottery shows that this city ceased about 1400 B.C.— according to the Biblical data at 1407 B.C. The fact that the west wall was damaged and the east wall quite destroyed, while the north and south walls are intact, indicates an east and west earthquake movement identical with the waves of the 1927–8 earthquakes at modern Jericho. Charred timbers, pockets of charcoal, reddened brick, layers of ashes, and the debris of house walls prove that the city was deliberately wrecked and burned. Pottery shows that there was no further settlement here for at least five hundred years, thus corroborating I Kings 16[34] that says Hiel of Bethel rebuilt the town in the time of Ahab (876–854 B.C.).

The mounds of Bethel, Hazor, Keriath-Sepher and Eglon also indicate destruction by war in the 14th–13th centuries before Christ.

36. **The Accounts of Other Conquests.** The other stories found in Joshua are extremely interesting and full of hints about primitive ways and peoples. The first city to fall after Jericho was Ai, well up toward the watershed on the

trail to Bethel. The ancient stratagem of an ambush and a pretended retreat deceived the inhabitants into leaving their town unguarded, and the Hebrews took and devoted it. They now held both ends of the road that led from their base by the Jordan to the hill-country they coveted. The next incident shows that the Canaanites, too, were not ignorant of stratagems. An embassy of wayworn travellers presented themselves to Joshua at Gilgal and asked him to make a treaty of peace with them on the ground that they lived in a far country, and having heard of what the God of the Hebrews had done for them, wished to enjoy the favor of this great tribe and its powerful divinity. Joshua lost his head for the once—doubtless not having heard much flattery hitherto—and immediately made a treaty. The next day he found that the far country was Gibeon, just over the hill, only six miles from Ai! The elders were for breaking the dishonestly made bond, yet Joshua kept to it, as far at least as to spare the lives of the Gibeonites, but he compelled them to pay a tribute of forced labor and to furnish slaves for the sanctuary of Jehovah.

Later tradition adds that certain southern kings were by this time aroused to the menace of the Israelites. Jerusalem, Hebron, Jarmuth, Lachish, and Eglon leagued together and attacked Gibeon, the new Hebrew ally. Joshua rushed to the rescue, and with the help of Jehovah, who "cast great hailstones from the sky," drove the five kings twenty miles down into the plain, while, in the language of the old war-song, "the sun and moon stood still," that the Hebrews might have daylight in which to complete the slaughter. The five kings who had taken refuge in a cave were discovered and hanged. Certain northern kings, led by Jabin of Hazor, next took fright; but Joshua surprised them before they were completely mobilized and routed them by the Waters of Merom. Now, according to the book of Joshua, the land had rest; and by means of the sacred lot each tribe received its inheritance.

37. **The Stories Interpreted.** In trying to understand what actually took place during the conquest we are somewhat confused by two contradictory points of view presented in the books of Joshua and Judges. Joshua states that all the tribes went into the land as a unit and in a

Fɪɢ. 39—LETTER FROM THE KING OF JERUSALEM

Written by King Abd-Keba, to Amenhotep IV of Egypt, about 1360 ʙ.ᴄ. One of the nearly four hundred clay tablets found at Tel el-Amarna in Egypt, in 1887. They were unearthed by a peasant woman and sold to an antiquity dealer of Luxor for about $10, who later sold them a few at a time at prices ranging from $5 to $750 each! They are now mostly in the British Museum. They all tell of an invasion of Palestine by a people called the Khabiri, who, as we now know, wrested all Palestine from the control of Egypt.

single war conquered the entire country; that all the inhabitants were ruthlessly destroyed and the land was divided among the twelve tribes; that then the people renewed their promise to be faithful to Jehovah, and Joshua made his farewell address and died. But it is easy to see that the book of Joshua is not history in our sense of that word. It is idealized history, written to teach later generations that the success of the Hebrews in conquering Palestine was the direct reward of their faithfulness to Jehovah. The first two chapters of the book of Judges, on the other hand, give us hints of a far different conquest extending over a much longer time. It tells the story of the filtering in of a people, of single clans and tribes attempting with more or less success to gain a foothold here or there, of conquest by compromise and intermarriage and assimilation, the decision hanging long in the balance as to which side would ultimately prevail. It becomes evident that the Hebrew conquest should be identified with the invasion of the Khabiri or Habiru mentioned in the Amarna tablets of the fourteenth century. These fighting Bedouin clans began to penetrate western Palestine in the sixteenth century or earlier, became increasingly troublesome, destroyed but did not at first reoccupy many Canaanite towns and finally became sedentary in the thirteenth and twelfth centuries. The clans that occupied southern Palestine came to be called Judah, Simeon and the Kenites, all of whom probably came in directly from the southeast some time before the invasion under Joshua. The Mount Ephraim invaders became the Joseph tribes of the later tradition. The minor clans north of Esdraelon came in from the north several generations earlier, were never in Egypt at all, and only with difficulty were amalgamated into the religious and national consciousness of the more southern clans. But whether early or late comers they were all racially of the same stock and together with the Canaanites spoke Canaanite-Hebrew, as is revealed by texts unearthed at Ras Shamra (north Syria) and Bethshemesh (Judea).

The so-called Canaanites were earlier on the ground and were well intrenched when Joshua arrived. The central Hebrews could not conquer the plain because the Canaanites had chariots of iron; and everywhere the more strongly fortified cities defied the invaders, like Jerusalem, Beth-shan, Taanach, Megiddo and Dor. These barriers prevented the Hebrews from acting in concert and delayed their conquest. All through the period of the Judges we see the struggle going on. Not until the time of David were the Canaanite lines broken and the divisions healed. Then for a brief century the Hebrews were a united people, the undisputed masters of central and eastern Palestine.

VII

THE STRUGGLE FOR INDEPENDENCE

38. **Israel's Dangerous Position.** Realizing as we now do that the conquest was not an act but a process, we are in a position to trace in detail the dangers that surrounded the Hebrews.

The first danger was the possibility of extermination. The tribes had deliberately come among hostile foes who now ringed them completely about. Between the Hebrews and the eastern desert lay the Arameans (north), the Ammonites (centre), and the Moabites (south). Cutting them off from the southern steppe land lay the Edomites (southeast) and the Amalekites (southwest). Between them and the sea lay two powerful peoples, the Philistines (south) and the Canaanites (centre and north). Moreover, as we have seen, the Canaanite cities quite cut them in two at the plain of Esdraelon, and nearly so at the valley of Ajalon in the south. The Hebrews must do or die. They must strike root and grow till their neighbors are crowded off the map, or they themselves will wither and be absorbed. Which alternative will result is bound to be determined by the relative physical and moral strength of the Hebrews and their neighbors.

The second danger lay in the change in occupation that the conquest made necessary, and the consequent adjustment to new conditions of life. Hitherto the Hebrews had been nomads and shepherds; henceforth they must become farmers, vine-dressers, artisans, tradesfolk. It was a question whether they could stop roving, whether they could master the difficult art of husbandry in a land of variable and often doubtful rainfall; whether they could give up tents and live huddled together in unhealthy stone villages and survive the new forms of disease that would surely come. The change was a test of intelligence, of physique,

FIG. 40—VINEYARD OF HEBRON

Note how the soil had to be cleared of stones. Each vine is about five feet long, the free end propped up on shears. The branches are pruned off close to this stump each season so that all the strength of the vine shall go into the grapes. August is the month for gathering. Hebron has always been famous for its grapes, since the time of the spies (Num. 13^{23}).

of courage, of staying power. Some of the tribes could not meet the test: Simeon relapsed to nomadic life, the half-tribe of Manasseh, east of the Jordan, was largely absorbed by the Arameans, Reuben by the Moabites, and Asher changed the plough and the ox goad for the oar, becoming practically Phœnician.

The third danger was a political one. We have seen that from the earliest days the Hebrews had been thoroughly democratic The families or clans were all on the same level of rights and opportunities, with special privilege for

none.   Their free nomadic life for two generations had confirmed their love for their democratic life and institutions.
But now they had come into close and hostile contact with
the Canaanites and the Amorites, whose type of government was a petty autoc-
racy in which a ruling
family or the appointee
of some military despot-
ism like Egypt owned all
the inhabitants as mere
vassals and used them to
defend or extend his
power. We know from
the Hebrew records that
the existence of these
kings and their success
in war was a powerful in-
centive to the Hebrews
to drop their loose tribal
form of government and
copy the nations round.
In time they yielded to

FIG. 41—A THRESHING-
FLOOR

Every village has a bare level place, preferably a ledge of rock, on which the
  grain is threshed. The most primitive method is to turn in a group of
  cattle, tied together, and drive them
  around through the spread-out sheaves
  till their hoofs have crushed the wheat-
  heads. For another method, see Fig.
  42.

this influence, but never completely.   The democratic spirit
in Israel never died.   Indeed, Israel's subsequent history is
largely the story of how this instinct for democracy fought
for expression and refused to die even when the political
life of the nation was blotted out by Babylon and by Rome.

The fourth and greatest danger lay in the realm of religion.   Coming fresh from the desert, with enthusiasm still
burning for the God who had delivered them from the perils
of Egypt and the wilderness, the Hebrews had at least this
bond of union among themselves and this difference from
their neighbors: they were Jehovah-worshippers, with a
simple and relatively pure morality adapted to their mode
of life.   But now they had come to a land over which Jehovah was believed to have no jurisdiction.   They were in a

land of Baals.   Every spring and hilltop and village tree
had its divine or demon proprietor who must be fed and
otherwise made comfortable if the newcomers wished any
peace or prosperity.   Jehovah was a shepherd's god, to be
worshipped with the firstlings of the flocks; Baal was a
farmer's god, to be honored with the first-fruits of the soil.
Being no longer shepherds and in a foreign land, many of
the Hebrews felt that they were no longer under any practical necessity to be loyal to Jehovah.

39. **Jehovah's Rival.**   Let us imagine a definite case.   A
Hebrew stakes out a claim in the hollow to the south of
Bethel and begins to till the soil.   He buys or steals his seed
from a Canaanite neighbor, sows it by guess, and sits down
to wait for the harvest.   Somehow the harvest does not
come; the grain turns yellow before it heads.   He goes
anxiously to his Canaanite friend, who asks him: "Did you
make sacrifice to the Baal who owns the field and lives in
the big tree at the end of it?"   The Hebrew confesses that
since he is a Jehovah-worshipper he did not.   Whereupon
he is told that he may expect no crops till he sacrifices to
Baal.   Not being rich enough to stand a second loss, he
takes his friend's advice next season, allows the Canaanite
to teach him the correct method of worship and incidentally
to give him some valuable points on how and when to sow and
how to take care of his field.   Next harvest-time there is a
bumper crop.   The Hebrew shows his joy by buying the
Canaanite's daughter as a wife for his son, and by becoming
a constant worshipper at the Baal-tree.   Of course he worships Jehovah, too, for old time's sake; but he understands
that the god whom it pays to cultivate, now that he has
become a farmer, is Baal.

This little episode makes real the crowning danger.   There
was not a feature of the new life the Hebrews had to lead
that was not connected with Canaanite religion—for religion
in those days was not a separate function but a vital part
of all living.   It was necessary to appease the Baal when a

new house was built, when seed was sown, when grapes and olives were gathered, when sheep were sheared, when children were born, when people married or died. Every one firmly believed that all calamities came to men because of

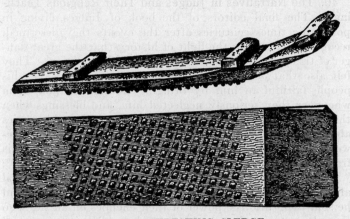

FIG. 42—A THRESHING SLEDGE

Made of planks, in the under side of which are inserted stones. The driver rides on the sledge as the cattle drag it over the grain spread out on the threshing-floor. The stones tear the straw and the grain falls out of the heads.

some slight to one of the gods. It behooved everybody, therefore, to keep on the best of terms with all possible divinities; which in plain words means that every Hebrew had to become an idolater. He had to worship the local gods of whatever part of the land he occupied, as well as the larger gods—like the sun, moon, and stars—who controlled the weather. At the same time he must faithfully bring offerings to his tribal god, Jehovah, and to the spirits of his ancestors, as represented by the teraphim, or household gods. Is it any wonder that the poor Hebrew forgot Jehovah more or less! The danger lies just here: If he forgets Jehovah he has nothing left to distinguish him from his neighbors. His

morals, influenced by the example of his neighbors and by
the debasing rites with which the Baals are worshipped, will
become corrupt, and in three generations there will be no
Hebrews.

**40. The Narratives in Judges and Their Religious Teach-
ings.** The final editors of the book of Judges, living in
post-exilic times centuries after the events they described,
recognized clearly in the light of history that the great danger of this period was loss of their distinctive religion.   They
felt also that Jehovah had tried in every way to keep his
people faithful to him by bringing calamities upon them
whenever they seriously neglected him, and blessings when
they were faithful.   They therefore took the old stories
about the heroes and champions and set them into a framework that tended to bring out this theory of history.   This
framework without any illustration is given in Judges 2¹³ ¹⁹:
"And they forsook Jehovah, and burned sacrifices to Baal
and Astarte.   And Jehovah was incensed against Israel, and
he sold them into the power of their enemies on all sides, so
that they were no longer able to withstand their foes.   And
Jehovah raised up judges, and delivered the Israelites from
those who despoiled them, for Jehovah was moved to pity
by their groans.   But when the judge died, they would
slide back and act worse than their fathers in running after
other gods."   In reality these stories tell how the Hebrew
instinct for freedom, the right of self-determination, refused
to be crushed, and how out of the ranks of the people themselves arose the patriots who saved their tribe.   They present a picture of democracy creating its own saviors.

A condensed account of what the five most important judges
or deliverers accomplished is here given.   See Appendix IV.

41. The Moabite Oppression.   The Moabites, who a generation earlier had tried to get rid of the Hebrews by magic
(Sec. 27), now under King Eglon found courage to try the
sword.   Their success was not large, but they probably retook the old Moabite cities that Israel had captured north

of the Arnon, and occupied Jericho with its adjacent lands
and fords, which belonged to Benjamin. For eighteen
years little Benjamin paid its tribute of oil and wine and
wool; then the "spirit of Jehovah" stirred up a man named
Ehud, who planned a bold stroke for liberty. He made him
a rude double-edged sword fourteen
inches long, without a guard on it,
and being left-handed he hung it
under his sheepskin jacket on his
right side. Having gone with others
in charge of the yearly tribute, he
sought a private audience with King
Eglon on the ground that he had a
message for him from Jehovah.
When the king reverently stood to
receive the message, Ehud delivered
it pointblank and beyond the hilt!
The assassin then made his escape,
rallied his forces, seized the fords of
the Jordan and so rid the land of
its oppressors.

FIG. 43—WINNOWING
Small wooden shovels are
used to throw the mixed
grain and chaff into the
air. The strong wind
that blows in harvest
time drives the chaff
away while the grain
falls to the ground.

42. **The Canaanite Oppression.**
The story of the defeat of the Canaanites concerns chiefly the north-
ern tribes on both sides of Esdraelon. This was the region
of greatest Canaanite strength, and the persecution to which
they subjected the Hebrews was cruel. People no longer
dared to travel the regular roads for fear of robbery and
violence, but took to secret paths. The first to break this
yoke of fear was the prophetess Deborah, and she used the
only rallying-cry that could have been effective in the case:
"Come up to the help of Jehovah against the mighty!"
She saw too that fidelity to Jehovah, and that alone, meant
national existence. With this conviction she inspired Barak
of Kadesh-Naphtali to assemble on Mount Tabor some 10,-
000 men of the northern and central tribes, and to try con-

clusions with their oppressors.   Sisera, the Canaanite leader, met the revolt promptly with 900 chariots of iron and many men.   Their rendezvous was Harosheth, that guarded the western exit of Esdraelon, where the Kishon breaks through

FIG. 44—MOUNT TABOR

This well-rounded dome is 1,843 feet high.   It is dotted all over with scrub-oaks, and surmounted by a Latin and a Greek monastery built because of the tradition (unfounded) that the Transfiguration took place here (Matt. 17[1-2]).

between the hills of Galilee and Mount Carmel.   The Canaan-ites took the offensive.   They marched eastward along the highway that joined their strong cities of Megiddo and Taanach and Bethshean, in order to cut off any help the Hebrews might receive from the south and to enable them-selves the more easily to absorb the conquered fragments. Barak held his men in leash until the long line of their foes had advanced far out across the soft, alluvial plain—all easily seen from the summit of Tabor.   Then, just after the van-guard of the Canaanites had crossed the narrow, treacherous

FIG. 45—PLAIN OF ESDRAELON

A wonderfully beautiful triangular plain, 15–20 miles on a side. You are standing at Jezreel and looking west. The dark patches are cloud-shadows. The light patch near the centre, to which the paths lead, is the village of El-fuleh, a station on the Haifa-Damascus railway, the junction of the new military branch to Egypt, and the focal-point of all the caravan lines that cross the plain. The hills in the distance are those near Nazareth (right) and Mount Carmel (left). The break where these two meet is the place where the river Kishon passes through to the sea.

This is the famous Armageddon, battle-ground of the nations. In addition to the biblical fights and the Roman and crusading campaigns, Napoleon was beaten here at El-fuleh, and in Sept., 1918, General Allenby captured the same town from the Turks on his victorious final campaign.

ford of the Kishon, like a thunderbolt he launched his columns full at Sisera's centre.   Providentially at the moment of impact there burst a tremendous thunder-storm which turned the soft-soiled plain into a quagmire.   The horses plunged, the iron chariots sank to their hubs, the soldiers caught panic from the storm, which they attributed, as did the Hebrews, to the wrath of some god, and soon the battle became a Canaanite rout in which the swollen Kishon and the miry plain claimed more victims than the sword.   Sisera the general fled, only to meet death treacherously at the hands of a woman in whose tent he took refuge.   This battle was one of the most important in Hebrew history, for it settled the question of supremacy in the whole central region in favor of the Hebrews and the Hebrew God, and left them free to establish their democratic institutions in the land of their adoption.

43. **The Midianite Oppression.** The Midianites came first within the Hebrew horizon during the wilderness wanderings.   They were a Bedouin tribe whose special grazinglands were east of the Red Sea, but who evidently ranged at times along the whole northwestern edge of the Arabian desert.   In the story in Judges we find them making annual raids upon central Palestine just when the inhabitants had harvested their grain, and taking it all away, while their countless cattle ate up all that was left in the fields.   Jehovah spoke to a powerful farmer named Gideon and in a vision placed before him his great opportunity to save Israel.   Immediately Gideon called upon the men of his clan to follow him.   By a personal night reconnaissance he assured himself that his enemies were as nervous as his own men.   He then devised the stratagem of a night attack with torches and horns, by which he made the enemy think that his three hundred soldiers were three hundred captains, each with a regiment at his back.   By taking the precaution to surround on three sides the right flank of the Midianites he forced them to flee down the valley eastward.   The

flight became a rout. Gideon did not desist in the pursuit until he had driven what was left of the Midianites across the eastern plateau to the desert. He slew their two kings with his own hand and took their clothes and their jewels as a trophy. On his return, when the men of his tribe sought to make him king, with true democratic spirit he declined,

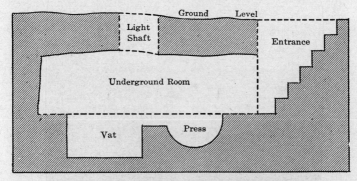

FIG. 46—UNDERGROUND WINE–PRESS

Excavated in the limestone rock about an hour's walk northwest of Ramallah. The grapes were trodden in the circular press, and the juice ran over into the square vat, whence it was dipped out into skins. In such a place Gideon beat out his wheat and winnowed it with a wing-fan, so that the puffs of chaff that usually rise from the out-of-door threshing-floors would not tell any tales to the Midianites (Sec. 43, and Jd. 6[11]).

taking instead the earrings that his soldiers had stripped from the slain—1,700 shekels of gold (about seventy pounds' weight). So great, however, was Gideon's prestige that his half-Amorite son, Abimelech, was made king after his death. This was the first instance in which the despotic Amorite idea of government overcame the Hebrew intolerance of all hereditary authority. But Abimelech's autocratic reign was short-lived. Democracy could not be downed so easily.

44. **The Ammonite Oppression.** When they came up from the south along the edge of the desert, the Hebrews had avoided conflict with the Ammonites. Instead, they

dispossessed Sihon and thrust themselves in between Ammon and the Jordan. The Ammonites proved a thorn in Israel's side for many generations even down to Roman times.

FIG. 47—GIDEON'S FOUNTAIN

You are looking south across the valley of Jezreel to Mount Gilboa, which is a range of bare hills in crescent form (see contour map of Esdraelon). The straight line across the centre is the railroad from Haifa (right) to Beth-shean and Damascus (left). The cluster of houses belongs to a Jewish colony. The hole in the hill at the extreme right of the picture is Gideon's Fountain or the Well of Harod, where, according to a late tradition, Gideon put his warriors to their famous test (Jd. 7[1, 4-7]). On this mountain Saul and Jonathan lost their lives (I Sam. 31[1-6]). *Cf.* Fig. 53.

They began by making the unreasonable demand that all the east-Jordan territory that Israel had taken from Sihon be returned to them on the ground that it was originally theirs; and they were backing up their claim by raids on the Hebrew farmers, even west of the Jordan, accompanied by acts of the utmost cruelty. Affairs at last reached the breaking-point, and the elders of Gilead picked out to lead them against their oppressors a rough half-breed outlaw named Jephthah. He made a successful drive and rid his country of them for a generation or two—till the time of King Saul. His victory brought a crushing grief to him, however, for he felt compelled to sacrifice to Jehovah his daughter, an only child, in consequence of a rash vow that he had made before going into battle. The leadership that Jephthah thus obtained over Gilead was virtually that of a military dictator, but, like Abimelech's, it was short-lived. The people were not yet ready to surrender their freedom.

45. **The Philistine Oppression.** The Philistines have long been hovering on the western and northern horizons of Palestine. Racially they connect themselves with the Homeric Achæans who descended upon the Ægean lands before 1300 B.C., gradually throttled the brilliant Cretan civilization by capturing its outposts like Mycenae and Troy, and at last the old capital of Minos at Knossos. Driving fragments of ancient people before them, some of these bands came to the Delta and to the Syrian coasts. Recognizing their valor the Egyptian Pharaohs had used many of them as mercenaries and stationed some in their strongholds in Palestine. When they became a real menace, Ramses III defeated them in a great sea battle about 1188 B.C., but he could not prevent their continued coming. He enlisted more of them in his service and made them keep the peace among the new arrivals. As Egyptian power waned we find these Philistines peacefully slipping into the Egyptian strongholds and gradually taking over the suzerainty of the lands round about. Thus a new danger for the Hebrews was introduced: two hardy nations of different ancestry came into hostile contact. The stories in Judges tell of the advance skirmishes that took place between the Hebrews and the Philistines in the hill country where the central mountains break down into the plain.⁋ Little Dan, that had settled in this dangerous border-land, first felt the pressure,

and in the person of their burly hero Samson, fought the Philistines single-handed. Samson bears all the marks of a popular hero. He was not heroic enough to accomplish anything for his nation, but was just strong enough and had just enough bravado to keep himself in the limelight. The stories that have been preserved of him are the most tangy in Hebrew literature. By their mingling of wit, marvel, and racy encounter they give proof that generations of story-tellers have enlivened with them the camp-fires and homes of the people.

46. **The Samson Hero Tales.** According to Hebrew tradition Samson's birth was attended with supernatural signs, and as a mark of his special character his parents made him a Nazarite, that is, made it unlawful for him to eat certain meats and drinks and to cut his hair. His first encounter with the Philistines comes in connection with a Philistine girl from Timnath. On account of his parents' protest he cannot have a home wedding, and so he arranges for the ceremony at Timnath, with thirty young Philistines for bridesmaids. Samson opens the week's festivities with a riddle based on a recent adventure of his with a lion, and makes a bet of thirty suits of clothes that his friends cannot guess it in seven days. Anxious to outdo their rival, they frighten the bride into wheedling the secret out of Samson; so that when the appointed day comes they give him the correct answer. Samson loses his temper, pays his bet by killing thirty Philistines and confiscating their clothes; then leaves town before the matrimonial knot is tied. The prospective father-in-law, to cover his chagrin and to save future expense, marries the girl on the spot to Samson's best man! A few months later Samson repents and comes down to complete the ceremony; but when the father explains that the girl has been placed elsewhere, Samson takes revenge by catching three hundred foxes, tying firebrands to their tails and turning them loose in the Philistine grain-fields. As a Roland for his Oliver, the Philistines proceed

to burn up the girl, her father, and his household; whereat Samson proves that he has been genuinely in love by killing Philistines until he is tired!

Fig. 48—A LOOM

The weaver sits on the floor of his house with his feet in a pit.   There he works the treadles by which the warp-threads are shifted so that the shuttle may pass between them now on one side and now on the other.   The shuttle is thrown by hand.   A plank that swings from above drives home the woof-threads.   This driving is sometimes done by a big wooden stick called a "pin" (Jd. 16¹⁴).   The finished cloth is wound upon a horizontal roller. Find in the picture as many of these details as possible.

When Delilah wove Samson's hair into her loom, Samson pulled all of the posts of the loom out of the ground and walked away with them hanging to his hair (Sec. 46, and Jd. 16¹⁴).

The Philistines now make a raid in reprisal.   The Judeans therefore persuade Samson to let them bind him and deliver him to his enemies.   Samson no doubt enjoys the joke, for when the transfer is made, he breaks his bonds as if they were tow, and seizing the jawbone of an ass he slays a thousand of them.

In his next adventure at Gaza, where his foes imagine that they have entrapped him, he carries off the city gates, and leaves them at Hebron forty miles away!

His final matrimonial venture proves his undoing. His new wife, Delilah, is bribed by the Philistine chiefs to find out the secret of Samson's marvellous strength. Samson deceives her for a time, and no doubt enjoys to the full the discomfiture of his enemies as they come upon him bound with enchanted bowstrings, or magic new ropes, or lying with his long hair woven fast into the web of Delilah's loom, only to see him snap his bonds or pull up the loom by the roots! But at last he tells her the truth: his strength lies in his uncut hair. Delilah proceeds to relieve him of his locks during his next nap, and the shorn and fallen hero is seized and blinded.

The lords of the Philistines now hold high festival before their god Dagon, to thank him for the capture of their enemy, and they bring out Samson to amuse them. Samson's hair, however, has had time to grow, so that as he feels the pillars that hold up the temple roof, he knows that he has one last chance for vengeance! With a prayer to Jehovah for strength, he presses the columns apart and brings the house down upon himself and his captors.

47. **The Result of the Oppressions.** A glance at Map No. 9 will make clear one result at least of these various oppressions. Delivered as they were on all sides like triphammer blows upon a loosely compacted people, the inevitable consequence was to weld Israel together. The logic of events was gradually proving to them that single tribes could not cope with foes so persistent and so powerful; Israel had to unite or die. One more and a mightier argument was needed; and the Philistines furnished that argument when a little later they captured the very palladium of Hebrew independence, the ark of Jehovah. For the probable chronology of this period, see Appendix IV.

VIII

DEMOCRACY UNDER SAMUEL AND SAUL

Saul (c. 1015–c. 1000 b.c.)

48. **The Philistine Domination.** Samson's selfish career brought no deliverance to his nation. That weak strong-man had no vision, saw no menace to anything but his own pleasure, and therefore rallied none to the support of Israel. The Philistines steadily stalked northward and eastward across the plain of Sharon to Mount Carmel, devouring the Canaanite farmers, and striking their talons into the foot-hills; and at last they crouched to spring upon the mountain fastnesses of Judah and Ephraim. The Hebrews met the attack bravely at Ebenezer, but went down at the first shock. Then they thought of the ark of Jehovah, which to their minds represented the very presence of Jehovah him-self, the Lord of the hosts of Israel. If their God could be with them in person, they would conquer. So they took the ark from its shrine at Shiloh, no doubt repeating the ancient prayer of their ancestors:

> "Arise, O Jehovah, and let thine enemies be scattered;
> Let them that hate thee flee before thee!"

But their hopes were vain. The ark aroused the Philis-tines to greater valor, and the Hebrews met a crushing defeat. Shiloh, the sacred resting-place of Jehovah, was raided and destroyed forever, the bonds of slavery were laid upon all central Palestine, and the God of Israel went with his ark into captivity among the Philistines.

The story of the adventures of the ark belongs to the realm of legend rather than history, but it serves to show

85

the religious ideas that were common in those days.   When the Philistines placed the ark of Jehovah in the temple of their god Dagon at Ashdod, Dagon mysteriously tumbled off his pedestal and was shattered.   Soon the men of Ashdod were smitten with boils, and in terror they sent the ark to

Copyright by Underwood and Underwood, N. Y.

Fɪɢ 49—SHILOH

You are looking northeast.   Behind the mountain lies the Jordan valley; not far to the left is the watershed.   The valley across which you look is the one where the Benjamites stole their wives (Jd. 21²¹⁻²³).   The little platform beyond the tree may once have held the tabernacle where Eli and Samuel ministered (I Sam. 2, 3).   The tree is held sacred by the natives, as evidenced by the rags that deck it.   In ancient days such trees were supposed to be the residence of Baals (Sec. 39); now they are sacred to some saint.   The ruins of the old town of Shiloh may be seen scattered on the hill to the right.

Gath.   The plague broke out upon Gath, and Gath sent on the ark to Ekron, which was forthwith afflicted with the same malady.   The rulers of the Philistines in dismay called for their diviners, who advised sending the ark of Jehovah back to the Hebrews with suitable apologies, which in this case consisted of golden mice and boils—imitations of things associated with their plague.   By a well-known rule of magic the sending away of these symbols was sure to remove the disease itself.   The ark was accordingly sent up the nearest valley to Bethshemesh.   But the infection was not yet out of it, for it smote the Hebrews of Bethshemesh, who curiously looked into it, and they passed the dread Thing on to the Philistine stronghold of Kiriath-jearim, where the mountain air purified it and made it harmless.   Here it remained in obscurity until a generation later David broke the Philistine yoke and took it to his capital.

49. **Samuel the Seer.**   While the ark was in captivity, a youth was growing to manhood who was destined to lead Israel out of their new bondage.   Samuel of Ramah in Ephraim, born of pious parents and early dedicated to the priesthood, began to develop clairvoyant powers and to gain a reputation thereby; so that when the son of a rich farmer of Gibeah lost a drove of asses, it was natural for him to turn in to Ramah and risk a quarter-shekel in consulting the seer.   But Samuel was more than a clairvoyant, he was a prophet; that is, he was one who had insight as well as second sight, who saw meanings as well as facts, who read characters as well as fortunes.   When, therefore, he saw this stalwart young farmer, Saul, standing before him, head and shoulders taller than himself, and felt in his sensitive soul the power of Saul's dormant personality, the seer dismissed the question of the asses with a wave of the hand and took the young prince to his housetop that he might show him a vision of his country's need and of his own unused power.   How the young man's heart must have burned within him as Samuel pointed out Gibeah garrisoned by the Philistines, Bethlehem in the grip of the foreigner, Shiloh prostrate, and the ark of Jehovah himself waiting to be rescued from its long exile.   Saul's spirit began to stir under the inspired eloquence and the piercing eye of the seer; so that when the morning broke, and Samuel anointed him in the name of Jehovah and sent him away, he was in a state bordering upon ecstasy.   Indeed, when he shortly met a band of Jehovah-worshippers, coming down from the

high place with music and dancing, Saul was caught by their religious and patriotic frenzy.

50. **Saul's Vigorous Beginning.** The plan which Samuel proposed to Saul was wise: possibly word was quietly passed round that the leader had been selected and anointed in the name of Jehovah, but action was to be deferred till occasion offered. That occasion came from an unexpected quarter. Israel's old enemy, the Ammonites, made a raid on Jabesh in Gilead, and insolently demanded that its inhabitants not only ransom themselves but have their right eyes gouged out as a warning to their kinsmen. The men of Jabesh, having begged a few days' delay to consider matters, sent news of their plight to their relatives on the west of Jordan. Saul saw his opportunity. By a threat of vengeance if they refused, he summoned the Hebrews to follow him to the relief of Jabesh, made a forced march all that night, surprised the Ammonites and delivered the city. Men then saw that Samuel's choice was justified; here was a leader of power. With one accord the elders assembled at Gilgal, the ancient sanctuary upon the hills west of Shiloh, and there elected Saul their national counsellor and leader in peace and war.

51. **The Bold Strike for Freedom.** Saul now realized, as the Philistines did, that the struggle for Hebrew independence had begun. Whether Saul would have taken the offensive is a question, but his valiant son, Jonathan, apparently precipitated the war by slaying the Philistine officer in charge of Gibeah. Both sides mustered to the attack. Saul stationed his picked men, who had helped him at Jabesh, in three divisions, one near Bethel, one with himself at Michmash, and a third with Jonathan at Geba. He also sent out a call for reinforcements. The Philistines scored the first success, driving in the advance-guard from Bethel and causing Saul to evacuate Michmash. The defeat was evidently severe, for Saul's new recruits melted away; some took refuge in caves and thickets, while others crossed

the Jordan. Saul, with only six hundred men left, thought it best to retire to Geba, and the Philistines, certain that they had scattered the Hebrews, started out in three bands

FIG. 50—GORGE OF MICHMASH

You are looking east down the valley toward the Jordan. The Philistine fortress was on the cliff to the left, the Hebrews were on the right. (Sec. 51.) It was country like this that made the capture of Palestine so difficult for General Allenby.

to plunder. They left a garrison, however, at Michmash, just opposite Geba.

Again the valiant Jonathan showed the way to victory. Secretly, and alone but for his armor-bearer, he descended the canyon in front of Geba, climbed the crag of Michmash, and, while his foes were aghast with astonishment, he killed some twenty of them. A providential earthquake inspired the Philistines with supernatural dread, and a panic ensued.

Saul was at the moment consulting the oracle to see whether he should attack; but the commotion among the enemy made an oracle unnecessary, and he ordered a general advance. The battle swept westward, while the Hebrew slackers came out of their hiding-places to swell Saul's victorious and pursuing army. The rout passed by the Beth-horons in the valley of Ajalon and so out upon the Philistine plain. Saul had won his title as national leader and the Hebrews their independence from the galling Philistine yoke.

There were still foes to be faced. Though beaten, the Philistines kept harrying the borders of Israel and must repeatedly be repelled. On the east the Ammonites, on the south the Moabites, Edomites, and Amalekites, and on the north the Arameans stood ready on the least pretext to attack the young Hebrew commonwealth. Only in one direction was the ring of spears not complete: the Phœnicians, bent on trade instead of conquest, paid strict attention to their shipping, and thus established a tradition of friendship that Saul's successors found very useful. Throughout his reign Saul's court was a camp and his symbol of power a sword.

52. **Saul's Break with Samuel.** Because of confusion and contradiction in the sources, we cannot tell with certainty what occasion led to the break between the two leading men of Israel, but there is no doubt of the fact and of its serious consequences. At first Samuel seemed to be not only the discoverer and inspirer of Saul, but his loyal supporter, and this means that besides his personal backing he threw into the support of the new state the whole group of religious zealots of which he was leader. The band of prophets whom Saul met near Gibeah were primarily Jehovah-votaries, but from other references to them we know that they were intense patriots as well—ardent advocates of democracy; indeed, this crisis seems to be the earliest instance in history where religion and patriotism were consciously de-

voted to creating a public sentiment and to furthering national ideals. The Semitic race is particularly susceptible to leadership of this kind. Samuel, Isaiah, Mohammed, the Mahdi, and the recent kings of the Hedjaz are familiar illustrations. It was vital to Saul's success that he maintain a sympathetic connection with this group; but in some way he failed. It may be that his too advanced ruling that all wizards, necromancers and mediums be banished from the land trod too closely upon the practices of some of these religious zealots. It may be that, as one story implies, Saul was too little considerate of Samuel's prestige, and attempted himself to offer sacrifices in Samuel's stead. Or it may have been Saul's occasional rashness or his growing melancholia that convinced Samuel of a fatal weakness in the new ruler; or that Samuel, as guardian of Israel's democratic spirit, feared that Saul was becoming an autocrat rather than the chief counsellor that his title implies.

The achievements of Saul and David should not blind us to the debt Israel owed to Samuel. Without his insight and courage and earlier wisdom, the Philistine yoke would probably never have been broken. But Samuel saw in the rulership as exercised·by Saul a danger to the liberties of Israel, and he saw only too truly.

53. **The Rise of David.** The Bible gives three accounts of the way David was introduced to public life. In one of these Samuel goes, by divine suggestion, to the house of Jesse in Bethlehem and anoints the youthful David, the youngest of his sons, to be Saul's successor. In the second and earliest account, Saul's advisers suggest that he find a harper to soothe him during the paroxysms of his increasing mental trouble, and David is brought to court on account of his skill in music. His ability as a warrior soon wins for him the enviable position of royal armor-bearer. In the third, David goes to visit his brothers while they are in Saul's army fighting the Philistines, and by slaying the giant Goliath he becomes a popular hero whom Saul finds it

advisable to attach to his retinue. Whatever the manner, Saul and his successor are brought into personal contact, and the former quickly conceives a jealousy that goes beyond

Fig. 51—VALE OF ELAH

The broad and fertile valley where the Hebrews and Philistines confronted each other. Find the brook where David got his pebbles (I Sam. 17⁴⁰). On a contour map find the location of this valley with reference to Bethlehem and Gath. Why should the Philistines choose such a valley for their raid?

all bounds and finally drives away one who ought to have been, with Jonathan, his chief supporter. The ground for that jealousy undoubtedly lay in David's wonderful skill in war, though his skill as a manipulator of men constituted a

FIG. 52—ENTRANCE TO THE CAVE OF ADULLAM

The "cave" of I Sam. 22[1] is probably a stronghold on a hill. Yet the hill which most modern scholars believe to be Adullam has caves in it, of which this picture shows one. How many entrances can you find? How good a hiding-place would this be? The grotto of Saint Chariton, near Bethlehem, identified by the crusaders as the cave of Adullam, contains seven chambers on different levels which run 660 feet into the mountain. Southern Palestine is full of such places.

truer basis. The fact that the crown prince, Jonathan, in spite of his father's insane dread of David, became and continued to be his staunch friend, argues great ability in David as well as splendid magnanimity in both.

Saul's evil intention against David showed itself by his twice throwing a spear at him while David was playing the harp, by his assigning David to dangerous work in connection with the Philistines, and by ordering his servants to assassinate him.   David's friend Jonathan interceded for him and brought about an apparent reconciliation; but soon the old fires broke out, and David fled from Saul's court never to return.   He stopped at the sanctuary of Nob on his way south and, giving the priests there the impression that he was still in the employ of Saul, took the sword of Goliath for his personal use, and proceeded to his native Judah to hide himself in its wilderness.   His clan joined him at the cave of Adullam, which for a time became the centre of his outlaw life.   We need not follow in detail his various adventures, his marriage to a rich widow which gave him added prestige with the southern tribes, or his pursuit by Saul and the magnanimous refusal of David to rid himself of his enemy by assassination.   Suffice it that Saul's persecution was so relentless that David had to take refuge with the Philistines, because they were the bitterest enemies of his own enemy.   Achish, king of Gath, received him kindly, glad of this chance to anger Saul and to strengthen himself. David was assigned at his own request to a district on the southern border, where he could keep the Amalekites from troubling Achish and could, without the knowledge of the Philistine king, distribute the plunder he obtained from them among his friends in the cities of Judah.   At the same time he kept up the fiction of loyalty to Achish by pretending that his plunder came from raids among the Hebrews. This position was one that must have been irksome to David's loyal nature.   It was bound not to last.

54. **The Tragedy of Gilboa.** Rumors of Saul's mental condition no doubt stirred the Philistines to a final attempt to regain their mastery over Israel.   Achish called upon David to perform a vassal's duty and go with him to battle as captain of his body-guard.   David actually started north-

ward with the troops, but fortunately the other Philistine leaders, out of suspicion of his loyalty, made Achish send him back; and thus they relieved David of a very awkward situation. The Philistines then moved northeastward through the passes into Esdraelon, and pitched by Shunem. Saul massed his opposing troops on Mount Gilboa. Saul's condition was indeed desperate. His malady had grown upon him, his insane temper had cost him the loyalty of his bravest warrior, and on the eve of the battle many chiefs of Manasseh had deserted him; Samuel, though dead, still thwarted him through the religious group known as the sons of the prophets, and the consciousness of failure had cut him off from his old happy sense of divine approval. Even the oracles, through which the people determined the will of Jehovah, were silent when he consulted them, a powerful hint that the priests who had charge of them were no longer his friends. To crown all, his old enemies had come to make war on the broken king and to snatch his kingdom away. In his despair he went by night around the sentinels of the Philistines to the wretched village of Endor, where his friends assured him he could find a medium. His object was to know by supernatural means the issue of the battle. Of her he demanded that she call up Samuel the Seer. The narrative of this scene is wonderfully vivid and psychologically true to the details of the situation. The medium went into a trance, in which she visualized Samuel to herself, and apparently interpreted Saul's desperate fears as a message from his dread enemy: "Jehovah will deliver Israel also with you into the hand of the Philistines; and to-morrow you and your sons shall be with me!" So absolutely did she harp Saul's fears aright that the king swooned; and the kind-hearted medium, coming out of her trance, pitied the weakness of the man whom she now knew to be her king, and begged him to take a little bread. Thus revived, he staggered out into the night, and back to his foredoomed battle.

Had Saul not lost the battle before he went into it, he
might not have been beaten, for his position on Gilboa was
well-nigh impregnable.   But the troops, sharing the hope-
lessness of their king, and probably few in numbers, were

FIG. 53—VALLEY OF JEZREEL AND MOUNT GILBOA

Compare Fig. 47, which shows a view of the mountains farther to the right
  (west).   This scene shows the broad mouth of the valley near where it joins
  the valley of the Jordan.   Bethshean, where the Philistines hung the
  bodies of Saul and Jonathan, is off the picture to the left.   Note the rank
  vegetation and cf. Gen. 49¹¹⁻¹⁵ in which both the quality of the land and its
  openness to invasion are poetically given.

soon thrown into a rout that all the desperate valor of Saul
and Jonathan could not stay.   Steadily the Philistine archers
drove them over the crest and down the swift descent of
Gilboa, even to the gulf of the Jordan.   Jonathan and
his two brothers died fighting like lions, and Saul, badly
wounded, fell upon his sword to escape capture.   The Philistines next day came upon Saul's body as they were stripping
the slain.   They sent his armor as a trophy to the temple of

Astarte in Beth-shan, they cut off his head and fastened his corpse and the bodies of his sons to the walls of the city. But the men of Jabesh Gilead, remembering what this man had done for them in the bright dawn of his career, at the peril of their lives stole the corpses from their ignominious place and reverently buried them under their own village tree. For the Astarte temples in Beth-shan see Appendix III.

55. **Saul's Character.** Saul deserves a higher place in the roll of Hebrew heroes than the writers of the Old Testament have assigned him. In the light of succeeding events they indeed had cause to reckon the kingship a failure, and they allowed their judgment of condemnation to fall heavily on the first member of the succession, while they exalted and glorified the prophetic Samuel, who represented in their eyes the ideal democratic leader under Jehovah. But if one reads all the data impartially, one sees clearly that Saul was at worst only the victim of a mental disorder which wrecked his career and made him at times an irresponsible despot instead of the chief counsellor of the elders. It could not, however, wholly obscure his many and great talents. It was his courage that launched the attack on Ammon and created courage in the Hebrews. It was his skill as a warrior that kept the Philistines at bay for a generation, so that central Israel at least was free from attack, and that so chastized their old oppressors to the east and south that later they more easily fell a prey to David's conquering sword. Something in his nature was so compelling that in his lifetime, up to the very eve of the catastrophe, no prominent Israelite, except David, openly broke away from him, a fact most extraordinary when one considers the anarchy that preceded him, and the inability of the great David to hold his throne unassailed. There are not wanting signs of a religious insight beyond his age; for his order against witchcraft and kindred arts, which in that day were universally practised, and his own almost anxious devotion to the oracle of Jehovah, show that he appreciated the fact that

disunion lay in the one and the road to his nation's highest good lay in loyalty to the other. That at times he was rash and that his jealousy of David was sheer folly cannot be denied. Yet David was nearer right than the biased chroniclers of a later time when he twined the names of Saul and his noble son in one garland of praise:

> "Saul and Jonathan, the loved and the lovely,
> As in life so in death they were not divided.
> They were swifter than eagles, they were stronger than lions.
> How are the mighty fallen in the midst of the battle!"

DAVID THE ORGANIZER OF THE HEBREW STATE
David (c. 1000–c. 955 B.C.)

56. The Vassal Fragments of Israel. At Ziklag, his Philistine headquarters, David received the news of Saul's defeat and death. His first acts were calculated to clear away any suspicion that he held a personal grudge against Saul: he slew the messenger who claimed to have killed the king, and he composed a noble elegy which enshrined his truest feelings about Saul and Jonathan and his grief at the nation's calamity. Then in obedience to an oracle he went with his men to Hebron, chief city of the Judah clans, and was there anointed as their leader. It is impossible to see how the Philistines could have allowed this, unless as a reward for David's apparent loyalty they let him reign as a vassal. In like manner they evidently gave their consent that the northern tribes should have a king of their own east of the Jordan, of course in vassalage to themselves. Abner, Saul's general, therefore elevated to the precarious throne a son of Saul named Ishbaal, who was not only a vassal to the Philistines but a puppet in Abner's hands. In this double-headed Hebrew state the Philistines saw the prospect of civil war, and rejoiced in it. David's problem was now threefold: First, how to win over the northern tribes; second, how to retain the loyalty of the powerful and jealous Judah while coquetting with its rivals to the north; third, how to extricate himself from his vassalage to the Philistines. It took him nearly eight years to find a solution.

The Philistine hopes were soon realized. Abner came across from Gilead with what fighters he could muster, and David's rough nephew, Joab, undertook to champion the cause of Judah's king. Though a state of civil war continued for some time, there is no record of contests except one at Gibeon and the general struggle of personalities.

FIG. 54—HEBRON

A town of hoary antiquity, containing before the war, 22,000 inhabitants. Of what are the houses made and why? The large building with the minarets is the mosque over the cave of Machpelah. Christians are not admitted. Why is this spot revered (Gen. 23$^{17-20}$; 25$^{8-10}$; 50$^{12-14}$)? The pool of Hebron is at the foot of the slope, to the right (II Sam. 4^{12}).

Abner pushed to the limit his mastery over his puppet king, and then, breaking with him over a personal matter, opened negotiations with David to transfer the whole northern kingdom to him. Overjoyed as David must have been, he did not lose his masterful grip on himself and the situation; he demanded that Saul's daughter, Michal, his first wife, who had been given by Saul to another man when he quarrelled with David, should be returned to him before any other business was discussed. In this way he secured for himself, as Saul's son-in-law, a certain title to the leadership of all Israel. Abner made Ishbaal issue the requisite order, and Michal was restored. Abner then proposed to the elders of the northern tribes that they transfer their loyalty, and he came personally to David at Hebron to report progress. David feasted him and sent him away enthusiastic, no doubt having promised to reward him generously for his services. But Joab was yet to be reckoned with. He was not at Hebron at the time, but, coming back shortly after Abner had left, he heard of the royal favor that had been heaped upon his rival. Smarting with jealousy and stirred with the thought of revenge for Abner's killing of his brother at Gibeon, and reckless of the disaster he might bring on David, he sent word for Abner to return to Hebron and then treacherously slew him. Only by the most skilful acting did David avert calamity. He dared not put his powerful captain to death, but he pronounced a solemn curse on him and his posterity, made him and his brother Abishai and all of their soldiers put on mourning and follow Abner's bier, while he himself wept copiously over the grave, uttered a funeral dirge, and refused to eat. Some of this may have been acting, but the situation was desperate enough to call for something of the sort, for Joab had wrecked a piece of delicate diplomacy when it was nearly completed. At any rate, everybody was convinced that David had no hand in the murder.

With their strong man dead, the northern elders realized that the rule of Ishbaal was destined to be short-lived. Two of Ishbaal's captains, however, hastened its downfall by assassinating him and bringing his head to David. They hoped for reward, but instead lost their own heads, hands, and feet, which were hanged up by the pool in Hebron as a warning that David did not accept assistance of that kind from anybody. The inevitable now occurred. All the northern tribes sent a formal invitation to David to be their chief counsellor and leader. In Hebron, therefore, he was anointed a second time.

57. The Nature of the Hebrew Kingship. It is highly important that we understand at the outset the nature of this kingship. We must note that the holder of it is summoned by the voice of the people through the sheiks of the tribes. He receives his authority from the people, and to them it returns with his death. As the Hebrew term (*melek*) implies, this king is primarily the chief counsellor of the people, in reality a president, whose personal ability has led to his elevation to power. The office was not hereditary in theory nor was it always in practice, for the people chose for themselves the new ruler or approved the choice made by the former king. While in the southern state the choice always fell within the family of David, the one elected was not necessarily the eldest. It must be further noted that the people retained the right of veto over the king's acts. This is most strikingly shown in the case where Saul condemned his son Jonathan to death for breaking a foolish command of his, but the people refused to let Jonathan die. (1 Sam. 14$^{44-45}$.) They also contrived to bring the pressure of public opinion to bear on an erring king either through a spokesman (Nathan and David, the wise woman of Tekoa and David, Elijah and Ahab), or by organized revolt (Jeroboam and Solomon). Though circumstances or the ability of individual kings often overrode this popular check, they never crushed out the ideal. At the first opportunity it reasserted itself, as we shall see in the later narrative.

58. David the Strategist. David was now thirty years old and full of ambition for the great game of statecraft. The Philistines promptly started the game, for while David as vassal ruler of Hebron might be tolerated, David as king of united Israel might not be. David could do nothing but retire to his old stronghold of Adullam. The Philistines broke through to the very summit of the range, to the plain of Rephaim southwest of Jerusalem; but David attacked them twice, the first time capturing their gods whom they had brought into the battle, and the second time driving them out of the southwestern highlands.

With a statesman's insight David now saw that the possession of a capital city situated nearer the northern tribes would be an advantage. Avoiding possible jealousies if he should choose an Israelite city, he chose one of the unconquered cities still held by the Amorites, the little fortress of Jerusalem, built impregnably upon a spur of limestone near the watershed. David himself devised the method of capturing it —to uncover the spring and climb up to the

FIG. 55—PLAIN OF REPHAIM

You are looking north. A bit of Jerusalem appears to the right over the tree. The hill to the left is part of the watershed of Judea. This fertile field represents the broad top of the plateau. About a mile to the left the narrow Valley of Roses begins to sink down toward the west, carrying the railroad past Bethshemesh and Gezer to the Philistine plain and Joppa. Behind you, twenty miles, is Hebron; to the right, twenty miles, is the Jordan. What evidences of prosperity do you find here?

very heart of the city through the water tunnel, such as has been described in Section 34. The part of the captured city that had been the Jebusite fortress he renamed Davidsburg, and promptly built there his royal residence. Thus Jerusalem enters upon its career of romance and blood that has made it the most significant city in the world.

59. David the Conqueror. David knew that the peace he coveted for his people lay only in his reducing to helplessness their ring of foes. Saul had adopted the same policy but was able to carry it out only in part. David, through the more complete loyalty he commanded and doubtless by

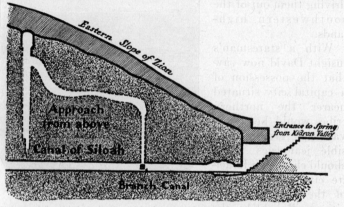

Fig. 56—ROCK CUTTINGS UNDER THE JEBUSITE FORTRESS

A cross-section of the hill Ophel, running east and west. The spring Gihon lies at the foot of the steps. The water flows to the left through the canal and comes out on the western side of the hill at the pool of Siloam (see plan, Fig. 98). The passage leading up to the surface of the rock is undoubtedly that by which Joab and his men gained entrance to the Jebusite fortress (II Sam. 5⁷⁻⁸). The surface of the Kidron valley was once about forty feet lower than at present, having been filled up with débris.

greater generalship and the aid of his mighty men, was able to accomplish it. First he carried war into Philistia and took Gath, the head of the Philistine league of cities. This country henceforth remained inoffensive. Next he trampled Moab into harmlessness by capturing its whole army and putting to death two men out of every three. Ammon next received chastisement. David had sent a friendly embassy to the new king of Ammon to express sympathy on the death of his father, who had evidently favored David during the war with the old Ammonite enemy, Saul. The young king was suspicious of David's motives and chose to insult the ambassadors. Knowing that war would follow, he hired his Aramean neighbors to the north to join with him in crushing the young Hebrew before he had grown too powerful. David drafted every available man and sent Joab into the enemy's country at once. Joab showed excellent judgment, put the Aramean allies to rout and compelled the Ammonites to take refuge in their capital city, Rabbath. Since it was too late in the year to conduct a siege, he retired to Jerusalem, but the following spring returned to complete the conquest. He took the lower city, cut off the water-supply from the citadel, and sent for David to share the glory of the final capture. All of the Ammonites were made bond-servants and were doubtless employed thereafter in David's building enterprises.

The Arameans who had helped Ammon were next subdued, though there is considerable doubt whether David ever extended his sway as far north as the Euphrates, or even took Damascus. Turning south, David broke the power of Edom and their Bedouin neighbors, the Amalekites, and thus completed the circle of conquest. He had no desire to conquer the peaceful, commercial Phœnicians, for they had been consistently friendly. Indeed, now that David's conquests had made him rich and had filled Jerusalem with gold and silver and brass and precious woods—the peculiar treasures of kings—the cunning workmen of Phœnicia proved indispensable in turning the loot into buildings and equipment for the increasingly ambitious ruler. Thus it came about that within a few years David had built up a little empire that extended from the territory of the Philistines and Phœnicians on the west to the desert on the east, and from the Gulf of Akabah on the south to Damascus on the north. Following the conquests came trade, and with trade came more wealth and a broader outlook. The Hebrew farmers were in a fair way to become citizens of the world.

60. David the Organizer. David next turned his attention to the internal development of his commonwealth. He had shown from the beginning of his career unusual skill in organization. While ruling at Hebron he had established two orders of knighthood among his soldiers in order to inspire the utmost daring and loyalty. The lowest rank, called the "Order of the Thirty," was bestowed upon warriors who had shown conspicuous bravery in presence of the foe—winners of the "Croix de Guerre." The chief of the order was Abishai, Joab's brother, who won his spurs by killing three hundred of the enemy with his own spear. Next in merit came Benaiah, who slew a lion in a pit in time of snow, and who with only a staff attacked an Egyptian eight and a half feet high, wrested his spear out of his hand and slew him with it. It was to this order that the three "Paladins of the Well" belonged, who broke through the Philistine hosts to get David a drink from the well of his boyhood at Bethlehem. Uriah, the first husband of Bathsheba, was also a member.

The other and most exalted company was known as the "Order of the Three." The commander of the order, a certain Ishbaal, won his distinction by killing with his axe eight hundred Philistines at one time. The second was Eleazer, who fought so long on one occasion that his hand refused to let go his sword; the soldiers who followed in his wake had only to pick up the spoil. The last member was Shammah, who at Lehi planted himself in a field of lentils while his men were in full flight and personally stopped the advance of the Philistines. David had also eleven captains from the tribe of Gad, of whom it is said: "He who was least was equal to a hundred, and the greatest to a thousand." It was this military organization that was the groundwork of his empire. With men like these for his veterans, David might well command the respect of his foes. Joab, though not a member of either order, was commander-in-chief of the army, which consisted of the professional soldiers mentioned, and the militia that was called out for special occasions.   Benaiah, second knight of the Thirty, was commander of David's body-guard of Philistine mercenaries.   David must have formed a high opinion of the courage and loyalty of the Philistines or he would not have intrusted his person to them.   The fact that he used mercenaries at all is clear indication that he feared either the tribal jealousies of the Hebrew clans or, more likely, their suspicion that their chosen leader was becoming a master.

61. **David the Grand Monarch.**   All of this success in war and in organization now began to turn David's head and caused him to forget both his humble origin and the ideals of his people.   Love of power grew with the exercise of power, and love of display kept pace with wealth.   David began to play the Grand Monarch.   In accordance with ancient practice, he himself was chief justice and held court for the benefit of any who wished his personal decision.   He was likewise chief priest.   But he began to add other officers.   He appointed one Jehoshaphat as grand vizier, or as we say in the West, prime minister, whose duties were to take charge of the general mass of public business and jog the royal memory at the right time.   Sheva the scribe was his private secretary and kept the official records.   Two priests, Zadok and Abiathar, were put in charge of the ark of Jehovah, and another priest, Ira, looked after the king's private chapel.   A significant officer is Adoram, overseer of the royal labor gangs.   That such an officer was needed is proof that David was beginning to strengthen his kingdom with works of defense, and adorn his capital with works of magnificence, and that his war captives were largely used for that purpose.   In addition we read of a board of counsellors called "Friends of the King," who ate at the king's table

David's increasing ambition is also seen in the growth of his harem.   While yet at Hebron he had six wives; now that he was both king and conqueror he must needs take others, princesses from the tributary kings round about and favorite ladies at home. His final establishment of some twenty or thirty wives looks small beside Solomon's thousand, as Solomon's was modest compared with that of Shah Jehan the

Fig. 57—SACRED ARK

Amen-hotep III, of Egypt (1411–1375 B. C.) offering incense before the ark of the god Amon-Ra. Observe that the ark is carried on the shoulders of priests, by means of poles (cf. Ex. 25$^{13\text{-}15}$). The shrine is in form of a boat with the symbol of the god, a ram's head, on both prow and stern. It was made of cedar of Lebanon overlaid with gold (Ex. 25$^{10\text{-}11}$). Overshadowing it is the winged disc of the sun, while on the side of the ark is a beetle—another emblem of the sun—protected by the outstretched wings of two little figures representing Righteousness and Truth (cf. Ex. 25$^{18\text{-}20}$; also Righteousness and Justice are the foundation of his throne, Ps. 97^2). On the boat are miniature fan-bearers and other symbols. Amen-hotep holds an incense-burner in his left hand, while with his right he drops incense into the flame. Behind the ark the king is again seen. Find the king's names in their cartouches. Notice the king's scanty dress, the tail, the serpent-crown, and the overshadowing goddess, Mut, as a vulture.

Mogul. But in all these cases the harem was the Oriental expression of wealth and dignity. By all these means, then, David sought to strengthen his hold upon the imagination and the loyalty of his own people and to consolidate his power throughout his newly acquired empire. They succeeded only in part. The people began to scent the approach of tyranny.

62. David the Devotee. One event in David's reign proved in the light of succeeding history to have the most far-reaching consequences. Having established himself in his new capital while the Philistine wars were in progress, he resolved to rescue the sacred ark, which since the ill-fated battle in Eli's time had been under Philistine guardianship. This involved a campaign in which 30,000 men were used, and it resulted in clearing the Philistines out of all the mountain and hill-country to the west of Jerusalem. The ark was then brought to the capital with high ceremony, David himself leading the procession with music and dancing. One accident marred the joy of the occasion: as the ark entered the city, the oxen slipped on the steep slope; one of the attendants tried to steady the ark, but at that moment fell dead. The death was attributed to the anger of Jehovah, the ceremonies were interrupted, and the ark was placed in the nearest house, belonging to Obed-edom, one of David's Philistine mercenaries. When Obed-edom began to prosper, David was emboldened to risk another attempt, and this time brought the ark safely within his royal home. David's desire was partly selfish and partly political: he wanted to secure for himself the blessings that he felt sure would flow from his personal devotion to Jehovah, and he saw that this devotion to the nation's God would greatly increase the loyalty of all Israel to his dynasty. Having the ark in his possession, also, he could carry it when necessary on his campaigns, as we know he did. David had no intention of making Jerusalem in any sense the one centre of worship. There were countless shrines in the land that continued to be used for three hundred years; the ark only made peculiarly dear to him his own religious establishment. Nevertheless we can now see that this act was the first of that long series which made Jerusalem the Holy City of the Jews, then of the Christians, then of the Moslems, the pivot about which so many of the wars and the great movements of history have turned.

David had now reached the zenith of his career. From his youthful entrance into public life he had carried himself discreetly, and his course had been a steady rise to a point of success and power that no Hebrew had hitherto attained. If he could have died at this time he would have been fortunate indeed.

X

DAVID'S WANING POPULARITY

63. The Approach of Nemesis. David's gradual loss of popularity seems to have been due largely to a combination of forces that he could not wholly control, yet there were elements in the case for which he may justly be blamed. During the Ammonite war he was guilty of an act that involved adultery and murder, and while in most Oriental despotisms such acts would excite only passing comment, in Israel, where the kingship was never intended to be a despotism but rested squarely on popular approval, they produced a strong feeling of condemnation. His people had cause also to resent the laxness with which he governed his household; for the outcome of it was a generation of passionate and self-indulgent princes who disgraced the royal name and brought civil war on the kingdom. Yet while such things furnished the occasion, the real causes of David's decline were deeper. They lay in the mutual jealousies and feuds of the Hebrew tribes which David with all his diplomacy had not been able to heal, and in the growing suspicion that the freedom that once was theirs was fast becoming slavery under the king's successes and organization.

64. Absalom's Waywardness and Ambitions. David's first serious trouble centred round his son Absalom. This prince was a handsome and high-strung youth who first murdered his half-brother in revenge for the wronging of his sister and then fled from home to escape punishment. After an exile of two years he was allowed to return, at the intercession of Joab, but was not allowed to see the king's face for two years more. During this time of half-forgiveness he conceived the ambition to take his father's throne.

Such a thought would have been folly had he not known
the strong undercurrent of dissatisfaction that was loosening
the people's loyalty to David. When at last he was restored

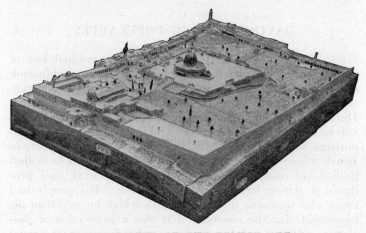

Fig. 58—MODEL OF THE TEMPLE AREA

This wooden model, constructed by Dr. Conrad Schick, of Jerusalem, represents
the Haram, or Temple area, as it appears to-day. Note on the near end
of the model the dark section that represents the contour of the hill Ophel.
The sag to the left is the Tyropean valley. Off the model to the right lies
the Kidron valley. The ridge of the hill Ophel ran north and south
between these two valleys. Within the enclosure note two levels:- (1) the
larger one that runs next the walls, (2) the inner square one on which the
octagonal building rests. In Solomon's day the area did not extend north
of the farther side of level No. 2, nor did it include the left-hand corner over
the Tyropean. Solomon's palace and public halls lay along the crest
of the hill, beginning about where the three little openings are seen in the
near wall of the enclosure and extending northward to the near side of
level No. 2. Just under the dome of the octagonal building, "the Dome of
the Rock," is to be seen the naked crest of the rocky hill, called Mount
Moriah. On this bit of rock Solomon's brazen altar of sacrifice stood,
while his temple stood a little to the left (west), facing the altar. (Cf. Fig.
150.)

to full favor by his father, he began to use the arts of the
politician, impressing the people with the splendor of his
public equipage and currying favor by personal attentions.
Standing at the city gate he made friends with all who came

in from the country, inquired into their cases if they had come to have wrongs righted, and by no modest hints gave people to understand that things would be different if there were only a younger ruler on the throne. In this way he "stole the hearts of the men of Israel."

65. **Absalom's Rebellion and Death.** At the end of four years Absalom considered that his hour had struck. Asking royal permission to go to Hebron to sacrifice to Jehovah, he raised there his standard of revolt. Hebron was no doubt selected because its people had never forgiven David for removing the capital from there and because the southern clans were increasingly jealous of the growing influence of the northern tribes. Absalom sent messengers everywhere to summon his friends to his side. Leading men had been caught in the net of intrigue, including two hundred from Jerusalem. David's ancient and greatly trusted counsellor, Ahithophel, was among them, induced no doubt by the hope of wiping out the disgrace (see page 111) David had brought on his family in the matter of Bathsheba and Uriah. Each day the cause of Absalom grew stronger, so that by the time the news of the conspiracy reached David, the latter had no alternative but to flee.

It seems incredible that David should have had so few supporters in this crisis. We read of no move to save him on the part of Jerusalem itself, or of Judah his tribe, or of Ephraim, the strong tribe to the north whose friendship he was supposed to be cultivating. This was the answer a free people gave to David's autocratic ambitions. The forsaken king had to leave his capital accompanied only by a handful of court officials and by his faithful body-guard of mercenaries. Zadok indeed brought the ark of Jehovah along, but David feared to provoke Jehovah's anger by seeming to force him to take sides, and he sent it back. The flight to the Jordan was full of dramatic scenes, each significant of the deeper current of affairs. In particular, the curses that Shimei heaped upon David were the expression of the hostility which his whole tribe of Benjamin felt for one who had deprived that tribe of its leadership under Saul. Followed by both blessings and cursings, David came at last to the Jordan and crossed over to the city of Mahanaim, where he knew he could count on some degree of loyalty on account of the peace he had brought to that region by the destruction of Ammon. The governor whom he had placed over the Ammonites did indeed send provisions for himself and men.

Absalom occupied Jerusalem without opposition, and took over the property of his father, including the harem. He then held a council to consider the next move. The proposal of Ahithophel to pursue the fleeing king immediately was defeated by the crafty arguments of Hushai, a trusty friend whom David had sent back to Absalom for this very purpose. "You know," said the astute Hushai, "that your father and his men are mighty men, and they are chafed in their minds, as a bear robbed of her whelps in the field; and your father is a man of war." The contrast between this description and the facts is ludicrous, but the argument went home. In the delay that followed, David had a chance to get his bearings and to rally some help. At last Absalom took the field in person and advanced into the east-Jordan region. Joab opposed him with the loyal troops. The defeat of the usurper was absolute, and Absalom, contrary to the king's orders, was killed by Joab's own hand while caught in the limbs of a great oak under which he had been fleeing. Joab saw the necessity, as the father did not, of ridding the land once for all of this menace.

66. **The King's Folly.** David's reception of the news was a revelation of an old man's weakness. His one thought was personal grief at the loss of a beloved though erring son. The lamentation reached such a pass that Joab was forced to tell David that he would have no supporters left on the morrow if he did not at once show some appreciation of the victory. David then pulled himself together for the cere-

mony of thanking the
soldiers. He next pro-
claimed a general par-
don to all who had
taken part in the re-
bellion; but the tribe
of Judah was slow to
accept the reconcilia-
tion. Not until David
secretly sent special
messengers among
them and even offered
Joab's post of com-
mander of the army
to Amasa, who had
just led the rebel host,
did their elders come
to meet the returning
king at the Jordan and
renew their oath. But
David's favoritism to
Judah, who had fur-
nished most of Absa-
lom's supporters, so
exasperated the north-
ern tribes that before
David had reached
Jerusalem they broke
out in a second revolt
under a certain Sheba.
David ordered the
new general to get
the warriors of Judah
together to put down

FIG. 59—TOMB OF ABSALOM AND
MOUNT OF OLIVES

You are standing on the southeast angle of
the temple wall (Fig. 58) and are looking
east   What is this valley called? How
far below you is the bottom? The square
building with the conical roof is the so-
called Absalom's Tomb. It dates from
the Græco-Roman period. However,
Absalom was buried not far from here.
(II Sam. 18¹⁸.)
The road between high walls running across
the centre of the picture takes one to
Jericho. The steeper paths above take
one to the summit and on to Bethany.
The countless white stones that dot the
ground are Jewish graves. According to
Jewish tradition the judgment is to take
place here. These forehanded ones have
secured front seats!

the rebels. Amasa's slowness, however, was interpreted
by Joab as disloyalty, so that on their first meeting Joab

killed Amasa and recommissioned himself commander in his stead. That David did nothing about this murder and insult to his authority is proof that he was as putty in the hand of his dauntless but unscrupulous nephew. Joab pursued Sheba and his diminishing band till he caught him in a town in the extreme north. To save themselves from destruction the inhabitants killed Sheba and threw his head over the wall to Joab. The backbone of the rebellion was now broken, but the whole experience with Absalom and Sheba shows that David had lost his grip.

67. **The Famine and the Plague.** Two further incidents in David's reign throw light upon David's character and upon current ideas about religion. The first was a three years' famine caused by a drought. David consulted the oracle to find why Jehovah was wroth, and the answer came that it was because of Saul's bloody house: the Israelites had taken no revenge for Saul's endeavor to kill the Gibeonites, contrary to the ancient treaty (Joshua 9[15]). David accordingly took seven of Saul's descendants and allowed the Gibeonites to impale them as a sacrifice on their highplace. With this gory sacrifice the Hebrews believed that Jehovah was appeased, for the October rains fell as usual.

The second was a plague that took off 70,000 men. Plagues as well as famines and other calamities were always supposed to be sent by Jehovah in punishment for some insult or slight. In this case the cause was thought to be a census that David had just taken, though according to the writer of II Samuel Jehovah's anger was kindled against Israel for some unknown reason and he stirred up David to take the census so that he might have an excuse for sending a plague. These incidents show how undeveloped and crude the religious ideas of the time still were. A few centuries later such ideas about Jehovah had been outgrown (see Sec. 115). The story states that when David discovered his error in having ordered the census, Jehovah gave him a choice of three forms of punishment, and he chose the plague. As his angel was about to smite Jerusalem, Jehovah repented of the destruction and stayed the plague. David saw in a vision the destroying angel as he paused over the threshing-floor of Araunah the Jebusite, and in gratitude he bought the floor and offered there a sacrifice. It was this spot in Jerusalem that became the site of Solomon's temple, and is revered in our own day as a most sacred shrine by three great religions: Jewish, Christian, and Moslem.

68. **The Intrigues for the Succession.** As David advanced in years he withdrew more and more within the seclusion of his harem, until at last his weakness made him unfit to reign. Then arose the important question of a successor. In Israel there was as yet no well-defined rule in such matters. However, in the matter of property and family rights among the Hebrews, the oldest son had first claim, and at the same time it was generally recognized that the dying ruler might at least nominate his own successor. With this general haziness as to the correct procedure it is not strange that there should have been two contestants in the present case: Adonijah, the king's eldest surviving son, and Solomon, the ambitious and accomplished son of David's favorite wife, Bathsheba. The important men of the kingdom had been for some time lining up on either side, the first clear case of party politics in Israelite history. With Adonijah went Joab, the intrepid commander-in-chief, and Abiathar the priest, both of them David's loyal friends. With Solomon were Nathan the prophet, who had been for years David's trusted adviser, Zadok the priest, and Benaiah, the captain of the body-guard. It was an open secret that David favored Solomon.

Adonijah had been for some time bidding for popular favor; and now, thinking that the time had come for action, he sent an invitation to his chief friends to dine with him at a place called Serpent's Rock, well below Jerusalem in the valley of the Kidron. The coup was to consist of a sudden anointing, a presentation of the new king to the people of

Jerusalem for their approval, and then no doubt a seizure of the palace. While the feast was in progress, a report of it came to Nathan's ears. He and Bathsheba brought the news to the helpless king, reminded him of his promise to name Solomon his successor, and roused him to act before it was too late. David ordered his own mule to be brought. They set Solomon on it, took him down to the spring Gihon just under the eastern wall of David's city, and there Zadok and Nathan anointed him in the presence of all the people. The trumpets were blown, the people shouted "God save King Solomon," and the faithful six hundred of the body-guard became at once the invincible power behind the *viva voce* vote. Adonijah heard the shouting and knew at once that his cause was lost. He fled to the sanctuary and clung to the horns of the altar until the new king promised him his life; the other guests scattered to cover, each in his own way.

David now gave Solomon his parting commands, chiefly directions about avenging him of his enemies and rewarding his friends; then after charging him to be faithful to Jehovah, he "slept with his fathers."

69. **Summary of David's Character and Reign.** The personality of David made a profound impression upon the men of his own and later times. At the root of this admiration undoubtedly lay David's personal charm and his capacity for friendship. Throughout his earlier career we see him playing a difficult rôle with marked success, because he knew how to make himself personally acceptable to such widely different characters as Samuel, Achish, Jonathan, and Joab. For the most part his personal friends stuck to him to the last: Nathan served him for years and became the support of his old age; Abiathar, Zadok, and Hushai grew old with him, and Joab's loyalty—his one redeeming trait—survived even the king's curses and the loss of his office. David must have been also a man of extraordinary strength,

courage, and skill in arms to command the unswerving obedience of his "mighty men."

We know too that David was generous to friends and magnanimous to enemies. All this is a just basis of success. With maturity came the developed capacity for organization, for skilful planning and the choice of efficient means and men. Because of this power he held unwilling vassal states in unwavering subjection, and moderated for a time the feuds and rivalries of his Hebrew subjects. But when with advancing years the charm and strength of youth disappeared, and when increasing seclusion within his palace cut him off from the opportunity of impressing himself personally on the new generation, he lost his hold upon his people's loyalty.

David had also a strongly religious nature. Late biblical writers may have exaggerated the work he did in developing a ritual of worship; but throughout even the older sources one reads of his constant devotion to Jehovah. His respect for Saul was based on the thought that Jehovah had anointed him. No public or private act of importance was undertaken without consulting the divine will. As soon as it was physically possible he rescued the ark from its exile and provided for it a special sanctuary. He enrolled among his advisers both the prophets Nathan and Gad and the priests Abiathar and Zadok, and he consecrated his sons to be priests, all in the endeavor to keep continually and perfectly in touch with Jehovah's will. Even in the days of his might he carried the ark into battle, and his refusal to take it with him when he fled from Absalom, as well as his attitude of pious resignation during that painful experience, shows even more clearly his reverence for Jehovah and the intimacy of his trust in him. It is quite evident, however, that David's religious ideas were of a primitive type: his god was a being who might break out with disaster on the slightest provocation, and who had to be appeased by sacrifices, even human ones. In these matters David was a man of his time. Our admiration is aroused only by the depth and strength of his devotion, not by his intellectual conceptions of what God is like.

David had one accomplishment that has endeared him to all time: he was a poet and musician. His harp first brought him to the notice of Saul; his deepest emotions took naturally the form of poetry, and the inspiration he gave to the lyric side of worship so impressed the imagination of later ages that they ascribed to him nearly all of the psalms in their Psalter. Only a few poems in our Bible are certainly his, like the "Dirge over Saul and Jonathan" (II Sam. 1$^{19-27}$), the "Lament over Abner" (II Sam. 3$^{33-34}$), and possibly the "Last Words of David" (II Sam. 23$^{1-7}$); but most of the psalms breathe the spirit of joyous confidence in Jehovah that was David's religion. He at least was the inspiration of many of their authors.

There is a darker side to David's character. Like most Orientals, he was at times cruel, vindictive, and sensual. His laxity with his own children brought upon his declining years the great tragedies of his career, and his example as Grand Monarch clearly pointed the way to his son Solomon's fatal policy. Yet these defects were in part balanced by the greatness of his virtues, so that in the large one may say with Professor Cornill: "He is the most luminous figure and the most gifted personage in Israelitish history, surpassed in ethical greatness and general historical importance only by Moses."

It is hardly possible to overestimate what David did for the Hebrews. He found them disorganized, discouraged, only slightly conscious of their unity of blood and their common destiny, holding on to a precarious existence in the midst of determined foes. He left them a nation, united as they were destined never to be again, their loyalty centred about a dynasty and capital city, conscious of a physical and moral superiority over their neighbors, the dominant race of that century in southwestern Asia. This is an accomplishment worthy of the highest genius. We can easily understand how the affections of Israel should so centre about this figure that a second David became the dream and hope of Israel's future.

XI

SOLOMON THE AUTOCRAT

Solomon (c. 955–c. 935 B.C.)

70. Solomon's Sinister Beginning. The outwitted and defeated Adonijah might have lived out his natural years in private but for a sudden desire to marry the pretty Shunammite nurse who had been secured to comfort David's last days. Knowing that there was risk involved in asking Solomon for a member of the royal harem, he induced Bathsheba, the queen-mother, to petition her son in his behalf. But Solomon saw in the request a scheme on Adonijah's part to seize the throne, and he suspected that the former conspirators, Joab and Abiathar, were behind Adonijah. Solomon's anger at once flamed out. He sent Benaiah, his captain, to put Adonijah to death, he banished Abiathar to his little home-town of Anathoth, and when Joab fled in terror to Jehovah's altar and refused to be coaxed away from it, Solomon commanded Benaiah to kill him even in that sacred place. Solomon salved his conscience—if he had any—by stating that he had thus executed a righteous sentence on the murderer of his father's friends, Abner and Amasa; but in reality he was glad of an opportunity to put a dangerous enemy out of the way. Shimei also, who had been unfaithful to David, was put to death on a flimsy pretext. These executions served notice on the kingdom that Solomon would stand no interference. More than that, they mark the change from a rule based on popular approval—as David's was at the beginning—to the iron rule of an autocrat.

71. His Policy of Magnificence. Solomon came to the throne with the fixed intention of having his own way. He was a young man of extraordinary and varied powers, and

122

taking the cue from his father's attempts at splendor and from the ways of other great monarchs, he set for himself the ideal of magnificence.   Lacking his father's moral capacity and political insight, he did not see that a course of unbridled selfishness, such as he proposed, would run counter to the best interests of his subjects and in the end to his own interests.

Outward splendor is based on the possession of wealth, and to get this now became Solomon's supreme ambition. To this end the state, which ought to serve the common good, was made an instrument for exacting and collecting wealth for the ruler.   If there was anything done in Solomon's reign to strengthen the people in material or intellectual ways, if there was any endeavor to purify religion or elevate morals, we do not know of it.   No heroic or noble act is recorded of any one while Solomon was on the throne.

72. **Territorial Losses and Their Result.**   At the outset of his reign Edom revolted.   The leader was one Hadad who had managed to escape when David nearly exterminated the nation, had taken refuge in Egypt, and now, with a king of different temper ruling at Jerusalem, returned to free his country from the oppressor.   Solomon was not a warrior; he let Edom go.   Taking courage from Edom's success, Moab revolted likewise.   Next Rezon the Aramean tried his hand.   He, too, had escaped the sword of David, had been an outlaw-chief for a generation, and now plucked up courage to enter Damascus and declare its freedom from Israelite control.   Solomon was powerless to stop him. Rezon thus laid the foundation of that Aramean kingdom of Damascus that was destined for two centuries to be Israel's bitterest foe and temporary master.

One can easily see that a large part of Solomon's income vanished with these revolts.   To recoup himself he had resort to forced labor and oppressive taxes at home.   At first the blow fell upon the non-Hebrew inhabitants of Palestine, the Canaanites, Ammonites, Jebusites, Gibeonites,

and the like who, since the conquest, had been living along-
side their conquerors. All of them became state slaves, in
precisely the way that five centuries previous to this the
Hebrew shepherds of Goshen had been enslaved by Thutmose I. Next the Israelites themselves were forced to supply 30,000 men for the royal levies, in relays of 10,000 each.

Fig. 60—COLLECTION OF TAXES

This world-old method of collecting taxes by use of a stick was employed not
only by the Pyramid builders, as here shown, but by Solomon and all other
autocrats down to 1890, when in Egypt at least it ceased to be used by
government. Of the six clerks-of-court, how many have desks to write
on? What are the writing materials? The three victims are village
officers who have not brought in the taxes due. The four deputies have
stout sticks, which will be stoutly applied if the money is not forthcoming.
The inscription reads: "Seizing the town rulers for a reckoning."

One month they worked for the king and two months they
worked for themselves at home. In addition Solomon levied
a direct tax on the people for the support of his palace.
This service and these taxes must have been galling to the
freedom-loving Israelites who were caught in the toils.

73. **The Organization of His System.** Solomon put his
schemes through by his consummate organizing ability. He
disregarded the old tribal divisions that had obtained hitherto, and substituted twelve administrative districts, nine
west of Jordan and three east. Over each he placed a pre-
fect of high rank. These men had for their special duty the
collecting of produce for the king's maintenance, each district furnishing the supply for a month. The amount they
collected daily is stated to have been three hundred and thirty
bushels of fine flour, six hundred and sixty bushels of meal,
ten fat oxen, twenty oxen from the pasture, a hundred sheep,

besides what miscellaneous delicacies in the way of gazelles, roebucks, harts, and fat fowl they could pick up. There was also barley and straw for the royal stables. This supply would take care of at least 35,000 persons. Since his establishment included his standing army, officials and servants of various kinds, this large quantity was doubtless required.

Some further details about Solomon's court have come down to us. He had now a high priest in addition to the regular priests; he kept his father's grand vizier, added a private secretary, making two; established the office of superintendent of the palace; kept up the circle of the "king's friends," and created for the son of the prophet Nathan the office of general supervisor of the various departments. The office of overseer of the labor gangs was perpetuated, as of course was that of the commander of the army. The character of the army, however, was changed by the introduction of chariots and horses, which hitherto had been unknown. His war horses were said to number 40,000, his mounted knights 12,000, his chariots 1,400. These he kept at Jerusalem and at certain fortified cities that he built or remodelled at strategic places as store-depots and centres of authority from which he could repel invasion or put down insurrection. The introduction of chariots would necessitate vast outlays for the construction of military roads, since hitherto in the hill-country at least there had been only the roughest kind of trails. Thus the expenses grew by leaps and bounds.

74. **Solomon's Building Enterprises.** To house his growing court, as well as properly to symbolize his growing state, Solomon now decided to build a palace. He chose for it a site to the north of his father's city, on the slope of the hill later called Mount Moriah. The plans included also a temple for Jehovah. The relative magnificence and extent of the two structures is shown by the fact that it took thirteen years to build the palace and only seven and a half to

build the temple.   Since no Israelite was capable of planning and executing such works as these, Solomon turned to
Hiram, king of Tyre, who, being the head of an industrial

Fig. 61—A GROVE OF CEDARS

One of the few groves of the cedars of Lebanon, as it was before the war.
  It lay 6,300 feet above the sea and contained about 400 very old trees.
  Notice the wall that was erected to protect it.   Formerly the trees
  formed a huge forest, and were a most valuable property of the Phœnicians
  who sold them or were forced to contribute them for centuries to the kings
  of Asia and Egypt.   The Crusaders attempted to introduce them into
  Europe.   One still grows at Warwick castle, England, after 800 years.
  Practically all the cedars were cut down in 1914–1919 to supply fuel for
  the Beirut-Damascus railway.

rather than an agricultural people, was glad enough to
undertake the contract both for timber and talent.   What
Hiram furnished in both kinds was to be paid for by a yearly
delivery to him of 220,000 bushels of wheat and 180,000
gallons of the best olive-oil.   This general summary does

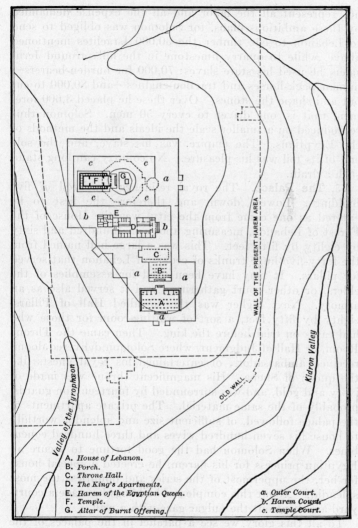

Valley of the Tyropœon

WALL OF THE PRESENT HAREM AREA

OLD WALL

Kidron Valley

A. House of Lebanon.
B. Porch.
C. Throne Hall.
D. The King's Apartments.
E. Harem of the Egyptian Queen.
F. Temple.
G. Altar of Burnt Offering.

a. Outer Court.
b. Harem Court.
c. Temple Court.

FIG. 62—PLAN OF SOLOMON'S PALACE

(According to Stade)

not represent all the labor and all the expense demanded
by these ambitious plans, for Solomon was obliged to send
to Lebanon to cut timber the 30,000 Israelites mentioned
above, while to quarry limestone in the hills around Jerusalem he used his state slaves: 70,000 for burden-bearers—
human pack-horses and traction-engines—and 80,000 to cut
out and shape the stones.   Over these he placed 3,600 fore-
men, that is, one driver to every 50 men.   Solomon thus
reproduced on a smaller scale the ideals and the methods of
the Egyptians.   The empire was his slave, and the sole
end of its toil was his pleasure.   No country can long stand
such a drain.

75. **The Palace.**   The royal residence consisted of five
buildings.   Lowest down, and therefore the first to be
entered as one came from the city, was the House of the
Forest of Lebanon, measuring about one hundred and sixty
by eighty by fifty feet.   This was a large hall named from
the forty-five huge trunks of cedars of Lebanon that served
for pillars.   It may have been used for assemblies of the
elders, or other court gatherings, and it served also as an
armory.   Next higher was the so-called Hall of Pillars,
eighty by fifty feet, a sort of waiting-room for those who
had cases on trial before the king.   Then came the Throne
Room, or Hall of Judgment, where Solomon delivered doom,
received ambassadors, or entertained his royal guests like
the queen of Sheba.   His magnificent throne was made of
ivory and gold, and was surrounded by fourteen lion guards,
probably of the same material.   The private apartments of
the palace followed, of sufficient size and splendor worthily
to house his seven hundred wives and three hundred concu-
bines.   When Solomon had the good fortune to secure an
Egyptian princess for his harem, he erected a special house
for her, the uppermost of the series and doubtless the most
splendid.   About this complex of buildings he made a courtyard and kept out the vulgar gaze with a wall.

To all this glory we see a parallel in the palaces of the

Moguls at Delhi and Agra. Shah Jehan had his Hall of Public Audience (like the House of the Forest of Lebanon), his Hall of Private Audience (Hall of Judgment), and his

FIG. 63—A CEDAR OF LEBANON

Note the superb background of snow-clad mountains. The wood of these trees is cream color and resembles white pine. It was used for interior finish, for furniture, and shrines. Tall straight trunks were used for pillars, as in Solomon's Hall of Audience, and for the timbers and masts of Egyptian and Phœnician ships. The wood is almost indestructible. The cedar roof of the temple of Diana at Ephesus lasted 400 years, and that of the temple of Apollo at Utica lasted 1,170 years.

famous peacock throne, the back of which was formed by the spread tails of two peacocks composed of precious stones, while between the peacocks there perched a life-sized parrot cut from a single emerald.

76. **The Temple.** The description given in the Bible of the house of Jehovah is very elaborate but not altogether

clear. Though we know something of its plan we can only conjecture what it looked like. It was no doubt copied from similar structures in Phœnicia and Babylonia. There

Fig. 64—JAFFA

The sand-dunes that form all the southwestern shore of Palestine here give place to a rocky hill, on which Jaffa is built. Just off shore a few yards you may see a row of black ledges. These form an imperfect shelter behind which small boats may lie. This is the only harbor south of Mount Carmel. For this reason, the log rafts shipped at Sidon for Solomon's temple were towed in here as the only possible haven, and from this point sent over-land to their destination. Steamers to-day anchor half a mile out, and their cargoes are lightered in. Landings are frequently impossible in winter.

was first the sacred enclosure protected by a wall, then a house with porch, antechamber, and shrine. It was not large, only a hundred feet long by about thirty wide. About the central rooms were grouped tiers of tiny chambers, doubtless robing-rooms for the priests, storage-rooms for the temple equipment, and safety-deposit vaults for the state and temple treasure. (See plan.) The Bible writer

lavishes great attention on the bronze work, which was
evidently a novelty in his day. Possibly his imagination
supplied some of the elaborate details. A cunning workman

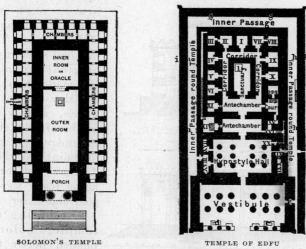

SOLOMON'S TEMPLE

TEMPLE OF EDFU

FIG. 65—SOLOMON'S TEMPLE COMPARED WITH TEMPLE
OF EDFU

The idea underlying ancient temples is always the same: a temple is the
palace or home of the god, and the priests are his servants. There is first
the sacred enclosure beyond which common people must not come. Then
there is the impressive approach—a porch with large pillars, or in Egypt
a "hypostyle hall." Royalty and privileged people may enter here. Beyond are the antechambers where priests only are allowed, while in the
inmost recesses of the temple, in darkness, the deity resides in his holy of
holies. Ranged about the central rooms are chambers in which to store
the clothing for the god, the vestments and standards for the festal processions, and usually gifts or other temple treasure. In appearance Solomon's temple may have been Assyrian, but in plan it is more nearly
Egyptian, as the above plans show.

named Hiram chose a clay bottom in the Jordan valley and
cast there the two huge pillars, Jachin and Boaz, that stood
before the entrance, like the obelisks of Egyptian temples.
These were thirty feet high, cast hollow, and had queer tops
that looked like pineapples without the leaves, festooned with

pomegranates. Undoubtedly these pillars had a religious significance, for they supported nothing. Then he cast a huge sea or reservoir, holding 16,000 gallons. It rested on the backs of twelve brazen oxen that faced the four points of the compass. This, too, had some mythological meaning. He made also ten smaller lavers on wheels, and a vast number of tongs, shovels, and other utensils for use in the sacrifices. All the vessels for the house itself were of gold and silver.

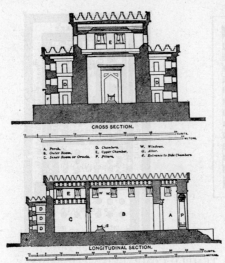

CROSS SECTION.

A. Porch. D. Chambers. W. Windows.
B. Outer Room. E. Upper Chamber, G. Altar.
C. Inner Room or Oracle. P. Pillars. E. Entrance to Side Chambers

LONGITUDINAL SECTION.

FIG. 66—CROSS AND LONGITUDINAL SECTIONS OF SOLOMON'S TEMPLE

In erecting this temple, Solomon builded better than he knew; for the priesthood that gathered about this royal shrine became the chief support of the dynasty of David, and its prestige attracted to it the love and the devotion that enabled Judah later to survive the shock of the exile.

77. **Solomon's Ventures in High Finance.** Solomon found it difficult to pay the bills thus contracted. Rather than risk a revolt by further taxes and levies he went into business. According to I Kings 10[29] he sold horses to the kings of the Hittites and the Arameans, and doubtless made a good profit. His chief venture, however, was in the Far East. Since the Hebrews knew nothing of ship construction or navigation, he had recourse again to Hiram's men. The Phœnicians built for him a fleet of "East Indiamen" on the

Red Sea, and sailed it to Ophir (eastern Arabia or western India). The recently discovered copper mines in the Arabah, between the Dead Sea and the Red Sea, which were indubitably worked at their maximum in Solomon's time, may have

Fig. 67—PHŒNICIAN GALLEY

A two-decked war-galley with two banks of oars (bireme). Note the long sharp prow on or below the water-line, designed to ram other ships. The soldiers have hung their shields along the rail. Is this salt or fresh water?

supplied him with his chief article of export. Solomon got what he wanted, namely, gold, and that in such quantity that the bottom dropped out of the silver market at Jerusalem: a later historian declares that silver had little value in the days of Solomon. One can hardly believe the report in I Kings 10[14] that Solomon's annual receipt of the yellow metal was $20,000,000—in purchasing power the equivalent of $300,000,000! Tradition declares that he made a display of part of this by fashioning five hundred shields of gold for his body-guard to use on state occasions, and by hanging them as ornaments in the House of the Forest of Lebanon.

Besides this, Solomon levied tariff on all goods shipped by caravan across his territory. With Egypt and Arabia to

FIG. 68—EXPEDITION TO PUNT

Upper register: Queen Hatasu's five ships arrive at the land of Punt. Find sailors furling sail. Find the "bridge." How are the ships steered and propelled? How does the officer in charge go ashore? Notice that the ships have curved bow and stern, the latter terminating in a lotus. How are the ships braced to stand rough weather?

Lower register: The ships loading at Punt. What are being carried on board? What are already aboard? How many articles imported by Solomon are here found? See also Fig. 69 from the same relief.

the south, and Phœnicia and the kingdoms of the Tigris-Euphrates valley to the north, the trade must have been considerable and the revenues large. Even so, Solomon could not keep pace with his outlay, and he fell back upon borrowing. The ever-ready Hiram of Tyre made to him various loans that finally amounted to $3,750,000—or in purchasing power about $56,000,000—a figure that gives

Hiram a very fair financial rating! Hiram became a little frightened at the pace his extravagant neighbor was setting, and called the loans. Since Solomon had not the cash to pay, he made over to him twenty cities in Galilee. Hiram took the towns because he knew he would not see his money again, but when he came down to look them over, he found that he had been cheated! Later generations, looking back upon this magnificence, imagined that Solomon must have been the richest man in the world; but they forget that he did not pay his bills.

78. **Solomon's Reputation for Wisdom.** The reputation for wisdom that Solomon has always enjoyed is not deserved, but it has some justification. Solomon was no doubt brilliant, with the personal charm of his father and the almost uncanny fascination of his mother. He had that ready wit, that flash of insight, that knack of pointed and apt speech, in which the Oriental especially delights. Hosts of stories in Hebrew and Arabic regale us with his shrewd judgments, his solutions of riddles, his striking nature-comparisons. The Bible editors attributed to him nearly all the anonymous sayings that had come down from the wise men of the race—two entire books of the Old Testament and one of the Apocrypha. In particular the visit of the queen of Sheba appealed to the story-teller's imagination. Though coming from a prosperous commercial nation in south Arabia and being herself a woman of no mean accomplishments, she had to confess that the half of Solomon's wisdom and splendor had not been told her. But granted all that has been claimed for him in these superficial ways, the results of his example and his policy upon the nation give the lie to any claim for true wisdom—unless to bring industrial and political ruin upon one's people while working first, last, and always for one's self is wisdom. Solomon was a brilliant fool.

79. **His Legacy of Idolatry.** The crowning evidence of his essential folly is found in his attitude toward religion:

FIG. 69—SCENES IN THE LAND OF PUNT

A wonderful relief on the colonnaded wall of Queen Hatasu's mortuary temple
    at Thebes, built about 1450 B.C.—five hundred years before Solomon.
Lower row: The soldiers with their commander have landed in Punt (Somali-
    land). What armor do they carry? Find the King of Punt. Why are
    his arms raised? (The King's enormously fat wife stood behind him).
    How far inland is this meeting? In front of the Egyptians is a box, some

he did not even know enough to avoid shocking his people's religious ideals. Jehovah was Israel's God and his father David's God. To be sure, since the conquest Jehovah had absorbed many of the qualities of the Canaanite Baal, even at times his name; and he was worshipped with many of the old rites that clung to the Canaanite high places. But in essential ways Jehovah still bore a likeness to the God of Moses, and he still claimed first place in the affections of Israel. Solomon openly placed by the side of Jehovah, even in the courts of his new Jehovah temple, the many heathen gods of his foreign wives, gods of nations whom the great David had conquered, gods who were pleased with forms of worship that outraged the moral sense of the Hebrew. Solomon in his wisdom may have felt that it was a necessary state policy to strengthen his foreign alliances in this way, but his unfaithfulness to the national God had a determining influence on the course his people took after his death.

80. **Solomon's Death.** The autocratic monarch was able to keep his people under until the very end. Only once was there an attempted insurrection, but that was quickly put down, and Jeroboam, the instigator of it, forced to flee. Solomon died peacefully in his palace at Jerusalem, having

---

bracelets, a dagger, an axe, and some strings of beads. What are these for? The inscription expresses the astonishment of the men of Punt at the coming of the Egyptians.

Second row: (left) A tent, in front of which is a large pile of incense, gold rings, and other valuables. What are these for? In the tent, according to the inscription, the Egyptian officers gave a feast of "bread, beer, wine, meat, fruit, and everything that is found in Egypt." Why was this done?

Third row: The Egyptians carrying off the incense-trees in baskets. They are to be transplanted in the temple garden at Thebes—the mud-brick tubs for which are still in place!

Top row: (not clear) Egyptians are climbing trees gathering eggs in baskets from the nests.

It is interesting to compare the enumeration of the cargo with the list of Solomon's imports given in I Kings 10[11], [14], [22]:

"The loading of the ships very heavily with marvels from the land of Punt: all goodly fragrant woods, heaps of myrrh-resin, with fresh myrrh-trees, with ebony and pure ivory, with green gold of Amu, with cinnamon-wood . . . incense, eye-cosmetic, with apes, monkeys, dogs, with skins of the southern panther, and with natives and their children."

From Olmstead: History of Palestine and Syria.

Fig. 70—SOLOMON'S STABLES, MEGIDDO

The mound of Megiddo occupies a strategic position in the plain of Esdraelon where the trade route from Egypt to Mesopotamia breaks through a defile in the Carmel range. It has been inhabited since neolithic days. City after city was found superimposed within it, as the excavators of the Oriental Institute, University of Chicago, lifted off the layers of debris. In the level that represents undoubtedly the age of Solomon were found the stumps of rows of square pillars, pierced with tie-holes, arranged in such fashion that their use in stables was quite evident. One of the staff, Mr. Lind, constructed this model on the basis of the evidence. In the cut, these stumps appear on the right. On the left are two completed sections of the stable as they originally appeared. In the right centre is a half-section that shows how the horses stood facing each other across a corridor where the grooms walked. This stable would hold 300 horses.

not even the wit to see, as Louis XV of France saw, that after him would come the deluge. To Solomon belongs the doubtful honor of having set the Hebrew world a standard of regal magnificence and selfishness, and by the perversion of great talents of having for a time changed a free people into slaves.

THE REVOLT AGAINST AUTOCRACY

Rehoboam (935–916 B.C.)   *Jeroboam* (935–912 B.C.)

81. **The Popular Recoil.** The tears that were shed over Solomon's grave were insincere. The joyful news that the tyrant was no more was carried instanter to Jeroboam, the exile rebel in Egypt. Solomon's son, Rehoboam, was quick to have himself proclaimed king by his faithful friends at Jerusalem, and he hoped at Shechem to have all Israel approve his nomination. But the northern tribes had stood all of Solomon's methods they could endure. If the young Rehoboam was willing to return to the less oppressive methods of David or Saul, they would be content to let him become their king; but if not, then their loyalty would go elsewhere. Before confirming his election they demanded a clear statement of policy: "Will you remove your father's yoke, or will you not?" Rehoboam saw that they were determined, and he took three days to consider.

His father's advisers realized the danger and counselled moderation. His young friends, who saw the advantages but not the dangers of vast wealth and autocratic power, bade him assert his authority. In his ignorance, the latter counsel seemed good to Rehoboam, and at the end of his three days he returned an autocrat's and a fool's answer: "My father chastised you with whips, but I will chastise you with scorpions." Large words for a sixteen-year-old! The people's reply was instant and decisive:

> "What portion have we in David?
> To your tents, O Israel!"

Rehoboam assumed his father's manner and ordered Adoniram, the overseer of the labor gangs, to set the people to work. The people stoned the overseer to death. Not knowing what to do next, Rehoboam fled. The ten northern tribes then elected Jeroboam head of the northern state,

FIG. 71—NABLUS—ANCIENT SHECHEM

You are facing east. What mountain is on the right? On the left? The olive groves furnish the chief article of export from this city—olive-oil soap. Twenty-two springs make the environs very fertile. The ancient city, mentioned so frequently in the Old Testament, lay a trifle to the east of the present city, where the mountains come almost together. Omri abandoned the site for one more easily defended—Samaria.

The ancient temple of the Samaritans built by Sanballat II (sec. 191) and destroyed by John Hyrcanus, 129 B.C. (sec. 221) stood on the peak above the centre of the picture. In the hollow just to the right, the Samaritans observe their passover (cf. Fig. 134).

which took the name Israel. The fateful breach was consummated.

82. **Jeroboam's Training.** The new ruler of Israel had been a protégé of Solomon. While the latter was fortifying Jerusalem, his attention was called to this young man of industry and ability, and he advanced him to the office of

supervisor of the labor gangs of Ephraim. Soon after this a prophet named Ahijah came across Jeroboam and, seeing his talent, was moved to sow in his mind the seeds of ambition, even as Samuel had earlier done in the mind of Saul. Meeting him alone as he was returning from Jerusalem, the prophet tore into twelve pieces a new mantle he was wearing and gave Jeroboam ten of them, saying: "Thus says Jehovah, the God of Israel, Behold I will wrest the kingdom out of the hand of Solomon and will give ten tribes to you." Whether he read in the young officer's mind some sympathy with the sufferings of his fellow tribesmen, or whether he discovered there a slumbering ambition, his words, like those of the witches to Macbeth, roused Jeroboam to action. He planned a revolt. Unfortunately the time was not ripe, and as stated in the previous chapter, he fled to Egypt. There he was sympathetically harbored by King Shishak. We have no means of knowing whether from that safe distance he kept up any agitation among the sheiks of the north, but he did not allow them to forget him. To him they turned at once in the great crisis, and thus fulfilled the daring forecast of the prophet of Shiloh.

83. **Causes and Consequences of the Division.** The broad material and political causes underlying the great rift have been already noted. Solomon had run counter to the primitive instincts for freedom and democracy which his people had inherited from their desert ancestors, and had made life bitter through forced labor and oppressive taxes; he had broken the spirit of the contract that David had made with their fathers when they consented to accept him as their ruler (II Sam. 5³). He had also shocked the strongly religious part of the nation by his idolatries. That this was a fertile source of discontent is shown by the fact that it was a prophet who instigated the abortive first revolt, and that one of the first acts of Jeroboam was to make adequate provision for his people's religion. But one must go even deeper and say that Solomon's oppression was merely an

excuse for the reappearance of a deep-seated and ancient jealousy, the jealousy between Judah and Joseph, the south and the north. Judah, in the persons of David and Solo-

FIG. 72—INSCRIPTION OF SHISHAK

On the south wall of Karnak. It commemorates the victory of Shishak I over Rehoboam about 931 B.C. (I Kings 14²⁵⁻²⁸). The figure of King Shishak smiting his foes was to have been placed on the blank stones to the right, but was never put in. Find the kneeling Asiatics with their hands raised for mercy. Standing to the left is the tall figure of the god Amon, with the crown of two feathers. In his right hand he grasps a curved sword; in his left the ropes by which he leads captive the conquered cities of Palestine. (See Fig. 73.)

mon, had gained the ascendancy over his kinsmen; this ascendancy was hateful to the powerful and high-spirited Joseph tribes. What Sheba's rebellion could not accomplish, Jeroboam's did: the northern tribes became their own masters. Judah held faithful to Rehoboam, partly because he was their kinsman while the rebel was an Ephraimite, and partly because the priesthood instituted by Solomon and supported by his lavishness set itself strongly to support his dynasty.

In this division Israel obtained the lion's share. The line of cleavage ran stright across the central highland through the valleys of Michmash to the east and Ajalon to the west, giving Israel fully three times the square miles that Judah retained. In Israel's land were all the fertile valleys and copious springs. There was the larger population. There ran the great roads, bringing trade and ideas from the four corners of the world; and next to her lay wealthy and peaceful Phœnicia. Judah, on the other hand, was rocky, dry, isolated, and exposed to the raids of the Bedouin. But Judah had spiritual assets that Israel lacked. She had the great traditions of David and Solomon, the prestige of having ruled; to her belonged Jerusalem, now splendid and well fortified; to her belonged the temple of Jehovah and the royal palace, strong rallying-points for Hebrew pride and loyalty and religion.

Whatever either Hebrew state may have gained, they lost immeasurably by the division. Instead of one, there were two; instead of harmony, discord; instead of a united front to the foe, intrigue with him by each against the other. The history of both states is a long death agony, and they both finally fell before the resistless advance of Assyria and Babylonia.

84. **Civil War and Invasion.** Rehoboam, having returned to Jerusalem and having found that the tribe of Judah would stand by him, resolved to make war on Israel and force her to accept his rule. It is stated in I Kings 14[30] that there was war between Rehoboam and Jeroboam continually. No incidents of this war are recorded. Five years after the division, Shishak I of Egypt profited by the weakness of the warring kingdoms to make a raid into Palestine. Since the fact is recorded in connection with the

reign of Rehoboam, we might think that Shishak spared
Israel on account of his former friendship for Jeroboam.
But this was not so.   In the large inscription that Shishak

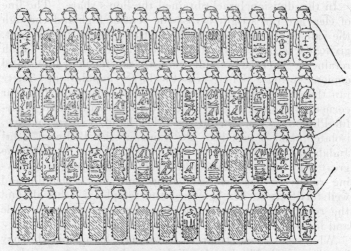

FIG. 73—CITIES CAPTURED BY SHISHAK

Detail of Fig. 72. On that picture, find the location of these ovals behind
     Amon.
Each oval here stands for a town in Palestine, and has its name in hieroglyphics
     carved upon it.   Rising from each is the body and head of an Asiatic, arms
     tied behind the back and rope round the neck.   Originally there were 156
     names, many of which have been effaced.   Among these are found Gath,
     Gibeon, Beth-horon, Ajalon, of the kingdom of Judah, and Taanach,
     Shunem, Beth-shean, Mahanaim, Megiddo, Edrai, Magdala, of the king-
     dom of Israel.

caused to be made on the walls of the temple of Karnak at
Thebes are found the names of more than sixty Ephraimite
cities along with more than ninety Judean towns.   It may
be that the tribute was exacted from Jeroboam by diplomacy, whereas it was collected from Rehoboam by force;
it may also be that Jeroboam, being at first worsted by

Rehoboam on account of the latter's inherited army and treasure, hired Shishak to attack his enemy. But at all events, the two quarrelling rulers became vassals to the ambitious Pharaoh.

Shishak's raid was a far greater blow for Rehoboam than for his northern neighbor, for all of the treasure that Solomon had managed to store up in the temple, and the five hundred gold shields that adorned his armory, were carried off. This must have left Rehoboam practically bankrupt. Jeroboam had no such treasure to lose. The evil that Solomon did in the matter of idolatry lived after him. His son kept up the foreign cults and even popularized them, until all Judah was worshipping by means of stone pillars and wooden poles on every high hill and under every green tree.

85. **The Royal Sanctuaries.** Jeroboam's main concern seemed to be to render his people independent of Judah in the matter of religion. Solomon's temple must have been a source of pride to the whole nation, and for the northern tribes now to be cut off from visiting it was a sentimental loss of vital import. To console his people, and also to give them no excuse for ever going to Jerusalem, Jeroboam built two royal shrines, one in Bethel on the southern border and on the highroad to Jerusalem, the other in the extreme north at Dan. Both of these places were sanctuaries of immemorial antiquity. Jehovah was represented here under the form of a bull of gold—the bull being an ancient Semitic symbol of divinity which Aaron was reputed to have used and which the Canaanites often employed for their Baals. He also appointed priests for these shrines and established a calendar of feast-days, duplicating Judah's. Jeroboam had no thought of substituting other gods for Jehovah; he merely was trying to make the worship of Jehovah convenient for his people.

This endeavor to solve the religious problem was not wholly satisfactory. There is a late tradition that a prophet from Judah took the trouble to come up to Bethel and curse

the place in Jeroboam's presence. An earlier story goes to
show that the prophets of Israel saw in Jeroboam's images a
source of danger; for Ahijah, who years before had inspired
Jeroboam with the thought of kingship and was no doubt

Fig. 74—"THE FIELD OF ABRAM"

Geographical name in the list of Shishak I at Karnak, containing the earliest
occurrence of the name of Abram.

his right-hand man in establishing the kingdom, turned
against him and cursed his house. There is no doubt that
the Jehovah images caused an increase of idolatry, because
the people soon forgot that they were only symbols; but
the king hardly merits the wholesale condemnation the
biblical writers mete out to him. It would seem from the
scant data given that Jeroboam was a ruler of strength and
sagacity, in every way devoted to the welfare of his sub-

FIG. 75—THE HATHOR COW

Jeroboam, who "made Israel to sin" by erecting calves at Bethel and Dan, may have gotten the idea of animal-worship while he was in Egypt (I Kings 11⁴⁰), where the cow, sacred to Hathor, was worshipped, and the bull, sacred to Serapis-Apis. More likely, however, he used the bull as an old Semitic symbol of strength and generative power. To his mind it represented Jehovah.

The statue above, found at Thebes, represents the goddess Hathor coming through the marshes of the West-land to welcome and protect the soul of the king. Find the marsh. Find two representations of the king. How is eternal life given to the king? Comment on the workmanship shown.

jects. For over two decades he was able to maintain his kingdom intact, and the people accepted his son as his successor.

86. Biblical Estimates of Character. A caution ought to be given at this point against accepting in general at their face value the estimates passed upon the kings of Judah and Israel by the biblical writers. These writers do not pretend to give us the full history of the period, but only to sermonize about certain events of the period. They are careful to mention the original sources for the benefit of any reader who wishes a detailed history: the *Book of the Acts of Solomon*, the *Book of the Chronicles of the Kings of Judah*, and the *Book of the Chronicles of the Kings of Israel*. They are interested chiefly in showing the state of Jehovah-worship in the two kingdoms and in proving from any incidents available that fidelity to Jehovah always brings blessing and infidelity brings disaster. In particular they endeavor to show that it was Jehovah's purpose all along to have his people worship exclusively in the temple at Jerusalem, avoiding all high places and all substitute shrines. From this point of view only do they judge both rulers and events. It is not strange therefore to find that every king of Israel, good or bad, is condemned, and the reason is usually stated: "He did evil in the sight of Jehovah, and walked in the way of Jeroboam, and in his sin wherewith he made Israel to sin." In estimating the kings of Judah the usually favorable judgment is modified in all cases but two by the sentence: "Nevertheless, the high places were not taken away." The modern historian, who is interested in economic and political and cultural history as well as religious history, and who has other standards of judgment, usually reaches a different conclusion about the various rulers and reigns

King of the   Kheper-sekhet-Rā,   son of   Shashanq meri Amen.
North and   setep-en-Rā,   the Sun,   *(Shishak.)*
South,

FIG. 76—NAME OF SHISHAK

In the right-hand oval, notice the two hieroglyphs that consist of alternate buds and blossoms of the lotus. The sound *sh*, which they represent, may have been suggested by the wind blowing through them. The letters literally transcribed are SH SH N K, to which are prefixed the words "Beloved of Amon."

XIII

EXPERIMENTS WITH MILITARY DESPOTS

RULERS OF ISRAEL

Nadab (912–911), son of Jeroboam. Murdered by Baasha during a mutiny in the army.

Baasha (911–888). Killed all descendants of Jeroboam. Fought a losing war with Asa and Benhadad of Damascus.

Elah (888–887), son of Baasha. Murdered while drunk by Zimri.

Zimri (887. Reigned but seven days). Committed suicide while besieged by Omri's troops.

Omri (887–876).

Ahab (876–854).

RULERS OF JUDAH

Abijam (916–914), son of Rehoboam. Successful war with Israel.

Asa (914–874), son of Abijam. Ten years of peace and prosperity. Purified worship.

Jehoshaphat (874–850).

87. **Enter the Sword and Dagger.** The fifty unhappy years that followed the division of the state show all too clearly the results of disunion. Mutual suspicions, rivalries, wars, both civil and foreign, sapped the material resources of both kingdoms and checked any political or intellectual or moral growth that might have occurred under a strong government. Judah was more fortunate than Israel. Asa seems to have been an able ruler whose long reign of two generations brought some peace to the people and considerable wealth to himself. Moreover, he seriously tried to undo

the danger to his people's morals that the idolatrous worship of Solomon and Rehoboam had caused. Israel, on the other hand, went from bad to worse. In thirty-seven years she had six kings, three of whom died violent deaths. Only twice was father succeeded by son. These rulers were in reality petty military despots whom the people raised to the throne in the hope that military force might save them from foes without and anarchy within. It did neither, but rather increased the difficulty. In fact the necessity of keeping so many free Israelites under arms brought about a change in the centre of power. The soldiers rather than the civilians became the kingmakers. The first case in which they exercised that power was Omri's. When the soldiers at the Philistine front heard that King Elah the sot had been murdered by one of their own number, Zimri, a captain of chariots, they refused to accept Zimri's self-nomination and promptly elected their general Omri king. Omri went in force to capture his rival, but Zimri, finding that he had no chance to win, locked himself into the palace and set fire to it. This relieved Omri of the necessity of killing him.

This election of Omri reflects still the democratic ideal of the Hebrew, but it illustrates also the almost universal tendency of a limited ruling class to usurp the rights that belong to the whole people. It is a step on the road to despotism; it helps a king to maintain a rule of might instead of a rule of right. But it is very significant of the temper of the Hebrews that the old order did not pass without a struggle. Those who still believed that the sword should be the servant, not the master, promptly nominated a man named Tibni for the throne. They were forced, however, to defend their choice by arms, and for four years the wasteful contest went on. The length of the struggle shows how determined both sides were; in fact, the numbers on each side were even. Tibni at last was slain, and Omri kept his throne.

88. Omri the Soldier-King.

The biblical writers have little to say about this able and energetic monarch. The Moabite Stone, however, of the ninth century B.C., tells us that Omri conquered Moab and exacted a yearly tribute. In the days of his son Ahab this tribute consisted of the wool of a hundred thousand lambs and a hundred thousand rams. Omri also occupied the Moabite cities, whether by Israelite colonists or by garrisons is not stated. We have also several inscriptions from Assyria that testify to Omri's greatness. The Assyrians thought that Omri was the founder of the kingdom of Israel, for they evidently had never heard of it until his day. The usual Assyrian designation of Israel from this time down to the time of Sargon (721 B.C.) is "the land of the house of Omri." Even Jehu, the destroyer of Omri's dynasty, is called by Shalmaneser III the "son of Omri." A man of small ability or of mean accomplishment could never have made such an impression upon far-off Assyria. Omri was the founder of the one great ruling family of Israel.

FIG. 77—MOABITE STONE

Found at Dibon in Moab about 1868. While the French and Prussian consuls were outbidding one another for its possession, the Arabs broke it up to make amulets for themselves, supposing that such a valuable stone must have magic virtue. The pieces were afterward bought up by M. Clermont-Ganneau and fitted together. The stone is now in the Louvre, Paris.

The stone bears the inscription of Mesha, king of Moab, a contemporary of King Ahab, and is written in one of the most ancient styles of Hebrew writing—the characters being in fact Phœnician. It was set up about 850 B.C. to commemorate his delivery from the yoke of Israel. (II Kings 3⁴⁻²⁷.)

89. **The New Capital.** The single fact mentioned about Omri in the Bible is his transfer of the capital from Tirzah to Samaria. With the eye of a soldier he saw that the hill of Shomer, the "watch-tower," was wonderfully adapted for a fortress and a royal city. It rose some three hundred feet from the plain and stood so far from its ring of mountains that an enemy could not reach it with any weapons of assault. Its situation was beautiful; and when Omri had surrounded it with walls and towers, it merited the description Isaiah later gave it:

> "The proud coronet of the drunkards of Ephraim,
>   And the flower of her beauteous adornment,
>   Which crowns the fat valley."

Omri's judgment is approved by the fact that Samaria was taken by the skilled Assyrian armies only after a siege of three years.

90. **Omri's Foreign Relations.** In only one direction did Omri meet with reverses. The Aramean kingdom of Damascus on his northeast frontier had been rapidly expanding and at last came into conflict with Israel. We have no knowledge whatever of the details, only the statement of Benhadad (I Kings 20[34]) that his father had taken from Ahab's father (Omri) certain cities, and compelled him to grant trading rights in the city of Samaria to the Damascenes. With an eye to future need Omri looked around for alliances and found Ethbaal, king of Tyre, a willing friend. To bind the treaty, Ethbaal's daughter, Jezebel, was married to Omri's son Ahab. The need for a compact was undoubtedly sensed by both of these kings; for not only was Damascus likely to be troublesome, but the great Assyria, under Ashurnaçirpal, was rousing from her sleep of a century, and in the year Omri died, 876, her armies had reached the Lebanon mountains. Omri, Ethbaal and all the neighboring kings made haste to lay tribute at the Assyrian's feet in order to

FIG. 78—THE HILL OF SAMARIA

Its elevation is 330 feet above the plain, and 1,542 feet above the sea, which is visible 23 miles away through a cleft in the hills. Discuss the fertility of this region. What kind of trees are these? The palaces of Omri and Ahab stood on the western (left) part of the hill (**Fig. 84**). Herod built above their ruins his temple to the divine Augustus (sec 235). His street of columns ran quite round the crest of the hill just below the temple. The wretched modern village of Sebastiyeh occupies the eastern edge of the ancient city. Find a mosque. It was once a crusaders' church, built over the supposed tomb of John the Baptist. Why would a fortress here to-day be less formidable than in Bible times?

avert a catastrophe. This is the first appearance of that power which was destined to throw an ever-deepening shadow over Israel for a hundred and fifty years, and at last to blot her out of existence.

91. Ahab's Reign (876–854). Ahab inherited his father's ability and had some of his own besides. On the whole he was the ablest monarch that Israel produced, far-seeing, energetic, politic, and for the most part just. The great religious crisis which occurred in his reign should not blind us to Ahab's essential greatness.

The order of events in his reign is not at all clear. It seems probable, however, that the religious crisis preceded the wars with Damascus, and that during practically all of his reign Ahab paid tribute to Benhadad. This did not prevent his laying the foundation of a commercial empire based on friendship rather than war. The beginning his father had made for him with the Phœnician Ethbaal stood him in good stead, and now his conciliatory policy with Judah secured his southern frontier from attack and gave the proper peace basis for expansion. That trade was one of his objects cannot be doubted in view of the treaty he made with Benhadad later. That he was successful is shown by his ability to build an ivory palace at Samaria, one in which ivory was the chief material of decoration. We know from the Moabite Stone that Moab paid tribute during his whole reign and thus supplied him with raw material to sell to the Tyrian weavers and dyers. Thus he devoted the first eighteen years of his reign to constructive enterprises.

92. **Jehoshaphat of Judah.** In Judah the able Asa was followed by his equally able son Jehoshaphat. Prosperity continued. Some of the Philistine cities brought tribute of silver, while Arabian tribes sent tribute of flocks. Eying with suspicion the growing power of Ahab, he began to strengthen his garrison towns on the northern border. But Ahab was too wise to join in a contest that was bound to exhaust both kingdoms, especially since he needed all his strength to fight greater powers to the northward. He therefore induced Jehoshaphat to make an alliance. To seal the pact, Ahab gave his daughter Athaliah in marriage to Jehoshaphat's son Jehoram. This alliance proved to be most unfortunate for Judah: it nearly cost the king his life, it paved the way for the introduction of Phœnician Baal-worship into Judah, and between the reformer Jehu and the murderous Athaliah it almost extinguished the royal family.

93. Ahab and His Northern Neighbors. War was forced
upon Ahab. The occasion seems to have been a piece of
insolence on the part of Benhadad. Not content with his

FIG. 79—DAMASCUS

You are standing on the slope of the desert Jebel Kasyun and are looking southeast over the oasis and city of Damascus toward the Arabian desert.
In the foreground are Mohammedan graves, then come the houses of a
suburb, then the gardens of fig, apricot, and walnut, and finally the clus-
tered white houses of the city in which the great barracks, the ancient
castle, and the mosque are conspicuous. Damascus, seen from this point,
has been described as "a handful of pearls in a goblet of emeralds."
Damascus is the oldest city in the world that is still inhabited. It exists
only because of the rivers Abana and Pharpar (II Kings 5¹²) that flow
from the Lebanons and create this oasis.

tribute, and coveting some of the wealth Ahab had been accumulating, he commanded Ahab to open up Samaria for
him to plunder. Ahab refused. The result was a defeat for
Ahab and a siege for Samaria. But following the advice of
an unnamed prophet, Ahab sent a force of picked men in a

sally against the camp of Benhadad while the latter was drinking himself drunk, and they put the host into disgraceful rout. Next spring Benhadad repeated his assault, this time on the plateau near Aphek in the Hauran. Again Ahab won, and forced his enemy to an unconditional surrender of his army and himself. Ahab showed astonishing leniency. When Benhadad offered to restore all the captured Israelite cities and to give a whole bazaar in Damascus to the Israelite merchants for their free use, Ahab accepted and gave Benhadad his freedom. People of narrower views than Ahab possessed criticised him most severely for freeing his bitterest foe; in fact, the bands of the prophetic dervishes who had now risen to prominence sent one of their number to the king to denounce his policy and to curse him. But the king had a reason.

That reason was Assyria. It will be recalled that in Omri's day Assyria had reached the horizon of Israel for the first time. Ahab knew that the present reigning monarch, Shalmaneser III, was planning to repeat his father's raid. He decided that a counter-thrust by the united kings of the west was the surest way of parrying Assyria. He and Benhadad therefore undertook at once to form a league. From Shalmaneser's own records we know the result. They confronted him at Karkar on the river Orontes in the year 854 B.C. with an army of 13 kings, 1,900 horsemen, 3,940 chariots, 1,000 camels, and 71,900 men. In this battle Ahab furnished 2,000 chariots and 10,000 men. Shalmaneser claims a sweeping victory, but he evidently felt that a victorious retreat was less risky than an advance ! It took him twelve years to recover his courage for a second attack.

94. **Ahab's Death.** Ahab felt that this was a good time to insist that Benhadad completely fulfil his treaty of Aphek and restore to him the city of Ramoth Gilead which up to now, on some pretense or other, he had retained. Benhadad refused and Ahab went to war immediately.

In order to make sure of victory, Ahab invited his friend

Jehoshaphat to a feast in Samaria and persuaded him to join forces with him for the siege of Ramoth. Benhadad met the two kings in force. In consequence of a prediction of

FIG. 80—DAMASCUS FROM WITHIN

You are standing on a minaret of the Great Mosque and looking west toward Mount Hermon. Notice on the right the long, roofed street, called the Greek bazaar, in the dim interior of which long caravans of camels pass silently between gaudily decked shops and hurrying buyers of divers races. The "Street called Straight" (Acts 9[10-11]) crosses this at right angles beyond the two dark cypress-trees. This was undoubtedly the street given to Ahab's merchants, for the Jews still live in it. In the foreground, the structure of many domes is a *khan*, or warehouse whither merchants and caravans resort. Important buildings, like this, are built of stone. Other houses are framed with poplar poles, cut along the banks of the Abana, the spaces filled in with mud and chopped straw, and whitewashed. All roofs are of mud and have to be rolled frequently to prevent leaking.

death made by one of his prophets, Ahab was a little nervous and sought to disguise himself as a private soldier. Jehoshaphat wore his kingly armor. It is significant of Benhadad's fear of Ahab that before the battle he instructed his soldiers to kill Ahab if they killed no one else. Seeing the royal arms of Jehoshaphat, the Arameans made for him and would have slain him but for the timely discovery that he was not the king they wanted. But a common soldier, drawing his bow at a venture, unfortunately pierced the joints of Ahab's armor just in time to snatch victory from him. The brave Ahab fought on in his chariot until night, though conscious of a mortal wound. When he died his army melted away, and Jehoshaphat returned to Jerusalem.

So perished a warrior and a statesman, but withal one who had not a full realization of the fact that a nation needs pure religion and democracy as much as it needs material prosperity.

FIGHTING THE PHŒNICIAN PROPAGANDA

95. Ahab's Evil Genius. Ahab would have gone down to history as a king no worse, at least, than many others had it not been for his wife. As the biblical writers saw, she was his evil genius. She came by her masterful qualities naturally enough through her father. He had been a priest of Baal; but finding little scope for his talents in that rôle he assassinated his king and seized the throne of Tyre for himself. Under the name of Ethbaal (about 888 B.C.) he ruled for thirty years. His daughter Jezebel was no ordinary woman, but possessed energy, intellect, zeal for religion, exalted ideas about the personal rights of kings, and in general a dominating personality. She regarded intrigue and murder as quite permissible if they brought the results she desired. In accordance with the customs of the time, Ahab allowed her to bring to his court the worship of her native god, Baal Melkart. Being busy with what he regarded as more important interests—war, foreign relations, trade, and building enterprises—he gave her free rein to develop her Baal cult as she chose. She chose to make it the prevailing religion of the land, and she nearly succeeded. She had temples built to Baal in Samaria and elsewhere, she increased the number of his priests and gave them the chief place at court, and she tried to kill off the prophets of Jehovah. Everybody who wanted to enjoy the favor of the powerful queen became a Baal-worshipper.

We must not suppose, however, that Ahab was a Baal-worshipper or that the whole country had gone over to the Tyrian god. Ahab had a band of Jehovah prophets at his court to consult on important matters, and even named his three children after the state god: Ahaziah, "Jehovah is strong"; Jehoram, "Jehovah is exalted"; and Athaliah, "Jehovah is great." Jehoshaphat of Judah, who was a strenuous worshipper of Jehovah, never would have consented to so close an alliance with Ahab if he had been a heathen. But it looks as if to keep peace in his family he had to let Jezebel do as she pleased with her Baal cult. Her success in destroying and in making converts aroused Elijah.

96. **What Baalism Meant.** It is necessary to distinguish between two kinds of Baals. We have already seen (sec. 39) that when the Hebrews entered Canaan they found the agricultural Canaanites paying homage to certain nature-gods who were thought to own the land and to give it fertility. These were the local Baals, gods who lived in the springs or in trees, or even gave rain. When the Hebrews brought their God Jehovah to live beside the Baals, in the course of years they lost the distinction between them. Jehovah himself even came to be called the Hebrew Baal, and when men named their children, they used with equal readiness compounds containing both names for God, "Jah" or "Baal." Saul and Jonathan were not Baal-worshippers, but they named their sons "Ish-baal" and "Meri-baal." Until the time of Elijah this Jehovah-Baal, a mixture of the nomad god of their Hebrew ancestors and the agricultural god of the Canaanites, excited no particular suspicion, and continued to be worshipped down to the end of the Hebrew state.

But Baal Melkart of Tyre was a different divinity. He was the god of a powerful foreign state. The friendship that had been begun in Saul's day between the Hebrews and the Phœnicians had strengthened into a political alliance under Solomon and now had become virtually a rivalry for supremacy. The great commerical empire of Tyre was the stronger partner. Jezebel's ambition apparently was to rivet the Tyrian bonds so firmly that Israel could never snake them off; to extend the domain of Melkart and rob Jehovah of his; to make the pleasant valleys of Israel merely a Tyrian back-land, so that the Israelite oil and flax and barley and wool which Tyre now had to buy could be taken in taxes. The menace was political as well as religious; Israel's independence was at stake.

There was also a moral menace. Melkart, like most Canaanite gods, was worshipped with obscene rites that were hateful to the relatively clean desert races; and with Melkart came his goddess-wife Ashtoreth, whose worship was little more than an orgy of lust. Jehovah had never tolerated an impure worship; and although some of this immorality had crept in when Jehovah became an agricultural god—the Hebrew Baal —yet the moral instinct of the Hebrews kept the practices in check. The

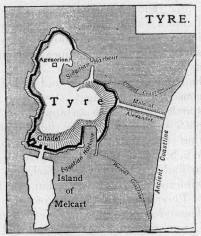

From Bury's History of Greece. Courtesy of Macmillan Company.

Fig. 81—MAP OF TYRE

On this rocky island was the palace and capital city of Hiram, friend of David and Solomon, and of Jezebel the wife of Ahab. Its two tiny harbors were the physical basis of the great commercial empire of the Phœnicians. Alexander captured the city 332 B.C. by constructing a mole to it from the mainland, large enough to carry his siege engines. Since his day the island has became a peninsula through the silting up of the mole.

burning of children as sacrifices, for example, was especially abhorrent to a Hebrew, yet this form of offering was particularly pleasing to Melkart. If Baal Melkart should become the Hebrew god, Hebrew morality was doomed. Elijah was the first to see clearly that the religions of Baal and

Jehovah were absolutely and fundamentally hostile, and could not exist side by side. Baal was sensual and Jehovah was moral. No man could serve two such masters. Israel must make a choice.

97. Jehovah's Champion. The Jehovah of the desert found a valiant and fitting champion. Elijah was a rough, impetuous, religious zealot from east of the Jordan, one who shunned society and appeared comet-like from time to time as a harbinger of disaster. He was a wild-looking man who had never cut his hair and beard, and whose only clothes consisted of a shaggy sheep pelt. No wonder Ahab was startled when such an apparition leaped out of his hiding-place by the path where the king was riding, uttered a curse that presaged a drought, and as suddenly disappeared. When the curse was fulfilled Ahab made desperate attempts to find the troubler of Israel, but Elijah took refuge in the wilderness beyond the Jordan, and later in an obscure village of Phœnicia. At the end of three years he reappeared and demanded of Ahab that he assemble all Israel on Mount Carmel in order that Jehovah and Baal might demonstrate which had the power to break the drought. According to popular story Ahab complied. Jezebel's god was represented by four hundred and fifty prophets while Jehovah had Elijah only. All day the priests of Baal called upon their god without avail; but when Elijah prayed, lightning fell from heaven and consumed the sacrifice he had prepared. The awed assembly followed the prophet's commands, took the priests of Baal down to the river Kishon and killed them all. Then Jehovah proved himself to be superior to Baal in Baal's own province of rain-bringing by sending a deluge. Ahab rode back in haste in his chariot to Jezreel, and Elijah in the strength of his religious frenzy ran the whole eighteen miles in front of the horses.

Queen Jezebel was not to be balked by even a popular revolution. To be sure, the reaction Elijah had created against her was so strong that she did not dare to kill him outright, but she sent a threat that frightened him out of the country. He fled southward to Beersheba, and there in the depression that followed upon his wild exaltation at

FIG. 82—ROCK OF BURNING, MOUNT CARMEL

This is the eastern end of the long ridge of Carmel that runs 13 miles northwest to the Mediterranean. You are looking northeast to the hills of Galilee. A glorious panorama unrolls on all sides from this point embracing the plain of Esdraelon, with Gilead, Samaria, and the plain of Sharon. Elijah could have selected no spot for his contest so conspicuous as this. (I Kings 18^{19}). The river Kishon flows directly past the base of the mountain (I Kings 18^{40}).

Carmel, he lost confidence in himself and his mission, and wished that he might die. Nor did he recover his poise until he had made a pilgrimage to Mount Horeb and met face to face the historic God of Israel on the very spot where the

Hebrews had first made their covenant with him. The picture of this meeting given in I Kings 19⁹⁻¹⁸ is impressive and dramatic. By this experience Elijah was made to realize that though his own personal accomplishment had been

958 Le Mont Carmel et la mer. — View of mount Carmel and the sea.

FIG. 83—MOUNT CARMEL AND THE SEA

This is the extreme western end of Carmel where it leaps into the sea. The building on the brow is a lighthouse. That to the left is a monastery used by Napoleon as a hospital in 1799. The original building on this site was the house of the order of Carmelites (1156 A.D.). Below the high altar in the church is a grotto said to have been used by Elijah (II Kings 4²²⁻²⁵). What is the name of the bay to the right? The city off the picture to the right? Of the famous city across the bay to the north?

small, Jehovah would still bring success to his cause by means of terrible judgments to come, and that others must be inspired to become the ministers of Jehovah's vengeance. These ministers were to be Elisha, Jehu, and Hazael; the work was still to be political as well as religious; and the instruments were to be revolution, war, and murder. A revelation of these aims shows us how imperfect as yet was even a prophet's interpretation of God's will.

98. **The People's Champion.** Jezebel had brought with her from Tyre something besides the worship of Baal Melkart; she brought the idea that kings had the divine right to do as they pleased. Her father had practised that theory of government, and though her husband had inherited from his Hebrew ancestors a very different notion of kingship, she was bound to make him over into an autocrat. Here again she was thwarted by Elijah.

A certain Naboth owned a fertile vineyard close to Ahab's palace in Jezreel. Ahab wanted to enlarge his grounds and so offered to buy the vineyard. Naboth refused to sell, for the reason that it had long been in his family. Ahab recognized the legality of Naboth's position, but was so disappointed that he went home and threw himself on his bed in a fit of sulks. Jezebel found him thus, and with a sneer at the king's cowardice, she proceeded in true Lady Macbeth style to get the vineyard for Ahab. Using the king's seal, she wrote letters to certain of the great ones commanding them to arrest Naboth on the charge of blasphemy and treason, and to have him stoned, together with his sons. This judicial murder was forthwith committed. Jezebel then turned the property over to Ahab. That was her conception of the divine right of kings. Elijah met Ahab in the flush of his guilty satisfaction, as he went down to take possession of the vineyard. There was no uncertainty in Elijah's words. He called Ahab a murderer and a thief, reminded him of his infidelity to Jehovah, and pronounced the curse that his whole family should be wiped out. Ahab was frightened. When Elijah saw that his penitence was genuine, he modified the curse so that it should not fall in Ahab's day but in that of his children.

Elijah is here the defender of the personal rights of the common man, as previously he had been the defender of the ancestral religion of Israel. We have seen how the Hebrews had become a nation by means of a revolt against oppression, and that they had ever been sensitive to tyranny; as Burke said of the American colonists: "They snuff the approach of tyranny in every tainted breeze." We have seen how they chafed under the yoke of even an elected king like David; how they had actually thrown over the son of Solomon because of the oppressions of his father. And now under the growing military power of the house of Omri, and especially under the dominance of Jezebel, the commoner was again running the risk of being crushed, might was fast destroying right, royal will was in a fair way to take the place of the consent of the governed. Elijah had the insight to see that this piece of tyranny was in reality a crime against the religious heritage and the moral sense of the nation, and he had the courage to denounce the tyrant face to face. As Moses was the first, so Elijah was the second great champion of social justice and democracy.

99. **Elijah's Limitations.** The remaining stories of Elijah, while legendary in form, are true in essence. They reveal both the strength and the weakness of this fiery prophet. Ahab's son Ahaziah was now on the throne. He had received a mortal injury through a fall and was sending messengers to Baal-zebub the god of Ekron to see if he should recover, when Elijah met the men and sent them back with the stern word: "You shall surely die!" The enraged king sent soldiers to seize the prophet, but the man of God called down fire from heaven and consumed two successive companies of them. Going, however, with the third band, he denounced the king face to face because of his faithlessness to the God of Israel.

Being warned that his own departure was at hand, with his new disciple Elisha he made a farewell circuit of the various prophetic settlements. Then the two went over Jordan together, the master having cleft the water with a stroke of his sheepskin jacket. Somewhere in the Moab wilderness he was caught up to heaven in a chariot of fire, leaving to his astonished disciple Elisha the mantle as a token that he should carry on the prophetic work.

These stories confirm the earlier ones. The fire that he so readily called down from heaven, and that caught him

FIG. 84—RUINS AT SAMARIA

Part of the citadel excavated by Harvard University in 1908
9a—Herodian retaining wall of the temple of Augustus.
8, 8—Seleucid wall enclosing street.
6—Wall of the Babylonian colonists, 720–670 B.C.
2, 8, 9—Miscellaneous Hebrew, Greek, and Roman houses.
The foundations of the palaces of Omri and Ahab are on the summit to the right, underneath the temple of Augustus.

away from earth at last, symbolizes his whole career. Elijah was uncompromising and destructive. He had two great ideals: that Jehovah is the only God for Israel and that justice is greater than the kingship. One might almost say that Elijah's work was a protest against the entire Canaanite civilization—against life in towns with their vice, against agriculture and trade with their luxuries, against the kingship with its tendency to tyranny, against every departure from the freedom and the simplicity and the narrowness of nomad life. "Back to the desert" was in reality Elijah's slogan. These ideas became the basis not of constructive work but of denunciation, vengeance, murder. He had no ability to reform but only to clear the path for reform; not to build up the good by patient teaching, but to protest against the bad; not to work with kings for the good of the nation, but to arouse the hostility of kings and so destroy any chance of inaugurating a constructive policy. Yet in preserving the old religion for Israel he proved to be what Elisha said he had been: "The chariots of Israel and the horsemen thereof." He was a bulwark against the onslaughts of Baalism and tyranny. It was his uncompromising and aggressive loyalty to Jehovah that led the Jews of a later day to place his name at the head of all the prophets, even as Moses was chief of lawgivers, and that caused Jesus and his contemporaries to see in the fiery John the Baptist a second Elijah.

XV

THE PEOPLE'S BLOODY EXECUTIONER

The half-century following the death of Ahab is marked politically by petty wars and religiously by the maturing of the great plot for the overthrow of Baalism and the house that fostered it.

ISRAEL

Ahaziah (854 B.C.), son of Ahab.   Moab revolted. See Moabite Stone.

Joram, or Jehoram (854–843), brotner of Ahaziah. Petty wars: one offensive against Moab and one defensive against Damascus.

Jehu (843–816), destroyer of the house of Ahab.

JUDAH

Jehoram, or Joram (850–843), son of Jehoshaphat. To be distinguished from his brother-in-law, Joram of Israel. Edom revolted.

Ahaziah (843), son of Jehoram. To be distinguished from Ahaziah of Israel, Ahab's son. His mother was Athaliah. He met his death while visiting his uncle Jehoram of Israel.

Athaliah, wife of Jehoram, mother of Ahaziah, murderer of her grandchildren, and usurper of the throne from 843 to 837.

100. **A Patriotic Revolution.** The most significant event of Joram's reign does not appear on the surface. It was the campaign of education carried on by the prophets of Israel under the direction of Elisha, the maturing of the seeds of revolution planted by Elijah. The propaganda was worked

by the so-called schools of the prophets, communities of religious enthusiasts that had grown up round the old sanctuaries of Gilgal, Bethel, Samaria, and the like. They were religious in the sense that they looked to Jehovah for their inspiration, which showed itself in an uncontrolled ecstasy brought on by music; but they were at bottom patriotic, for their purpose was the overthrow of the dynasty of Ahab and all that Ahab stood for in the way of tyranny and Baalism. These guilds first came to notice in the time of Samuel (sec. 49). Since his day they had grown in numbers and influence, and with the increase of foreign elements in the life of Israel they had become more intense in their opposition. By this time they were hotbeds of revolution—societies whose avowed purpose was to knife every foreign institution. Outside of the guilds also there was a strong feeling of revolt fostered by such men as Jehonadab, who so applauded Jehu's work and whose descendants were found later by Jeremiah still clinging tenaciously to their peculiar and old-fashioned customs. The aim of such people was to preserve without change the old nomadic religion of Jehovah, and they were therefore bitterly opposed to that Canaanite civilization which had been adopted by the rank and file of the northern Israelites. They stood as a permanent protest against the corruption, intemperance, and luxury which they saw were engulfing their nation and which they felt had been greatly increased under the influence of Jezebel and her Tyrian Baal. These jealous champions of Jehovah, both in and out of the circles of the guilds, now began to enlist a wider following from the mass of the nation. By the time Joram had reigned ten years, the leader of this movement felt that the hour had struck for a national house-cleaning.

101. The Character of Elisha. Elisha must be regarded as the moving spirit of all this work. His inspiration had come direct from the great champion of Israel's earlier ideals who had personally called him from the plough and given him six years of companionship. But he was a man of different temper from the explosive Elijah. In appearance he differed. Elijah was hairy, half naked, impulsive. Elisha was bald, clothed in the usual manner, and composed. When he desired the ecstatic trance he brought it on by music.

Fig. 85—THE GREAT MOSQUE OF DAMASCUS

You are standing on the minaret mentioned in Fig. 80 and are looking northeast over the oasis to the long range of Anti-lebanon. The main roof of the mosque is seen at the right; beyond this is the court surrounded by two-storied cloisters. There are three minarets, the one shown here being named "The Bride's."

The mosque was built by the Caliph Welid (705–715 A.D.) by making over the magnificent church of St. John, which the emperor Theodosius I (379–395 A.D.) had constructed out of a Roman temple to Jupiter. This temple, in turn, was the successor of the old Aramaic temple to Rimmon, the thunder god. The site therefore has a continuous history as a holy place for at least 2,800 years. To this temple used to come Naaman the Syrian on whose arm the king of Damascus leaned. (II Kings 5¹⁷ ¹⁸.)

Elijah was solitary. Elisha was a companionable man who loved society and frequented the cities and the homes of Israel. He was a man of incessant activity, appearing now here and now there, in Israel, Judah, Phœnicia, Moab, Damascus, and always with work on hand that furthered his mission. The Bible stories that so charm us testify to his

constant spirit of helpfulness and show a fundamental good-
will, which was no doubt the basis of his popularity and of
his success as a revolutionist.

Unlike his predecessor, Elisha was a friend of kings both
at home and abroad. Which kings of Israel he especially
served the sources do not always tell us, but we know that
he was active during the reigns of Joram, Jehu, Jehoahaz,
and Joash. Since he lived forty-five years after the revolution of Jehu, we may well suppose that the stories about
his helpful clairvoyancy against the invading Arameans belong to this latter period, when of course his opposition to the
government had ceased. It is interesting to compare him
with Elijah in this regard: Elijah seemed to Ahab and Ahaziah to be a personal enemy, one to be hunted and put out
of the way; Elisha, though held in awe because of his prophetic powers, was sent for, consulted, and loved alike by
rulers and people.

102. **Elisha the Revolutionist.** The object that lay next
to Elisha's heart was the overthrow of Baalism and the
iniquitous house of Ahab. We can only infer the means he
used to educate the people, aside from his patronage of the
schools of the prophets. But we know that he was a keen
observer of current affairs. When he considered the time
ripe for action, he acted. He did not limit his activity to
Israel, for one of his most unaccountable and far-reaching
acts was the instigation of Hazael to murder his master
Benhadad and seize the throne of Damascus. He must
have seen in this event some hope of furthering his great
ambition to overthrow the house of Ahab, but the sequel
proved most disastrous. It was this same Hazael who forty
years later brought Israel to the very verge of annihilation.
The crowning act of Elisha's career was the anointing of
Jehu, by which the whole mine of revolution he had been
laying was fired.

103. **The Ripening Plot.** Elisha worked and waited more
than ten years before he felt that the time was ripe. Then

the situation and the man came to hand. King Joram of Israel had been campaigning against the Arameans at Ramoth Gilead, the old bone of contention between his father Ahab and Benhadad. Joram had been wounded and had returned to Jezreel to recuperate, leaving his army and his captains in the field in charge of a young cavalry officer, Jehu. Elisha evidently knew the temper of the army, as he certainly knew Jehu, for without the backing of the one and the aggressive leadership of the other the revolution would have been a failure. He therefore sent one of his young disciples to tell Jehu that "the day" had come. The prophet found Jehu and the other captains in council. Calling Jehu into an inner room he poured oil on his head, proclaimed in Jehovah's name that he was king, and disappeared. When his fellow captains learned what the prophet had done they at once hailed Jehu as king, and the entire army accepted the revolution.

104. **Jehu the Reckless.** Jehu's action shows at once his impetuous and clean-cut executive quality; his first thought determined his first act. Leaving orders that none should depart from Ramoth Gilead to tell the news, he took a chariot and a small body-guard of cavalry and started post-haste for Jezreel, thirty miles away. The guard on Jezreel tower saw a cloud of dust whirling up from the valley road to the eastward and reported to the king. Joram ordered two successive couriers to ride down and find the nature of the embassy, but they were not allowed to return. This was suspicious. The watchman now guessed from the furious driving that it was Jehu. The king, fearing that affairs had gone wrong with the army, mounted his chariot and, together with King Ahaziah of Judah, who had come up on a visit to his convalescing uncle, rode out to learn the worst. They met Jehu in the field of Naboth, which was a fitting scene for the culmination of the revolt. In answer to Joram's question, Jehu sent an arrow through the king's heart. Ahaziah turned his chariot to flee. Jehu ordered his

men to kill him also; so they overtook him and wounded him as he entered the hill-country at Ibleam. Fearing to continue by the direct road, his servants took a long détour by way of Megiddo, where Ahaziah died. Thence the body was taken to Jerusalem by the maritime plain, avoiding the bloody territory of Israel.

Jehu now turned to the palace. The queen-mother Jezebel had heard the news and understood at once the fate that was awaiting her. She resolved to die like a queen. Putting on all her robes of state she appeared boldly at the window as Jehu drove into the palace yard. With the stinging taunt "You Zimri!" she placed him where he belonged among the assassins. Then at Jehu's command she was thrown head-long to the ground by the servants. Jehu drove his chariot over her and went in to dinner. When later he bethought himself of his duty to bury her as a queen, he found that the dogs had relieved him of that trouble.

105. **Athaliah's Brief Usurpation in Judah.** When the body of the murdered Ahaziah reached Jerusalem, the unexpected happened. Fearing that the death of her son, brother, and mother meant the overthrow of her influence in Judah, the queen-mother Athaliah at once took the initiative in an act that showed her to be a true descendant of Ethbaal and Jezebel. She seized the throne and had all of her son's children killed (as she supposed) in order that there might be none to dispute her claim. For six years (843–837) Jerusalem tamely submitted to the murderer. One little year-old son of Ahaziah, however, was rescued from assassination by his aunt, who had married the high priest Jehoiada, and was reared by her in secret until the time should be ripe in Judah to treat the house of Ahab as it was treated in Israel.

106. **The Bloody Slaughter.** But Jehu had hardly begun his task of killing in Israel. He wrote letters to the elders in Samaria challenging them to put a prince of the house of Ahab on the throne and fight it out. Seeing at a glance that with the whole regular army at Jehu's back they had no

possible chance to win, the elders sent an abject submission. Jehu then ordered them to prove their loyalty to him by sending him the heads of all the descendants of Ahab, seventy men. Next morning the baskets filled with heads were delivered in Jezreel, and Jehu used them as an argument with the men of that town that it would be unwise to meddle in his plans. Then he proceeded to murder everybody in Jezreel who had any connection by blood or friendship or official position with the house of Ahab. Starting for Samaria, Jehu fell in with a company of Judean princes on their way to visit their royal cousins of Israel. Coming by the direct road north they had not met the corpse of their brother nor heard of the revolution. Jehu had them all killed.

Next Jehu met Jehonadab the son of Rechab, the fanatical founder of that religious group whose aim was to reject all customs that the Hebrews had adopted from the Canaanites —wine-drinking, stone houses, Baal-worship, and all. Jehu recognized him as a kindred spirit, took him into his chariot, and said: "Come, see my zeal for Jehovah!" Riding thence to Samaria, Jehu repeated his orgy of blood against all Ahab's relatives and sympathizers. Then assembling all the priests and worshippers of Baal in their temple, under pretext that he himself had decided to out-Ahab Ahab in his zeal for Baal, he gave signal to his soldiers to kill every one. The temple was destroyed and the site desecrated. Thus Tyrian Baalism was destroyed root and branch, together with the house of Ahab that had introduced it. Jehu's sword had accomplished what Elijah's lightning and Elisha's plottings had not been able to effect.

107. **Estimates of Jehu's Work.** The biblical writers who held the theory that prosperity and adversity were the signs of Jehovah's pleasure and displeasure felt that Jehovah was pleased with all this killing because he allowed four descendants of Jehu to sit on the throne after him. But, seeing also that he was badly beaten in the wars with Damascus, they

Fig. 86—BLACK
OBELISK OF
SHALMANESER III

Set up by Shalmaneser
in his palace at Nim-
rud about 825 B.C.
and inscribed with an
account of his thirty-
one years of cam-
paigning in the West-
lands. It is now in
the British Museum,
London. Each of the
five divisions, carried
round on four sides,
pictures the tribute
brought by a separate
nation. The section
next to the top is de-
voted to "Jehu, son of
Omri, king of Israel."
For details, see Figs.
87 and 88. What ani-
mals do you discover
on the monument?

concluded that Jehovah was displeased
because he had not gone far enough in
his religious house-cleaning to remove
Jeroboam's calves at Bethel and Dan!
(Sec. 86.) But these simple-minded
judgments were reversed by the great
moral teachers of Israel who soon came
upon the scene. Hosea looked upon this
unatoned guilt with horror and boldly
proclaimed that God would punish not
only Jehu's dynasty but the whole
kingdom. It is quite clear to us that
Jehu's reforming zeal was worse than
unholy; it was destructive and insane
fanaticism that cared not what might become of the state provided only that a
certain type of worship might prevail.
His holy massacres were forerunners of
Saint Bartholomew's Day, the Inquisition, and the crucifixion of Armenia.
Nor did the revolution accomplish anything permanent for democracy. There
is no doubt that the people were behind it, but by killing off the strong men
of the nation in true Bolshevist style
they laid their country open to the most
crushing foreign tyranny it had yet experienced.

108. **The Revolution in Judah.** While
Jehu's revolution had been at once successful in ridding Israel of the house of
Ahab, it brought to the front in Judah
one of the worst members of that house.
Athaliah, as we have seen, ruled tyran-
nically for six years. But the leaven of
hatred of the foreigner was at work in

the popular mind. Those who encouraged and directed the hatred were not the free-lance, irresponsible prophets, as in Israel, but the priests of Jehovah, led by the high priest Jehoiada, himself, who irked to see the priests of Baal rivalling them. As in the north, the conspirator made sure of armed backing before he struck. Jehoiada took into his confidence the officers of the palace guard, showed them the young prince Joash, now seven years old, and laid before them his carefully planned stratagem. Accordingly on a Sabbath day, at an hour when the guards were changed, all the detachments of troops assembled in the temple area, the child was presented to them and crowned. The queen, hearing the shouting, hastened to the temple, but the guards turned her away from the sacred precincts and put her to death in the palace. King and people then renewed their covenant of loyalty to Jehovah and to David's dynasty, and proceeded to tear down the altar of Baal and kill his priests. Thus, though belated, the ideals which Elijah had initiated thirty-five years before were fully realized. Palestine for the Hebrews, the Hebrews for Jehovah, and kings responsive to the popular will. But at what cost!

109. **The Bitter Fruits of Jehu's Revolution.** Jehu's zeal for Jehovah now began to reap its natural harvest; he had sown to the wind and the whirlwind was approaching. In 842 B.C., on the very heels of his wholesale killing, the inveterate Shalmaneser put in an appearance beyond the Lebanons. Jehu knew full well that he had no means of resisting the conqueror; the leading men of the nation were in bloody graves; all who had had experience in state affairs were no more; Athaliah, whom his zeal had unexpectedly placed on the throne of Judah, was his sworn enemy; Hazael of Damascus was too powerful to be a safe ally, and Jehu's inability to aid him against Assyria had made him angry. There was only one thing to do and that was to buy off Shalmaneser. Though the Bible is silent on this matter,

TRIBUTE OF JEHU, SON OF OMRI   SILVER

GOLD   BOWLS OF GOLD   CHALICES OF GOLD

FIG. 87—TRIBUTE OF JEHU

Details of Fig. 86. Upper panel: Find Shalmaneser, fan-bearer, attendant,
Jehu (or his chief envoy), an emblem of the sun-god, two Assyrian officers.
Lower panel (a continuation of the upper one, to the right): Note details
of dress.

Shalmaneser has given us the full story. On his black
obelisk in the British Museum we see Jehu on all fours
before the conqueror, his forehead on the ground, waiting
for the Assyrian to put his foot on his neck in symbol of

CUPS OF GOLD   BUCKETS OF GOLD   LEAD

A ROYAL SCEPTRE   STAVES   I RECEIVED

FIG. 88—TRIBUTE OF JEHU

Details of Fig. 86 and continuing the series of Fig. 87. Identify as far as possible the objects mentioned. The English printed under each panel is a
translation of the cuneiform text above it.

overlordship, while behind follows the train of Jehu's servants bearing the price of Israel's disgrace.

Hazael of Damascus seems to have been able to turn

Assyria, though he lost everything but his capital city. For the next thirty years he made good his losses at the expense of Israel and the other nations to the south. He fulfilled all the visions of evil that Elisha had foreseen of him. First he ravaged the east-Jordan territory, not only Hebrew but Moabite. His barbarity knew no limit: cities were pillaged, men were pitilessly slain, women were ravished, and children were dragged off to cruel slavery (Amos 1³). West of Jordan he swept over the maritime plain as far south as the Philistine city of Gath. Joash of Judah knew that he was powerless to resist and therefore tried gold. He stripped his palace and the temple of all the treasures that had been accumulating since Asa's day (Sec. 92). Thus both kingdoms were brought low, and Jehu was to blame. Never was there a more significant illustration of the principle that they who take the sword shall perish by the sword. And the evil that Jehu did lived after him.

XVI

THE PROTEST AGAINST GREED AND PRIVILEGE

ISRAEL

Jehoahaz (816–800), son of Jehu.
Jehoash (800–785), son of Jehoahaz.
Jeroboam II (785–745), son of Jehoash.

JUDAH

Joash (837–798), son of Ahaziah.
Amaziah (798–790), son of Joash.
Uzziah or *Azariah* (790–738), son of Amaziah.
(Jotham regent, 749–738).

In the period covered by this chapter, from the death of Jehu in 816 to the death of Uzziah in 738, the two kingdoms were on the downward road, each suffering from the excesses and weaknesses of the past; then, with the release from foreign oppression, came a rebound to great apparent prosperity. What an individual or a people does in its moments of freedom is highly significant of character. In this period the material ideals that had all along been growing in the Hebrew civilization at last had an opportunity to come to fruitage. They were wrong ideals and they brought forth death.

110. **The Power of the Priests in Judah.** One incident in the reign of Joash shows a new tendency in religion. When he undertook to repair the temple he discovered that the priests were profiting by the income of the sanctuary but were quite unwilling to share in the expense of maintaining it. Joash therefore made definite regulations by which certain classes of income should go by right to the priests and certain others to the maintenance fund administered by lay-

181

men. The incident shows that the temple at Jerusalem was no longer merely a royal shrine but was becoming a popular place of worship, and that the priests had become a powerful body with vested interests in that worship. Judah, even at this early date, was becoming churchly and priest-ridden as Israel never became. The power of the priest is no doubt shown by the fact that when Joash in the latter part of his reign somewhat relaxed his zeal for Jehovah-worship and put to death a son of the high priest who criticised him, he was promptly assassinated.

111. **The Reigns of Jehoahaz and Jehoash.** Hazael the Aramean continued to crush Israel during the reigns of Jehu's son and grandson. The only territory that he left to Jehoahaz was a few square miles around Samaria; while he limited the entire military establishment of Israel to 50 horsemen, 10 chariots, and 10,000 infantry.

In the first part of the reign of Jehu's grandson, Jehoash, the land reached the depths of humiliation. Judah also was laid under tribute. But with the death of Hazael a change came. First, the hitherto obscure kingdom of Hazrak in northern Syria became strong and, while Assyria was busy elsewhere, gave Damascus so much trouble that Damascus let Jehoash alone. Then Assyria, under Adad-nirari III, swept down in 797 and caught in her drag-net of tribute Edom, Philistia, Damascus, Tyre, Sidon, Israel, and probably Judah. Damascus, which had proved so stubborn in the past, was the special object of the expedition. It was forced to pay an enormous indemnity which permanently crippled it. As soon as the Assyrian armies had withdrawn, Jehoash proceeded to pay off old scores with Damascus; he won three victories and retook several cities his father had lost. Meantime Judah, too, felt the release from Aramean pressure and began to expand. Edom was first reduced, in order no doubt to gain control of the trade routes to the south and to make Elath a Judean port. This touch of success made Amaziah, who had succeeded his father Joash, so conceited that he dared Jeho-

FIG. 89—EGYPTIAN CHAIR

Found by Mr. Theodore Davis in the tomb of Iouîya and Touîyou, the parents of Queen Ti, wife of Amenhotep III (c. 1400 B.C.). It is made of stained wood, with lion feet. The two sculptured heads were gilded. On the chair-back is shown a Nile goddess receiving a necklace from the princess who owned the chair; this done in relief and gilded. On the arms, four women bring gold and offerings and gods dance. The seat is of woven leather. Other pieces of furniture of this period show beautiful inlay of semi-precious stones.

Against the introduction of luxuries like these the prophet Amos preached (Sec. 114, and Amos 6 1-6).

ash of Israel to hold him any longer in vassalage. Jehoash was now in position to accept the challenge of Amaziah. Taking his army into Judean territory, Jehoash defeated and captured Amaziah, tore down a large section of the north wall of Jerusalem, looted the palace and temple, and took hostages to insure future good conduct. Judah remained henceforth a vassal of Israel until Israel was destroyed.   Israel was now well on the up grade.   Damascus had been crushed, Assyria was busy with wars to the north, especially with Armenia, and Jehoash could leave to his son a free kingdom and great hopes.

112. **The Strong Policy of Uzziah of Judah.**   The folly of Amaziah in attacking Israel caused a popular insurrection. The king tried to flee but was caught and assassinated.   The insurrectionists then put on the throne his sixteen-year-old son, Uzziah or Azariah.   Between the priests and the people kings in Judah were having many trials.

The youthful king proved to be an exceptionally able ruler.   Without attempting to throw off the overlordship of Israel, he set himself to strengthen his kingdom internally and to extend his power abroad.   He fortified Elath on the Red Sea.   Philistia he conquered and colonized.   The trade routes that crossed his domain he made secure with garrisons and watch-towers.   He strongly fortified Jerusalem, and made use of artillery for throwing stones—the first Hebrew to do so.   Jerusalem proceeded to grow by leaps and bounds. Realizing that prosperity comes primarily from the soil, he took an active hand in agriculture and cattle-raising.   Wealth increased.   In Judah it seemed as if permanent prosperity had at last arrived.

113. **Israel's Indian Summer.**   It is singular that the longest and most brilliant reign of Israel should receive hardly any mention in the biblical narratives.   We know only that Jeroboam II, the son of Jehoash, extended his political sway over practically all of David's kingdom from Hamath on the north to the Dead Sea on the south; and counting Judah as vassal, the limit of his power southward was Egypt.   Naturally, the one condition that made this burst of power possible was the inactivity of Assyria.   By a strange coincidence both Israel and Judah were ruled by brilliant and able kings, whose long reigns were contemporaneous.   For a whole generation, therefore, the Hebrews enjoyed what has been called an Indian summer of prosperity.

Fig. 90—DIADEMS OF A TWELFTH DYNASTY PRINCESS,
FOUND IN HER TOMB AT DASHUR. (Cairo Museum.)

These delicate pieces of jewelry illustrate the foreign luxuries against the introduction of which the Hebrew prophets cried out. The upper crown
consists of a delicate framework of gold threads springing from four
Maltese crosses of gold, carnelian and blue faience. Tiny flowerets of
red, blue, and gold are scattered among the threads. The lower crown
is of gold, lapis-lazuli, carnelian, red jasper, and green felspar, and is made
in an alternating pattern of rosettes and lyres.

114. A Glance Beneath the Surface. While the his-torians are silent regarding internal conditions in both Judah and Israel, a flood of evidence pours in from the writings of the prophets Amos and Hosea. From them we learn that a great social transformation had been going on. When the tide of the Aramean wars turned back, out of the Israelite conquests came abundant spoils to enrich the kings and their favorites. Peace enabled the nobles and richer classes in Israel to develop their country's naturally great resources, and in Judah the same thing happened, only on a smaller scale. Commerce also brought to them rapidly increasing wealth, for across the broad valleys of northern Israel ran the main trade routes which bore the rich products of Egypt and Babylonia, of Phœnicia and Arabia; and Judah controlled all exits to the south. Thus during the first half of the eighth pre-Christian century the Hebrews ceased to be simply a nation of shepherds and farmers. Cities took the place of villages, and the fruits of commerce completed the sudden transformation. The powerful nobles and richer classes transferred their homes to the capital or to the larger cities. Meantime, as a result of the vicissitudes of war, the middle class had been either killed off or largely reduced to serfdom. Obliged to borrow of the rich nobles at exorbitant rates of interest, they had not only lost their mortgaged lands but their freedom. Heavy taxation and unjust decisions in the law courts, over which the rich and ruling classes presided, had completed their enslavement. The love of luxury and display had rendered the rich insensible to the sufferings of the poor, who were the victims of their greed and legalized injustice. To all external appearances both kingdoms were prosperous and powerful; but the majority of their citizens were sad and sodden, crushed by the small ruling class that wrongfully exploited them. Their social problems were those of the modern city and of a developed commercial civilization: special class privilege, misuse of authority, unjust distribution of the

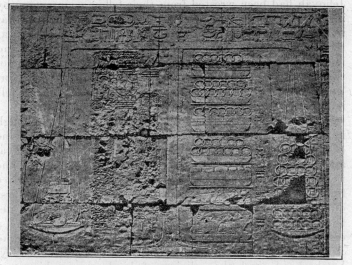

Fig. 91—WEIGHING GOLD

Section of the beautifully carved "Expedition to Punt" in the colonnade of Queen Hatasu's temple at Thebes. Note the great scales, with the indicator hanging from the beam near the pivot. In the right pan, are piled the rings of gold to be weighed, while near by are rings and other objects together with groups of weights in the form of oxen. The inscription tells us that "silver, lazuli, malachite, and every splendid costly stone" was also weighed. In the left pan are the ox-weights. Many weights of this kind have been found in Egypt, oxen and ducks having been the medium of exchange before weights were invented. The ox was regarded as a unit of value everywhere in the East; so that in Rome the word for a head of cattle, *pecus*, became *pecunia*, money. The figure of the weigher has been chiselled out because of the spite of Queen Hatasu's successor, Thothmes III.

burden of taxation, and the wicked exploitation of the masses.

To make matters worse, the old popular Semitic conception of religion still prevailed. As long as the rulers brought rich sacrifices to the sanctuaries and faithfully met the demands of the ritual, they felt sure of Jehovah's favor and protection. Though the very offerings they brought to

Jehovah had been wrested from their fellow countrymen by injustice and oppression, they felt confident that all was well, since Jehovah was prospering them. Even at the great religious festivals there were gluttony, drunkenness, and immorality; and yet they believed that by the splendor of their ritual they were purchasing Jehovah's continued favor. The poor, who had no such offerings to bring, must have felt indeed that Heaven was against them.

115. **Preachers of Social Righteousness.** Amos, though not a priest or a prophet but only a herdsman, felt a divine call to go to Bethel at the time of a great national festival and cry out against all this wickedness. He denounced the rich and ruling classes, the grafters who used public office for private gain. He fearlessly proclaimed that the first duty of rulers is to protect the rights of the poor and defenseless; that riches gained by exploiting the poor are a disgrace and a menace; and that God cannot be bribed to wink at evil, even by the richest sacrifices. Democracy, brotherhood, and the religion of kindness are his great teachings. These are all the greater because in Amos they are clearly heard for the first time in Hebrew, if not in world history.

It seems as if the genius of the Hebrew people, balked in its attempt to realize a true democracy in the forms of government, had now burst out in the moral realm. All its pent-up passion for justice and brotherhood, finding at last a mouthpiece in Amos, leaped at once to revolutionary expression and demanded in the name of Jehovah, the God of righteousness, a full recognition of its claims. There is no more dramatic passage in literature than the words of Jehovah as uttered by Amos (5^{21-24}):

"I hate, I despise your feasts, and I will take no delight in your solemn assemblies. Even though you offer me your burnt-offerings and cereal-offerings, I will not accept them; neither will I regard the peace-offerings of your fat beasts. Take away from me the noise of your songs; for I will not

hear the melody of your viols. But let justice roll down as
waters, and righteousness as a mighty stream.''

Besides marking the high-tide of literary art, this passage
proclaims the revolutionary truth that God is on the side

Fig. 92—BETHEL

One of the most ancient Amorite shrines, taken over by the Hebrews (Gen. 29¹⁹)
and used especially by Jeroboam I and his successors (I Kings 12²⁸⁻³³).
Why should such a site be chosen for a sanctuary? Notice the terraced
hills, suggesting to the sleeping Jacob the staircase to heaven (Gen. 28¹¹⁻²²).
What kinds of trees?   The tower is the guest-room in the house of the
sheik, or head-man of Bethel.   Bethel stands 2,890 feet above the sea.

of the downtrodden and the poor, and that any religion
which does not concern itself with the welfare of one's fellows is no religion at all. This is a great discovery, one that
outranks any discovery or invention in the realm of science
in its possible effect upon human civilization. In thirty
centuries we have not yet lived up to it; it still stands as a
protest against most of our civic and social institutions, and
as a great ideal yet to be attained.

This same period produced a second prophet who ranks even above Amos in insight and moral power. Hosea, a native of northern Israel and a thorough patriot, boldly proclaimed that the social life of the nation was corrupt and that Jehovah had no choice but to punish. His denunciation is specific and terrible (Hos. 4$^{1-3}$):

> "Hear the word of Jehovah, O Israelites,
>   For he has a charge against the inhabitants of the
>   land;
>   For there is no fidelity nor true love,
>   Nor knowledge of God in the land,
>   But perjury, lying, and murder,
>   Stealing, adultery, and deeds of violence,
>   And acts of bloodshed follow in quick succession.
>   Therefore the land mourns,
>   And all its inhabitants languish."

But Hosea's positive teaching shows the greatness of his genius. He taught that the only corrective for such crimes is love—not a sentiment or an emotion but a principle of action; love that shows itself in righteousness, justice, kindness, fidelity. Finding in his own heart the presence of such love even toward his unfaithful wife, he reached the bold conclusion that God must love even while he punishes faithless Israel. God's justice and his love thus become the great arguments why men should love and be just. Hosea anticipated by eight centuries the teaching of Jesus that love to God and love to man are essential to the formation of a perfect society. His teaching is only another expression of the democratic spirit that all along had underlain Hebrew society; for we know now what havoc the principle of love always works with distinctions of caste, with aristocracies, oligarchies, plutocracies, and other manifestations of selfish individualism. Love is as dangerous to vested privilege as T N T powder.

It is hardly too much to say that all the sufferings the Hebrew nation endured from outward oppression and inward sin were not too great a price to pay for these sublime ideals that have permanently enriched mankind.

XVII

THE COLLAPSE OF THE NORTHERN STATE

ISRAEL

Zechariah (745), son of Jeroboam. Reigned but six months.
  Assassinated by Shallum.
Shallum (745). Reigned but one month. Assassinated by
  Menahem.
Menahem (745–736). Paid tribute to Assyria.
Pekahiah (736–735), son of Menahem.
Pekah (735–732). Assassinated Pekahiah; himself deposed and
  killed.
Hoshea (732–722).

JUDAH

Jotham (749–735), son of Uzziah. (Regent for his father to
  738.)
Ahaz (735–720), son of Jotham.

116. **The Reign of Anarchy.** In their arraignment of
Israel Amos and Hosea beheld an ominous background: they
saw Assyria with sword in hand waiting for Jehovah's
command to punish faithless Israel. Never was there
greater opportunity for a strong monarch to plunder a
rich and helpless country, for at the death of Jeroboam II
anarchy broke loose. In fourteen years there were six
kings in Israel, four of whom were assassinated and one
captured in battle, while only one was succeeded by a son.

117. **Menahem's Rule.** In the year Menahem seized the
throne (745) there came to the throne of Assyria the most
able conqueror and organizer that empire had yet produced, Tiglath-pileser IV. The conditions in Israel were

too tempting to be resisted. In 738 he therefore invaded Palestine. Menahem was evidently having difficulty in managing chaotic Israel. Rather than offer resistance, he hastened to pay Tiglath-pileser an enormous tribute, in return for which Tiglath helped him retain his throne against his enemies. The Assyrian must have smiled as he pocketed his "easy money"—about $2,000,000 in metal, in purchasing power equal to $30,000,000 to-day. And Menahem smiled sardonically as he turned upon his rich and re- bellious fellow countrymen and recouped himself at their expense! He took 50 shekels from every landed proprietor —and there were 60,000 of them. The Assyrian bribe en- abled Menahem to keep his crown for ten years and hand it on to his son, Pekahiah.

But the party in Israel that opposed the paying of tribute to Assyria decided to get rid of Pekahiah, the Assyrian vassal-king, and so assassinated him. Pekah, a military man, did the bloody work for them and was rewarded with the crown.

118. **The Puppet Kings of Judah.** Jotham, who had been regent in Judah for eleven years during his father's illness, now became sole ruler. He appears to have been an able and pious king. According to a late tradition he strengthened Jerusalem, built fortresses in various parts of the kingdom, subdued Ammon which had revolted on the death of his father, and for three years collected therefrom a handsome annual tribute, $200,000 in silver (equal to $3,000,000 to- day), 110,000 bushels of wheat and the same of barley.

For some unaccountable reason his son Ahaz broke with the religion of his fathers and became an out-and-out idol- ater. He introduced into Judah the heathen rite of child- sacrifice. He was a degenerate who was unable to rule or to take advice. The surrounding nations proceeded to take advantage of him. Edom attacked him on the south, the Philistines recaptured all their cities which Amaziah had taken, and Israel under Pekah and Damascus under Rezin

Fig. 93—SARGON AND HIS VIZIER

From the palace at Khorsabad; now in the
    Louvre. King's costume: Crown of
    cloth embroidered and ornamented
    with rosettes, and culminating in a
    peak. Underdress reaching from neck
    to ankles, edged with a fringe of tas-
    sels and a fourfold border of pearls;
    the skirt is richly patterned. Mantle
    with broad fringe embroidered with
    rosettes. Sandals that protect the
    heels only. Toe-rings. Earrings.
    Large rosette-bracelets on the wrists
    and spiral bracelets above the elbow.
    Sword with heavily ornamented han-
    dle and scabbard. Note the heavy
    beard and hair, with curls natural
    or artificial.

Vizier's costume: A band about the hair,
    undergarment like the king's but
    plainer, overgarment that hangs from
    one shoulder leaving the right arm free,
    jewels and hair like the king.

resorted to violent means
to induce him to join a
new league against As-
syria.

Ahaz, who was secretly
planning to throw him-
self into the hands of Assyria, refused their de-
mands, and these two
firebrands from the north
invaded his country.
The result was little less
than a catastrophe for
Judah. Rezin and Pekah,
according to the late tradition in II Chronicles,
killed or enslaved great
numbers and captured
Elath, the Red Sea port.
Ahaz was thoroughly
frightened and sent a
distress call to Tiglath-
pileser, promising trib-
ute and vassalage if he
would pull Pekah and
Rezin off his back. The
prophet Isaiah suspected
that something of this
kind would happen, met
the king as he was in-
specting the water-sup-
ply of Jerusalem, and
promised him that Je-
hovah would save him if
he would only rely on him
and not needlessly sacri-

fice his country's independence. But Ahaz had not much
respect for Jehovah; besides, the messengers had already
gone to the Assyrian king and much silver and gold had
gone with them.

Tiglath-pileser was doubtless pleased to get pay for what

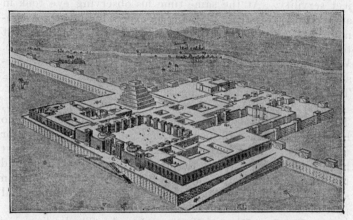

FIG. 94—SARGON'S PALACE, RESTORED

Erected at Khorsabad, several miles above Nineveh, in 706 B.C. Probably
    this was the most magnificent palace ever built, covering as it did more
    than twenty-five acres. The rooms were of immense size, the walls
    wainscoted with sculptured alabaster slabs, the entrances guarded by
    colossi. It was discovered by M. Botta, French consul to Mosul, in 1842,
    and excavated by the French government.
The wall extending from the palace forms one side of the great royal park a
    mile square. Within the enclosure were lakes and pleasure-houses. The
    terraced pyramid is a temple for sun-worship. Note the platform, 46 feet
    high, on which the palace rests; also the inclined planes by which chariots
    could mount. Find the main entrance, the Court of Honor, the Halls
    of Audience, the private apartments.

he had intended to do at his own expense. He came down
post-haste and with an overwhelming force (734–733). Israel
was the first to suffer. He took all the east-Jordan territory
and all Galilee as far as the southern border of Esdraelon, and
carried away into slavery tens of thousands of the inhabitants.
Turning to Damascus, he crushed and absorbed that realm.

From this time on the Aramean kingdom disappears and Damascus is a provincial Assyrian city.

After the defeat of Pekah and Rezin, Ahaz hurried to Damascus, where Tiglath-pileser had made a temporary headquarters, and proceeded to fawn on the conqueror with abject servility. At the same time his observing eye took in an altar of new pattern. Being an expert in matters of ceremonial worship, he had drawings made of it, which he sent to Jerusalem with instructions to duplicate it for the temple. When he returned home he dedicated the new altar personally, and cast Jehovah entirely out of his own shrine. The gods of Assyria were good enough for him!

Nevertheless, the Assyrian favor was an expensive luxury. To pay the annual tribute Ahaz was at last forced even to break up the brass furnishings that Solomon had made for the temple. True patriots like Micah and Isaiah must have shed bitter tears as they saw Jehovah dethroned and their king a bankrupt vassal. But they had to weep in secret. Ahaz had no patience with Jehovah-worshippers and patriots.

119. **The Last King of Northern Israel.** The leading men of Israel, seeing now that they had made a mistake, murdered their king Pekah who had gotten them into this trouble. Hoshea was their tool. He promised Tiglath-pileser that he would be loyal, and the Assyrian let him rule over the shrunken kingdom. This favor cost him $300,000 in gold and $2,000,000 in silver—equal to $35,000,000 today!

Hoshea's loyalty, however, had a time limit. When Tiglath-pileser died Hoshea promptly intrigued with Egypt, which in the degenerate days from Shishak to the present crisis had pretty effectively kept out of world politics. Backed by Egypt's promises, Hoshea refused tribute to Assyria; as a matter of fact, he had no money to pay. The new king, Shalmaneser IV, forthwith invaded Israel, defeated the rebel's little army, and took Hoshea prisoner. Marching thence to Samaria he besieged it, determining to put an end forever to all trouble from this quarter. Thanks to Omri's skilful choice of its site, the city held out for three years. Shalmaneser died before it

Fig. 95—COLOSSUS FROM SARGON'S PALACE

These composite creatures, usually of gigantic size, guarded the entrances of the palace. They represent supernatural beings and were supposed to keep away evil spirits. The elements of which they are composed probably stand for qualities or functions. For what would the human head stand? the wings? the lion's body? How many legs has the creature, and why?

fell, and his son Sargon II completed the conquest (722 B.C.). The conqueror deported over 27,000 of its inhabitants, all of the wealthy or aristocratic class and any who he felt might make trouble. These he scattered in northern Mesopotamia and Media, in accordance with the Assyrian policy of conquest. The partly depopulated land of Israel was refilled with colonists from abroad, especially from

northern Syria and Babylonia. Thus the national spirit
was completely broken and the area of the northern kingdom was absorbed into the Assyrian empire. The kingdom
of Israel became the Ten Lost Tribes, not that they were

Fɪɢ. 96—HEBREW CAPTIVES
Brought in under guard to do homage to the conqueror.

lost in the sense of being misplaced and forgotten; they
merged into the life of other races and lost their identity.
They dissolved like salt in water.

120. **The Significance of Israel's Fall.** The fall of Israel
made a profound impression upon the Hebrews who survived. Naturally they sought for a cause, and the religious
ones, who held the idea that Jehovah was primarily a re-
warder of goodness and a punisher of evil, saw in the catastrophe a crowning proof that Israel had been bad. According to the priestly writers of the biblical narratives, that
badness consisted in infidelity to Jehovah. "Idolatry,"
said they, "brings catastrophe; catastrophe comes only as
a result of idolatry." But according to the prophets,
Israel's real guilt was the injustice and oppression wrought
by the rich on the poor and other kindred social sins. Both
sets of interpreters were partly right and partly wrong.
The punishment did not come wholly in consequence of

badness nor was it a piece of vengeance on Jehovah's part. We believe to-day that God works through the channels of law, whether physical, economic, social, or moral; and as we look at the fate of Belgium and France, for example, in the Great War, we are quite sure that all catastrophes are not the consequence of the victim's sins. Two different forces were at work here in two different realms of life, accomplishing two different results. Israel fell because her wealth excited the greed of Assyria, because she lay in the path of Assyria's conquering ambition; these were economic and political reasons that had no relation to Israel's deserts. But Israel fell in a deeper and more significant way—had, indeed, been falling for years before the final crash. Greed, materialism, and lust had destroyed national and individual character and substituted debasing Canaanite forms of worship for the ethical worship of Jehovah; for that reason her fall meant extinction. When the great catastrophe came, Israel had nothing worth saving— not an ideal nor a God. Assyria destroyed her political identity, but sin had already destroyed her soul.

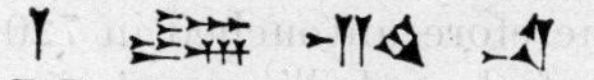

D.P. Shar - gi - na

Sargon.

Fig. 97

D.P. means Determinative Prefix, showing that a name is to follow.
The name forms a sentence, "God has established the king."
Sargon reigned over Assyria, 722–705 B.C. He conquered Israel (722 B.C.), defeated So of Egypt in league with the Philistines (720 B.C.), conquered Ashdod in Philistia (711 B.C.; Isaiah 20[1]) and Merodach-baladan who intrigued with Hezekiah (II Kings 20[12-13]). His son Sennacherib succeeded him.

XVIII

JUDAH'S NARROW ESCAPE

Hezekiah (720–692), son of Ahaz.

121. **The Shadow of Assyria.** The great calamity that had wiped out the kingdom of Israel affected all the kingdoms of the west. Judah seemed to herself to be a brand plucked from the burning. The youthful king, Hezekiah, who now came to the throne knew himself to be no match for the great Assyrian, and he wisely attempted nothing. His only hope lay in absolute submission to the dread overlord whose aid his father Ahaz had invoked and who was now claiming all the world in vassalage and nearly making good his claim. For nine years Hezekiah paid tribute faithfully. He was therefore untouched in 720 when Sargon put down the revolt of the rebellious princes of the West-land, and at Raphia on the Egyptian border punished Egypt for meddling with politics in general and Hoshea in particular.

What Hezekiah did in these nine years is partly a matter of conjecture. Being by nature religious, and perhaps having been tutored by the prophet Isaiah, he may well have begun some of those reforms that toward the close of his reign he carried out with great thoroughness. It was doubtless in this period also that he caused the tunnel to be dug from the spring Gihon, east of the City of David, through the hill to a reservoir called Siloam on the west side of David's city but within the walls of Jerusalem. (See Fig. 98.) With an eye to future needs he also strengthened the national defense, repaired the walls and fortifications of

Jerusalem, fitted up arsenals, built cities, and encouraged trade and agriculture through the erection of shelters for sheep and cattle and of storehouses for produce. He followed in all these things the example of his great-grandfather Uzziah. The significant events of his reign, however, grew out of his relations with Assyria and the prophet Isaiah.

122. Hezekiah a Near-Rebel. Trouble began about the year 711, when Egypt succeeded at last in stirring up the Philistine cities to a revolt. Shabaka, an Ethiopian king, had managed to get possession of Egypt, and now his ambition expanded to take in western Asia, or at least to form a series of independent buffer states between himself and Assyria. The time seemed favorable. A certain Merodach-baladan, who had risen to power in a small Chaldean state at the head of the Persian

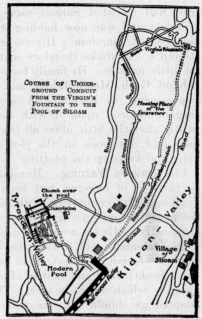

COURSE OF UNDERGROUND CONDUIT FROM THE VIRGIN'S FOUNTAIN TO THE POOL OF SILOAM

FIG. 98—THE SILOAM TUNNEL

Be careful not to confuse the roads, which run on the surface of the ground, with the tunnel that is cut beneath them. The workmen began cutting at both ends and met in the middle. Notice the uncertainty of the engineers as the two parties of excavators neared each other.

This is probably the conduit constructed by Hezekiah in anticipation of Sennacherib's invasion (II Kings 20^{20}; II Chron. 32$^{1-4}$). It is 1,700 feet long and is six feet high. It brought the waters of Gihon (the Virgin's fountain), which lay outside the city walls, to a pool within the walls, so that the inhabitants could, in case of siege, fill their water-jars without exposing themselves.

The church shown above just north of the pool was built about 450 A.D. by the empress Eudocia.

Gulf, had defeated Sargon some years before, had seized Babylon, and was now holding it against all comers as an independent kingdom. His success argued well for other attempts. Shabaka therefore sent out his agents to stir up the little nations. He finally formed a league in which were Ashdod, Gath, Moab, Edom, and Judah. Fortunately the league came to nothing. Ashdod did indeed revolt, but Sargon pounced upon it with such a large army and so swiftly that the little allies all beat to cover and pretended they had not been in the plot at all. Egypt could only fume and keep up the plotting.

123. **Isaiah's Warning.** Hezekiah had been nearly caught by this net of intrigue, but his escape did not teach him wisdom. The coquetting with Egypt kept on. Now for the first time in ten years the prophet Isaiah suddenly became active. He set himself steadfastly to hold his king true to his vassalage and thwart the intrigues of the Egyptian envoys. Isaiah was statesman enough to see that Egypt was a broken reed and that in all of this plotting Egypt had a purely selfish object in view. The method of agitation he adopted we should call sensational. He took off his shoes and his prophetic mantle of sackcloth, and in this condition went about the streets of Jerusalem. This spectacular campaign of education he continued for three years, in summer's heat and winter's cold, while he took pains to publish the meaning of it everywhere: "Thus saith Jehovah, As my servant Isaiah has walked unfrocked and barefoot three years for a sign and a portent against Egypt and Ethiopia, so shall the king of Assyria lead away the captives of Egypt and the exiles of Ethiopia, young and old, stripped and barefoot." This was nothing less than an appeal to the people over the heads of the king and his court, over Shebna the grand vizier and his pro-Egyptian party. It was an attempt to form a public sentiment so strong that the men in power must yield to it, a sentiment against putting any trust in the flattering promises of a big, blustering

country, once powerful but now utterly incapable of defending itself against Assyria, to say nothing of delivering Judah.

This protest of Isaiah's was measurably successful. While it did not wholly stop the intriguing, it kept Hezekiah from taking any positive step not only in the Philistine re-

FIG. 99—THE SILOAM INSCRIPTION

Carved by Hezekiah's workmen near the Siloam end of the tunnel (see Fig. 98). It is the oldest Israelitish inscription of any length that has come down to us. It was discovered in 1880 by the bright eyes of an English boy, a missionary's son, and reported to the authorities. The text was afterward cut out by a Greek villain who hoped to profit by it; but he was punished. It is now preserved in the museum at Constantinople.

volt of 711 but also in the more favorable opportunity of 710. In that year Sargon had the fight of his life with Merodach-baladan, a fight that was nothing less than a contest for the sovereignty of the world between Assyria and Babylon. Assyria won, and Merodach-baladan disappeared for a time. In this crisis Judah remained true to her overlord. This much, at least, Isaiah had accomplished.

124. **Hezekiah's Sickness and World Politics.** The dreaded Sargon was murdered in 705 by his son and successor Sennacherib. Immediately his empire burst asunder and Sennacherib had to prove his fitness to rule by bringing the separate pieces again under his sway. It took him four years, but he did it. He first gave attention to Babylon, a province so great that only the turn of a hand might de-

termine whether it or Assyria should rule the world. Merodach-baladan was again attempting to establish himself
there. Until Sennacherib had settled with him he could
not attend to western Asia. In the meantime throughout
the West-land there was a mighty "trembling in the tents

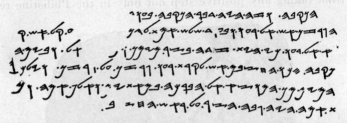

FIG. 100—TEXT OF THE SILOAM INSCRIPTION (FIG. 99)

"The tunnel [is completed]. And this is the story of the boring through:
While yet they plied the pick, each toward his fellow, and while yet there
were three cubits to be bored through, there was heard the voice of one
calling to another, for there was a crevice in the rock on the right hand.
And on the day of the boring through, the stone-cutters struck, each to
meet his fellow, pick upon pick; and the waters flowed from the source to
the pool for a thousand and two hundred cubits, and a hundred cubits
was the height of the rock above the heads of the stone-cutters."

of Kedar," an excitement of intrigue, embassies hurrying
from state to state, and a common rising against the common oppressor. From far-off Ethiopia came the tall, shin-
ing ones to tempt Hezekiah into their league in which the
Ethiopian king hoped to be chief. From Egypt also and
Edom and Philistia they came, all making Jerusalem their
rendezvous because it was the one impregnable fortress in
all the rebel lands. Here from 705, when Sargon died, until
701, when Sennacherib was at last free to deal with them,
was the true centre of gravity of the western revolt. Hezekiah was the king-pin—or thought he was—but Isaiah was
the true bulwark of his country's safety. Jerusalem was
for the prophet as a watch-tower from which he could survey all the nations and truly judge of the great political and
moral forces that were at work beneath the surface of events.

Isaiah believed that Sennacherib was destined to be the master of the world. To the mind of the prophet all of these plottings and engineerings and revolts were the sheerest folly; and he did not hesitate to denounce the pro-Egyptian party and all of its works. This was the most strenuous period of Isaiah's life.

In the midst of this agitation Hezekiah fell seriously sick with an abscess. Feeling that he was going to die, he sent for Isaiah. The prophet saw the desperate nature of the case and told the king that he must die. This announcement threw Hezekiah into an agony of prayer. He knew the perilous times into which he had fallen, and he knew that there was no son to succeed him on· the throne. He begged Jehovah to spare him. Even while he prayed, word came to Isaiah to return and announce to Hezekiah that his prayer had been heard, and that Jehovah would also save the city from the hand of Sennacherib. The prophet then ordered a fig poultice laid on the abscess and the cure began.

This sickness and recovery were the excuse for Merodach-baladan's sending to Hezekiah an embassy of sympathy. In reality the mission was political. Merodach was for the moment succeeding in his attempt to regain the throne of Babylon, and for the space of nine months held Sennacherib at bay. But he needed all the help he could get, and he thought he might be able to distract Sennacherib's attention if he could push the revolt in Palestine. The scheme did not work. Sennacherib conquered Babylon in 704, and Merodach-baladan dropped out of sight. But the embassy gave Isaiah a text for a political warning to Hezekiah.

"Who were these men?" asked the prophet, "and what have they seen?"

Hezekiah confessed that they were from Babylon, and that he had showed them all his treasures and his arsenal.

"Hear the word of Jehovah," said the aged and angry prophet; "Behold, the days are coming that all that is in

this house and that which your fathers have laid up in
store unto this day shall be carried to Babylon."

Isaiah saw that Hezekiah had done two rash things; he had
fully committed himself to the revolt against Assyria, and
by showing his resources he had excited the greed of Babylon. The first brought swift vengeance. The latter came
to naught; for though a century later Babylon took Jerusalem, the king was not Merodach-baladan nor was the
event connected with Hezekiah's foolish pride. Isaiah now
worked unsparingly to undo the folly of the war party.
He knew full well that Hezekiah was only pulling chest-
nuts out of the fire for Egypt and Babylon, and that disaster stared his country in the face. He had a religious basis
also for his condemnation, for to put trust in princes meant
to fail to put trust in Jehovah. Isaiah knew only too well
that the official religion in Judah was a farce; even the priests
at the altar were drunk while they ministered and their
power of vision was hopelessly dulled. Not until they were
crushed by a great calamity could they appreciate the
plain truth the prophet had spoken and be ready to put
their faith in the Holy One of Israel.

125. **On the Verge of Destruction.**   The day of vengeance
was now at hand. Sennacherib had conquered Babylon, had
suppressed the rebels farther east in Elam, and now he fell
like a thunderbolt upon the league that Egypt had gotten together. He began with the Phœnician cities. The king of
Sidon ran away; Tyre was shut up on her island. Then he
struck Philistia and one by one took her cities. Edom and
Moab became frightened and sent their submission. Ekron
was next besieged—for all of the towns on the plain had to
be reduced before an army could safely venture into the
mountains of Judah. While Sennacherib was busy with
Ekron, the very thing happened which Hezekiah and all
the league had been trusting would happen—Egypt came
up with an army. Sennacherib relaxed his grip on Ekron
for the moment and turned upon the new foe. The forces

FIG. 101—CYLINDER OF SENNACHERIB

Six-sided baked clay cylinder describing eight campaigns of Sennacherib from about 705 to 691 B.C. It records the defeat of Merodach-baladan and the sack of his city (Sec. 124), the invasion of Palestine and the siege of Jerusalem. Partial translation:

"I drew nigh to Ekron and I slew the governors and princes who had transgressed, and I hung upon stakes round about the city their dead bodies. . . . I brought their king Padi forth from Jerusalem [Hezekiah had evidently taken him prisoner earlier] and I established him upon his throne. . . . I then besieged Hezekiah of Judah who had not submitted to my yoke, and I captured forty-six of his strong cities and fortresses and innumerable small cities, with the battering of rams and the assault of engines and the attack of foot-soldiers and by mines and breaches. I brought out therefrom 200,150 people both small and great, male and female; and horses, mules, asses, camels, oxen, and innumerable sheep I counted as spoil. Hezekiah himself I shut up like a caged bird in Jerusalem, his royal city. I threw up mounds against him, and I took vengeance upon any man who came forth from his city. His cities which I had captured I gave to the king of Ashdod, and Padi king of Ekron. . . . The fear of the majesty of my sovereignty overwhelmed Hezekiah, and the Urbi and his trusty warriors whom he had brought into his royal city of Jerusalem to protect it deserted. And he despatched after me his messenger to my royal city Nineveh to pay tribute and to make submission with thirty talents of gold, eight hundred talents of silver, precious stones, eye-paint, ivory couches and thrones, hides and tusks, precious woods, and divers objects, a heavy treasure, together with his daughters and the women of his palace, and male and female musicians."

met at Eltekeh, and Egypt was beaten. With a crash
down went the hopes of Hezekiah and all who leaned on that
"broken reed." Jerusalem was in a panic, and the panic
grew as the fires of blazing cities drew nearer and the fugitives from the fast-falling Judean towns poured into the
capital. With feverish haste the engineers put Jerusalem
into a state of defense. But when the Assyrian soldiers
actually appeared before the walls all courage failed; those
who had brought on this calamity by their persistent clamor
for rebellion fled from the city, and Hezekiah was forced to
play his last desperate card—abject submission and an
enormous indemnity. He stripped his treasury, his palace,
the temple, he even took off the gold from the doors and
pillars of the house of Jehovah. This, with his most humble
apologies, was sent to Sennacherib at Lachish. It was a
fair sum of money—30 talents of gold and 300 talents of silver (Sennacherib says 800), equivalent in purchasing power
to-day of $22,800,000. And besides, Hezekiah's own daugh-
ters and various others of his household had to go to swell
the conqueror's harem at Nineveh. Sennacherib sent as-
surances that the city should be spared, and withdrew his
army. Hezekiah had thus saved his crown and his city, but
practically nothing else. His former territory was divided
among Sennacherib's Philistine vassals.

126. **Isaiah's Vindication.** This was the hour of Isaiah's
victory. Through all the conflict of parties and the clash
of world-powers and the stress of invasions he alone had
seen facts as they were and had advocated in vain the one
policy that would have brought deliverance. He had
labored for more than thirty years to keep Judah true to
her allegiance, and when Judah had revolted, trusting in
Egypt, he had proclaimed swift punishment. All this had
now been accomplished. The prophet had proved his right
to be called a statesman and a watchman of Jehovah.
But what booted it? His country was laid waste, and only
the cowed and humiliated Jerusalem was left, like a booth

in a vineyard. It was time now to bind up the wounds and to re-establish on true foundations the faith of a people in the God that they had abandoned. That was Isaiah's next task.

and to re-establish on true foundations the faith of a people

XIX

THE DEMAND FOR CLEAN POLITICS AND RELIGION

127. Accumulated Rubbish. Before we recount the reform measures undertaken by Hezekiah and the prophets
it is well to examine the moral and religious conditions that
made such a reform necessary. We have already outlined
the state of affairs in Israel in the days of Amos and Hosea.
(Sec. 114.) They were practically the same in Judah at the
time of Uzziah's death, when Isaiah began his preaching.
Under Uzziah's successors things became worse. Ahaz, as
we have seen (Sec. 118) became an out-and-out idolater.
He introduced all kinds of curiosities into his museum of
religions at Jerusalem, and ended with the practical ejec-
tion of Jehovah from his own temple. All of this had a
debasing effect upon popular religion and morals. When
Hezekiah came to the throne there was some attempt at
reform, for he had a deeply religious nature and no doubt
through early contact with Isaiah, who was perhaps related
to the royal house, had been trained in the faith of his ancestors. But the reforms had not gone very deep, and the
ideas that underlay the ordinary religion of the common
folk looked more like magic or atheism than they did like
religion. In the prophecies of Micah and Isaiah we get pictures that are really cross-sections of the whole structure of
Hebrew social life and thought. Conditions in the year
701 B.C. may be thus summarized:

Rulers.—Micah and Isaiah both call them cannibals, mercilessly eating the people whom they should have protected; haters of good and lovers of evil.

210

Judges and Priests.—The majority are corrupt and mercenary; full of hypocrisy, uttering cant about Jehovah's care for them even while they plunder the poor. Graft is written all over Judah's public life.

The Wealthy.—Lust for money and power had utterly destroyed the ancient manhood of Israel. There was no longer any brotherhood; love of country had become mercenary patriotism. The one satisfaction in life was to get and to hoard. He was the best man who could steal most and still keep within the law.

Class Legislation.—Laws were made for the benefit of the rich. Particularly they favored the acquisition of real estate contrary to the old customs of inheritance. Land monopoly resulted; one master grasped a whole domain.

FIG. 102—EGYPTIAN AMULETS

1. Two fingers (obsidian) used in the ceremony of "opening the mouth" of a mummy. 2. Builder's square. 3. The "Ankh," a symbol of life. 4. The "backbone of Osiris," giving the wearer strength to rise after death. 5. A head-rest supposed to "lift up the head" in the other world. 6. An Osiris (?). 7. The eye of Horus, protecting from disease and all kinds of misfortune. 8. A heart. 9. (?). 10. A scent-bottle. Assyrian and Babylonian amulets, which the Hebrews copied, were numerous and varied—sometimes astronomical. (Isaiah 3 18-23.)

Drunkenness.—Drunken Ephraim has gone into captivity, but drunken Judah remains. Even priest and prophet, while performing their religious duties, "reel with mead. They reel during their visions, they totter while giving judgment" (Isaiah 28 7).

Idolatry.—Micah is so absorbed with the wrongs of the poor that he has little to say about the forms of religion, but Isaiah gives us hints of the degeneracy caused by foreign cults—the sacrifices on high places, burning incense to heathen deities. Even the ornaments of the women take the form of magic amulets, little suns and moons, ear-drops, nose-rings, girdles, and veils.

128. The Protests of Isaiah and Micah. Against all of this the reformers now turn, both with the spoken and the

FIG. 103—ASSYRIANS ASSAULTING A CITY

This cut gives some details of warfare not shown in Figs. 104 *ff*. Notice that the beam of the ram is suspended from a tower and is worked by men who are protected from attack by a thatch of shields. The officer in charge has a "conning-tower" from which to direct operations. On the same mova-ble platform is another tower by which the Assyrian sharpshooters are raised high enough to pick off the defenders on the wall. The king personally engages in the assault, accompanied by his two armor-bearers and an official. His powerful bow will shoot an arrow from 1,000 to 1,400 feet. This picture fairly describes the Assyrian operations against Jerusalem (Sec. 125) though it dates from the ninth century B.C. Note the childish way of representing men nearly as tall as the city towers.

written word. Isaiah relies upon pleading as well as upon denunciation:

"Wash you, make you clean,
 Let me see the evil of your doings no more.
 Seek out justice, chastise the violent.
 Right the orphan, plead for the widow.
 Come now and let us argue together, says Jehovah.
 If your sins be as scarlet, they may become white as
   snow;
 Be they red as crimson, they may become as wool."

Micah, sprung from the people and full of the violence of the revolutionist, denounces and threatens:

> "Hear this, you heads of the house of Jacob,
> And you judges of the house of Israel,
> You who spurn justice,
> And make all that is straight crooked,
> Who build Zion with acts of bloodshed,
> And Jerusalem with crime.
>
> The heads render judgment for a bribe,
> And her priests give oracles for a reward,
> And her prophets divine for silver;
> Yet they lean upon Jehovah and think,
> 'Jehovah is indeed in our midst,
> Evil cannot overtake us.'
>
> Therefore for your sakes
> Zion shall be plowed as a field,
> And Jerusalem shall become a heap of ruins,
> And her temple mount a wooded height."

It was the fire of Micah that touched off the train of reform. The public conscience was aroused and the king had to act.

129. **The Temple Cleansed.** It is easy to imagine the task that confronted the reformers in the temple. Idolatry had been rampant for fourteen years when Hezekiah came to the throne, and even if the clean-up took place in the first year of his reign, there was enough to do. But if, as seems probable from the study of the prophets, the reformation did not occur until after 701, there were thirty-two years of neglect for which to atone. The cleaners began with shovels and scrubbing-brushes. There was not only the refuse from the sacrificial altars to remove, but all kinds of rubbish that had been thrown into the temple court as an

intentional pollution of Jehovah's precinct. It took them eight days to clear out the court. They then undertook to clean the temple itself. Eight days more were required to remove the dirt, find, clean, and arrange the furniture and utensils, and lastly to make everything ceremonially holy by a sort of spiritual fumigation—by washings in holy water, by uttered charms or formulas, and by prayers, to drive away the taint which the worship of foreign gods had left. Then everything was ready for the ceremony of rededication, which took place with great pomp. Following this Hezekiah proclaimed a wonderful Passover feast, to which all Judah was invited. He even sent messengers to the various towns of Israel to ask all who were still faithful to Jehovah to join in the festivities. Unfortunately, the peasant Israelites who had escaped deportation under Sargon had lost interest in a god who, they thought, could not protect his people, and they made sport of the whole affair. Nevertheless, Judah celebrated the ancient feast with great ceremony. So great was the enthusiasm gener-

FIG. 104—DESTRUCTION OF LA-CHISH

This cut and Figs. 105 and 106 are from the famous series of slabs on which Sennacherib describes the campaign against Lachish. They were taken from his palace at Nineveh, and are now in the British Museum.

In this picture find the flames of the burning city, soldiers destroying (what tools do they use?), soldiers carrying off loot, soldiers eating and drinking, a sentinel. Notice that the city is on a hill. See Fig. 13.

ated by this feast that the people undertook the destruction of all idols and other accompaniments of the strange gods, the stone pillars and the poles on the high places, the altars and all the heathen symbols. Hezekiah destroyed in particular one venerable object that the people of Jerusalem had worshipped for many generations: it was the serpent that Moses was said to have made in the wilderness. Whatever its origin, it had become an idol. Hezekiah branded it as "an old brass thing" and broke it up with the rest. Thus was Jehovah enthroned again as the national God, and all his rivals were swept into the rubbish heap.

130. **The Deeper Reformation.** This was a good beginning, but it was after all a surface affair. The prophets knew very well that ritual and sacrifice had little to do with true religion. Amos forty years before had voiced Jehovah's disgust with feasts and new-moon assemblies, with the smell of burning flesh and the noise of viols. Now, Isaiah points out the same weakness in the popular religion:

> "What care I for the great number of your sacrifices?
>   says Jehovah;
> I am sated with burnt-offerings of rams, and fat of
>   fed beasts,
> And in the blood of bullocks and lambs and he-goats I
>   have no delight.
> Your new moons and your set days my soul hates;
> They are an encumbrance to me; I am tired of bear-
>   ing it.
> If you spread forth your hands I will hide mine eyes
>   from you;
> Even if you make many prayers I will not hear; your
>   hands are stained with blood."

And Micah, still more dramatic in his speech, puts the absurdity of immoral religion into pointed questions:

> "With what shall I come before Jehovah,
> Bow myself before the God on high?

> Shall I come before him with burnt-offerings,
> With calves a year old?
> Will Jehovah be pleased with thousands of rams,
> With myriads of streams of oil?
> Shall I give him my first-born for my guilt,
> The fruit of my body for the sin of my soul?"

The answer is swift and clear:

> "It has been shown you, O man, what is good;
> And what Jehovah demands of you:
> Only to do justice and love mercy,   .
> And to walk humbly with your God."

We have the testimony of Jeremiah that Micah's insistence upon morality had an immediate effect. From the king down there was an endeavor to put their house in order. Abuses were corrected, the powerful were restrained in their attempts to grind the weak. Something like a reign of brotherhood was introduced. At least, in the latter part of Isaiah's life, we hear none of those fierce denunciations of social wickedness that fell so constantly from his lips in former days; and in the sermons of the prophets who followed Isaiah social problems ceased to occupy the central place. There was an attempt also to gather up the fragments of religious literature belonging to the past and preserve it for purposes of instruction or ritual. According to Proverbs 25[1] part of our book of Proverbs was collected under Hezekiah (chaps. 25-29); the Talmud ascribes to him and his associates the writing of certain other books of the Old Testament. Thus the teachings of all the great reformers of the Assyrian period bore fruit in the heart of this king and in the conscience of the people.

131. **The Great Test.** Some time after the great reformation, though just when we are not able at present to determine (probably in 692), the new faith of the people of Jerusalem was put to a severe test. Sennacherib again

marched westward, evidently for the purpose of conquering
Egypt, the arch-plotter and disturber of his peace. The
army had reached the Philistine plain when Sennacherib
decided that it was unwise military strategy to leave in his
rear a strong fortress like Jerusalem; if it should revolt, it

FIG. 105—VICTORIOUS SOLDIERS AT LACHISH

What kinds of trees are shown? How many soldiers carry human heads?
Find a captive woman and child; a soldier cutting off a head; other
prisoners. All are marching toward the king seated in Fig. 106.

might cut off his retreat. He accordingly sent a detachment
of his army under the Rabshakeh (commander-in-chief) to
demand the surrender of the city. Three Hebrew officials
came out to treat with the Assyrians but found them inso-
lent in their demands. The Assyrians even talked loudly
in the Hebrew tongue so that the common people on the
wall might hear and take panic. Their argument was:
"Surrender, and let us transplant you to a more fruitful
land where you can prosper and be happy. If you resist
we will tear you to pieces. Trust not that your god Jehovah
will deliver you, for you see what we have done to the gods

of all the other nations." When the officials brought the
Assyrian demands to Hezekiah, he went into the temple to
spread them before Jehovah, and he sent for his best friend,
Isaiah. The prophet assured him that Jehovah would not
allow his city to be violated:

> "He shall not come into the city,
>   Nor shoot an arrow into it;
>   I will guard this city that I may rescue it,
>   For my own sake and for my servant David's sake."

Isaiah was strengthened in his faith by his consciousness
of his people's virtue. They had paid their tribute faithfully, they had purged away idolatry and had reformed
their wicked ways in accordance with their best light.
Sennacherib had no moral right to make these demands,
and therefore it was right for Jerusalem not to yield. The
prophet, who forty years before had warned Ahaz not to
make alliance with Assyria, and who for thirty years after
the compact was made had counselled absolute fidelity to
Assyria, now in the light of Assyria's perfidy boldly chal-
lenged the great empire and threw himself on Jehovah's
protection. It is a sublime spectacle of faith and courage.

The prophet's faith was justified by an extraordinary
event. When the Rabshakeh returned to Sennacherib with
his report of Jerusalem's defiance, he found that the Assyrian
army had advanced to the border of Egypt to attack Tirhakah, the Ethiopian king. Here a pestilence broke out, or,
in the language of the scripture, "an angel of Jehovah slew
in the camp of the Assyrian 185,000 men." Sennacherib
was frightened and beat a hasty retreat, ordering home at
the same time the detachment that was about Jerusalem.
The city was saved, and the aged prophet became after all
his trials and labors the most honored and beloved citizen
of the nation.

132. Summary of Isaiah's Work and Character. Isaiah's
career as prophet covers four reigns, five Assyrian invasions,
and three periods of special activity, divided as follows:

Fig. 106—HOMAGE TO SENNACHERIB

The background represents the stony hills of Palestine. Find Sennacherib
on his throne set in a grove; his fly-drivers; his waiting chariot; his general and captains reporting their victory; the elders of Lachish begging
for mercy. The little panel of text in front of the king reads: "Sennacherib, king of hosts, king of Assyria, sat upon his throne of state, and the
spoil of the city of Lachish passed before him."

1. Preaching social reform and hostility to any Assyrian
alliance. This period coincides with the invasion of Israel
by Tiglath-pileser IV in 734–733, and the destruction of
Samaria by Sargon in 722.

2. Preaching fidelity to Assyria and hostility to Egyptian
projects for revolt. This period covers the campaigns of
Sargon in 711 and of Sennacherib in 701.

3. Preaching reform and counselling resistance to Sennacherib, 700–692.

While Isaiah was the most versatile of all the prophets, it is upon his work as a statesman that his reputation with later generations chiefly rests. He was the greatest statesman of Hebrew history. Through repeated crises he offered counsels which if followed would have brought peace and comparative prosperity to little Judah. His principles of action were founded upon a clear idea of justice and on a deep religious faith, and therefore he could endure opposition and disgrace—as during most of his life he was obliged to endure them—he could challenge iniquity in high places and labor unceasingly for the redemption of his nation. He was primarily a prophet of action. Though he made no new contribution to the religious thought of Israel, his belief in the righteousness and majesty of Jehovah was so strong that it became henceforth a transforming force in the national life. That Judah did not at this period cease to exist under the impact of Assyria and like Israel leave no trace behind but endured for a full century, until its religious life was so strengthened and purified that it could endure the shock of exile, is due in large measure to Isaiah.

THE RETURN TO HEATHENISM

Manasseh (692–638), son of Hezekiah.

133. Assyria the World Overlord. The kingdom that Manasseh inherited from his father was a microscopic one, and he held it for fifty-five years simply by permission of Assyria. The territory was so small that the Assyrian Esarhaddon speaks of it as the "*city* of Judah." Among the great states that made up the empire, Judah was almost a negligible quantity. Yet it paid Manasseh to be loyal; he had his head in the lion's mouth. During his reign he enjoyed peace because he paid his tribute faithfully. No longer was there coquetting with Egypt; rather, when Ashurbanipal undertook a campaign against Egypt in 688, Manasseh sent a contingent of troops and ships to help him like a dutiful subordinate. Yet Manasseh had temptations enough to revolt. Tirhakah of Egypt and his successor gave Assyria plenty of trouble from 676 to 660, necessitating not only the conquest of Egypt but repeated punishments and the destruction of Thebes. Sidon revolted in 678, Tyre in 668, Babylon in 652, and her example roused to similar action northern Arabia, Edom, Moab, the Hauran, and upper Phœnicia.

Manasseh or his advisers must have exercised great self-control not to have been drawn into these whirlpools of rebellion. They, no doubt, felt what we now know to be a fact, that the great Assyrian empire was at the height of its power, the summit of its culture and of its ability to stamp that culture upon its subject peoples. The hands of Esarhaddon and of his son Ashurbanipal were everywhere—destructively if there was resistance, constructively if there was

co-operation. Everywhere there was Assyrian administration. Officers from Nineveh were resident in each province to see not only that governmental affairs ran smoothly, but that Assyrian ideas and ways of doing things were introduced. At Gezer, for instance, have been found tablets recording in the Assyrian language, and under an Assyrian notary, the deeds of sales of land. We know that Esarhaddon established his officials and his gods at Sidon. By numerous other signs we know that ideas flowed freely along the arteries of traffic throughout the western world, from Thebes and Arabia on the south to Cappadocia and the Caucasus

Fig. 107—ESARHADDON, KING OF ASSYRIA, 681–668 B.C.

The king stands with a libation vase in his right hand, while he worships the various gods represented before his face. In his left hand he holds a sceptre and the leash by which his two captive kings are secured. A hook passes through their lips. The larger figure represents Baal, king of Tyre; the smaller Tirhakah (Ethiopian king of Egypt 704–663 B.C. II Kings 19⁹). The monument was set up at Senjirli in northern Syria 670 B.C. In his inscription he mentions Manasseh of Judah among his conquered kings.

on the north, and well up into the Zagros mountains on the east. Nineveh was the heart of the empire, and the life blood was Assyrian authority and culture.

134. Assyria the Heir of Babylon. Yet Assyria was herself the inheritor of an older culture, a culture begun by the Sumerians, absorbed and passed on by the Babylonians in their early city states and in their great empire under Hammurabi, and now brilliantly revived by the broad-minded enthusiasm of Esarhaddon (681–668) and Ashurbanipal (668–626). The city of Babylon, which we saw trying to assert its independence under Merodach-baladan (Sec. 124), was finally destroyed by Sennacherib; but Esarhaddon saw its value to the world and rebuilt it. Ashurbanipal especially became interested in its literature and its religion, had

FIG. 108—BABYLONIAN FLOOD TABLET

One of the 20,000 books from the library of Ashurbanipal (668–626 B.C.) found at Nineveh and deposited in the British Museum. The clay was inscribed with a three-sided instrument made of wood, metal, or ivory, and then baked in an oven so that the inscription might be permanent (see Fig. 125). The king sent scribes to the ancient cities of Babylonia and Assyria where libraries existed, to make copies of rare and important works for his own library. In this way were preserved for us the ancient literature, science, and social documents of the Sumerians and Babylonians. Among these books are certain Creation tablets and Flood tablets which give another version of the stories in Genesis.

translations of its old books made into the Assyrian language, and assembled a great library which to-day, for the most part, lies in the British Museum and which has brought back as from the dead a lost civilization. Assyrian culture was therefore Babylonian. It was this culture embodying the work of the oldest Semitic civilization in the world that was now poured into Palestine, into little Judah, not only add-ing elements that, though old, were new to Hebrew thought, but bringing back to life the beliefs and practices that lay buried deep in the Semitic nature of the Hebrews. Small wonder that Manasseh yielded to the tide, that he made his peace and his crown secure by drifting with the currents that set so strongly from Nineveh.

135. **Enter the Host of Heaven.** Babylonian religion had a basis in the worship of the heavenly bodies. From the most ancient days the dwellers on the plain of Shinar had been astronomers, and it was but a step from science to re-ligion, where the objects of study were so wondrous and so beautiful; in fact, religion came before science. These Babylonian gods the Assyrians inherited and were now spreading throughout their broad dominions. It became as much a badge of loyalty to offer homage to their gods as in the early Christian days it was to sprinkle salt on the altar of the divine Cæsar. Manasseh promptly opened the courts of Jehovah's temple to the host of heaven, and in par-ticular to Ishtar, the planet Venus, the queen of heaven. Surely there was provocation in the very situation of Jeru-salem, lying high on its mountain ridge with the sky so near, with the clear-cut horizon of Moab thirty miles to the east from which the planets nightly spring, and with the desert air to magnify and glorify the radiance of every star. The new worship spread like wild-fire. Many a housetop became an altar from which incense ascended, even a family altar; for, as Jeremiah says (7[18]): "The children gather wood and the fathers kindle the fire and the women knead the dough to make cakes to the Queen of Heaven." Nor was this purely a relapse and a denial of Jehovah. In the minds of many was the thought that Jehovah was still being wor-shipped, that he who had formerly been called the Lord of the hosts of Israel, might now be called Lord of the hosts of heaven. This was a seductive and dangerous mingling of the new and the old. The strength of the new worship lay

not in the fact that it was introduced and made popular by
imperial command, but that it appealed to some of the most
fundamental instincts of man, among them the instinct for

FIG. 109—A ROYAL LION HUNT

This represents the most perfect period of Assyrian art, characterized by vigor,
skill in composition, and a fidelity to nature excelled by no ancient race.
The royal chariot holds four people: the king, the charioteer and two
assistants. The horses go forward at full gallop, while the king shoots the
lions which his hunters have beaten up. One dead lioness lies behind the
chariot; her wounded mate springs at the king, but is killed by the spears
of the two assistants.

nature-worship in its most alluring form, approved, to be
sure, and stimulated by the court.

136. Re-enter the Old Gods. When the doors of the
Hebrew conscience opened wide enough to admit the host
of heaven, they admitted also the host of the earth. Out
from their hiding-places they came, from the memories of
old grand-dames, from the uncanny ravings of clairvoyants

and wise women, from the springs and trees and the caverns of the wilderness. All the old Semitic stock of gods, whose altars and sacred poles Hezekiah had scrapped, now trooped back for a final fling before the great prophets and the scourge of the exile should drive them out forever. Baal led the way, or rather the host of the Baalim, and they set up their poles again on every high place that Hezekiah had dismantled. Next

> "Moloch, horrid king, besmeared with blood
> Of human sacrifice, and parents' tears;
> Though, for the noise of drums and timbrels loud,
> Their children's cries unheard that passed through fire
> To his grim idol."

Him they worshipped in the valley of Hinnom to the south of the city. Shrines arose like magic: to Thammuz, the Phœnician Adonis, type of the reviving vegetation of spring; to the gods of their Semitic neighbors, Chemosh and Milcom. The courts of Jehovah, the houses of the city, the valleys and the Mount of Olives were soon covered with the spawn. Now, instead of inquiring at Jehovah's oracle, the people practised augury, tried to learn the future by the "sound of the movement in the mulberry-trees," or the hum of insects or of flies; or they consulted mediums who called up from the dead their familiar spirits; or they sought a magician who by means of spoken words of power controlled demons or jinn that could stop the winds or dry up a spring or cause an enemy to pine away and die. Worse than this, when the people lost their grip on Jehovah, who insisted on morality, they dropped back into the licentiousness that has always gone hand in hand with the crude faiths of crude civilizations. The morals of Judah took a swift fall, backslid to the days of Ahaz that had so incensed Isaiah. It truly seemed as if the abyss had swallowed up the prophetic teachings and even Jehovah himself.

137. **The Underlying Reasons for the Reaction.** We have suggested that political interest caused Manasseh to open his land to the Assyrian gods. But undoubtedly other causes were at work. We must remember that Manasseh was only a lad of twelve years when he was crowned, which means that he personally did not shape the destinies of his kingdom for at least ten years. Who was the power behind the throne? There is not a hint in the Bible. We know, however, that in all eastern courts the harem plays a large part, especially in intrigue. The royal household of Judah contained women from many lands and of many faiths. They were undoubtedly ignorant, superstitious, and revengeful, as well as vain and licentious. They had no special sympathy with the reforms of the late king, and they had a very lively hatred for the old prophet who had held their vanity and their immorality up to such public scorn (Isaiah 3^{16-24}). There is every reason to suppose that these women used all their influence to get their boy king out from under the control of the puritanic Isaiah and his party. And they had plenty of helpers, all the old grafters and pleasure hunters whom Hezekiah had overthrown. The good old times was all they asked for, especially if in bringing them back they could get even with their enemies Isaiah and Micah.

Then the reforms of Hezekiah had been undertaken late in his reign and in a way under pressure. The marvellous deliverance of Jerusalem from Sennacherib in accordance with Isaiah's word had hypnotized everybody into a temporary declaration for Jehovah. But, on further thought, they saw that Jehovah had not saved the forty-six fenced cities of Judah, and that the gods of Assyria had laid waste and plundered and killed and carried captive about as they pleased. The country places were then, as always, less advanced in religious ideas; and when the invasion of Sennacherib drove thousands of villagers into Jerusalem for refuge, they merely swelled the number of superstitious jinn-worshippers who could never help a reform, but who could always be counted on to favor a reaction. Hezekiah's reform had been accomplished largely by proclamation instead of conversion. As King Olaf of Norway preached the gospel with his sword, with the result that on his death Odin

Copyright by Underwood and Underwood, N. Y.

FIG. 110—VALLEY OF HINNOM

This is the valley made infamous by the idolatrous worship of the kings of Judah, beginning with Solomon and ending with Amon. It was polluted by Josiah so that it might never again serve as a place of worship, and thenceforward its name, changed to Ge-henna, became a symbol of the dumping-place of the moral refuse of humanity (Hell).

The great hill to the left is Zion, the highest portion of ancient Jerusalem, though now outside the walls. The southeast angle of the city wall appears to the right of it, above the almost indistinguishable hill of Ophel. To the right of this sweeps down the steep valley of the Kidron, which on the extreme right rises the Mount of Olives.

and the other Norse gods came promptly back, so Hezekiah preached his gospel by edict. The new truth lacked grip on the popular mind. Isaiah's only God, high above the earth and holy, did not satisfy the plain citizen who needed a god that could help him earn his bread and butter and could scare away the devils from his sheep and his olive-trees. So the old gods and the new ones won out.

138. **Manasseh's Shame and God's Opportunity.** The
hatred of the pious folks by the old grafters and idolaters
whom Isaiah and Micah had succeeded in banishing must have
been intense. They were not satisfied until they had driven
every last reformer to cover. Manasseh as their tool signed
the death-warrant of many a preacher of righteousness: "he
shed innocent blood very much, until he had filled Jerusalem
from one end to the other." Tradition says that the aged
Isaiah fell in the slaughter—as well he might fall. But the
blood of the martyrs became, as always, the seed of the new
faith. Those who escaped the sword and could no longer
preach their belief, wrote it. In those dark hours of persecution the biblical books of Amos, Hosea, Isaiah (chaps.
1–33), and Micah took substantially their present form. A
new history of the Hebrews, embodying the great moral
lessons that were illustrated by the stories of the race, was
compiled out of the old Judean and the old Ephraimitic
historical material; and the beginning also was made on the
book of Deuteronomy, which puts down in the form of
definite laws the reforms of Isaiah and his fellows and which
appeared for the first time in the reign of Josiah a few years
later (Sec. 141). There was certainly no more important
period of literary or spiritual activity, prior to the exile, than
this bloody reign of Manasseh. Conviction was ripening
and deepening, roots of faith were striking down into the
structure of the moral universe, and strong branches were
reaching upward to a clearer heaven. Hereafter there will
be more preachers of righteousness.

XXI

JUDAH'S NEW DEMOCRATIC CONSTITUTION

Amon (638–637), son of Manasseh.
Josiah (637–607), son of Amon.

139. The Reformers' Fresh Grip. Nothing is recorded of
the brief reign of Manasseh's son Amon except that he followed in the footsteps of his father and that he was murdered. What was the cause of the assassination we do not
know. The murderers belonged to the court, and those who
avenged the murder and set the young Josiah on the throne
were the public at large. The quarrel was evidently a
private affair and had nothing to do with the great change
of policy that ensued.

There must have been a good deal of quick manœuvring
behind the scenes when Amon suddenly dropped out, for
his successor was his son Josiah, a mere child of eight. He
was too young to show any significant traits, but not too
young to be directed by some one and trained to a definite
ideal. We do not know how it came about, but somebody in
sympathy with the persecuted prophetic party won the
necessary control and took the little king in hand. It may
have been Hilkiah, whom Josiah later made high priest;
more likely it was Zephaniah who wrote the biblical book of
that name. We know that he was of royal blood, being a
descendant of Hezekiah, and therefore on the inside of
palace politics. This initial victory of the prophetic party
was of prime importance, for it enabled them to come back
slowly but surely, as the young king was trained into their
ways of looking at things. By the time Josiah was sixteen
years old and ready to make decisions for himself, he frankly
avowed his sympathy with their policies, and before he was
twenty-six he was actually leading in reforms.

230

140. **The Scythian Scare.** About 626 something happened that sent the shivers through Judah and made people recall all the prophecies of dreadful things that Isaiah and Micah and Amos had ever made. It awoke to life two new prophets also, Zephaniah and Jeremiah. This was a deluge of Scythian hordes that poured out of Europe across the Caucasus into Media and Asia Minor and Armenia. Unfortunately, in the same year the great Ashurbanipal died and was succeeded by a weakling. There was nothing to stay the onward sweep of this tidal wave of barbarians. The Scythians lacked the skill to conquer strongly fortified cities, but all other places which they touched they plunged into blood. Both Zephaniah (chap. 1) and Jeremiah (chaps. 4–6) boldly announced that this was the scourge of Jehovah, the day of doom that Jehovah had promised to idolatrous Judah. The hordes spread southward along the coastal plain of Palestine, blotting out the Philistine towns. Their ultimate aim was to plunder the rich valley of the Nile. But a new dynasty had arisen in Egypt, the twenty-sixth, and Psamtik I, a vigorous and ambitious king, turned back the tide at his frontier either by the sword or with gold. Jerusalem on her mountain perch was not touched, but the terror she felt was a mighty aid to the reformers. It was a glimpse of hell-fire.

141. **The Happy Find.** By 621 the reformation had gathered some headway. Josiah was having the temple repaired and sent his secretary to audit the counting of the money which the people had cast into the collection boxes for that purpose. When the job was done, Hilkiah the high priest told the secretary that he had discovered a law-book in the temple, and he gave it to him to read. The secretary took it to Josiah and read it to him. The king was profoundly impressed and so alarmed that he tore his clothes, for the book gave in detail the curses that would fall upon Judah if Jehovah's law were not scrupulously obeyed. Hastily the king sent five of his most trusty advisers to

From a photograph by Dwight L. Elmendorf
FIG. 111—OLD CODEX AT SHECHEM
(See description on opposite page)

the prophetess Huldah to see if Jehovah would say through her whether the doom might in any way be averted. The answer came that repentance and thorough reform might at least postpone the crisis. The king thereupon set on foot a complete revision of all the religious practices of the realm, a great house-cleaning more thorough than even Hezekiah's had been.

This discovery suggests interesting questions that can be answered only by inference. What was this book, how did it happen to be written, and why was it discovered and brought to the king's attention at such a propitious time? When we consider the fears that the curses of the book aroused and the nature of the reforms that followed, it seems certain that the book was essentially the oldest portions of our book of Deuteronomy, chapters twelve to nineteen. It was that recasting of the older legislation ascribed to Moses upon which the prophets of Manasseh's reign had been secretly at work. They had not dared to publish it over their own names, for that would have killed its influence and might have cost them their lives. They therefore used the literary device of putting the new legislation into the mouth of Moses, the great lawgiver; in truth, it was in accord with the prophetic spirit of that founder of Israel's faith. Then, when they felt the time was ripe, some one apparently hid it in a temple storeroom where they knew it would be discovered during the repairs. Possibly the high priest was in the secret, but not necessarily so. He was at any rate in sympathy with the movement it represented

---

This is Jacob, son of Aaron, High Priest of the Samaritans, holding their most sacred copy of the Law. The Samaritans claim it was written by the great-grandson of Aaron, but scholars say that it is only about 2,000 years old. It is written in the old Phœnician character as used by the Jews before the Captivity. It consists of the Pentateuch and Joshua, books that form the constitution of the Samaritan faith and nation, as one of them, the book of Deuteronomy, was the earlier constitution of the Judean commonwealth. By changing the text of Deut. 27⁴ from "Ebal" to "Gerizim" they claim that Mount Gerizim is the one sanctuary chosen of Jehovah, and that the claims of Jerusalem are false. (Sec. 143 and John 4²⁰.)

and was shrewd enough to get the book into the king's hands without delay. The royal fears and the royal enthusiasm did the rest.

142. **The Great Reform.** Josiah threw all his youthful energy into the task of cleansing. First he called a grand assembly of all the free men of Judah. They thronged to the temple courts and there listened with wonder while the king himself read the entire book, its curses and its blessings. The people were so impressed, or so pliant in the king's hands, that they and Josiah together vowed to make the new-found book the law of the land. The book thus became the first written constitution the Hebrews ever had, and by far the most fateful both for good and ill.

Josiah then began to put into execution every one of the new statutes. He found there the command to worship Jehovah alone and to use in that worship neither idol nor symbol. Jerusalem was still filled with the abominations of Manasseh his grandfather and the sacred poles, standing stones, and other Canaanite devices with which the Hebrews had long worshipped Jehovah. These now all went by the board. The priests brought them out from the temple, burned them, and scattered the ashes in polluted places. The Queen of Heaven, the bronze horses and chariots of the sun, the roof altars, the House of the Satyrs, and all the shrines by which Solomon had kept the peace in his overfeminine household, all were ground to powder. Henceforth Jehovah should be dissociated forever from the debasing rites of the Canaanite religion and should have no rivals. This destruction of idols was the first step toward reformation.

143. **The Abolition of the High Places.** Josiah found also the command that all high places should be destroyed and the worship transferred to Jerusalem. This was not such a large undertaking as might at first seem. Many high places had already been destroyed by the Assyrians, and the territory of Judah was now so small that only a few

square miles were included within its boundary. Going to
Jerusalem was not a difficult task, for a man could easily
walk there in a day or two from the most remote corners of
the land. The prophets since Hosea had felt that these

Fig. 112—A HIGH PLACE

The "cathedral-altar" of Petra, on the highest summit within the rock-city.
In the top of the rock a platform was sunk, 47 x 20 feet.   On its west side
two altars were cut out, the main square one occupying the right centre
of the picture.   There is a depression cut in the top for libations.   The
dark hole cut in the rock to the left is a pool, perhaps for washings.   Beyond this is a round altar for bloody sacrifices sunk also in the rock.
We must imagine that a Hebrew high-place was similar, with the addition of
stone pillars or poles.

shrines were a constant danger to pure religion, for, though
Jehovah was invariably worshipped there, the sanctuaries
themselves were originally Canaanite or even prehistoric.
They had been built for Baals; all the accompaniments and
traditions of Baal worship still clung to them. It was useless to think of leading the people to a purer worship or to a
loftier ideal of Jehovah's character if these compromising
shrines remained. The simplest and most thorough pro-

ceeding was to abolish them entirely; this Josiah did. He not only dismantled them, but polluted the ground so that they could never be used for religious rites again. High places ceased forever. Those who had been their priests were allowed to come to Jerusalem and serve the temple on equal terms (on paper, at least) with its regular priests. Practically, however, those who came at all were relegated to second place. These were henceforth called Levites.

144. The Feasts Centralized. A third great change had reference to the national festival, the Passover. Hitherto it had been a family feast. At the time of the spring moon every household throughout the land had killed its lamb and sprinkled the blood and eaten the sacred meal. Now all of this was made illegal, and every one who wished to join in the rite must come to Jerusalem to the great celebration at the temple. Josiah inaugurated the new form of the Passover with impressive ceremony, and thus started that long series of pilgrimages that for seven centuries brought Jews from the four corners of the earth each year to the sacred city, until in 70 A.D. Rome quenched forever the sacrificial fire.

145. Love the Principle of Religion and Conduct. The great glory of this reformation and of the book that caused it rests in the elevation of love as the cardinal principle of both religion and morals. The Hebrew was commanded to love Jehovah as the only God whose character could command respect, and to love man because only so could justice be done. All the heavenward-soaring fervor of Hosea and Isaiah and all the humane outreachings of Amos and Micah here found expression. Indeed, so wonderfully did these early thinkers of Israel penetrate to the heart of the universe that Jesus himself was able in the words and spirit of this book to sum up the whole of religion:

"Thou shalt love the Lord thy God with all thy heart and with all thy soul and with all thy mind and with all thy strength; and thou shalt love thy neighbor as thyself."

It was to break from his countrymen the damning and stifling bonds of ceremonial law and to lead them back to the freedom of this great conception of duty that the greatest of prophets gave up his life.

It will be interesting to see how this book, so instinct with the higher spirit of religion, was gradually perverted into an ironclad set of religious rules, until the living prophet of God came to be of no account and the petty, hair-splitting scribe became the dictator of a nation's fate. This was the great tragedy of the Hebrew race.

146. **Crumbling Empires.** Following the grand revival came twelve years of happiness and prosperity, the noblest period in Judah's history. Josiah was himself the embodiment of the virtues he taught, a strong, patriotic and high-minded ruler. Under him the borders of Judah were somewhat enlarged until they included much of the land of Israel, at least as far north as Samaria. But events without were moving swiftly and disastrously. Assyria had passed her zenith. The empire of Ashurbanipal was tottering under the impact of the Scythians and of the Medes who were now pressing in from the east. Babylon too had revolted and her Assyrian viceroy, Nabopolassar, had not only proclaimed himself king, but had leagued with the king of the Medes for the destruction of Nineveh and the dismemberment of her vast domain. The west felt instinctively that things were about to happen. The prophet Nahum sensed the coming doom and sent up to heaven a shout of exultation (Nahum 3). That great city was about to be punished for its years of cruelty to little Israel and Judah. The instruments of Jehovah's vengeance were Nabopolassar of Babylon and Cyaxares of Media. Together they placed their engines under the walls of Nineveh, and the city fell with a crash that shook the world (612 B.C.). The two conquerors then proceeded to divide the empire, the Mede taking the lands east of the Tigris and the Babylonian taking those to the west.

147. **Death of Josiah.** Egypt now leaped to a brief supremacy. The new dynasty that had arisen in the person of Psamtik had been able by the aid of Greek mercenaries to subjugate all the land of the Nile. Necho II, who succeeded Psamtik in 609, seeing that the fall of Nineveh had for the moment left the west defenseless, resolved to snatch Syria for himself before Babylon and Media could take it. With his army he started northward in 608. Josiah had been a faithful vassal of Nineveh, but he too resolved that since Assyria had gone to pieces no king but a Hebrew should rule Palestine. He therefore attacked Necho, determined to beat him back to Egypt and restore the glories of an independent Israel. But Josiah's poorly trained handful of troops were no match for the disciplined and skilled Greek soldiers that Necho had hired and in the first skirmish at Megiddo Josiah was killed by an arrow. Necho swept northward victoriously to the Euphrates, while an army of mourners trooped back to Jerusalem with Josiah's lifeless body, to mingle their tears with those of an agonized city. The best-beloved ruler Judah ever knew seemed to have been forsaken by the very God he had championed, and the sun to have fallen from the sky.

King of the North and South, Nem-ảb-RÅ, son of the Sun, Nekau. (*Necho.*)

Fig. 113—NAMES OF PHARAOH-NECHO II

XXII

THE ROAD TO RUIN

Jehoahaz (607, three months), son of Josiah.
Jehoiakim (607–597), son of Josiah.
Jehoiachin (597, three months), son of Jehoiakim.
Zedekiah (597–586), son of Josiah.
Gedaliah (586–581).

148. **The Overthrow of Democracy.** The tragic death of
Josiah did not quench the spirit of patriotism. The people
promptly put on the throne Jehoahaz, a younger son of
Josiah's, passing by the natural heir evidently because he
had some leanings toward Egypt. But Necho did not propose to have an independent Judah. As soon as he had secured his hold on northern Syria he sent a summons to
Jehoahaz to meet him at Riblah on the Orontes, where he
had made his headquarters. There he put him in chains, and,
after a reign of but three months, sent him to Egypt. In
his stead he put on the throne of Judah Jehoiakim, an older
son of Josiah's who was willing to rule as a vassal of Egypt.

Jehoiakim's first duty was to pay Necho a war indemnity. He got the money by squeezing the nobles, and they
in turn promptly squeezed the commoners. It was a heavy
tax and the people suffered. Nevertheless, the covetous and
selfish king proceeded to tax them further in order to build
an elaborate palace for himself. It soon became evident
that the wise policy of the just and pious Josiah had gone
forever. And the worst of it was that many were glad of
it, glad of the chance to oppress the under-dog once more
and to push their get-rich-quick schemes. If Jehovah did
not like these schemes, so much the worse for Jehovah!
There were plenty of other gods who did not object. While
the reforms of Deuteronomy still existed on paper as statute

law, men did practically as they pleased. And the frivolous and despotic Jehoiakim led the way.

149. **The Supremacy of Babylon.** Pharaoh-Necho now hastened to the Euphrates to defend his newly conquered

Copyright by Underwood and Underwood, N. Y.

Fig. 114—RUINS OF NINEVEH

The mounds in the foreground represent Nineveh, the capital of the Assyrian empire from about 900 B.C. to 607 B.C. What is the modern city across the Tigris? What significance had it in the Great War?

possessions, while the Babylonian crown prince Nebuchadrezzar hastened to meet him. The hosts clashed at Carchemish (604 B.C.). Necho was routed and fled southward with Nebuchadrezzar at his heels. He would have lost then and there his whole kingdom, including Egypt, had not Nabopolassar happened to die and force Nebuchadrezzar to return to Babylon to make his succession sure. But any one with discernment could see that the Egyptian grip on Palestine was broken and that when the Babylonian lion chose to return, all he had to do was to seize the prey. The battle of Carchemish had made Nebuchadrezzar the master of the West-lands.

150. **Jehoiakim's Treason.**   When Jehoiakim found that his overlord Necho had been beaten and was out of the game, he lost no time in making peace with Nebuchadrezzar. The Chaldean took him and his money at their face value, and let him continue on the throne as his vassal. But Jehoiakim intended to be loyal to his new master only until he could find means to break away. Those means he at length thought he had found, and he withheld his tribute.

Nebuchadrezzar could not, at the moment, attend to the little rebel, so he ordered the governors of the various neighboring provinces to let loose upon Judah bands of guerilla warriors, Edomites, Ammonites, Samaritans, and what few Chaldean soldiers they could spare from their garrisons. These bands harried the countryside and drove many people into Jerusalem, but they did not touch the arch-rebel. In fact, Jehoiakim was destined not to be caught. By the time Nebuchadrezzar could appear in person with a Chaldean army, the king had died and his son Jehoiachin succeeded him.

151. Jeremiah the Faithful Counsellor. Just one man in all Judah saw the folly of this revolt. This was the prophet Jeremiah, a native of little Anathoth, whom the Scythian

From Breasted's "Ancient Times."

FIG. 115—PLUNDER FROM A CITY

This scene shows two scribes taking dictations from an Assyrian officer, who recounts the amount of plunder seized from an Asiatic city. Notice how captive women and children are treated. A shepherd drives off the flocks. Two different methods of writing are here indicated. Find the scribe who is using a clay tablet and stylus, and the one using papyrus and pen. Which is the outgoing and which the incoming method? (Figs. 119 and 127.) What would be the language written on clay and what the one on papyrus?

scare (Sec. 140) first inspired to rebuke Judah for its sins and who later moved to Jerusalem where he might be Jehovah's watchman, as Isaiah had been. He warned the king to be faithful to his Babylonian overlord and combated the crazy notion, inherited from Isaiah's time, that Jerusalem could never be taken. But all to no purpose.

His first roll of sermons was cut to pieces by the king personally, he was put in the stocks, his life was plotted against both in Anathoth and in Jerusalem. Jerusalem was hopeless in her follies and her sins. From this time on Jeremiah became the relentless prophet of doom.

152. **The First Deportation.** With the appearance of Nebuchadrezzar the straits of Jerusalem became desperate. Within there was divided counsel, some boldly proposing to fight it out, some advocating surrender. Jeremiah was busy night and day preaching from the same text the same practical sermon: "Judah has sinned beyond forgiveness; Jehovah is bound to destroy the city. While there is time, make your peace with the king of Babylon." Jehoiachin soon saw the folly of resistance, and at the end of three months voluntarily surrendered himself and his family into Nebuchadrezzar's hands (597 B.C.). The unfortunate boy—for he was only eighteen years old—was sent at once to Babylon, where he passed the next thirty-seven years in prison. Nebuchadrezzar made a careful investigation of the personal resources of the city, and in order to cripple it, as he thought forever, he took back with him to Babylon all the court, the aristocracy, the wealthy men, the standing army, and the skilled workmen; in all about ten or eleven thousand people. The city was sacked, the treasury emptied, and all the gold and silver vessels used in the temple service were carried as prizes to the gods of Babylon. Jeremiah escaped deportation, possibly because Nebuchadrezzar felt that the prophet was the greatest guarantee of future peace he could leave in the city.

153. **The Left-Overs.** It is difficult to realize the change that came over Judah as a result of the deportation of its chief men to Babylonia. The orders of the conqueror were quickly carried out; the prisoners of war had little time to adjust their affairs and dispose of their property. City houses must have sold for a song, good olive and fig orchards and valuable vineyards were turned over to the first bidder

at any price. In countless cases there was no sale of property made; lands and houses were simply abandoned and
business firms put up their shutters without realizing a penny
on their stock or good-will. Those whom the conqueror left
behind proceeded to take possession of what remained.
The man who a few months ago was worth a few shekels
of silver, now found himself a landed proprietor; the down-
and-out man suddenly woke up rich. The men who grabbed
while the grabbing was good became leading citizens, regardless of any personal qualifications for leadership. In
short, a new social class sprang up, the class of the newly
rich. They were ignorant, superstitious, of no ability, and,
as one might expect of such folks suddenly possessed of
wealth and position, horribly conceited, arrogant, intolerant.
They felt that since Jehovah had punished the sinners with
exile, they themselves who had been spared and given this
new start in the world must be the apple of Jehovah's eye.
But Jeremiah sized up their characteristics in one graphic
phrase, "bad figs." All the good figs were in Babylon.

154. **A Vacillating King.** Over this scrambling crowd of
incompetents Nebuchadrezzar made Zedekiah king. He
was a son of Josiah and therefore the uncle of Jehoiachin.
It was a bad choice, but possibly the best that could be made.
Zedekiah was a weak man who listened to everybody's advice and switched the policies of state about in accordance
with the latest opinion. While he himself was of royal
blood, his court were necessarily all common people without
any previous experience in affairs and with no statesman's
outlook upon the troubled world. For four years Zedekiah
paid his tribute regularly. But he was constantly goaded
by his upstart court, who trusted in the strength of the de-
fenses of Jerusalem, and by the false prophets who preached
everywhere Jehovah's protection of his city and temple; so
that when ambassadors came from Moab and Ammon, Tyre
and Sidon to tempt him to make secret league with them, he
yielded; even the official prophets of Jehovah joined in

approving this breach of honor. While Zedekiah did not actually revolt at this time, he came so near it that he was obliged to go to Babylon to explain his conduct. Nebuchadrezzar gave him another chance.

FIG. 116—PROCESSION OF PRISONERS

Taken by Thothmes III in one of his seventeen Asiatic campaigns The prisoners are brought from the ship to the prison-pens at Thebes They are in pairs, held individually by Egyptian servants of the Pharaoh. Of the latter note the carefully arranged hair and the scant dress of linen. Study the faces of the prisoners. Are there any intelligent ones? Why are they all so old? Note their long matted beards—an abomination to the Egyptians—and the heavy masses of black hair. Note also their heavy dresses made of gayly colored wool stuff such as an Egyptian would never put on. Find a woman carrying two children, and note the method.
Processions like this have streamed for thousands of years from every captured city to the capitals of the conquerors.

155. The Fatal Revolt. Four years later a new king of Egypt arose, Hophra by name, who actively renewed the old intriguing. The pro-Egyptian party again got the ear of the king and this time put their scheme through. Zedekiah revolted in 589. Nebuchadrezzar threw his army into Palestine at once and tightly encircled Jerusalem in January, 588. Again Jeremiah hurled his denunciations against the faithless and foolish king: "What can you hope for? Will Jehovah come to the rescue of one who breaks his oath, and will feeble Egypt save you? Surrender at once to Nebuchadrezzar; it is your only hope." But the king had popular support and he stood firm. The city was strongly fortified, the defenders were full of spirit, and they felt sure that Egypt would come to their relief. In order to insure without fail the favor of Jehovah they even set free all the Hebrew slaves which many of them had been holding contrary to the statutes of the new law-book (Deut. 15$^{12-15}$). Apparently Jehovah was well pleased with this, for almost immediately an Egyptian army appeared on the frontier for their relief, and Nebuchadrezzar was compelled to raise the siege. The city went wild with joy. Jehovah had again rescued his holy city as he did in Isaiah's day! But in their enthusiasm they did something that exposed their absolute lack of honor even in dealing with their God; they re-enslaved their Hebrew brethren whom they had just set free. This act convinced Jeremiah that Judah's fate was irrevocable; she was not worth saving. He sent word to Zedekiah that Nebuchadrezzar would return and fulfil every syllable of the doom Jehovah had pronounced.

As the prophet foresaw, Nebuchadrezzar scattered the Egyptian army and returned to the siege. Conditions in Jerusalem now became hopeless. The food-supply soon was exhausted and disease broke out. Jeremiah managed somehow to get out of jail, where his enemies had put him, but they arrested him again on the charge that his constant advice to surrender was weakening the defense of the city— as it certainly was. This time they put him into an old cistern full of filth, where he nearly died. But a negro slave took pity on him and pulled him out, though he could not set him free. Again the distracted king asked for an oracle of hope, but again came the stern word, coupled nevertheless with the assurance that Jerusalem should one day rise from its ashes and be again the home of Jehovah's true worshippers.

Fig. 117—JEREMIAH AT THE FALL OF JERUSALEM

By Eduard Friedrich Bendemann (1811–1889)

Find the following: troops blowing trumpets of victory, runners throwing palm branches, the conqueror (what is in his hand?), king Zedekiah bound to a chariot, the captive ark, the smoking ruins of the temple, priests, soldiers lashing trains of captives (what are the prisoners carrying?), Jeremiah, Baruch (why have they rolls?), chained musician and other men (what are they doing?). Why are women and children fleeing toward Jeremiah? A man and a child, fallen in the foreground, are symbols of what? Why is Jeremiah so calm in the midst of the confusion? Read his thoughts.

156. **The Capture and Destruction of Jerusalem.** The morale of the city now began to break. The timid ones began to steal out by night and surrender themselves to the tender mercies of Nebuchadrezzar. The battering-rams

thundered unceasingly against the northern wall until in July, 586, after a siege of a year and a half, a breach was made and the enemy poured in. The panic-stricken king fled with his guards by the opposite gates southeastward, and did their best to reach the Jordan and the safety of the desert. But the Chaldeans were not to be balked. They overtook the company at Jericho and carried them to Riblah on the Orontes where Nebuchadrezzar had his headquarters. The king's sons were killed in his presence, his own eyes were put out, and they all were carried in chains to Babylon. To awe the nation still further, seventy of the leading citizens were also taken to Riblah and put to death. Jeremiah was brought before the authorities and questioned; but the Chaldeans evidently knew all about him and gave him the choice of going to Babylon or staying behind. He chose to stay.

At Nebuchadrezzar's order the Chaldean soldiers then stripped the city of everything of value, even breaking up the brass of the temple equipment. They burned the royal palace, the temple, and many of the private houses; they broke down the walls so that they might never again harbor a revolt, and they carried into exile nearly the entire population of the city, possibly 25,000 people. What was left in Judah was the poorest of the land—the dregs, as far as energy and wealth and brains were concerned, leaderless groups of peasants, to be sure far outnumbering the 35,000 who had been deported in the two great siftings, but disorganized and discouraged.

157. **Judah Becomes a Babylonian Colony.** Nebuchadrezzar had no thought of depopulating Palestine and letting it fall back into the jungle, but only of breaking the power of the land to revolt again. To keep up some form of organization he appointed one Gedaliah as governor (586 B.C.), a man of noble birth and a friend of Jeremiah. It speaks well for Nebuchadrezzar's friendly attitude that he should choose a native rather than a Chaldean. Gedaliah

was the best possible choice. He was a man of character and of a conciliatory spirit. Since Jerusalem was no longer habitable, he chose for his capital the tall hill of Mizpah, six miles northwest of Jerusalem. Thither came the heads of the wandering guerilla bands and the sheiks of the country villages to swear allegiance to the new government. Gedaliah induced the scattered peasants to return to their homes and to undertake again the cultivation of the soil. Many who had fled to Moab, Ammon, and Edom came back to share in the process of rebuilding the nation.

Things went excellently for a few years, when suddenly a rascal who claimed to have descended from David and therefore to have a better title to rule, encouraged by the jealous king of the Ammonites, murdered the unsuspecting Gedaliah (581 B.C.). This threw the community into a panic. They feared that now Nebuchadrezzar would certainly blot them off the map. After a few days of chaos the more energetic among them fled to Egypt, taking Jeremiah with them by force. They settled for a while in the town of Tahpanhes, a frontier city where foreigners of various kinds were allowed to live. Jeremiah felt that even so they would not escape the heavy hand of the Chaldean, for he predicted the conquest of Egypt by Nebuchadrezzar. The prophet was shocked also at the ease with which his fellow exiles threw away Jehovah and took up with any heathen god that was offered them. The last cry that has come down to us from Jeremiah's lips is his bitter denunciation of the idolatry of this Egyptian remnant. A late tradition says that for his faithfulness to the truth he was stoned to death by his own people.

158. Jeremiah's Career. No one can study the history of this period without forming the judgment that Jeremiah was the noblest patriot and the greatest prophet of his epoch. For nearly a half-century his personality completely overshadowed that of kings, prophets, and priests. Called in his youth to interpret the will of God to man, throughout his long life he spoke unflinchingly what seemed to him the truth, even though his voice sounded alone and though the truth brought him persecution, disgrace, and martyrdom. With the grasp of a statesman he saw the certain trend of world politics, he assessed the true weight of world-powers that struggled for the mastery, and he announced as Jehovah's will those policies that would have kept little Judah in peace and safety. With the insight of a prophet, also, he saw that what his country needed was morality founded on true religion: a morality that would bind men to their duty, to their covenants and to their fellow men; a religion that would enthrone Jehovah as the only God and worship him not with the debased and half-heathen ritual that was used even in the reformed temple, but with the sincere love of the heart. These teachings were not popular; they did not tickle the vanity or fill the pockets of either king or commoners, and in the strenuous times of war they sounded like treason. Hence his lifelong martyrdom, a martyrdom that so impressed succeeding generations that Jeremiah became for them the embodiment of the heroic and self-sacrificing genius of Israel. His character and services were undoubtedly in the mind of the great prophet who painted the matchless portrait of the suffering servant of Jehovah:

"He was despised and rejected of men; a man of sorrows and acquainted with grief; and as one from whom men hide their face he was despised and we esteemed him not. Surely he hath borne our griefs and carried our sorrows; yet we did esteem him stricken, smitten of God, and afflicted. But he was wounded for our transgressions, he was bruised for our iniquities; the chastisement of our peace was upon him, and with his stripes we are healed."

If this noble soul could still follow after his martyrdom the fortunes of his people and could see his truth march on to the end of time, cheering, inspiring, guiding men into fuller faith, he might well appropriate to himself those closing verses of the same great elegy:

"When thou shalt make his soul an offering for sin, he shall see his seed, he shall prolong his days, and the pleasure of Jehovah shall prosper in his hand. He shall see of the travail of his soul and shall be satisfied."

TRANSFORMATIONS BY THE RIVERS OF BABYLON

159. The Scattered Nation. The Hebrew people were by no means annihilated by the fearful experiences through which they had passed. Northern Israel, to be sure, was now being absorbed by the races among whom the Assyrian had scattered it, and it was destined never to reappear in history as an independent nation; but Judah was still living, though torn into three parts.

The Palestine Fragment. The largest of these three parts was still to be found in Palestine. When conquerors carried people away, as Sargon and Nebuchadrezzar had done, they took the city dwellers, those who had amassed wealth or acquired skill in workmanship and trading, or had been connected with the king and the aristocratic families. They hardly touched the poor or the country dwellers. These latter, scattered like sheep without a shepherd, had to shift for themselves. And a difficult time they had of it, between earning a living in a devastated country and defending themselves from enemies who now swept in from the borders to pick up the lands and the opportunities which the exiles had left behind. Ammonites, Moabites, Philistines, and Edomites all swarmed in; and besides plundering and settling they took dire vengeance on the defenseless Judeans for the raids they and their ancestors had suffered under Judean kings. The Edomites were particularly cruel and aggressive, partly because they were being pressed out of their own lands by the desert Nabateans, and they seized southern Judea as far north as Hebron. Ezekiel, the priest who had been carried with the exiles to Babylon and there became their pastor, utters a curse upon the Edomites

(Ezek. 25$^{12-14}$), as indeed he does upon all the invading nations. This group of peasant Hebrews nevertheless survived and became an important factor in Jewish life after the return from exile.

160. **The Egyptian Fragment.** The next largest group of Hebrews was to be found in Egypt. A considerable body had

From Breasted's "Ancient Times."

FIG. 118—RUINS OF ELEPHANTINE

This town was built on an island in the Nile about four miles north of the first cataract. Some of these houses are as old as the twenty-seventh century B.C. How does it happen that buildings of sun-dried brick and documents of fragile papyrus have been so long preserved?

To this island came Jews in the days of Nebuchedrezzar or earlier, and formed an enterprising commercial colony. Later exiles increased their number to six or seven hundred. They built here a stone temple to Jehovah. This temple was destroyed by a mob led by jealous Egyptian priests, and its gold and silver vessels were stolen in the year 400 B.C., as is shown by the letter in Fig. 119.

fled thither after the assassination of Gedaliah (Sec. 157), taking the prophet Jeremiah with them. These settled in the frontier towns of Tahpanhes and Migdol, both fortress cities on the main highway between Egypt and Palestine; but when the Pharaoh Amasis withdrew trading privileges from the foreigners in these towns in 564 B.C., the Hebrews either returned to Palestine or joined others of their nation in upper Egypt. Of the existence of these other Hebrews in Egypt we now have ample evidence. Not only do Jeremiah and Ezekiel refer to colonists in Memphis and Pathros (upper Egypt), but recent discoveries on an island in the Nile River opposite Assuan confirm the fact that there was for more than a century a flourishing settlement there. The people had doubtless filtered in in small groups throughout the period of the later Judean kings, attracted by greater chances for wealth and comfort and peace than troublous Palestine could afford.

The discoveries include legal documents of various kinds, contracts, bills of sale, marriage records, and letters. One remarkable letter, dated November, 408 B.C., asks the assistance of the Persian governor of Judea—Bagohi by name —in rebuilding the temple of Jahu (Jehovah) which a recent outbreak of foreigners had destroyed. This temple, which is described as of considerable architectural worth, proves that within a generation after the destruction of Solomon's temple at Jerusalem the Hebrews in Egypt were an influential people, and it furnishes us with an explanation why in the time of Christ Alexandria in Egypt could become the chief seat of Jewish commercial power and the intellectual centre of the Jewish world.

161. The Home of the Exiles in Babylonia. The third and smallest group of Hebrews—the Judeans or Jews, as we must henceforth call them—was the band of exiles transplanted by the rivers of Babylon. Practically all of the wealth and culture, the brains and skill of the Jewish race was here, and on this soil grew those ideas and ideals that were destined to control the Jewish world down to our day. This group deserves our extended attention.

As a place to live in, Babylonia was far better than Palestine. Instead of a mountainous country where only by incessant terracing and cultivating one might wrest a living

from the soil, the Jews now possessed a rich alluvial plain
where crops grew almost of themselves. A stable government under wise kings had created and preserved impressive
irrigation works for the benefit of all. Great reservoirs like

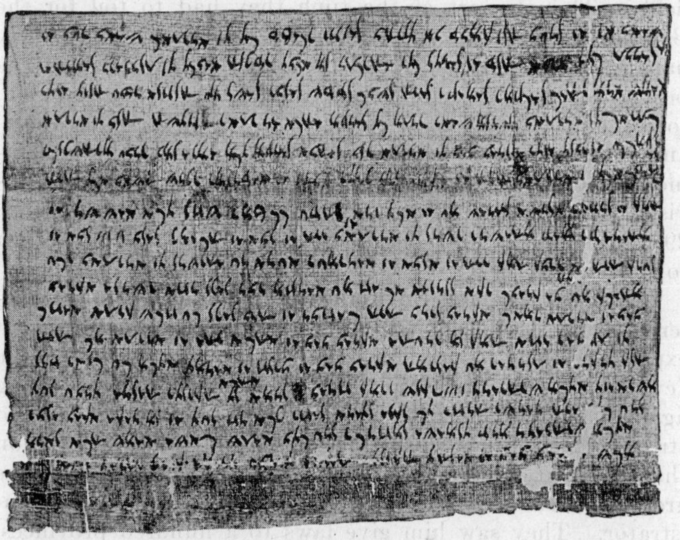

From Breasted's "Ancient Times."

Fig. 119—ARAMAIC LETTER FROM EGYPT

A piece of papyrus discovered in 1907 in the ruins of Elephantine (Fig. 118).
The letter tells of the destruction of the Jewish temple of Jehovah and
requests the Persian governor of Palestine to use his influence with the
Persian governor of Egypt to allow the Jews to rebuild. What is papyrus?
Why should the letter not be written in Hebrew (Sec. 192)? Compare the
characters with that of Fig. 100.

that near Sippar, huge navigable canals like the Kabaru
(the river Chebar of Ezekiel) that ran southeast from Babylon to Nippur, and smaller intersecting canals that meshed
the whole plain, were both life-bringers to the soil and arteries
of traffic. In the midst of this richness the Jewish exiles were

transplanted, with their families and social bonds hardly at all disturbed. They lived on little *tels* or artificial mounds made by the ruins of former cities, each named in some fanciful way, as Storm Hill, Salt Hill, Forest Hill, and from these they went forth each day to cultivate the surrounding fields. Though part of the time they had to toil for the Babylonian monarch, the Jews ought to have been relatively happy. So long as they paid the imperial tax and kept the peace they were free to keep up their customs and religion, to rear and educate their children, to traffic here and there, and even to rise to positions of responsibility in the government. Jeremiah told them that they were well off and advised them to settle down to business and grow rich (Jer. 29⁵). There was only one restriction: they could not return to Palestine.

162. **Their Cultural Environment.** To be suddenly transferred from the border to the centre of great affairs was an experience likely to shock into life whatever latent powers the Jews possessed. Hitherto they had been outsiders, plotting against a government of which they knew only its armed strength; now they were living in the midst of a civilization that touched all the interests of life. They now saw the great Nebuchadrezzar not as a conqueror but as an administrator. They saw him give laws to a hundred provinces, and rule a court where thousands of officials transacted the business of a vast empire. They saw him foster the welfare of his people by devotion to agriculture and commerce, establishing his throne upon a foundation of wealth and loyalty rather than upon the force of arms alone. They saw him rebuild and adorn Babylon and surround it by a double wall, the outer one fifty miles in circumference, defended by countless towers, broad enough at the top for four chariots to drive abreast. They saw him dedicate his sanctuary of Bel the sun-god—a huge pyramid of brick roofed with cedar of Lebanon and adorned with gold. They looked with wonder at his palace, decorated everywhere with brilli-

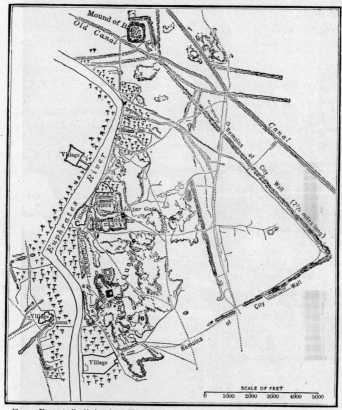

From Breasted's "Ancient Times."

Fig. 120—MAP OF BABYLON

Observe the great size of Babylon as compared with the cities of Palestine
(Figs. 13, 37, 78, etc.).   Find the former channel of the Euphrates, the
site of Fig. 121 and the site of Fig. 123.   The Hanging Gardens (Fig. 123)
were within the palace enclosure.   The city wall also enclosed a large
space on the other side of the river.

Fig. 121—THE ISHTAR GATE

(See description on opposite page)

antly colored tiles arranged in pictures and geometric designs, vast enough to form an exhaustless quarry of bricks for succeeding generations. They gazed with awe at the hanging gardens he built to solace his Median wife for the loss of the mountains of her childhood, itself a mountain built in terraces of brick, each terrace capped with a sheet of lead and a layer of earth, then planted with trees and flowers. On the topmost terrace shone a palace for the queen.

These symbols of wealth and power opened the eyes of the Jews. They saw the advantages that went with citizenship in such an empire, the possibilities that lay for them in education, commerce, government; and many of them responded with a vigor that has always been a badge of their race. The exile therefore was for the Jews a period of radical transformation. It wrought a fundamental change in their point of view, so that instead of being provincial and local in their interests they became interested in the whole world; and a change in their dominant activities from agricultural to commercial. The impression then stamped upon the national character has never faded out. The Jews have from that day to this been citizens of the world; they have powerfully shaped its history and largely dominated its commerce. Nearly every age has had its Disraeli and its Rothschild.

163. **Their Religious Transformation.** The most remarkable change that the Jews underwent was in their religion. They lost one faith and found another. Or more accurately, the ideas they once held about Jehovah and his relation to his chosen people gave place, under the preaching of the prophets and the stern trend of events, to those that were

---

The towers of this gate are the largest and most striking of the ruins of old Babylon. They are nearly 40 feet high and covered with reliefs in brick, some plain and some of colored enamel. Bulls and griffins alternate, 575 of them, each about a yard high. The bull was sacred to Ramman, the weather-god, and the griffin—a walking serpent with scaly coat and tail, and the head with a forked tongue—was the emblem of Marduk, the great god of Babylon. Nebuchadrezzar was the builder, about 600 B.C.

broader and more spiritual, more humble and yet more ambitious. Jehovah, the old national deity whose worship had
been exclusively theirs since Moses' time, was now seen to
be the God of the whole earth, whom any nation might worship. The disasters that had fallen upon their nation were

Fig. 122—COLORED BRICK LION

One of the many lions built into the wall bounding the street of Babylon that
led to the Ishtar gate. The road was made by Nebuchadrezzar for the
processionals of the god Marduk. The lions advance to meet the processions. Some are white with yellow manes, others yellow with red
manes. The background is light or dark blue. Each lion is six feet long
and there are sixty of them on each side of the street.

the means by which God was purifying them for a great
spiritual task; and that task was to make God and his service known to all men. Religion became the chief end and
occupation of life for many of the Jews, the true Israel became a nation of priests, the state became a church, Israelit-
ism became Judaism.

To be sure, all the Jews in Babylonia did not experience
this change. The fascination of the splendid ritual of Bel
worship took some away; some married Babylonian wives
and drifted into heathenism; some became absorbed in business, and the growing pile of shekels hid from their sight

gods of every kind. So the sifting process that began generations before, even in Elijah's day, continued through the
exile and after, until only the most intensely religious na-
tures were left to form the Judaism of the latter days.

Fig. 123—HANGING GARDENS OF BABYLON
An imaginative reconstruction.

Built by Nebuchadrezzar to please his Median wife. Find the queen; the
river Euphrates. The elephant and the camels are supposed to be alive;
other animals are statues. Does such a structure seem improbable?

164. **Biblical Testimony to the Change.** As we read certain portions of the Bible we can see this change in thought
clearly reflected. In the book of Lamentations (e. g.,
chaps. 1 and 2) we look upon the horrors of the siege of
Jerusalem and hear the groans of a people who are being
despoiled of their land and their God. It is the cry of cap-

tives who are leaving behind all that they hold dear; the wail of the deported and the hopeless, conscious only of their grief. In such Psalms as the one hundred and thirty-seventh we see the first recovery from the shock, the sullen anger that will not permit them to enter into the life of their captors but that curses the conqueror and longs for revenge:

"O daughter of Babylon—happy shall he be that re-
    wardeth thee as thou hast served us.
Happy shall he be that taketh and dasheth thy little
    ones against the rock."

Now the voice of another psalmist is heard (Ps. 130) calling from the depths of repentance to a God who can forgive iniquity; for the consciousness that the prophets of old were right and that Judah has brought this catastrophe upon herself has dawned upon him:

"If thou, Jehovah, shouldst mark iniquities,
    O Lord, who could stand?
But there is forgiveness with thee!

My soul waiteth for the Lord
More than watchmen for the morning."

As if in answer to this prayer the prophet Ezekiel has a vision. He sees a valley full of dry bones (Ezek. 37[1-14]). At the word of his prophecy the breath of the Lord blows upon them, and the men once dead rise again a mighty host. Even thus shall Jehovah become Judah's savior:

"I will put my spirit in you and you shall live, and I will place you in your own land; and you shall know that I, Jehovah, have spoken it and shall perform it."

While Judah is still incredulous that help will come, an unknown prophet (Isaiah 21[1-10]) scans the horizon and discovers world events that promise restoration to God's people. From **Elam and Media** in the east comes the sound of rumbling

FIG. 124—PORTRAIT OF CYRUS

The oldest known relic of Persian sculpture, set up about 538 B.C. at the royal residence of Cyrus, Pasargadae (Murghab), after he had conquered Babylonia. Note that the features are not Semitic but Aryan. The crown Cyrus wears is borrowed from Egypt and the four wings are those of an Assyrian cherub (*cf.* Ezek. 1⁵⁻⁹).

chariots and trampling horsemen. Like a whirlwind these forces gather and sweep on toward Babylon. They smite that great city with its gods and scatter it as dust of the thrashing-floor. But the winnowed grain of Judah shall not be harmed; rather it shall be precious seed for a new sowing.

So grief has passed through the phases of revenge and repentance to hope, and hope shall some day become a vision of service and blessing.

165. **The Master Mind of the Exile.** The master mind of the age was Ezekiel. He was a prophet by nature and a priest by education; a man of insight into spiritual values and a planner of definite methods for the expression and cultivation of religion. He dealt with the specific problems of his fellow exiles, analyzed the present situation as due to the inefficiency and greed and oppression of Judah's earlier rulers, cheered the people with promises of God's help, cursed their foes for them, pictured the glories of Palestine when God should miraculously reclothe it with verdure for their use, and drew up an elaborate and detailed plan for a rebuilded city and temple and for a temple ritual. In his view the whole nation, from prince and high priest down to the humblest Levite, should exist for the worship of God. Feasts and holy days, processions and sacrifices were all outlined, with the Sabbath the crowning day of all the week. It was Ezekiel who found the practical means by which a people who had ceased to exist as a state could still survive as a church. The Judaism of the next four centuries was the creation largely of this genius.

166. **The Literary Activity of the Exile.** Other minds in this period were keenly alive to the necessity of preserving Israel's religion and teaching the lessons that the disastrous past and present were meant to convey. Their method was that of history writing. They took the old stories that were common property of the Hebrews, the hero-tales, state chronicles and folk-songs that already had been written

down in a masterly way in earlier days, and set them into a framework of moral interpretation where we find them to-day—the books of Deuteronomy, Judges, Samuel, and Kings. The portraits and stories of the past now become the text of sermons intended to show how Jehovah had always rewarded faithfulness and always punished sin. The work of these unknown editors changed a book of history into a Bible; took facts and showed their meaning and moral value, so that all who read might shape their own conduct more righteously. We must therefore class these unknown humble writers among the permanent benefactors of the race; for certainly no book of history ever written has had a fraction of the influence exerted by the Old Testament narratives.

167. **The Rise of the Synagogue.** During the dark days of the exile was born an institution that was destined to have the greatest conceivable influence in shaping the thought and life of Jews. It was the synagogue. Bereft now of their homeland, of their rulers and their temple, the people reasserted in a new and purer form the democratic instincts that even overwhelming calamities had not been able to crush out. Each community became responsible for its own spiritual and, to an extent, its political life. On the returning Sabbaths all the people came together in an assembly in some specific place or building, and there the law and the prophets were read, instruction was given, alms were received and distributed, and the spirit of religion and brotherhood was kept alive. The name synagogue was applied to the institution itself or to the building in which the meetings were held. The synagogue was under the supervision of the elders in general and of a ruler of the synagogue in particular. When the Jews returned to Palestine they took this institution with them. Every village of Palestine came in time to have one; and when the nation was dispersed in Persian, Greek and Roman times, in fact even down to the present day,

wherever the Jew went, with him went the synagogue.
From India to Spain and San Francisco synagogues to-day
bear witness to the existence of that fraternal democracy
where all are equal under the law.

XXIV

CYRUS AND THE FAITHFUL PATRIOTS

168. The Rise of Cyrus.   When the great Nebuchadrezzar died there were only feeble hands to grasp his sceptre.   A succession of weak monarchs followed, the last of whom was more of an antiquarian than a ruler; for while he dug over ruins and restored ancient temples, his son Belshazzar attended to affairs of state.   This is why the book of Daniel (chap. 5) calls Belshazzar king.

But while the power of Babylon waned, a new star was rising on the eastern horizon.   It was Cyrus, king of a little province called Anshan, a dependency of Media east of the Zagros mountains.   Cyrus revolted against his overlord Astyages, doubtless for good reasons; and when the two armies came together, the army of the Mede went over in a body to Cyrus, taking its king along as prisoner.   Thus in the year 549 B.C. Cyrus without a blow became master of the Median empire with its capital city Ecbatana and its treasure.   This empire comprised modern Persia, northern Assyria, Armenia, and part of Asia Minor as far west as the river Halys.   Treating the Medes as allies rather than a conquered people, he held his course westward, seized northern Mesopotamia and attacked Crœsus, the rich king of Lydia who barred his way to the sea.   Having conquered him he made his capital, Sardis, the chief seat of power in the west, and from that base subdued the Greek colonists that fringed the western border of Asia.   In three years he had become master of nearly all southwestern Asia from the river Indus to the Ægean.

Cyrus next turned to Babylon which alone stood in the way of a united Asiatic empire.   In 539 B.C. he appeared before its gates, having been invited, it is said, by the priesthood of that city who were disgusted with the way their king had honored other gods than theirs. These priests opened the gates, the king's son and coregent Belshazzar was slain while feasting, and the king himself was captured and deported. Thus Babylonia, and with it southern Meso-

FIG. 125—DREAM TABLET

Found at Erech. It contains the interpretation of two dreams by a seer. They are dated, 548 B.C. Translation: "In the month Tebet, day 15th, year 7th of Nabonidus, king of Babylon, Shum-ukin says as follows: "The great star Dilbet, Kaksidi, the moon, and the sun I saw in my dream. It means favor for Nabonidus, king of Babylon, my lord, and favor for Belshazzar the son of the king my lord. May my ear attend to them." The second dream is similar. Compare the dreams in Daniel (4⁴⁻¹⁷) and the inability of the astrologers sometimes to interpret them (Dan. 4¹⁸, 5⁷⁻⁹).

potamia, Syria, and Palestine—all southwestern Asia—passed from the rule of the Semitic race to the rule of the Aryan. It was destined to remain in Aryan hands for a thousand years until the Arabs came in the seventh century of our era.

169. **The Policy of Cyrus.** Cyrus must be ranked with the greatest men of history not only because of high personal character, but because of extraordinary powers of heart and intellect and will. Magnanimous, tolerant, wise, daring, he swayed men and nations with equal ease. He had a genius for evoking loyalty. He made allies of all his conquered foes and treated all religions with respect because he saw in them feeble or perverted attempts to worship the one true God, who for him was the Persian god Ahura Mazda. He

thus favored the god Marduk of Babylon and rebuilt his shrine, and he honored Jehovah the God of the Hebrews when occasion offered. This policy was naturally very pleasing to the host of different races and religions within his empire. It was part of his broad conception that an empire should be founded upon goodwill. He believed in making peoples happy. Where the Assyrian Sargon was wont to conquer, deport to distant provinces, and destroy the identity of nations, as he did in Israel's case; and where the policy of the Babylonian Nebuchadrezzar was to deport but preserve peoples, as he did

From Breasted's "Ancient Times."

Fig. 126—PERSIAN SOLDIERS

Palace guards, as shown by their fantastic dress. What are they carrying on their backs? What are their weapons? The figures are made of brightly colored glazed brick, a method of decoration much used by the Assyrians and Babylonians and Persians (*cf.* Figs. 121 and 122).

in Judah's case; the Persian Cyrus sought to restore all conquered and deported peoples to their native lands and there develop their local customs and religions, so that they might bless the hand that prospered them. The royal governors of Cyrus proved, as a rule, not oppressors but benefactors.

170. **The Remnant of Judah.** As in the case of other deported peoples, the Jews were given prompt permission to return to Palestine and rebuild their sanctuary and city.

The edict was issued in 538 B.C. Not all availed themselves of it. In fact, the good news fell for the most part upon listless ears. A new generation had grown up that knew not Jerusalem, a generation born to the soil of Babylon and attached to it by many ties. Life had become prosperous and easy for many of them. They had acquired lands, they had trafficked along great rivers and across rich mountains. Babylonian wives were already rearing mixed children to Jewish fathers and Babylonian gods. The splendor of Marduk's temple ritual had led some away to his shrine and Jehovah had become only a name. So in spite of prophet and priest, in spite of Sabbaths and feasts and prayers, of warnings and pleadings, Judah had mostly gone over to strange gods or no god. It was an inevitable situation. Indeed, it was paralleled in our day before the Great War, when the appeal of the Zionists that the Jews should return to Palestine found a feeble response; for what prosperous Jew would exchange the opportunities for wealth and power and culture afforded by London and New York for the primitive and almost prohibitive conditions of modern Jerusalem?

No wonder the prophets spoke of those pious ones who still cherished their old patriotism as the faithful remnant. They were indeed but a fragment; yet it was the seed of a precious harvest for mankind. Renan says: "We may say that in the history of Judaism this is the critical hour, the hour which determined life or death. If the return had not taken place, Judah would have shared the fate of Israel; it would have blended with the East. The Hebrew scriptures would have been lost. Christianity would not have existed. The small troupe which crossed the desert therefore carried the future with it, and definitely founded the religion of humanity."

171. **The First Return.** In 537 B.C. the first little band started on the eight-hundred-mile journey from the river Chebar to Jerusalem; they were but a handful. There was Joshua the priest, descendant of Zadok the high priest under

David, and Zerubbabel, prince of the royal house of David. With them went their families, servants, friends, together with a few loyal Jews and many Levites. There could not have been more than a few hundred. After this first return there were doubtless many others straggling along the years; and yet we feel certain that the figure of 42,000 given in the book of Ezra applies to all the members of the Persian colony a century later, of whom the peasant population that had never been deported formed the largest part.

FIG. 127—CYLINDER OF CYRUS

It records the capture of Babylon by Cyrus 539 B.C. "Without battle and without fighting Marduk [god of Babylon] made him (Cyrus) enter into his city of Babylon; . . . and Nabonidus the king who feared him [the god] not, he delivered into his hand." The priests of Marduk were disloyal to Nabonidus and treacherously opened the city gates to Cyrus.

Cyrus is said to have aided the band with grants of money, to have ordered his governors across the river Euphrates to help, and to have sent back the sacred vessels that Nebuchadrezzar had taken from the house of Jehovah.   But the expense of maintaining the colony in the ruined city and the neglected land until they could become self-supporting fell upon the wealthy Jews who stayed behind in Babylonia. They no doubt felt that this was the best way of showing their loyalty to a good cause—to stay where they could make money and contribute to the well-being of their enthusiastic but visionary fellow religionists.   History is repeating itself in precisely this feature to-day: Palestine has long been financed by Europe and America, and must be for a long time to come.

172. **Jehovah-Worship Re-established.**   We can imagine the mingled joy and grief with which the exiles greeted their holy city.   There were some in the band who as children had played about its streets; and now with tottering steps they led the others through the ruined gates, over the heaps of former walls and houses until they stood within the sacred precinct on Mount Moriah and found the great rock of sacrifice.   This was the focal point of all their thinking and the true goal of their pilgrimage.   Here they scraped aside the débris of fifty years, rolled together a few stones for an altar, and once more offered an oblation to Jehovah on the spot where he had "set his name."   Now at last they had re-established connection between earth and heaven. Once more were they Jehovah's people, and Jehovah would now fulfil all the visions seen by his prophets of a new Jerusalem, the joy of the whole earth, and of scattered peoples flocking to it.

"It shall come to pass in the latter days that the mountain of Jehovah's house shall be established on the top of the mountains, and it shall be exalted above the hills; and peoples shall flow unto it.   And many nations shall go and say, 'Come and let us go up to the mountain of Jehovah, and to the house of the God of Jacob; and he will teach us of his ways, and we will walk in his paths. From out of Zion shall go forth the law, and the word of Jehovah from Jerusalem; and he will judge between many peoples and will decide concerning strong nations afar off: and they shall beat their swords into ploughshares and their spears into pruning-hooks; nation shall not lift up sword against nation, neither shall they learn war any more. But they shall sit every man under his vine and under his fig-tree; and none shall make them afraid; for the mouth of Jehovah of hosts has spoken it.' "—Micah 4$^{1-4}$.

Not yet, however, had the fulness of the time come. Delays and disappointments were still in store.

173. **The Struggle for a Temple.** The returned exiles first laid the foundations of their new temple (536 B.C.). In this project the people of the land wished to share, for they were partly at least Jews in blood and in tradition. But the returned exiles refused their offer. It may be that the racially pure Jews from Babylonia did not like to associate with those of mixed race and mixed religion—the descendants of the confused peoples whom Sargon and Nebuchadrezzar had left in Palestine; or it may be that they feared to forfeit their independence and their charter by admitting outsiders. At any rate, the refusal was unfortunate, for it made eternal enemies of the older inhabitants. The immediate result was that the latter blocked all transport of timber from Lebanon, and the building of the temple had therefore to cease. For sixteen years nothing was done, while the hatred grew.

174. **Zerubbabel's Hopes.** In the meantime things happened in the outer world. Cyrus died in 529 B.C. His son Cambyses had a short reign, following which came chaos. The empire seemed to be going to pieces. Even after Darius had been proclaimed king there arose nine pretenders in different parts of the empire who desperately disputed the throne with the newcomer, so that not until 519 did Darius

finally master the situation. This period of chaos set the hearts of the Palestinian community to fluttering. Might it not be that Jehovah would now liberate the Jews completely and restore to them the throne of their father David?

Two prophets, Haggai and Zechariah, arose to fan the hope into a blaze. They proclaimed that if only Jehovah's people would perform their vows and build his temple, he would do his part and establish his kingdom. Zerubbabel, their governor, was at hand, a noble prince of the Davidic line. He should be crowned. With feverish expectancy the people leaped to the task of completing their temple structure. Perhaps because the secret hope they were nursing leaked out, the Persian governor of Syria to whom Zerubbabel was subordinate attempted to stop the work. But the Jews claimed that they had authority in their original decree from Cyrus. The governor wrote Darius for instructions. Darius looked in the state records, found the decree, and gave orders that the temple-building should not be hindered. Accordingly the Jews pushed on the work and completed the structure in 516 B.C. But in the meantime Zerubbabel disappeared from sight. Whether his ambition became known to Darius and he was put out of the way, or whether he was removed because of a general change of policy, the fact remains that henceforth Palestine was ruled by a Persian satrap, as indeed all the provinces of the great empire of Darius were. The Messianic hope of the Jews was dashed to pieces and did not reappear until the days of the successful Maccabean revolt nearly four centuries later.

175. **What the Temple Meant.** Although in Josiah's reign (Sec. 143) the new law-book had declared that Jehovah should be worshipped henceforth only at Jerusalem, yet when his temple had been destroyed and his people scattered, the exiles in various lands felt at liberty to build other shrines. We know for certain of a Jehovah temple in Egypt (Sec. 160). The temple at Jerusalem therefore must have served primarily as a place of worship for the people of that

city and community. But there was a sentimental connection still between all Jews, wherever exiled, and their national home; and so the new temple became a rallying-point for Jewish patriotism and religion. To the old-new shrine gifts were sent across great deserts and sundering seas. To it pilgrims were attracted in greater and greater numbers through the years as the worship and ritual were developed, their caravans drawing thither to the great feasts from the four corners of the world. And here at length grew up that hierarchy of priests, sustained by a body of sacred law, that constituted the very life of Judaism. By the new temple the gulf of the exile and the dispersion was bridged: over it passed the tradition from the destroyed state to the coming church.

176. The Psalms of the Second Temple. The joy of having completed the temple gave rise to an outburst of song. Many of these poems have been preserved in our book of Psalms. They all speak of the nation's sense of gratitude for sin forgiven, their pleasure in the shrine upon the holy hill, their love for Jehovah who thus has prospered them, and their trust for the future. The opening lines of a few of them give a correct hint of their spirit:

"Jehovah, thou hast been favorable to thy land,
    Thou hast brought back the captivity of Jacob."
                                                —Psalm 85.

"His foundation is in the holy mountains.
    Jehovah loveth the gates of Zion
    More than all the dwellings of Jacob."—Psalm 87.

"O sing to Jehovah a new song,
    For he has done marvellous things."—Psalm 98.

"How amiable are thy tabernacles,
    O Jehovah of hosts!

My soul longs, yea, even faints for the courts of
Jehovah."—Psalm 84.

This period of enthusiasm was as brief as it was joyous.
When next the voice of the psalmist breaks upon the ear,
the garment of praise has given place to the spirit of heavi-
ness, the song has become a wail.

XXV

THE SUFFERINGS OF THE FAITHFUL

177. Palestine again Oppressed. Of the course of Persian history, of which Jewish history is now a part, we have a fairly full knowledge. Darius reigned from 521 to 485 B.C. This is that Darius whose satraps in Asia Minor could not prevent the Asiatic Greeks and the Athenians from burning Sardis, and who ordered his cupbearer to say to him three times a day: "Sire, remember the Athenians." This is he who invaded Greece and met defeat at Marathon in 490 B.C. After him ruled Xerxes, whose vast armaments raised for the destruction of Greece were shattered at Thermopylæ, and Salamis and Platæa. Then came Artaxerxes, who kept up a losing fight with the Ionians and Greeks and whose title to fame in Jewish history rests on his kindness to Nehemiah his cupbearer. Palestine in the days of all these kings was a Persian province governed by a satrap whose centre of power was somewhere in the north and who left local control largely in the hands of the high priest at Jerusalem.

Though the period of Jewish history that follows the rebuilding of the temple is very obscure, we know in a general way what the condition of the colony was. The lot of the Jews was hard. No merciful Cyrus watched over their interests, but satraps oppressed and hostile neighbors raided them. The second Isaiah well describes the plight of the faithful:

> "It is a people spoiled and plundered,
> They are all snared in holes,
> And hidden in prison houses.

They have become a spoil
With none to rescue,
An object of plunder
With none to say, ' Restore,' "—Isaiah 42²².

This period of wretchedness must have seemed to the pious
Jews to be hopeless. Not only was there oppression from

FIG. 128—"SHUSHAN THE PALACE"

A restoration of the throne-hall in the palace of Xerxes (485–465 B.C.) at Susa.
    It covered an area of two and a half acres and consisted of a pillared throne-
    room in which were 36 fluted columns 67 feet high.   The ceiling was of
    cedar of Lebanon.   Externally the building was adorned with columns as
    shown above, the capitals of which consisted of the heads and shoulders
    of oxen, back to back.   The cornice, as well as the various friezes of the
    interior were of enamelled brick of bright colors, forming rosettes, war-
    riors, lions and geometric patterns.   This is one of the many buildings
    that constituted the palace of Queen Esther.

without, but corruption within. The old enthusiasm with
which the remnant had returned from exile had waned; the
old devotion to the re-established temple had died down.
Sordid human nature had reasserted itself in priest and ruler,
and the old evils of class hatred and social injustice were
again intrenching themselves. The humble man who did
right and kept the faith was condemned to poverty and persecution and then confronted by the vicious theory that his
sufferings were Jehovah's punishment for his sins. The day
was indeed dark and the night starless.

178. **Nehemiah to the Rescue.** The story of Nehemiah breaks in upon the despondency of the times like a sunrise. This great patriot, born of course in exile, was cupbearer to the Persian king Artaxerxes I at Susa. To him there came a deputation from the inhabitants of Judea, bringing news of the defenseless plight of the holy city and the urgent need of help. The story of the sufferings of his fellow countrymen made Nehemiah so sad that when he next stood before the king his face showed traces of weeping. When the king learned the cause of his sorrow he was gracious enough to grant Nehemiah leave of absence, with passports to the governors beyond the river Euphrates and authority to make levies of wood in the king's forest and to rebuild the walls of the city. A military escort was also furnished. Arriving in Jerusalem in 445 B.C. Nehemiah found conditions that well might have discouraged him. The high-priestly rulers were suspicious and hostile because his authority superseded theirs. They and the wealthy class had been having things their own way with the people regardless of the claims of justice, and they feared to have light let in. There were also hostile neighbors who were little enough inclined to see Jerusalem become a strong and controlling city: Samaritans on the north first of all, then Ammonites on the east, Arabians on the south, and Philistines on the west. Couple this suspicion and hostility with the general poverty and lack of leadership in Judea itself, and the size of Nehemiah's task becomes apparent.

179. **His Efficiency and Bravery.** Nevertheless he went to work. He made a tour of the ruined city by night and then reported to those in authority that he would begin rebuilding without delay. For this undertaking he divided the wall into sections and placed each section in charge of a definite person—a priest or householder or head of family, so that responsibility and friendly rivalry might hasten the work. But when Sanballat, who ruled Palestine from Samaria as a sub-satrap, heard of this renewed attempt to

strengthen Jerusalem he violently opposed it. He let loose
upon the builders certain guerilla warriors from Samaria
and the bordering regions who harried the workmen without
mercy. Then Nehemiah organized the citizens of Jerusalem
for defense, stationed some of them with arms at strategic
places, gave weapons to the builders themselves so that they
could turn from trowel to sword without loss of time. A
trumpeter was stationed on the walls to give signal of the
point of special attack. Nehemiah himself was everywhere
all the time; he even slept in his clothes. In this way the
work proceeded with feverish haste until in fifty-two days
the whole encircling wall was completed. Sanballat was
chagrined to find himself outclassed. He tried four times to
entice Nehemiah out of the city on the pretense of a conference, planning to have him assassinated, but Nehemiah
was too wary. He tried to scare him by threatening to ac-
cuse him of treason before Artaxerxes. But all to no purpose.
Nehemiah then organized the city for permanent defense
and administration under his brother as governor. A census
was taken as a means of determining who were of strict
Jewish descent, and many Jews who had settled in neighboring towns were transferred to Jerusalem to help fill in the
vacant places behind the new walls. In these ways the city
was again put in habitable form after a hundred and fifty
years of desolation, and the external part of Nehemiah's
commission was accomplished.

180. **Nehemiah's Reforms.** But Nehemiah found it
necessary to strengthen the struggling colony in other ways.
During the building process the hard lot of the poor became
wofully apparent. Having left their farms and other profitable work to build the city's walls as a labor of love, they
found themselves out of bread. Some had mortgaged their
lands to wealthy men only to have their creditors foreclose
and take their lands away. Others had to sell their children
into slavery to raise money to live. Nehemiah called the
capitalists together, appealed to their common blood and

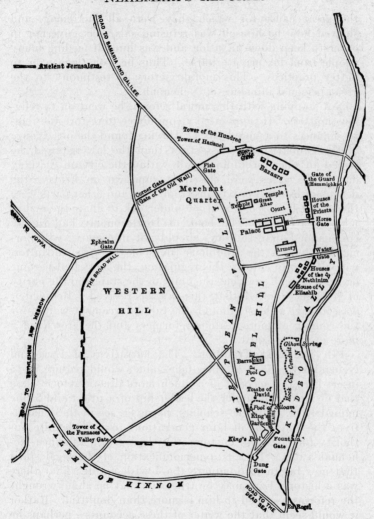

Ancient Jerusalem.

ROAD TO SAMARIA AND GALILEE

Tower of the Hundred
Tower of Hananel
Sheep Gate
Fish Gate
Bazaars
Gate of the Guard (Hammiphkad)
Corner Gate
Gate of the Old Wall
Merchant Quarter
Temple
Great Altar
Temple Court
Houses of the Priests
Horse Gate
Palace
Ephraim Gate
Armory
Water Gate
THE BROAD WALL
Houses of the Nethinim
House of Eliashib
WESTERN HILL
TYROPEAN VALLEY
OPHEL HILL
KIDRON VALLEY
Gihon Spring
Rock Cut Conduit
Barracks or Pool
Tombs of David
Pool of Siloam
STAIRS
King's Garden
Pool of King's
Fountain Gate
Tower of the Furnaces
Valley Gate
King's Pool
Dung Gate
VALLEY OF HINNOM
ROAD TO THE DEAD SEA
En-Rogel
ROAD TO JOPPA
ROAD TO BETHLEHEM AND HEBRON

Fig. 129—THE JERUSALEM OF NEHEMIAH

the great cause for which they were all sacrificing, and showed how he himself was refusing salary as governor in order to keep down taxation and was himself feeding many people from his private purse. Thus he won them over to better practices. This moral victory is testimony to the great personal influence of Nehemiah.

Not stopping with this moral reform, he went on to religious matters. He appointed a committee to restore the temple finances to a sound basis. Having found the observance of the Sabbath much less strict than the law required, he issued an edict forbidding trade within the city on the holy day. The gates were closed at sundown on Friday; the dealers in fish and provisions from Tyre and other parts were thrust out by force. Next, he undertook to abate the evil of mixed marriages. The book of Deuteronomy had rigidly commanded that Hebrews should not intermarry with foreigners; but in the troublous times of the exile and after, with no one to enforce this regulation, the Jews had become lax. Nehemiah saw that the unity of the state and the purity of religion required that this law be revived. Revived it was, in part at least, though the full enforcement waited for the coming of more zealous reformers and the growth of a more exclusive spirit.

181. **The Ezra Tradition.** The narratives of Ezra and Nehemiah, if taken at their face value, would require us to insert here the account of a much more drastic reform than that of Nehemiah under the leadership of a priest and scribe named Ezra. Modern scholars, however, see in these narratives the endeavor of later generations to give definite authority for laws and customs that had grown up since Nehemiah's day. Ezra is a personification of the legal spirit that now began to dominate the Jewish mind. That there was a historic Ezra may be true, but that he alone wrought the reforms ascribed to him is more than doubtful. Rather it would seem that the writer of these accounts—perhaps he who wrote also the books of Chronicles—projected the ideas

and institutions of his own day (c. 250 B.C.) back into the earlier period. The laws ascribed to Ezra should therefore be ascribed to many reformers scattered over two centuries of time and finally collected and attached to Ezra's name.

These laws all have to do with religion: keeping marriages free from outside mixture; regulating offerings, worship, Sabbaths and feasts. They mark the growth of that spirit that Jesus so condemned in his day, by which men tithed mint, anise and cummin, but left undone the weightier matters of justice and mercy. From this time on, the Jewish religion becomes less and less a matter of the heart and

FIG. 130—CYLINDER SEAL OF DARIUS

(British Museum)

Represents a lion hunt. The horses are leaping over a dead lioness, while the king discharges arrows at her ramping mate. Above, the symbol of the god Ahura Mazda protecting Darius. Inscription in Persian, Median, and Babylonian: "I am Darius the great king."

deed and more a series of rules about the details of worship.

182. The Religious Interpreters of Judah's Suffering. Out of the crushed and trampled life of this period has arisen the sweet odor of the most wonderful religious literature the world has known. Never did men look within more earnestly to find in their own sin the cause of suffering, nor look above so hopefully to find in God their salvation. A host of singers arose, all of them unknown by name, who left in our book of Psalms the record of their spiritual experiences. To read the Psalms with their historic backgrounds in mind is to get a new conception of their meaning and beauty. In some the note of despair is heard:

"My God, my God, why hast thou forsaken me?"— Psalm 22.

"O God, thou hast cast us off, thou hast broken us down."—Psalm 60.

"Out of the depths have I cried unto thee, O Jehovah."
—Psalm 130.

Now a hope arises that God will hear and save:

"Have mercy upon me, O God, according to thy loving-kindness."—Psalm 51.

"In thee, O Jehovah, do I take refuge."—Psalm 71.

"In my distress I cried unto Jehovah,
And he answered me."—Psalm 120.

With deliverance comes the note of praise, and delight in the worship on Mount Zion:

"Jehovah is my light and my salvation;
Whom shall I fear?"—Psalm 27.

"O give thanks unto Jehovah, for he is good,
For his lovingkindness endures forever."—Psalm 107.

"I love Jehovah because he hath heard
My voice and my supplications."—Psalm 116.

The voice of prophecy is now raised almost for the last time in Hebrew history. Malachi, pondering on the sins of priest and people alike, proclaimed the need for a great moral awakening and for a new priesthood who should teach the way of righteousness. The author of Job, as he thought on the mystery of suffering, taught men to reject the old theory that God always punishes sinners and prospers the righteous; for the righteous are more often to be found suffering, while the wicked prosper. Instead he taught that all of life, suffering included, is a mystery, and the righteous must trust God's wisdom where they cannot understand his ways: "Though he slay me, yet will I trust him."

183. **The Second Isaiah.** But the greatest voice of the age and one of the great voices of all ages was the second Isaiah, who rose on the wings of prophetic rhapsody as he saw in downtrodden yet purified Israel the "Suffering Servant of Jehovah." Well might a nation accept so hard a fate if out of it could come an insight like his—an insight into God's wondrous character, his sovereignty over all the world, his righteousness contrasted with Israel's sin, his forgiveness over against Israel's faithlessness, his redeeming love for Israel his servant, and through that suffering servant his promised redemption for all mankind. It was this unknown prophet—called the second Isaiah because his prophecies are bound up with those of the Isaiah of Hezekiah's day in our book of Isaiah (chaps. 40–55)—who put stars into the sky of Judah's night and directed men's faith toward distant horizons of hope and the sunrise clouds beyond. The visions of the prophet were destined not to be fulfilled in the sense in which he perhaps understood them, but they voice the eternal hope of man for better things, and they illuminate with brilliant significance the career of Jesus of Nazareth who showed men and is still showing them how through suffering they may help God establish, not a kingdom of David, but a democracy of redeemed humanity.

THE CHURCH ABSORBS THE STATE

184. The Last Century of Persian Rule. The Jewish people were perhaps never happier than during the century that followed the reforms of Nehemiah. Behind the new walls Jerusalem found courage, peace and security. The meagre resources of Judea were developed. Under favoring edicts from the Great King the borders of Jewry were extended northward and into the plain of Sharon. Still the colony never became large; and because of its racial exclusiveness and its aloofness from the outside world and from the great lines of trade it remained an almost unknown factor in the great empire. Herodotus, who tells us much about the East in this period, apparently never heard of the Jews.

Persia allowed Judea a large measure of self-government; in fact, about the only requirements laid on her were that she should pay a definite tax, furnish a levy of youths for the royal standing army, and keep the peace. The local governor at Jerusalem was responsible to the satrap at Damascus, and he together with nineteen other satraps who administered the Persian empire reported to the Great King at one of his four capitals, Babylon, Susa, Persepolis, or Ecbatana. Since the disappearance of Zerubbabel (Sec. 174) the governor of Judea had been the high priest. His office therefore became one of increasing dignity, especially after it became hereditary. The high priest was virtually the head of the Jewish state from now until that state disappears from history.

185. Organization and Income of the Priests. Below the high priest stood an aristocratic ruling class made up of (a) descendants of the old families of wealth and royal blood

in the pre-exilic period, (b) priestly families, some of them
tracing their line from David's or even Aaron's day. Gradually the priestly families gathered to themselves the offices
and positions of social influence, and so took the place of the
lay aristocrats. The whole gov-
ernment became priestly. It is
easy to understand how this
transformation came about when
one considers the wealth that
came to priests. The law spec-
ified that all the best of a man's
produce of every kind should go
to them, amounting according
to Jewish tradition to one-forti-
eth of the whole (Num. 18¹²).
Moreover, when this had been
deducted, one-tenth of the entire
crop had to be paid to the Levites (lower priests and temple
officials), whose duty it was to
pass one-tenth of that tenth to
those higher up. When grain
was ground and baked, one loaf
in twenty-five had to go to the
priest. To the priest went the
first-born of all cattle, or a
money equivalent; to him the
redemption money of every first-

Fɪɢ. 131—ASSYRIAN DUL-
CIMERS

The lower part is the hollow
sounding-box. From it the
strings run to an upright post,
by which device strings of
different lengths are secured
The whole is attached to the
player by a belt, and can be
played while marching. The
Hebrews used harps, of which
this is one variety, on all
kinds of occasions (Job 21¹¹·¹²,
Amos 6⁵, I Sam. 10⁵, 18⁶)
Who is said to have invented
the harp (Gen. 4 ²¹)?

born male ($3.25, equivalent to perhaps $30 to-day). When
a Jew killed an animal for food, the shoulder, two cheeks and
stomach went to the priest. When he sheared a sheep he
had to pay a tenth of the wool. A part of every sacrificial
animal and every meal-offering, sin-offering, and trespass-
offering became priest-fees. Other fines and vows went by
the same road into the priests' pockets. The punctual payment of all these dues became a matter of conscience, a pre-

eminent act of righteousness and a guarantee that Jehovah
would in turn bless the giver. No wonder that under such
a system it paid to be a priest, and even to intrigue and
bribe and murder one's way into the high priest's chair!

186. **The Written Law.** While the priestly class tended
more and more to control both the civil and religious life of
the Jews, nevertheless there was a limit beyond which priests
could not safely go. There was a written law. We recall
that in Josiah's day (Sec. 141), the people had adopted such
a law, the nucleus of our book of Deuteronomy. This book
had been enlarged by the priests of the exile, who having no
longer any temple to serve turned all of their zeal into per-
fecting and elaborating the traditions of their worship.
Other additions, especially along the lines of ritual, followed
the rebuilding of the temple in 516 B.C., and still others in
continuous procession down into the Greek period. This
written law became the standard for all civil and religious
life, and since it was binding alike on priest and people it
became a great bulwark of popular rights. It and the synagogue are the two institutions that have kept Israel democratic all through the ages.

187. **The Scribes.** Reverence for the law was destined
to work a fateful change in the structure of Jewish life.
Since the law was supreme over priest and people, he who
had perfect knowledge of the law and was skilled in inter-
preting it would gradually rise to a position of power and
dignity in the state. Men who were learned in this way were
known as scribes. At first they were all priests, but later
laymen entered the ranks. This class, who began to be
prominent in the Persian period, came at last to have a
wider popular influence than the hereditary ruling class. In
Jesus' day the scribe overshadowed the priest.

188. **The Jews Outside Judea.** It must not be imagined
that the Palestinian Jews made up at this period the bulk of
the Jewish race. There were still thousands of others who
were destined never to see Palestine and who in a way had

little part in this intense religious life that was developing in Judea. There was the host still in Babylonia, transplanted by Nebuchadrezzar to new fields and now actually rooted there. Caught by the commercial spirit of the times, many

FIG. 132—TRUMPETS

Made from the horn of the wild goat or of the ram. The horns were soaked in oil until they became pliable, then were worked into the desired shape. While the Jews had beautiful silver trumpets, these old-fashioned ceremonial ones were used on special occasion, their sanctity dating from the time of Moses (Ex. 19¹⁶, 20¹⁸). Note the carving on the upper one. Trumpet blowing was an important feature of Jewish ritual, especially on fast-days, New Year's, and Jubilee year.

had engaged in trade in the great capital cities of the world, in Susa, Ecbatana, Persepolis, the towns of Mesopotamia and Syria, and in the seaports of Asia Minor and the Egyptian delta. In upper Egypt also the ancient Jewish colonies continued to flourish. We must not forget the prisoners of war who had been scattered by conquerors all over the East, as Artaxerxes Ochus scattered them in 350 B.C. after a revolt, and the slaves kidnapped by Phœnician dealers and sold in Mediterranean ports. These individuals and groups were like seeds driven by the winds to strange soils, but, true to type, reproduced in the course of years communities of Jews that had a wonderful influence on the trend of events, especially on the spread of Christianity in the first century after Christ. These foreign-dwelling Jews came to be called "The Dispersion."

189. **The Book of Esther.** In our Bible is a book written after the close of this period which, though not strictly historical, reflects accurately the life of the dispersion. It is the book of Esther. Here we see large numbers of Jews living in the midst of foreign and often hostile races, subject to the whims of governors and royal favorites, yet managing to save themselves by their wits and even to retaliate on their enemies. It is not on the whole an edifying picture, but it is redeemed somewhat by the intense though narrow patriotism that shines through it.

190. **The Influence of the Dispersion on Judaism.** Growing out of these contacts with the world there now began to develop two opposite tendencies in Jewish thought. One may be called the inclusive tendency, which looked upon all peoples as possible Jehovah-worshippers. This view was based upon the ideals of the great prophet, the second Isaiah, with his vision of a Messiah's kingdom embracing all the world. The other tendency is the exclusive, growing out of the teachings of Nehemiah and his reforming successors. This view drew a sharp distinction between Jew and Gentile, the worshippers of Jehovah and the heathen, and made more intense the feeling of separation and even of hostility between them. The numerous genealogies found throughout the Old Testament are silent witness to this pride of race. In some of the biblical prophets we find traces of the belief that all the heathen will some day meet with disaster at Jehovah's hand (Isaiah 24–27, Joel, Obadiah, and Zech. 9–14). But there is one remarkable book that upholds the broader view, the book of Jonah. It teaches that God has a wider sympathy than man; that when his prophet refuses to preach to a heathen city and even tries to run away from his duty, God brings him back and through him calls the great Nineveh to repentance. In the lands of the dispersion, naturally, the wider conception of Jehovah's sphere of influence and grace

prevailed; but within Judea the narrower view won acceptance. It culminated at the end of the Persian period in the great split known as the Samaritan schism.

191. The Samaritan Schism. There had never been any too much love between the inhabitants of the land who had never been deported and the faithful remnant that re-

Fɪɢ. 133—CYMBALS

(British Museum)

They served to mark the time in dancing or singing, and were used frequently with trumpets (Ez. 3¹⁰, I Chron. 15¹⁹, Ps. 150⁵).

turned from Babylon. There was, however, one bond between the two—there had been a considerable intermarrying. But as the exclusive spirit grew stronger in Judea this right of intermarriage became a serious bone of contention and at last caused a crisis. Manasseh, brother of the Jewish high priest, had married the daughter of a Samaritan magnate called Sanballat II (not Sanballat I of Nehemiah's day). The narrower religious party demanded that he divorce her. Rather than do this, Manasseh withdrew from Jerusalem at the invitation of his father-in-law, taking many priests with him who were doubtless in a similar predicament, and with Sanballat's money established a rival temple on Mount Gerizim.

Henceforth these two religious groups developed side by side, each charging that the other was the more debased in blood, and hating each other more and more cordially until in Jesus' day it could be truthfully said: "Jews have no dealings with Samaritans." It was this condition that put such a sting into the parable in which Jesus made a good Samaritan rescue the highwayman's victim while the self-righteous priest and Levite passed by on the other side. Down to the present day the Samaritan group has persisted, though reduced to less than two hundred individuals. Jacob, their high priest, still worships at Mount Gerizim and uses a copy of the same old Pentateuch that his ancestor brought with him from Jerusalem. (Fig. 111.)

192. Changes in Language and Thought. While the religious life of the Jews in Palestine was growing more narrow and intense, in other respects the world was impressing itself upon the little community. Their language was the first thing to go. In those days Aramaic was the language of practically all the nations who surrounded them; it was the language of business and government throughout Syria. Gradually therefore, through necessity, the Jews substituted the Aramaic for the classic Hebrew, until in the course of time the Hebrew scriptures were an unknown tongue, and when read in public had to be translated, or " targumed," by the reader, verse by verse. For popular use there were copies of the law in Aramaic. These Aramaic targums formed that Bible which the Jew knew by heart. (See Fig. 119.)

Contact with Persia also introduced ideas that were destined to have a growing fascination for the Jewish mind. While the Persian religion with its good god Ahura Mazda helped to confirm the Jewish conception of only one God, it introduced the notion that there were countless semi-divine creatures who did his bidding. These the Jews adopted as angels, and in due course enlarged and systematized their duties until there was very little left for Jehovah to do. Parallel to these was a series of angels of opposite nature, taking their character from Ahriman, the great opponent of Ahura Mazda. These were demons, with Satan at their head. To this evil one were now transferred some of the characteristics of Jehovah that the growing moral conceptions of the Jews could not reconcile with the divine character. One interesting instance, already alluded to (Sec.

FIG. 134—SAMARITAN PASSOVER

At the Passover time the entire Samaritan community, living at Nablus and comprising 160 people, encamps for ten days on the top of Mount Gerizim (Fig. 71). On the evening of the Passover just at sunset the paschal lambs are killed, skinned and roasted, in accordance with the directions in Exodus. During the night the lambs are eaten in the tents. The heads of households dress in white for the ceremony. All before the Great War wore the red fez or cap, symbol of Turkish citizenship.

67), is to be found in the books of Samuel and Chronicles. In the former we read (chap. 24[1]) that in a fit of unprovoked anger Jehovah stirred up David to number Israel. But when the chronicler, who wrote long after the exile, came to record the same incident (I Chron. 21[1]), he ascribes that piece of venom to Satan!

193. Tendencies in the Persian Period. As we pass in review the two centuries of the Persian period it gives us the impression of a long and pathetic decline. Though the Jews returned from captivity with high hopes, they found themselves involved in a losing struggle with the wicked world. At first the voice of prophecy cheered and inspired them (Haggai, Zechariah, the second Isaiah), but within a century that voice was stilled forever. Turning then for satisfaction to the performance of the written law, the religious genius of the nation became narrower in its sympathies and more intense in its narrowness. Members of the Jewish community who were less exclusive dropped away or were driven away by persecution and became children of the dispersion or Samaritans, until at last a mere handful was left, petty, intolerant and absolutely devoted to the law and the temple. The religion of the heart, responsive to the guidance of a living God, had stiffened into a religion of form.

XXVII

WHEN GREEK MEETS JEW

194. **The Coming of Alexander.** Alexander the Macedonian burst into the world of Asia in the year 334 B.C. His object at first was to break the power of Persia that for a century had disturbed the peace of Greece by means of its armies and its spies; but in order to break that power he had first to secure possession of Asia Minor, then Syria, then Egypt. He thus cut rudely across a world that had hitherto been wholly Asiatic, and the consequences were full of fate. The first year he beat the generals of Darius at the Granicus and liberated from despotic sway the Greek cities of the Ægean coast. In 333, he took all Asia Minor and put Darius himself to flight at Issus. In 332 he moved down the Phœnician and Philistine coast, and by destroying Tyre wrecked the Persian sea power while by taking Gaza he secured the entrance to Egypt. In 331 he not only conquered Egypt but retracing his steps wrested northern Syria, Mesopotamia and Assyria from Darius's hand. Babylon and Susa, the great seats of Oriental power, became his. We need not follow him into Afghanistan, Bokhara, Sarmacand, India and Beluchistan, nor pause at his untimely death-bed at Babylon in 323. In ten years he had mastered the world in which the Jew lived. Henceforth the Jewish world faced the west rather than the east.

195. **His Successors.** At the death of the great conqueror a grand scramble for the fragments of his empire arose in which all the Macedonian chiefs participated. Thirty years of chaos followed, at the end of which the contestants were reduced to five, each carrying on the fight for supremacy and calling himself a king. Another generation passes

by and the five have been reduced to three, all but one of them descendants of the original fighters. Two of these three concern our story: (1) Ptolemy, who ruled Egypt, and (2) Antiochus, who ruled in the Mesopotamian region.

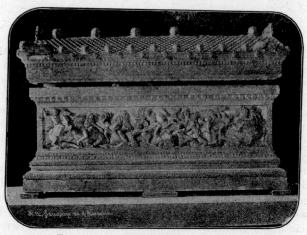

Fig. 135—"ALEXANDER'S COFFIN"

One of the most exquisite productions of Hellenistic art, found with many others in a rock-cemetery at Sidon in 1887. Coffin and cover are each one piece of pure white marble. It was made probably at Alexander's order for one of his generals. The wonderful frieze represents on this side Alexander fighting the Persians (at Issus?). Alexander is the figure on horseback at the left. On the other side, Alexander with Greek and Persian companions is hunting lions. All the figures were delicately tinted. Art of this kind was impossible under the Hebrew law (Ex. 20⁴).

This Ptolemy was a Macedonian chief who had been appointed governor of Egypt in 323 before the fighting began, and in the comparative isolation of that country between the deserts had managed to maintain himself. Using the newly founded city of Alexandria for his base, he had absorbed a large part of the sea power of the Mediterranean and the Red Sea. Thus enriched he was able to found a dynasty that continued three centuries, until Cleopatra, its last and most famous representative, fell before Cæsar Augustus.

Seleucus, the original ruler in the north, had been one of Alexander's generals who managed to outlive all his competitors and after fifty-three years of fighting nearly to grasp all of Alexander's empire, Macedonia and Egypt included. But he died a moment too soon. His son Antiochus managed to salvage everything but Egypt and Macedonia and to found the royal house of the Seleucids that lasted until Rome put an end to it. In a few years the borders of his realm fell away to revolting governors or native princes and the Seleucid kingdom settled down within the limits of Syria, Mesopotamia and Armenia, with its capital at the newly founded city of Antioch on the Orontes River. Both the Ptolemies and the Seleucids, it must be remembered, were Macedonians, educated in Greek ideas. They were always foreign tyrants to the peoples over whom they ruled.

196. **The Fate of Palestine.** Palestine was the unhappy frontier between these two kingdoms of Egypt and Syria and was the occasion of a standing quarrel between them. Ptolemy needed it, for it controlled the caravan routes to India and Arabia, and it grew the only timber in the Levant for the ships by which his wealth and throne were maintained. His ambition to keep up his sea power made it necessary for him to control Tyre and Sidon with the territory behind. He had claimed Palestine when first he became governor of Egypt, but when the chaos of 320 B.C. was let loose, Antigonus the temporary master of Asia Minor and Syria took it and captured and dismantled Jerusalem. When Antigonus was downed by a league of four kings in 301, Palestine fell again to Ptolemy. When at length Seleucus came to power in northern Syria he recognized the great value of Palestine to his kingdom, but generously refused to fight his old friend Ptolemy for it. In the next generation, however, war broke out between the two houses—a hundred years' war. Antiochus II extended his border as far south as Damascus, and then the two armies thrashed back and forth across the plains of Philistia and Galilee. Jerusalem, perched

on her rocky aerie, was a spectator of all this and passed from one control to the other, not especially disturbed by the rapid changes in the standards that gleamed over her gates.

In 223 B.C., a hundred years after Alexander's death, there came to the Syrian throne a man who finally settled the quarrel. He was Antiochus III, called the Great. He conquered Palestine in 218, lost it in 217 and won it again in 198 by a battle fought at Banias, near the source of the Jordan. With this event Egyptian control ceases, never to be revived except for a brief time or two in the Middle Ages.

All of these political and military events are the least significant parts of the history. What made this period fateful for the Jews was the introduction of Hellenism.

197. **The Meaning of Hellenism.** Alexander was vastly more than a conqueror, he was an apostle. While his primary object in the East had been to square old scores with Persia, he soon came to regard himself as a messenger of Greek civilization to a benighted and stunted world. Though himself a Macedonian and not a Greek, his education under the famous philosopher Aristotle had been nothing but Greek, and the ideas that had shaped the fortunes of Greece and produced the glories of Athenian art and literature and civic life appealed mightily to the imagination of this boy genius. He resolved to conquer the world for Greek culture. This Greek culture that took root beyond the boundaries of Greece is called Hellenism.

Alexander's methods of spreading Hellenism were truly Hellenic. The civilization of Greece was essentially a city product, evolved by the complex life of cities and best reproduced in cities. Therefore Alexander founded cities everywhere, naming them frequently after himself; Alexandria in Egypt, Alexandria on the shore at Issus, Alexandria in Babylonia, in Sogdiana, Oxiana, India. These cities were peopled wholly or in part by his veterans, and many other cities like Samaria in Palestine were given to them as well. Within twenty years from the time when Alexander crossed the Hellespont the Eastern world was studded with these fortresses of Greek culture; the great highways of the world were beaconed with them. Aping the ways of the

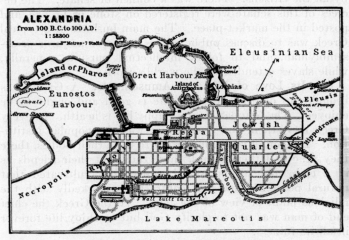

FIG. 136—MAP OF ALEXANDRIA

Alexandria was founded 331 B.C. Beginning with the first Ptolemy, 323 B.C., the city became the resort of artists and scholars and scientists. For the benefit of these a library was founded in the Museum, or University. It contained 900,000 scrolls by Cæsar's time, when it was burned. Jews settled here from the first. They lived under their own laws in the northeastern end of the town, separated from the other nationalities by a wall. In Roman times the Jewish merchants controlled the important grain trade by which the chief cities of the empire were fed (Acts 27[6], [38], 28[11]). The famous stone lighthouse called Pharos, built to facilitate commerce, was 370 feet high and lasted till 1326 A.D. During the second and third centuries of our era, Alexandria was the intellectual centre of Christendom, as it had been of Judaism in the first century and of classical culture in the first century B.C. For a description of the city of the fifth century A.D. see Kingsley's *Hypatia*, chaps. 2 and 5.

conqueror, the subject nations began to make over their cities after the pattern set before them.

198. **Its City Organization.** The East had always had cities, but they were for the most part mere groups of houses and men, places of safety from attack or collections of

bazaars for trade. They were ruled by a tyrant. Politically the inhabitants were slaves. On the other hand, the Greek cities were always free. Magistrates were elected annually by all the citizens. There was a council or senate. The decrees of this senate were registered on stone or bronze, and posted in the market-place. The main business of a typical Greek was to discuss public affairs, to serve as juror or assemblyman, and to follow intellectual pursuits generally, while slaves attended to the world's work.

199. **Its Love of Life and Amusements.** A Greek was brought up on the idea that life is good and ought to be enjoyed. The foundation of a happy life is health. In every Greek city, then, the gymnasium was the popular institution. Thither all young men went to train their bodies, there they practised their games, there they met their friends as in a club, and in this social centre they cultivated that natural point of view that contrasts so markedly with the religious point of view of the Jews. To the Greek the chief end of man was not to glorify God but to enjoy life forever in all its fulness.

The out-of-door life of the Greek tended to sport and play. Amusement there always was in plenty, but there was something intellectual about even the recreation of a Greek. His games were trials of skill rather than strength; his festivals usually had literary features: music, poetry, dancing. His great literature had grown up around the theatre as well as in the court-room and the council-chamber. In Palestine, on the contrary, we read of no sports nor physical or intellectual interests like these, except the social joys of a feast-day.

200. **Greek Art and Architecture.** The life and interests of a Greek tended to embody themselves in definite architectural forms. There had to be an assembly building and a court-house for the transaction of public business. There must be a theatre for dramatic presentations and shows of various kinds; a gymnasium for training, a stadium for athletic contests, a hippodrome for chariot-racing. Every

well-ordered city should have a colonnaded street where the
best shops are found; an *agora* or market-place where trade
and friendly discussion go hand in hand: a *stoa* or pillared
porch where gentlemen of leisure may lounge in the heat of
the day. All these types of building would also be adorned
with sculpture: statues of the gods, of great citizens, of ath-
letes, literary men and saviors of the city. A city without
art was unthinkable to a Greek. (See Fig. 140.) With all
this, contrast the huddled hovels of the East, the unadorned
and squalid streets of an Oriental city, the formless bazaars.
Only the king's palace and the god's temple stood out from
the general mass. In Jerusalem even these lacked sculptured
ornament, for the stern command, "Thou shalt not make
unto thee any graven image or the likeness of anything,"
shut the door in the face of art.

201. **Greek Language and Literature.** The Greeks had a
great and a justifiable pride in their language. It was an
instrument of precision and of beauty in comparison with
which all other speech seemed barbarous. With it they had
created great works of literary art which surpassed all other
literatures except the Hebrew and which have inspired men
down to our own day. The spread of Hellenism was therefore
largely dependent on the spread of the Greek language. It
is marvellous to see how this tongue blotted out the use of
all other languages of the East for cultural purposes. The
ignorant, of course, clung all along to their native dialects,
but the language of business, of government, of literature,
philosophy and art became Greek. Native literatures simply died. Lucian the Syrian (120–200 A.D.) puts down his
witticisms in the language of Alexander, while the Syrian
Meleager (60 B.C.) collected in his great anthology not a
single Aramaic poem, but only Greek ones, while his own
one hundred and thirty love epigrams are all in the Greek
tongue.

So universal did the use of Greek become for the Jews of
the dispersion that during the reign of Ptolemy Philadelphus

ΚΑΙΔΟΘΗΤΩϹΜΗΓ
ΜΑΚΑΙΗΛΟΙΠΗΕ
ΙΙΙΜΕΛΙΑΚΑΙΤΥΝΙΙ·
ΗΑΝΑΡΕϹΗ ΤΩΒΑϹΙ
ΛΕΙΚΑϹΙΛΕΥϹΕΙΑΝ
ΤΙΑϹΤΙΝΚΑΙΗΡΕϹΕ
ΤΩΒΑϹΙΛΕΙΤΟΓΙΡΑ
ΓΜΑΚΑΙΕΓΙΟΙΗϹΕ
ΟΥΤΩϹ
ΚΑΙΑΝΘΡΩΠΟϹΗΝ
ΙΟΥΛΑΙΟϹΕΝϹΟΥ
ϹΟΙϹΤΗΠΟΛΕΙΚΑΙ
ΟΝΟΜΑΑΥΤΩΜΑΡ
ΔΟΧΑΙΟϹΟΤΟΥΙΝΙ
ΡΟΥΤΟΥϹΕΜΕΕΙΟΥ·
ΙΟΥΚΕΙϹΑΙΟΥΕΚ
ϹΦΥΛΗϹΒΕΝΙΑΜΕΙ
ΟϹΗΝΑΙΧΜΑΛΩ
ΤΟϹΕΞΙΪΗΛΑΜΗΝ
ΗΧΜΑΛΩΤΕΥϹΕΝ
ΝΑΡΟΥΧΟΔΟΝΟ
ϹΟΡΚΑϹΙΛΕΥϹΚΑ
ΒΥΛΩΝΟϹΚΑΙΗΝ
ΙΟΥΓΙΩΙΙΛΙϹΘΡΕ
ΓΙΤΗΘΥΓΑΤΗΡΑΜΙ
ΝΑΔΑΒΑΔΕΛΦΟΥ
ΙΙΑΤΡΟϹΑΥΤΟΥΚΑΙ
ΤΟΥΝΟΜΑΑΥΤΗϹ
ΕϹΘΗΡ ΕΝΔΕΤΩ
ΜΕΤΑΛΛΑΞΑΙΑΥ
ΤΗϹΤΟΥϹΓΟΝΕΙϹ
ΕΠΕΔΕΥϹΕΝΑΥΤΗΝ
ΕΑΥΤΩΕΙϹΓΥΝΑΙ
ΚΑΚΑΙΗΝΤΟΚΟΡΑ
ϹΙΟΝΚΑΛΗΤΩΕΙΔΙ
ΚΑΙΟΤΕΗΚΟΥϹΘΗ
ΤΟΤΟΥΒΑϹΙΛΕΩϹ
ΠΡΟϹΤΑΓΜΑϹΥΝΗ
ΧΘΗϹΑΝΤΗΝΠΟ
ΛΙΝΥΠΟΧΕΙΡΑΓΑΙ

(250 B.C.) the sacred books of the Jews began to be translated into that language in Alexandria. By the beginning of the Christian era our entire Old Testament was finished, and the "Septuagint," as it is now called, became the Bible of the Jewish world. In Palestine itself this version largely supplanted the Aramaic ones. Jesus perhaps read from it in the synagogue at Nazareth. Paul always quoted from it. When therefore the New Testament was written in the first Christian century, its language throughout was that of the great Macedonian conqueror.

202. **Greek Manners and Customs.** Greek fashions fol-

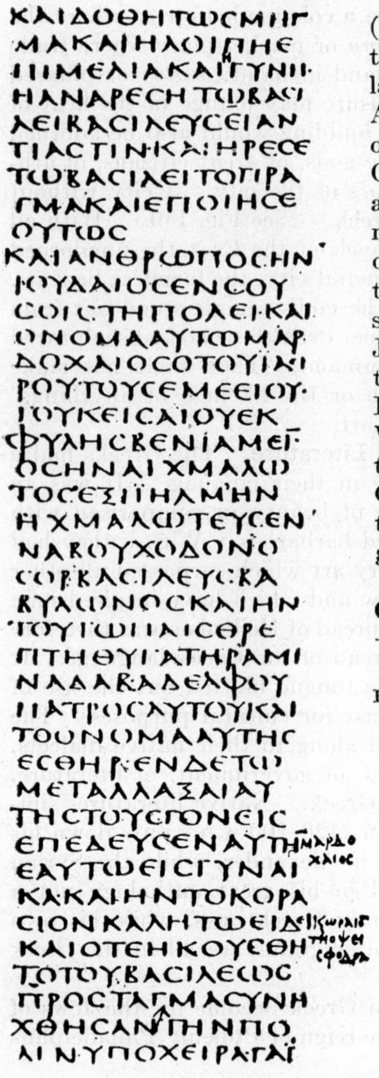

FIG. 137—THE SEPTUAGINT

Facsimile of Esther 2:3-8 taken from the Leipzic portion of the *Codex Sinaiticus* written in the fourth or fifth century of our era. Forty-three leaves of this manuscript were picked out of a waste-basket in the monastery of Saint Catherine on Mount Sinai, by the great biblical scholar Tischendorf in 1844. In 1859, under the patronage of the emperor of Russia Tischendorf again visited the monastery and recovered all that remained. The MS. consists of 390 quarto leaves of fine vellum, written in Greek uncials (capitals) four or two columns to the page. Originally it contained the whole Bible besides the Epistle of Barnabas and the "Shepherd" of Hermas.

lowed the conqueror. The months of the year were all renamed after the Greek style, and the year when Seleucus
conquered Antigonus (312 B.C.) became the point from which
dates were reckoned, and continued to be with the Jews down
to the Middle Ages. Personal names were often changed:
the Hebrew Solomon became the Greek Alexander, Joseph
became Menelaus, Judas became Aristobulus. Many inhabitants of Judea and Jerusalem even assumed the title
"Citizens of Antioch." All this looks like fawning on the
victor. Dress, too, assumed a foreign cut. Young Jews now
appeared in the Greek mantle and broad-brimmed hat, in
fact, joined the semi-political and semi-social guild of the
Ephoboi—Young Men's Greek Association—of which these
were the insignia. Well might the pious people of Jerusalem
think that the world was turning topsy-turvy.

203. **Hellenism and Judaism.** One must not imagine that
Hellenism was an unmixed blessing to the East, great as its
gifts were. Political freedom often meant political license,
it meant the arts of the demagogue, it meant squabbles in
politics, rivalries, and even assassinations. The gymnasium
meant too often an emphasis on lewdness and the life of the
beast, and an elevation of the athlete into a hero beside
whom the gods were pale. And in general, men admired
cleverness rather than righteousness. This tendency opened
the way for a decline in public and private life, until the
old-fashioned virtues of honesty, loyalty, sincerity gave place
only too frequently to trickery and vice. It was a rotten
Hellenism that debauched Byzantium and Rome and prepared the way in the fifth century of our era for the deluge
of the barbarians.

The means by which Hellenism slowly inundated the East
have been hinted in the preceding paragraphs. While Jerusalem, hugging its law-book and practising its narrow righteousness in its out-of-the-way mountain fastness, resisted the
influence for a long time, it felt at last the full impact of it.
The dispersion had already largely gone down under it. Alex-

andria became its special stronghold. There the Jew rapidly succumbed to Greek habits of life; indeed, he found it especially advantageous to do so, for thereby his varied talents could be used for advancement in business, learning, and the state. At Jerusalem the point of entrance for Hellenism was through the aristocratic classes. These people soon found that if they expected to get anywhere in the political world they must stand in well with Hellenism. Solicited on all sides in subtle and attractive ways, the young men of wealth conceived an ambition to be men of the world, to burst the bonds that held them in barren Judea and see the lands beyond, to know other and more famous civilizations, to take on a broader culture and to remove the reproach of being a peculiar people. Hellenism proved wonderfully attractive to all worldly minded Jews. Its paths seemed pleasant to the young, the idle, and the rich; but they knew not whither these paths led. They led to the greatest struggle the Jew ever experienced, in which his religion was all but extinguished.

THE DEATH–GRAPPLE FOR RELIGIOUS FREEDOM

204. The Rise of the Pious. While Hellenism was slowly penetrating the life and thought of the Jew, opposite influences were at work. As the aristocracy turned their sympathies toward things Greek, the middle and lower classes stiffened themselves to resist. More and more tenaciously they clung to the law and the customs of their fathers, and with hearts of foreboding they looked for some weapon with which to fight the incoming tide. There arose at length a new party that struggled with the old aristocracy for the control of the policies of state. They called themselves the Godly or the Pious, and they branded the Hellenists in derision as the worldly party. Some of the higher class were enrolled among the godly, including even the high priest, but for the most part the ranks were recruited from the poorer classes and from villages outside of Jerusalem. It is the old and never-ending story of liberals against conservatives.

205. The Villain of the Play. The contest of Hellenism with Judaism might have gone on without serious break until one side or the other won a peaceful victory. But just at the critical moment the great Antiochus died, and a period of assassination and civil war at length brought to the throne Antiochus IV, called Epiphanes (175 B.C.). He combined the most diverse characteristics. In youth he had been a hostage in Rome. After his liberation he studied philosophy and rhetoric at Athens and became an enthusiastic lover of Hellenism. Everything Greek became his passion. The year after his accession, he began to build at Athens one of the largest temples to the Olympian Zeus ever constructed, the remains of whose enormous columns still excite the admiration of the traveller. Highly impulsive and of tremendous will, he conceived schemes overnight and annihilated

From Breasted's "Ancient Times."

Fig. 138—MODERN ANTIOCH

The ancient city of Antioch was founded by Seleucus after he became master of Asia (301 B.C.) and named after his father Antiochus. It finally became a great commercial centre with several hundred thousand inhabitants, rivalling even Alexandria. For a vivid description of the city in the time of its glory, see Wallace's *Ben Hur*, Books IV and V. Antioch was the place where a Christian community was first formed independent of the Jewish synagogue, and here the members of the sect were first called Christians (Acts 11[26]). From Antioch, Paul started on his missionary travels (Acts 13[4]). Antioch thus became the cradle of Gentile Christianity.

The city has been repeatedly destroyed by fire and earthquake. Its present population is 28,000. Judging from the picture, what is their religion? Try to discover traces of walls. The building on the sky-line in the saddle is a castle built by the crusaders. The ancient city lay above the modern one, on the slope of the mountain.

whatever stood in the way of realizing them. A large measure of practical ability was his also; he was a good general and a consummate diplomat, largely because of a scandalous lack of honor. But there was a rift in his nature, indicated by his constant tendency to play pranks, and an insane conceit that led him to assume divine honors. On his coins he put the words, "Theos Epiphanes" (the god made manifest), which some wag, with more truth than fiction, promptly changed to "Epimanes" (cracked). He had the shrewdness to see that his ill-assorted empire could best be bound together by a common culture, and therefore he resolved to make Hellenism universal.

206. The First Move Against Judaism. The accession of Antiochus made an immediate difference at Jerusalem: it strengthened the hands of the Hellenizing party. The leader of this party was one Jason, a brother of the high priest Onias who was leader of the pious. By bribery at the Syrian court Jason had himself appointed high priest and his brother exiled. He procured at the same time permission to remodel the city along Greek lines. At once he built a gymnasium almost under the temple walls and instituted athletic sports. The young men of the aristocracy went over with a will to the new

Fig. 139—COIN OF ANTIOCHUS IV (Epiphanes)

King of Syria 175–164 b.c.

A silver *stater*, worth perhaps 67 cents, equivalent to four ancient Greek drachmas. In Jesus' time the stater was used interchangeably with the Jewish shekel.

point of view. They formed a guild of the Ephoboi and flaunted their Greek cloaks and broad-brimmed hats about the streets and in the temple area. To be an athlete became the craze. Even the priests caught the mania, regardless of the fact that the sports were instituted in honor of the demigod Heracles. According to the author of Maccabees, they left their sacrifices unperformed in order to see the sport in the stadium and to participate in the games. Naturally, the pious were scandalized. From our modern and largely Hellenic point of view there is nothing godless in athletic sports, but there seemed to be much that was godless for the Jew. It would be nearer the truth to say that it was the newness and the difference rather than the godlessness that shocked him. Yet the pious were essentially right. Judaism could not yield up its major interest in religion and its devotion to the moral law without running the risk of annihilation. If Hellenism succeeded in Palestine Judaism was doomed.

207. Further Irritations. One Menelaus—note that all the names are Greek—now supplanted Jason by bribing Antiochus, using for the purpose not only taxes newly wrung from the people but some of the temple treasure. In reply to the protests of the pious he caused their leader, the exiled Onias, to be put to death. Jerusalem was now ablaze with anger. At that critical moment (172 B.C.), war broke out between Antiochus and Egypt, and Antiochus marched into the delta. When report came that Antiochus had been killed in battle, the opponents of Menelaus and all that he stood for rose in rebellion and put an end to the hated ones by wholesale murder. The report about Antiochus, however, proved to be false. On his return from Egypt, Antiochus turned aside to punish Jerusalem, and punish her he did most mercilessly. Not only were the tables turned and the pious slaughtered, but the temple was wholly looted of its treasure. The avenger polluted the Holy of Holies by entering it in person, stole the golden altar, the candlestick, the cups, the censers, and even scaled off all the gold plating on the face of the building.

208. The Abomination of Desolation. Angered and embittered by later political events, Antiochus then decided to root out forever the Jewish religion that stood in the way of realizing his policy of Hellenizing the Jews. He made proclamation that all Jewish religious customs should cease: there should be no more Sabbath, no circumcision, no clean and unclean food, no sacrifice to Jehovah; and that whoever should be found to possess a book of the law should be put to death. He forthwith sent an army of 22,000 to carry his edict into effect. Taking advantage of the Jewish refusal to

Fig. 140—JERASH

One of the best extant examples of a Græco–Roman city. In the foreground
is a semi-circular forum adorned with 56 columns. Leading from this is
a street half a mile long, flanked by 520 columns of which 75 are still standing. The group of pillars on the left belong to a larger temple to Zeus,
on a terrace 527 feet by 344 feet. The columns are 45 feet high. The
four columns seen between this temple and the forum belong to the basilica
or law court (Fig. 148). The heap of rubbish above the forum to the right
is the baths, opposite which is the large temple of Artemis. Not shown in
the picture are a triumphal gateway (behind us), a hippodrome 170 yards
long and 60 broad, an elliptical circus 295 feet by 180, several temples,
two theatres—one of them with 32 rows of seats and the other with 19—
intended for gladiatorial shows, and four churches dating of course from
Christian times.

The city, lying east of the Jordan in the Decapolis, is first mentioned by Alexander Jannæus (104–78 b.c.): its freedom was restored by Pompey; its
most prosperous period was the second and third centuries of our era. Lying on the great Roman road, it was considered in the fourth century one of
the largest and strongest towns in Arabia. With the coming of the Arabs
in the seventh century its prosperity waned, while a decreasing rainfall
hastened its depopulation. To-day there are 1,500 people where once
there were at least 30,000.

fight on the Sabbath, the troops entered Jerusalem, dismantled the temple, pulled down the walls, looted and burned the homes, and sold into slavery hordes of women and children. Then adding insult to injury, in December, 168 B.C., they built an altar to the Olympian Zeus in place of Jehovah's great altar of sacrifice, put up in the sacred precinct a statue to the same pagan deity, probably bearing the likeness of Antiochus, and by force compelled the Jews to worship it by offering swine's flesh. This statue of Zeus was what the book of Daniel calls the "Abomination of Desolation." It marks the point of despair below which a Jew could not descend. To the pious it seemed as if the God were dead who could suffer such defilement without defending himself. Many of the Jews went over openly to the heathenism of the conqueror, while others of sterner stuff fled from the insults and the sword and took refuge in the caves of the wilderness. Antiochus had not reckoned with the temper of this adamantine remnant. The hunted people, brought at length to bay, were soon to turn and spring at the hunter like a tiger.

209. **Biblical Echoes of the Great Scourging.** In the darkness of this midnight hour we can best discover the heroic temper of the Jewish faith. It lights for us with sublimity the pages of scripture, both when it implores for divine help and when it boldly rises to claim victory. How the cry of anguish rings from Psalm 79:

"O God, the heathen have come into thine inheritance.
Thy holy temple have they defiled.
They have laid Jerusalem in heaps.
The dead bodies of thy servants have they given as food
    to the birds of heaven,
The flesh of thy saints to the beasts of the earth.
Their blood have they shed like water round about
    Jerusalem,
And there was none to bury them!"

The prayers go up like incense from many another Psalm, prayers for rescue, prayers for vengeance on their foes, prayers for forgiveness for the sins that have brought such terrible retribution (Ps. 74, 83, etc.). But the noblest product of this experience is the book of Daniel, a book impossible to understand except in the light of the tragedy that brought it forth. In the first six chapters the author seeks to encourage the faithful by reciting the noble deeds of their ancestors during the exile: of Daniel who would not defile himself with the king's meat nor cease to pray with his window open toward Jerusalem; of Shadrach, Meshach and Abednego, who endured the furnace rather than worship the king's golden image. Then he recites the history of the past in the guise of prophetic symbols and visions. By Nebuchadrezzar's dream and similar devices he shows the rise of Persia, Greece and Syria, culminating in the persecutions of Antiochus, and then proclaims the glorious hope that in these days shall the God of heaven set up a kingdom that shall never be destroyed. The significance of the book lies in the thought that throughout all history, even in its darkest hours, runs the divine purpose, and that faith in God will bring the dawn. Though the author did not know it, the dawn was already breaking.

210. **Mattathias and His Sons.** During the persecutions an aged priest named Mattathias had betaken himself with his five sons to his country residence at Modin on the borders of the hill-country toward Philistia. Officers of Antiochus, hunting everywhere for victims, at length came to Modin. They erected an altar for the king and required Mattathias as head man of the town to offer the first sacrifice, promising in return for his obedience much gold and the king's favor. Indignantly he spurned their blasphemous orders, and when a villager came forward to perform the heathen sacrifice, the old man flew upon him in a rage and killed him. Then he ran his sword through the royal commissioner, threw down the altar and issued his call to the

Fig. 141—THEATRE AT AMMAN

The modern Amman lies within a Græco-Roman city built by Ptolemy Philadelphus (285-247 B C.) on the site of the old Rabbath Ammon that David
captured (II Sam. 12²⁶⁻³¹) and named after himself, Philadelphia.   In the
days of its splendor it was an important member of the Decapolis.   Like
Jerash (Fig. 140) it contained the usual public buildings—temples, baths,
a forum, theatres, and colonnaded streets.

The great theatre is seen in the centre of the picture.   The seats are arranged
in three tiers, in the lowest of which five rows of seats are visible, in the
second fourteen and in the highest sixteen.   Between the second and third
sections and above the third are boxes for spectators.   The theatre easily
holds 4,000 people.   Its acoustic properties are excellent.   The stage has
disappeared.

The heap of ruins in the left foreground is the Odeum, a small theatre for musical performances.

The picture is taken from the citadel in the assault of which Uriah, the husband
of Bathsheba, was killed (II Sam. 11²³⁻²⁴).

men of Modin: "Whosoever is zealous for the law and loyal
to the covenant let him follow me." Thereupon the gallant
leader, his five sons and other daring men, fled to the
wilderness and proclaimed deathless war against the per-
secutor.

211. The Open Revolt and the Unequal Contest. A motley company soon gathered to them, men of all kinds, from desperadoes to the pious. Mattathias led them up and down the country, tipping over altars and punishing with the sword all renegade Jews wherever found. His headquarters was the nearest cave, his equipment and commissary whatever he could find. But the rough life was too much for the old man and he soon died, having first named his son Simon as chief counsellor and his son Judas as captain. Time revealed the father's good judgment, for Simon was indeed wise and Judas a born leader whose marvellous success soon won for him the name Maccabæus (the Hammerer). Indeed, there are few captains in the annals of time who surpass in military insight, albeit on a contracted field, the indomitable Judas.

Judas ought to have known that his cause, humanly speaking, was hopeless. His race, because of their peculiar customs and their unyielding exclusiveness, was already the most despised in the world. His band of followers was utterly untrained, unequipped and unsupported. Opposed to him were the trained armies of a powerful state, reinforced by Greek mercenaries with bronze armor and the best weapons made, led by generals who had acquired skill in world-wide campaigns. On every field the Syrians outnumbered the Jews six to one. In the enemy's ranks also were renegade Jews who knew the land with all its intricacies and who cordially hated the bigoted and short-sighted defenders of the law. Against them Judas could only oppose a desperate courage, a band of loyal and rugged followers, a superior knowledge of the wilderness and the mountain strongholds of Judea, belief in his own ability to inspire, plan and execute, and an undying faith in God. With these he would do the impossible.

212. The Four Victories. The king of Syria did not propose to be thwarted by a band of guerillas. He sent his general Apollonius with an army to annihilate it. Judas and his ragged handful met the army near Samaria and defeated it. The bodies of the slain furnished him with clothes and weapons. A larger army was at once sent down under General Seron. Advancing along the old road across Galilee and the plain of Sharon he took the first valley that led to Jerusalem—the valley of the Beth-horons. This was a fatal mistake. Within two miles the trail ascends 1,500 feet, and at points it is a mere crevice between rocks. At one of these Judas chose his ground and, like Joshua of old on the happy day when the sun and moon stood still over this spot (Sec. 36), utterly routed his enemy.

Judas now had a name among the nations. Seeing that he was a formidable antagonist, Antiochus next launched against him half his entire military strength, an army of 50,000 men, under three of his most accomplished generals. Avoiding the trap that caught Seron, they took the broader pass to the south, the Wadi Ali, up which the modern carriage-road winds to Jerusalem. Near the top of the range where the valley broadens a bit at Emmaus they pitched. Judas pitched against them on the heights of Mizpah (the watch-tower), famous in Hebrew story and full of inspirations for a patriot. So confident of victory were the Syrians that General Nicanor had brought with him a host of merchants to buy the Jewish slaves whom he expected to get, and to sell them abroad. Even the price of these uncaught slaves was posted in neighboring cities. As on a former occasion, the attack was made on the Sabbath. But Judas flung scruples to the winds, made a glorious speech to his soldiers full of patriotism and religion; like Gideon he sent home all those who were faint-hearted, and with his intrepid 6,000 he launched his attack. While one of the Syrian generals tried to turn his flank, he slipped away through a parallel valley in the opposite direction and at dawn struck the unsuspecting camp of the invader like a thunderbolt. The Syrians broke and ran and the Syrian merchants who had come down with such golden hopes fled home empty-handed.

Chagrined beyond measure at the defeat of his generals, Lysias himself, the regent of the kingdom, now took the field with 5,000 cavalry and 60,000 infantry. This time he essayed a still more southern pass, the vale of Elah, haunted by memories of David and Goliath. Here they penetrated to the top of the range a little north of Hebron, where they had as a rear protection the Idumeans (descendants of the Edomites), who in the restoration period had driven the Jews from this part of their inheritance (Sec. 159). At a place called Bethsura, Judas and his 10,000 met him, and again the "contemptible little army" won. The Syrian withdrew.

213. **The Temple Restored.** While Lysias was refitting his shattered battalions at Antioch, Judas turned his attention to Jerusalem. There was a garrison of Syrians and backslidden Jews in the Akra, or citadel, that overshadowed the temple from the south; but setting aside a portion of his troops to keep them harmless, he led the rest of his veterans into the sacred temple enclosure. Their first act was to tear their garments and mourn for the desolation that met their eyes, for the dismantled house, the overthrown altar, the rubbish and filth, the thorns and weeds, and the defilement of heathen sacrifice. Then with a pious zeal they went to work. All was repaired and cleansed, a new altar was built, gates, doors, courts, chambers were renewed, new vessels were furnished, and on December 25, 165 B.C., three years after the abomination of desolation had been set up, the temple was once more dedicated to the service of the God of Israel. This memorable date became a national holiday ever after, known in Christ's time as the Feast of Dedication (John 10^{22}), but in ours as the Feast of Lights.

214. **The Hammerer's Further Blows.** Antiochus Epiphanes died in 163 B.C. while hastening from Persia to punish Judas personally. Hence there was a brief breathing space. Judas seized the opportunity to gain elbow room for further

fights.   First he struck at the Idumeans, hereditary foes on
the south, and won a signal victory.   Next he turned to the
Ammonites east of Jordan who had oppressed the Jews
resident there.   In this campaign he took Bosra on the edge
of the desert and other towns on the headwaters of the Yarmuk River and in the Hauran as far as Damascus.   The decisive battle with the Ammonites was fought near Edrei.
Gathering up much spoil and as many Jews of the dispersion as he could find here and in Galilee, the victorious
Judas returned to Jerusalem.   He then defeated the Idumeans, capturing Hebron, and overran the Philistine plain
as far as Ashdod.   In an incredibly short time this peasant
warrior had won more victories against greater odds than
any other leader in Hebrew history.   David himself controlled hardly more territory.   While the results of these
conquests were short-lived, they made secure the fame and
fear of Judas, they rescued thousands of Jews from heathen
lands, and they laid the foundation of the kingdom that was
soon to rise.

215. **Psalms of Victory.**   This glorious deliverance from
the jaws of death was the signal for many a pæan of praise.
Some of these undoubtedly appear in the Psalter:

"Jehovah saith to my lord, 'Sit thou at my right hand,
Until I make thine enemies thy footstool.' "—Psalm 110.

"Not to us, O Jehovah, not to us,
But to thy name give glory."—Psalm 115.

"O give thanks unto Jehovah; for he is good;
For his lovingkindness endureth forever."—Psalm 118.

The hope of a restored kingdom under the Messiah again
blazed forth for the first time since Zerubbabel's day (Sec.
174), and apparently inspired the rhapsody found in Zechariah 9⁹⁻¹⁰:

"Rejoice greatly, O daughter of Zion; shout, O daughter of Jerusalem; behold thy king cometh unto thee; he is just, and having salvation; lowly, and riding upon an ass, even upon a colt, the foal of an ass. And I will cut off the chariot from Ephraim, and the horse from Jerusalem; and the battle bow shall be cut off; and he shall speak peace unto the nations: and his dominion shall be from sea to sea, and from the river Euphrates to the ends of the earth."

XXIX

THE HEROIC AGE AND THE UNHEROIC

216. The Attainment of Religious Freedom. While the
Syrian princes and notables were quarrelling over who should
be the next king of a dying realm, Judas thought it a good
chance to capture the citadel at Jerusalem. Some of the
garrison escaped through his net and implored Antioch to
help them. Lysias, having at length gotten a young prince
crowned as Antiochus Eupater, and himself made prime
minister, gathered a huge army and himself accompanied the
young king into Judea. They had 100,000 infantry, 20,000
cavalry and 32 elephants of war armed like tanks and
carrying a squad of soldiers in their conning-tower. They
again chose the southern pass of Elah and met Judas with
his 10,000 at Beth Zacharias, near Bethsura. The battle
is memorable not only for the terrific odds against Judas
but for the feat of Judas' brother Eleazar. He fought his
way up to the tallest elephant, supposing that it carried the
king, got beneath it and thrust his spear into its heart.
The hero was crushed by the elephant's fall. The odds
however were too great. Judas suffered his first defeat and
had to withdraw. But while Lysias was besieging Jerusalem
with the hope of ending the struggle forever, perilous news
from home compelled him to return to Antioch with his army.
He therefore made a hurried peace compact by which the
Jews were guaranteed religious freedom, though still politically subject to Syria. This pact marked a real and a glorious victory for the Jews and closed the first chapter of the
history of the Maccabean struggle. The Jewish religion was
saved; never again was there any question about the free-

dom of the Jewish faith. From this time on the struggle was for political independence.

217. The Death of Judas. The withdrawal of the Syrian army left the two old parties, the Hellenizers and the pious, just about where they had been before. The struggle for control began again, especially the struggle for the high-priesthood. The Syrian king had appointed a certain Alcimus, a Hellenizer, as high priest; but the people of Jerusalem refused to take him and thrust him out of the city. When the Syrians tried to put him back by force, Judas took arms to defend the popular cause, met the new army on the old field of Beth-horon and again won. But the Syrians within two months sent another force under another leader. Judas was forsaken by most of his war-weary band, was defeated and killed, 161 B.C.

Great was the mourning throughout Palestine, for Judas had been both chariots and horsemen to a lost cause. History has passed on him the judgment that he possessed courage, energy, unflinching determination, a tender regard for the welfare of his men, the power to inspire enthusiasm, and military skill that amounted to genius. He was the savior of the Jewish faith and the Jewish race, the last and one of the greatest of that line of saviors that included Deborah and Elijah, Isaiah and Nehemiah. But for his valor and devotion Judah would in his day have met the fate that the prophets had so barely helped her to escape on the plains of Babylonia and that had actually overwhelmed godless Israel. God had surely been keeping watch within the shadow.

218. Jonathan's Struggles. Emboldened by the loss of their great enemy Judas, the Hellenizers began a fearful persecution. But Judas' brother Jonathan took the popular side and after an almost complete failure was able to win the political and religious leadership of Judea by playing against one another the two rival claimants for the Syrian throne. He even added part of Samaria to his lands. Then Jonathan bought freedom from taxation by the payment of three hundred talents. In this rather inglorious fashion a kind of political independence was secured. Jonathan was murdered soon after by a Syrian general who hoped to be appointed ruler in his stead. But this crisis brought to the front the last and the wisest of the sons of Mattathias, Simon, who had been in all the ups and downs of the long struggle a strong helper and a counsellor. Before his enemy could act, Simon had gathered the power into his own hands.

219. **Political Independence at Last.** Again the weakness of the Syrian throne proved to be Judah's opportunity. The new king, Demetrius II, needed Simon's support. To gain it he broke the last bond that held Judea to Syria. Simon was recognized as high priest, all the covenants made with Jonathan were confirmed, and the payment of tribute was stopped forever. This pact marks a new era in Jewish history. The year 143 B.C. is the year 1 of Jewish independence.

Now began an era of prosperity the like of which the Jews had never known before. The Jews "tilled their land in peace, and the land gave her increase, and the trees of the plain their fruit. The old men sat in the streets, they talked together of the common good, and the young men put on glorious and fine apparel. Simon provided food for the cities and furnished them with the means of fortification—and he strengthened all the distressed of his people, he was full of zeal for the law, and every lawless and wicked person he banished. He made the sanctuary glorious, and multiplied the vessels of the temple" (I Macc. 14⁸⁻¹⁵).

As a ruler Simon was both moderate and wise. He assumed the state of a king but did not provoke prejudice by taking the title. For the first time in history Jewish coins were struck. We still possess shekels having on one side a cup and the words "shekel of Israel" and on the other a device interpreted as Aaron's rod with the words, "Jerusalem the Holy." Simon commanded the full confidence and love of his people. In a solemn assembly convened in 141 B.C. he was confirmed in the double post of governor and high priest, both offices being made hereditary in his family. From this assembly therefore dates the founding of the dynasty of the Hasmoneans—so called because the family name of Simon's father Mattathias was Hasmon.

FIG. 142—SILVER SHEKEL OF SIMON MACCABÆUS

Obverse : A cup, with inscription in early Hebrew letters, "Shekel of Israel"; above the cup, "Year Three." *Reverse :* Triple lily, or Aaron's rod that budded, and the inscription "Jerusalem the Holy."

220. Simon's Untimely Death. Simon owed his death to the unscrupulous ambition of his son-in-law. This rascal named Ptolemy coveted for himself the dignity and power that Simon possessed, and knowing full well that Simon's sons would naturally inherit these things, he conceived a plot to destroy them all. While they were on a tour of inspection among the cities of Judea, Ptolemy invited them to a banquet in his castle near Jericho, and having plied them well with wine, set assassins upon them. But Ptolemy was balked in seizing the power by Simon's third son, John Hyrcanus, who won the support of the people of Jerusalem before Ptolemy had time to do it. John therefore succeeded to his father's titles.

221. New Ambitions. A new king of Syria, Antiochus Sidetes, now tried to re-establish a claim on Palestine; but he soon died. Left free to do as he pleased, John began ambitious projects for conquest. With the aid of mercenaries he conquered additional east-Jordan territory, took Shechem and southern Samaria, and thereupon destroyed the Samaritan temple on the top of Mount Gerizim. Turning south, he captured the chief cities of the Idumeans, plac-

ing over them as governor one Antipater, himself an Idumean. Next he reduced the strong city of Samaria, since
Alexander's time a Greek stronghold; and last of all, took
Scythopolis, ancient Bethshean, at the mouth of the valley of
Jezreel. All of this does not look like the conduct of a high
priest. The last trace of the religious zeal that had so fired
the early Maccabean house had vanished, and in its place
had come the purely worldly desire to conquer. This course
could not fail to arouse protest on the part of those who had
religion at heart.

222. **Pharisees and Sadducees.** Back in Jonathan's day
there had arisen a party of separatists who had objected to
policies of state that did not advance the cause of religion.
Now these separatists, or Pharisees as they are henceforth
called, stepped openly into the light as opponents of John
and his worldly schemes. On the other hand, those who
favored the ruling house and its policy were known as Sadducees. It is evident that these parties were the descendants of the old pious and worldly groups of the pre-Mac-
cabean days, only their aims were changed. Now it was a
question of whether the state should be primarily religious
or secular.

Henceforth the Pharisees played a leading part in Jewish
life. In politics they were conservative, believing that the
policy of expansion and of alliance with heathen nations was
really disloyalty to Jehovah. In religion they were pro-
gressives, holding that the ancient sacred law must be interpreted and applied to new questions as they arise in
every-day life, and that the new interpretations and applica-
tions are of equal authority with the law itself. This gave
rise to no end of regulations, most of them petty and some
of them absurd, like those that applied to the keeping of the
Sabbath. A good Pharisee would not eat an egg laid on the
Sabbath, for example, because the laying involved work on
the part of the hen! Pharisees set before themselves the
keeping of every last jot and tittle of the law and the tra-

dition. They believed in immortality, the resurrection of the body and the coming of the Messiah; and since these beliefs were shared by the great mass of the people, the Pharisees became the natural leaders of the nation. They

FIG. 143—A PHARISEE AT PRAYER

The scarf worn over the head is part of the ceremonial of reading the Law; likewise the phylactery bound on the forehead (see also Fig. 144). The scroll is wound up by the right hand as it is unrolled by the left.

were the true representatives of Judaism, and their principles are still the foundation of the orthodox Jewish faith.

The Sadducees were few in number compared with their rivals. They represented both the old priestly aristocracy and the new nobility that rallied around the Maccabean leaders. They depended for their authority not on popular support but on wealth, prestige and the favor of the ruling house. They were really a political and not a religious party. They favored any policy that would further their own interests, and they had no sympathy with the scruples and endless discussions of doctrine that so occupied the Pharisees. They were selfish, often unscrupulous. They could produce, in the time of Christ, such characters as Annas and Caiaphas whose shameless grasping for wealth and power became a byword.

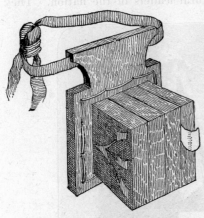

FIG. 144—A PHYLACTERY

A little box of leather, about two inches square, fastened to a leather band, by which it was bound on the forehead between the eyes. It has four compartments, in each of which is a piece of parchment bearing one of these four verses from the Law: Ex. 13⁹, 13¹⁶, Deut. 6⁸, 11¹⁸. Phylacteries began to be worn in the second century B.C. The Talmud directed every male Jew to wear one after his thirteenth year at morning prayers on Sabbaths and festivals. Their use grew out of a literal interpretation of the passages mentioned above, and became a mark of great piety. Jesus condemned the spirit that made a show of them (Matt. 23⁵). Compare also Fig. 143.

223. The Wreckers of the Jewish Democracy. John died just as the contest between Pharisees and Sadducees was becoming acute. Aristobulus his son, who followed him, was a brute whose inglorious reign lasted only a year. His only title to fame lies in his conquest of Galilee, which he colonized with Jews and so made it possible for Jesus to come out of Nazareth. His title to ignominy lies in his wholesale murder of the members of his own family.

With the accession of Alexander, another son of John Hyrcanus, we reach the low-water mark of the Hasmonean house, for he stopped at no act of perfidy or cruelty. His reign accomplished three things, all of them unfortunate: he drove the finest of the Jews into open hostility to the Hasmonean family, losing 8,000 by voluntary exile and 50,000 by civil war; he fanned the rivalry between Pharisees and Sadducees into a murderous hatred; and he depleted the treasury by fruitless wars of conquest. He was followed at his death by his wife Alexandra, whose folly was the undoing of her house. In the first place, she made her oldest son Hyrcanus high priest and gave her younger and more energetic son Aristobulus nothing to do—which was a fatal mistake. In the second place, she renounced the support of the Sadducees and favored the Pharisees, the party of the people. Now came in the golden age of the Pharisees; their exiles returned and they at last held the balance of power. But bent on humiliating their rivals, they began a series of persecutions and judicial murders that finally drove the Sadducees out of Jerusalem. Alexandra's son Aristobulus now saw his chance. Taking advantage of his mother's sickness—she was now seventy-three—he attached himself to the ostracized Sadducees, raised an army, and while his mother was dying he tried to get the throne.

224. **The Fatal Struggle Between Brothers.** Though the dying queen had willed everything to Hyrcanus, in the first encounter with his brother he lost everything except his life. He doubtless would have been content to remain in peace and privacy, but he was sought out by an ambitious and wonderfully able man named Antipater, who saw that he could use so weak a prince to advance his own ends. This Antipater was son of that Idumean who had been made governor of Idumea by John Hyrcanus (Sec. 221). Antipater persuaded Hyrcanus to flee to Petra, the rock-city of the Nabatean Arabs, whose king Aretas promised to put him back on the throne if Hyrcanus would restore to him twelve cities that his father had captured. Hyrcanus agreed, returned with the backing of 50,000 Arabs and defeated Aristobulus,

who fled to the temple and there defended himself. At this critical juncture the Roman eagles descended and Jewish independence became a memory of the past.

FIG. 145—COPPER HALF–SHEKEL OF SIMON MACCABÆUS

The inscription reads: (left) "Fourth year: One Half" (shekel); (right) "Of the Freedom (independence) of Zion." The old Hebrew forms of letters were used on the Maccabean coins, perhaps for patriotic reasons.

THE DESCENT OF THE ROMAN EAGLES

225. The Shadow of Rome. In the course of our history we have seen the sceptre of world-empire pass in succession from Babylon to Assyria, back to Babylon, then to Persia and to Greece. The centre of power still was moving westward, and while the fragments of Alexander's domain were wearing themselves out in fruitless struggles, Rome was sharpening her sword for conquest. By a wonderful series of successes and accidents Rome had absorbed Italy, then northern Africa, then Greece, and by the first quarter of the first century before Christ she was battling for the control of Asia Minor and Mesopotamia with Mithridates, king of Pontus, and Tigranes of Armenia who was now in virtual control of the ancient kingdom of the Seleucids. These kings were finally conquered in 65 B.C. by the Roman general Pompey, who became in the East a veritable king of kings, immensely rich and full of ambition for himself and Rome. Naturally he turned lustful eyes on Syria and Palestine not only for the spoils they would yield but because he needed them as a base of operations against the Parthians still farther to the east. He therefore sent his general Scaurus southward and in 64 B.C. "pacified" Syria as far as Phœnicia and Damascus. Hyrcanus and Aristobulus both hit upon the happy idea of asking Roman aid in their quarrel, and offered the same persuasion—four hundred talents each. Scaurus took a trip to Jerusalem to look the ground over, decided that he would back Aristobulus, and ordered Hyrcanus, Antipater and Aretas to drop the siege of Jerusalem. These left at once, for cause. When Pompey himself reached Damascus the grateful Aristobulus sent him a present of a golden vine worth five hundred talents, which Pompey forwarded to Rome to be put in the temple of Jupiter Capitolinus.

226. **Pompey the Dictator.** But when Pompey returned to Damascus the following year (63) he was met by envoys of Hyrcanus, Aristobulus, and also of the Jewish people, each with an axe to grind. The words of the last-named group sounded pleasantly in his ears, for they had been sent by the peace-at-any-price Pharisees to ask that the Jewish kingship be abolished altogether, so that under the protection of Roman law they might give their exclusive attention to religion. Pompey now decided to take a trip to Jerusalem to inspect conditions personally; whereat King Aristobulus said indiscreet things about obligations for gifts received and Pompey was sensitive enough to arrest him on the spot. As Pompey approached the holy city the party that favored Hyrcanus opened the gates to him; but the party of Aristobulus shut themselves in the temple and citadel, and defied him. The fortifications of the citadel were strong enough to hold back the Roman for three months. But by taking advantage of the Pharisaic scruples about fighting on the Sabbath, Pompey made a breach and began a massacre in which 12,000 Jews were slain, including many priests at the altar. Through such a sea of blood Rome made her entry into the sacred city. Henceforth she maintained her grasp on it for seven centuries, 63 B.C. to 635 A.D.

Pompey restored Hyrcanus to his high-priesthood and for civil power gave him the newly manufactured title of ethnarch. But the cities conquered from Syria by the Hasmoneans were all taken away; and Hyrcanus' territory was cut down to Judea only, and made subject to the Roman governor of Syria. The walls of Jerusalem were demolished, a Roman garrison was stationed in the citadel, and tribute was imposed. It was now that the Greek cities, mostly east of Jordan, were made locally free and were organized into a league known as the Decapolis.

Pompey was curious to enter the temple; he even lifted the veil and entered the holy of holies. Awed by the strange worship in which no image of the god was used, by the wonderful ritual and the costly incense, he withdrew without touching the immense treasure in the temple vaults—an astonishing thing for Pompey. The Pharisees, however, never forgot the profanation of their shrine, and when the chance came later they sided against Pompey with Julius Cæsar. Pompey now returned to Rome, taking as captives to grace his triumphal procession Aristobulus, his two sons Antigonus and Alexander, his two daughters, and multitudes of Jews. On the voyage Alexander escaped and returned to make mischief in Judea. Aristobulus and Antigonus escaped later from Rome and did the same thing. All the rest were in due time given freedom, and they formed the Jewish colony in Rome that figures afterward in the work and writings of Paul and Peter.

227. **Fighting the Inevitable.** The defeated party had no intention of giving up the struggle. First, the escaped Alexander collected and led a force against Jerusalem. Hyrcanus and his patron Antipater were overthrown. They then appealed for help to the Roman governor of Syria and managed to regain their grip (57 B.C.). Aristobulus and his son now escaped from Rome (56 B.C.) and tried their luck with a revolt, but they were captured and sent back. In 55 B.C. Alexander made a second attempt without success. In 54, Crassus was the Roman general in charge of the East. Needing money for his Parthian expedition, he came to Jerusalem and stripped the temple treasury of the hoard that Pompey had spared ($12,500,000). As soon as he was defeated by the Parthians, the Jews revolted; but his successor Cassius took swift vengeance on them by selling 30,000 of the rebels into slavery. When the rupture came between Cæsar and Pompey, who were struggling for the mastery of the world, Cæsar released Aristobulus and gave him two legions with which to start a revolt in Judea and so harass

his enemy. But friends of Pompey poisoned Aristobulus, and others killed Alexander about the same time (49 B.C.). Rome was still in the saddle, whatever became of her generals.

228. **The Schemes of Antipater.** The wise Idumean grand vizier of Hyrcanus saw that no one could rule in Judea without the help of Rome. He therefore ingratiated himself with whatever Roman was on top at the moment. When Pompey was defeated at Pharsalia in 48 B.C. and Cæsar, following him to Egypt, was in a serious plight at Alexandria, Antipater sent a force to help him out. The Idumean mouse helped the Roman lion. The lion never forgot it. Cæsar raised Antipater to the rank of Roman citizen and made him procurator of Judea, Samaria, and Galilee under Hyrcanus, while he confirmed Hyrcanus as high priest and made him hereditary ethnarch and a Roman senator. Cæsar also granted him the right to refortify Jerusalem and gave the Jews all over the world substantial privileges (47 B.C.). With an eye to the future, Antipater made his son Phasael governor of Jerusalem, and sent his son Herod, then twenty-five years old, to restore order in Galilee where desperadoes, robbers and religious zealots were defying the authority of Rome. When Cæsar was assassinated in 44 B.C., Antipater trimmed his sails to go over to Brutus and Cassius, the leaders of the conspiracy; but Antipater died before the leadership of the East was settled, leaving his sons Phasael and Herod to manage king Hyrcanus and the Romans as best they could.

229. **Herod the Tight-Rope Walker.** The assassins of Cæsar did not gather up the Roman world as Antipater thought they would. Instead they were beaten at Philippi, 42 B.C., by Mark Antony and Octavius (afterward Augustus Cæsar). Young Herod promptly patronized Antony, and by bribes and his own personal charm brought it about that when Antony became master of the East he confirmed Herod and Phasael as tetrarchs under the nominal rule of Hyrcanus.

The Jews protested, but in vain. Antony now went to Egypt to carry on his long financial and political flirtation with Cleopatra that was to end in disaster for both. The Parthians took this opportunity to invade Palestine (40 B.C.). Antigonus, son of Aristobulus II, came again out of his hiding and persuaded them to espouse his cause. Eagerly welcomed by the Jews, they captured Jerusalem and with it King Hyrcanus and Phasael the governor. Hyrcanus they deported to Babylon and so mutilated him that he could never again be high priest. Phasael committed suicide. Herod escaped and fled with his family to the fortress of Masada, southwest of the Dead Sea. Antigonus after all his unsuccessful attempts was now installed as ruler and high priest, and for three years had the semblance of power. But the Parthians soon returned to their mountain fastnesses east of the Zagros, leaving Antigonus to look after himself.

230. **Herod's Sudden Rise to Power.** Herod now escaped from Masada and fled by way of Egypt to Rome. He showed Antony and Octavius that Antigonus had become ruler of Judea only by aid of the Parthians, the Roman archenemy. He urged them to dethrone Antigonus and substitute one Aristobulus, a grandson of old Hyrcanus and a brother of his fiancée Mariamne. To his surprise, they decided that Herod himself was the proper candidate for the office and had the Senate confirm his appointment as king of Judea (39 B.C.). The Jews hated Herod. When he landed to claim his kingdom the leaders would not co-operate. But Antony had loaned Herod two legions of Roman soldiers, more soldiers were picked up in Galilee, so that when Herod appeared before Jerusalem to take his kingdom by force he had 100,000 men at his back. A six months' siege followed and a surrender. The upstart king Antigonus was sent to Antioch, where after making of himself a spectacle of cowardice he was beheaded by Antony. Thus the house of the Hasmoneans ended ingloriously in 37 B.C., one hundred and thirty years after the first victories of the valiant Judas

Maccabæus and seventy years after the assumption of the royal title by Aristobulus I. Herod the Idumean was now king of the Jews.

231. Jewish Hopes and Fears. This period of swift changes of Roman masters, of the rise and fall of local rulers, of invasion and plunder and massacre, was intensely trying to the Jewish people. The vast majority of them naturally had no interest in the course of events except in so far as it meant taxes or bloodshed for them. Their troubles only drove them more strongly to religion and to the longing for relief offered by the hope of a great deliverer—the Messiah. This hope, born in the period of exile, had centred first around Zerubbabel; then, suffering a long eclipse, it shone forth at the time of the early Maccabees. Each time it was doomed to disappointment, but the hope persisted, taking on more fantastic and miraculous shapes until by the beginning of Herod's rule it had become almost a passion in which patriotism and religion were indistinguishably mingled. The Psalms of Solomon, completed in the early Roman period, voice the ideals and longings of loyal Pharisees; they lament the desecration and bloodshed wrought by Pompey, and the sins of priests and rulers; they express belief in God's mercy toward Israel, his speedy gift of a Messiah to lead them again to freedom, and his reward of resurrection and immortality for the faithful. Thus did a distressed people seek release from the wretched present in dreams of a sudden and miraculous deliverance. Underlying all their Messianic hopes was their indestructible belief in justice, in democracy, and in the right of each man and people to enjoy life, liberty and the pursuit of happiness. They also believed—even though Rome seemed to give the lie to this belief—that a God of justice ruled in the universe.

XXXI

HEROD OF THE IRON HAND

232. The Personality of Herod. The Jews had occasion to resent the coming of one like Herod to rule over them. They feared him for his ability, for his severity, and for his unscrupulousness. As a young man, with not much more to help him than engaging manners and brilliant speech, he had succeeded in winning the friendship of Antony, the master of the East. When sent by his father to pacify Galilee, he straightway showed consummate ability as a commander, even capturing brigands who infested the caves in the precipitous cliffs of Arbela, by letting down soldiers in cages from above and smoking out and shooting the rascals. His punishments were meted out to desperado and pious zealot alike, and with such severity that the Sanhedrin or national council at Jerusalem summoned him before them to answer the charge of killing good Jews. Herod appeared in full armor with a company of soldiers behind him, and the gray-bearded cowards dismissed the case. In politics, as we shall see, he was a trimmer, his object being to make a safe port for himself, whatever way the wind blew. Of respect for the Jewish nation and its religion he had not a trace. These were the reasons why the wise ones at Jerusalem were not wild with joy over his accession.

233. His Early Cruelties. The suspicions of the Jews were confirmed when shortly after his accession Herod put to death forty-five of the leaders of the old aristocracy— fully half the Sanhedrin. His marriage with Mariamne, a princess of the Hasmonean house, instead of harmonizing the factions, intensified them and made his home life a per-

fect torment.   Mariamne was not only beautiful but a little
too conscious of her ancient blood, and Herod's sister Salome
—in fact, the whole Idumean family—took violent offense

FIG. 146—ROCK OF CÆSAREA

This site (30 miles north of Jaffa) was chosen for Herod's city because the mass
    of rock gave promise of sheltering a harbor on its northern side.   Herod
    made the harbor by building breakwaters, consisting of stones 50 x 18 x 9
    feet in size, let down into 20 fathoms of water.   The mole was 200 feet
    wide.   It took ten or twelve years to build this and the city.
Here Vespasian was named emperor by his soldiers, and Titus celebrated his
    brother's birthday by setting 2,500 Jews to fight with beasts in the am-
    phitheatre.

at her. Thinking to gratify the Jews, Herod appointed
Mariamne's young brother Aristobulus high priest, but the
appointment proved so popular that within a few months
after his first official Passover Herod had him drowned in
the swimming-pool of the palace at Jericho (35 B.C.).   Mariamne loved Herod less after that, and among the sympathizers

there were whispers of revenge. Salome's incessant lies and goadings at last roused Herod's fear that Mariamne was plotting. He had her murdered at Samaria (29 B.C.), and she was the only person he ever loved. In the reaction that followed, his remorse knew no bounds and in fact nearly resulted in his death. But his suspicions of her family continued and the next victim was Mariamne's mother Alexandra. Even old and mutilated Hyrcanus was brought back from Babylon and killed. Along with these were sacrificed many others who he thought were involved. By 25 B.C. he had killed off all possible claimants to the throne and terrorized all his subjects into submission.

234. **His Political Shrewdness.** Herod's political path also was a treacherous one: he had to keep his balance and his head amid the whirlwinds of Roman politics. He was devotedly attached to Antony. Cleopatra on the other hand hated him, and it was a question whether her hatred or Antony's friendship would win. When Antony fell out with Octavius, Herod vigorously supported his friend Antony. But when the battle of Actium (31 B.C.) showed him that Octavius was destined to be the master of the world, Herod went to Rhodes to meet the conqueror, taking with him his best wits and much gold. He argued that as he had been a valuable friend to Antony as long as Antony deserved friendship, so he could be a valuable friend to Antony's wiser conqueror. Octavius was duly impressed and confirmed Herod on his throne. After the conquest of Egypt he gave Herod also the whole Syrian coast from Egypt to Tyre, and added the cities of Gadara, Hippos and Samaria, and the territory northeast of the sea of Galilee.

235. **His Hellenism.** Having thus secured his throne from dangers within and without, Herod settled down to his policy of Oriental magnificence. In temper he was an Eastern despot, but in culture he was thoroughly Greek. Under him Hellenism came to its own. His court was full of Greek parasites. His most trusted adviser during the latter half

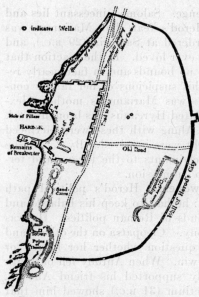

FIG. 147—PLAN OF CÆSAREA

Notice the walls of two towns: the outer circular wall of Herod's city three miles long, and the inner rectangular wall of the mediæval city built by the crusaders. The splendor of Herod's foundation made it the most important city of Palestine. The Roman procurators lived here. It was the port of entry for all southern Palestine and Arabia. St. Paul was a prisoner here for two years (Sec. 242). The great hippodrome had seats for 20,000 spectators.

of his life was a rhetorician of Damascus named Nicholas with whom he read Greek literature and talked of Greek philosophy and composed speeches in the style of Demosthenes. He even endowed the Olympic games in Greece and was made perpetual president of that institution. But his special passion was building Greek cities and adorning them after the classic style, and in showering benefits on famous centres of Hellenic culture. Nearly a score of the latter had cause to thank him, including Athens, Sparta, and Rhodes. Here it was a temple he built, there a stoa or a bath. In Antioch he built a colonnaded street of marble; temples to the divine Augustus went up all over Palestine. In Jerusalem he built a theatre and an amphitheatre, besides remodelling the fortress of John Hyrcanus northwest of the temple and naming it Antonia in memory of his first Roman friend. After the Hellenic style he also constructed his palace at Jericho and the palace and park on the high hill southeast of Bethlehem, known to-day as the Frank Mountain.

His crowning works of civic splendor were the cities of Sebaste and Cæsarea. The former was the ancient Samaria which John Hyrcanus had destroyed twenty-nine years

Fig. 148—HEROD'S LAW COURT

This imposing building, excavated by Harvard University in 1908, stands in the eastern part of Herod's city, just off the forum. Its floor consisted of marble mosaic. The columns divided the building into a central nave and a broad aisle on each side. You are looking across the western aisle and into the nave. Find the semicircular seats where the judges sat. The lighter portions of the columns show the depth of the débris which the excavators had to remove.

before and the site of which had been given him by Octavius. Herod rebuilt it magnificently, erected a gymnasium, basilica, double street of columns a mile long around the crest of the hill; on the acropolis he reared a temple to the emperor and in the year when Octavius assumed the title "Augustus" dedicated the whole to him and named it Sebaste—the Greek for Augustus. A still more magnificent offering to his imperial patron was Cæsarea, named also for this adopted son of Julius Cæsar. First he built a harbor by running a breakwater two hundred feet wide out into the open sea—a brilliant engineering feat in those days. Then the city rose superbly, its public buildings of marble adorned with costly pillars from abroad, as the relics now in the Piazzetta in Venice testify. There were the usual street and agora, a temple, a theatre, an amphitheatre and a palace. These splendid monuments strengthened the favor of Augustus and got Herod a name.

236. **His Judaism.** Though Herod despised the Jews and hated their religion, as king of the Jews he felt it necessary to pay some attention to his people's faith, at least in their chief city. He himself never exercised the functions of high priest. Instead, he raised to office various nobodies who did what he said, and removed them as he pleased. These dignitaries did not transgress the requirements of the ritual, and therefore the Pharisees endured them and him with a sort of sullen loyalty. In little things Herod always respected Jewish scruples. His buildings in Jerusalem and his coins bore no likeness of living things, there were no statues erected in the holy city, his daughters were married to none but Jews, and he used his influence with Augustus to protect the Jews of the dispersion everywhere. These things undoubtedly helped keep him on his throne. But his great bribe to the nation, as every one concedes, was the new temple at Jerusalem, the most sumptuous building the Jews ever owned.

237. **The Temple of Herod.** When Herod proposed to rebuild the temple there was consternation lest the sacred place be desecrated. But Herod began at once to train large numbers of the priests as masons and carpenters, so that they, rather than unsanctified workmen might perform the sacred task. First he enlarged the narrow summit of Mount Moriah by building a huge platform of stone, supporting it on piers and arches—now seen in the so-called Solomon's stables— and buttressing it with a wall of magnificent hewn stone.

This platform, about a thousand feet square and extending
on all sides but the north, quite covered up the site of Solomon's palace. All around the borders of this area he erected
beautiful colonnades of marble, row on row, and roofed

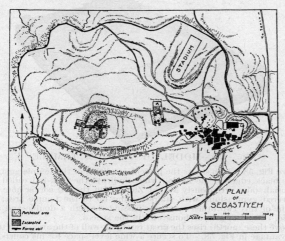

Fig. 149—HEROD'S SAMARIA

A good portion of the hill is here shown.   Note the outer defensive wall following the contours of the land; the western gate—no doubt the one outside
of which the lepers sat in Benhadad's day; the street of columns running
round the crest of the hill—monoliths of limestone about 18 feet high, in
four rows; the citadel toward the left, on which were the earlier palaces
and Herod's Augustus temple.   Between the citadel and the village lies
the rectangle of the basilica, while perhaps two hundred feet below to the
northeast, the gymnasium, called stadium on the plan, was built in a bay
in the hill.

them with cedar of Lebanon.   These formed the famous
porches or cloisters in which the citizens of Jerusalem could
walk or lounge and the rabbis hold their schools.   Solomon's
Porch was the eastern colonnade, the Royal Porch the
southern.   All the area so far mentioned was called the Court
of the Gentiles.   From this platform and these porches there
arose toward the centre various flights of steps leading to a

higher level. No one but Jews could enter here. Warnings were posted to that effect at the top of each stairway. On this higher level was another colonnade arranged as a hollow

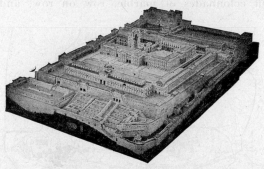

Fig. 150—MODEL OF HEROD'S TEMPLE

Compare Fig. 58, which shows the present condition of the temple area. Note the black edges of the model, which indicate the rock-hill called Mount Moriah (also erroneously Mount Zion). On the left corner note the uncovered gymnasium, with stairs leading up to the temple area; to the right of this two other entrances passing through a double and a triple gate. Rows of priests' houses fill in the spaces.

Just above these (north) rises the great retaining-wall of the area, seen to better advantage in Fig. 58. To secure a wide level space for his courts, Herod raised on vaultings a huge platform (see Fig. 58, the bright portion in the southeast, and Fig. 152, "Solomon's Stables"). Going north on this area you come to the Royal Porch—a long covered colonnade running east and west. You are now within the Court of the Gentiles—free to every one. Solomon's porch is the colonnade that bounds this court on the east.

Crossing this court toward the centre you come to a platform raised on fourteen steps. Beyond these steps Gentiles might not go (Fig. 151). The Court of Israel began here, surrounded by a high building in the form of a hollow square. This court was again subdivided into the Court of the Women (east) and the Court of the Men (west). In the latter was the Temple proper, with the altar of burnt-offering. .Notice in the picture the lofty façade of the temple, facing the rising sun.

square and the square itself divided into two parts by a wall of columns. The eastern portion was the Court of the Women. The western, approached through the lofty Gate Beautiful, was the Court of Israel, exclusively for men. All but the front edge of this latter area was reserved for the priests and those who assisted at the temple service. Within this for-

bidden section arose first the great stone altar of sacrifice,
and then the temple building proper, a house about ninety
by a hundred and twenty feet, with a large façade extending like wings thirty feet on each side of the front and rising a

FIG. 151—WARNING–STONE FROM HEROD'S TEMPLE

Discovered in 1871, now in the museum at Constantinople. It stood originally
at the top of one of the stairs that led to the Court of Israel. The warning,
written in large Greek characters, reads as follows: "Let no foreigner
enter within the balustrade and embankment about the sanctuary. Whoever is caught makes himself responsible for his death which will follow."

hundred and twenty feet into the air. The foundation blocks
of the house were nearly seventy feet by nine feet each, their
outer faces covered with gold. The internal arrangements of
the house were identical with those of Solomon's temple
(Sec. 76), only instead of the ark in the inner shrine there
was a slab of stone. The whole constituted a structure of
which the Jews everywhere were justly proud, and which
adequately housed the elaborate and dignified ceremonial
which the Pharisees had developed in the five hundred years

since Zerubbabel and his returned exiles had restored the
worship of their fathers. Yet their pride in the building was
no greater than their detestation of the builder: contemporary rabbis never mention his name in connection with it.

From a photograph.

FIG. 152—SOLOMON'S STABLES

Compare Fig. 58, and note how the floor of the temple area is raised high above
the hill. This floor is of stone, and is supported on long piers that run
down below the present level of the ground to the solid rock of the hill.
The present picture takes you beneath the floor and among these piers.
While Herod laid the foundations most of his superstructure has perished.
These particular piers were built by the emperor Justinian (c. 550 A.D.)
when he repaired the area and built the church of the Virgin Mary, now
used as a mosque (el-Aksar), and shown on Fig. 58 against the south wall;
or perhaps by the Arabs in the eighth century. The crusaders used to
stable their horses here, and the holes pierced in the stones to hold the
halter ropes may still be seen. In spite of the name, none of this work
has any connection with Solomon.

238. Herod's Last Years. It is difficult to find in history a more pitiful figure than Herod in his old age. As in-
firmities increased he became more suspicious, arbitrary and
unscrupulous. He knew how his people hated him and this
knowledge did not tend to soften him. His sons too began
to intrigue for the succession; and the various factions in
the harem and the palace were always informing on one another and receiving their rewards in scourgings, poisonings

and crucifixions. It was a living hell. Herod's two sons by
Mariamne had been sent to Rome for an education. When
they returned after six years they may have put on some
airs, and, being the very last of the old Jewish house of
the Maccabees, the thought of the people centred on them
too strongly for Herod's peace of mind. His son by an earlier marriage, Antipater, fanned his suspicions with lies until
Herod finally had the boys strangled at Sebaste (7 B.C.).
Later Herod found that Antipater was the real traitor, and
threw him into prison. Herod himself now fell mortally
sick. His ravings were terrible to hear and his orders for
executions blood-curdling. Antipater was the last victim of
his rage; which led Augustus when he heard of it to exclaim:
"Better be Herod's pig than his son." Five days later the
royal maniac died at Jericho (4 B.C.), having left an order
with his sister Salome to have all the notable Jews butchered
so that people might mourn at his funeral. Salome ignored it.

239. **The Effect of His Reign.** Herod would not have been
called the Great were there not substantial reasons. There
is no denying the greatness of his natural endowment, nor
the fact that under his iron hand the Jewish nation grew in
wealth and importance. Herod first of all gave peace to
Palestine. He was the first ruler since Simon Maccabæus
who was strong enough to keep order, to make the Pharisees
and Sadducees stop murdering one another. In the process,
to be sure, he extinguished the last traces of Maccabean
blood, but that removed one potent cause for quarrel.
Moreover, by denying the Pharisees any participation in
politics he freed them to develop their religious beliefs and
practices, to study and teach the sacred law, and thus gain a
hold on the minds and lives of the people that the Sadducees never attained. It was this influence that made the
Jews of Jesus' day so strongly religious—after their own idea
of religion. And, lastly, his gift of the temple gave the Jews
all over the world a rallying-place and a pride in both race
and religion, turned the feet of thousands each year to wor-

ship at his magnificent shrine, and helped bind them so inseparably to their faith that two thousand years of exile and persecution have not shaken it. Herod's Hellenism left no trace; his Judaism still lives.

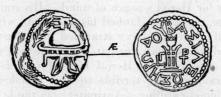

FIG. 153—COPPER COIN OF HEROD I

The inscription in Greek reads: (right) "Of King Herod."

XXXII

ROME'S DEATH THRUST

240. The Palestine of Jesus' Day. The life of Jesus (6 B.C.–29 A.D.) falls within the period we are now considering and gives it an interest and importance in the world's thought that it could not otherwise possess. The Jewish state is drifting—or rather, rushing—toward a cataract; its destruction is at hand. Rome does not stay the catastrophe, but rather hastens it through the excesses of her rascally officials. Centuries of fanaticism conspire with centuries of misrule to work the ruin of the Jewish nation.

Herod divided his kingdom by will among his three surviving sons: Archelaus was named king of Judea, Samaria and Idumea; Herod Antipas, tetrarch of Galilee and Perea; Philip, tetrarch of the northeast territory. Augustus after some delay confirmed the will though he styled Archelaus simply an ethnarch and took away some of his territory east of the Jordan. Archelaus was thoroughly bad. The Jews endured him for ten years and then in 6 A.D. made such a powerful complaint that the emperor banished him to France and placed his territory under a Roman procurator subject to the legate of Syria.

These procurators resided at Cæsarea, though at feasts and other important functions they stayed in Jerusalem, occupying Herod's palace which was henceforth called the Pretorium (John 18²⁸). They exercised supreme military and financial control and alone had power of life and death. They ruled, with a brief interim, from 6 to 66 A.D. In general they were a disgrace to the government they represented. Pontius Pilate, whose connection with the death of

Jesus alone makes him immortal, was procurator from 26 to
36 A.D., and furnished his full quota of torment for the Jews.
In Galilee Herod Antipas had a long reign of forty-three
years (4 B.C.–34 A.D.), a crafty, ambitious, and unscrupulous ruler whom Jesus characterized as "that fox." He is the

FIG. 154—JERUSALEM FROM THE NORTHEAST

"Jerusalem is builded as a city that is compact together." Ps. 122³. The
present walls are only half a mile on a side, enclosing therefore an area of
a quarter of a square mile. Within this space about 65,000 people live.
A modern suburb containing perhaps 35,000 has arisen to the north (right)
of the city. Find the valley of the Kidron, the temple area, the site of
Herod's palace.

tyrant who put John the Baptist to death and scoffed at
Jesus during his trial at Jerusalem. Philip (4 B.C.–34 A.D.)
seems to have been a good ruler, but his tetrarchy contained
practically no Jews.

241. **The Reign of Herod Agrippa I** (41–44 A.D.). The
rule of the procurators in Judea is broken only by the three-
year reign of King Herod Agrippa. This man owed his success to the fact that in his early days in Rome he gained the
favor of the emperor Caligula. When his uncle Philip died,
Caligula gave that tetrarchy to Agrippa, together with the

title of King. At the assassination of Caligula, Agrippa was
instrumental in placing his boon companion Claudius on the
throne, who as a reward banished Antipas to France and gave
his tetrarchy also to Agrippa. Soon after (41 A.D.), the emperor
added the territory of the Judean procurators, so that for
the last time in history a king ruled all of Palestine. Agrippa
was a fairly good ruler, tried to be a pious Jew and even
went so far as to persecute the rising Christian church in
order to please the Jews (Acts 12$^{1-3}$). He died shortly afterward at Cæsarea (Acts 12$^{18-23}$).

242. **Herod Agrippa II and the Apostle Paul.** The other
Agrippa mentioned in the book of Acts is Herod Agrippa II,
who was tetrarch of Philip's former territory, Gaulonitis, etc.
He comes into the narrative as friend of the procurator Felix
who married his sister Drusilla and who delayed his judgment in the case of the apostle Paul, hoping that Paul would
bribe him (Acts 23^{31}–24^{27}). Felix was one of the worst of
the Roman procurators. While Paul was lying in his dun-
geon at Cæsarea, the city was in open revolt against him.
After he was deposed, Agrippa kept up his friendship with his
successor Festus, perhaps the best procurator of the lot, and
with him had the pleasure of listening to Paul's famous speech
recorded in Acts 26. Festus had a sufficient sense of justice to see Paul's innocence; but Paul by this time had
taken the case out of the procurator's hands by appealing
to Cæsar.

243. **The Great Rebellion.** In all these changes of governors it is evident that the Jews themselves had no voice.
The nation that had been the first to embody in lasting institutions the true spirit of democracy, now through the
wicked ambitions of its chosen rulers found itself in the grip
of Roman military despotism. Under Rome's strangle-hold,
self-government died, but not the spirit of freedom. Driven
mad by their governors' utter disregard for all rights and
decency, the Jews broke into open rebellion in 66 A.D. First
they won some victories over the legions sent from Syria.

The emperor Nero realizing the seriousness of the revolt, despatched his best generals, Vespasian and Titus, to subdue it. Beginning in the north, they reduced Galilee after a year of severe fighting, then took the territory west and south of Jerusalem, and lastly closed in on the city itself in one of the most desperate sieges in history. We are indebted to the Jewish historian Josephus for full details of this entire period. Josephus was in command of Jewish forces in Galilee, but early surrendered to the Roman, used his influence to help the Roman cause, and after the great catastrophe retired to Rome with the emperor's favor to spend his declining years in writing the history of his people.

244. **The Siege of Jerusalem.** As the Roman armies closed about the sacred city the conditions within were indeed desperate. There were three different factions quarrelling over what should be done and who should lead. One held the lower town, one the upper and one the temple. The grain-supply in the Tyropean valley, enough to provision the city for a long siege, became a bone of contention between two of the factions, and after repeated fights and slaughterings the whole vast store was burned. Here indeed was a situation. A city dominated by three fanatical groups of soldiers who waged bloody war on each other and butchered all who called for surrender to the Romans, a city crammed not only with its normal population but with refugees from the country and with an immense crowd of pilgrims who had come up to the Passover. Estimates of this horde vary from 600,000 to 2,000,000, all jammed into that pitiful area of a single square mile, powerless to fight or run away and yet compelled to eat. Before Titus had fairly invested the city they began to die like flies.

Titus posted his tenth legion on the Mount of Olives to the east, the twelfth and fifteenth on Mount Scopas to the north, and the fifth on the west, opposite the present Jaffa gate. He then began the assault on the northern wall. For artillery he had the *ballista*, a gigantic sling-shot that could throw a stone weighing one hundred and thirty pounds a quarter of a mile. These stones he painted white so that the gunners could better follow their flight and judge the range. He used also the familiar battering ram, to supply

FIG. 155—JERUSALEM FROM THE SOUTHWEST

You are looking northeast from the valley of Hinnom at a place called "The Sultan's Pool." The pool is now used as a cattle market. The tower is a minaret rising from the Turkish barracks in the citadel. Solomon may have had a tower on that spot, but we know that Herod's palace lay there extending from his towers of Phasael, Hippicus and Mariamne on the north (left), along the wall southward for a thousand feet. The hill on which the wall seems to rest was made by the soldiers of Titus during the siege (Sec. 244). Beneath this earth the city wall rests on a scarp of solid rock, too high to be touched by rams.

timber for which and for his towers he cut down every tree within ten miles of Jerusalem. In order to bring his machines close to the wall, which rose high above the perpendicular sides of the valleys that surrounded the city, his soldiers raised huge mounds of earth with long inclines, the remains of which may be seen to-day along the west wall. (Fig. 155.) So after almost superhuman preparations the assault began. Day and night the north wall where the defense was weakest

trembled under the steady impact of the rams, while all
around was desperate fire and counter-fire and sortie, until
on the fifteenth day the biggest ram—old Nikon, "the conqueror"—breached the third or outer wall and Titus became
master of the new city quarter, Bezetha. Nine days more of
desperate fighting gave him the second wall and the lower
city.

245. **Horrors of the Siege.** The conditions within the city
were now pitiful beyond description. Men died until there
were none to bury and the bodies choked all the valleys and
the streets. Those who had strength left pillaged and killed
without mercy that they might obtain and hide away some
little morsel of food against worse days to come. The whole
city was filled with one passion, to possess just one mouth-
ful of something, until children killed their fathers, and
mothers their children, for the sake of the one scrap of bread
that was in their mouths. At night some of the wretches
would steal out into the valleys beyond the walls where the
dead bodies were rotting to gather perchance a few roots.
Those whom the Romans caught they crucified, five hundred
in a night. Those who returned to the city were robbed of
what they had found, or were murdered for its sake. And
yet neither of the two commanders hinted at surrender.
On the contrary, the defense continued with incredible
courage and effectiveness. The Jews even undermined the
Roman mounds, caused the collapse and almost total destruction of their engines, and sallied with such a whirlwind
of rage that Titus saw his legions waver before this half-
starved and haggard mob. The assault had failed. The
Roman had to wait for his ally, starvation.

Titus now built a wall of earth five miles in length, completely around the city and far enough away to be out of
range of the Jewish arrows. This work, vast though it was,
he accomplished in three days. The blockade was now absolute and the suffering of the wretched city was so intense
that it moved to tears even Titus, who called God to witness

that it was not his doing. Again and again Titus offered
clemency in return for surrender, but the city would not
listen.

246. **The Final Assault.** As the months passed and the
defense weakened, Titus renewed his assaults. One by one,

FIG. 156—SPOILS FROM JERUSALEM

A marble panel (restored) from the Triumphal Arch of Titus erected on the
Via Sacra in Rome half-way from the Colosseum to the forum, to commemorate the destruction of Jerusalem by Titus, A.D. 70. This panel
presents a procession of Roman soldiers crowned with laurel, carrying
the seven-branched candlestick, the table of show-bread, and the silver
trumpets, all from Herod's temple.

after desperate resistance, the remaining walls were taken.
Antonia succumbed and was pulled down. On July 17, 70
A.D., the deathless flame went out and the daily sacrifice in
the temple failed for the first time. But only after a month
more of fighting and engineering, and six days of continuous
play from the rams against the temple wall, did the Roman
win even the outer cloisters. John and his men made their
last stand in the inner temple and fought like demons; until
on August 9, contrary to the orders of Titus who hoped to
save the holy of holies, soldiers set fire to a golden window

through which there was a passage to the storerooms about the house. The noble temple was doomed. Titus and his staff did everything they could to save it, but the soldiers were mad. The entire building was consumed and all the ten thousand men, women, and children, priests and commons who were in the sacred enclosure perished either by fire or the sword.

All the city, but the upper section around Herod's palace, was now in Roman hands. But still the handful of its defenders scorned in their madness Titus' offers of clemency. Nearly a month more was necessary to raise new mounds, construct new engines, breach the walls, and take possession. But at last the end came. The Romans slew until they were weary, plundered until the corpses in the houses drove them into the street, and then killed again till every lane and alley was choked with blood and dead bodies. Then they set fire to the houses. Those whom the victor saved alive would better have died; they were made to fight wild beasts at Cæsarea or were doomed to perpetual labor in the mines of Sinai, a living death with none to pity. This fate to the conquered. To the victor, spoil uncounted, the grand triumph at Rome, the marble arch that still crowns the Roman forum, and the emperor's seat.

So ends a siege more heroic and more tragic than any in history.

247. **The Last Agonies.** With the fall of Jerusalem, the Sanhedrin, the party of the Sadducees and the entire priesthood as an institution perished forever, but Judaism itself remained. There was the dispersion found among all the great commercial cities of the world; there were the law, the synagogue, and the rabbis. These things kept Judaism alive. Many Jews were still left in Palestine, so that the government continued under a Roman prætor. These Jews gradually overcame the numbness of defeat and rallied around their rabbis at various places; first at Jamnia, where a sort of

"college of scribes" was formed after the pattern of the old
Sanhedrin. It was this group of rabbis who in A.D. 90 pronounced the book of Jewish scriptures complete—our Old
Testament as it now stands. Afterward the towns of Tiberias and Sepphoris in Galilee became centres of learned
authority. But the sullen hatred of Rome kept showing itself in Jewish settlements in various parts of the empire.
Messiahs were constantly appearing to fan useless hopes, and
the Roman arms had constantly to be called upon to put
down the revolts. Jerusalem still lay in heaps, peopled only
by the Tenth Legion. Under the emperor Hadrian who had
a passion for building and restoring, the Jews of Palestine
ventured to ask permission to rebuild their temple. Hadrian,
warned by the prevailing spirit of Judaism, refused the request
and announced that he himself was about to restore Jerusalem
as a Roman colony. This proposed desecration of their holy
city touched off a fanatical uprising, led by one Bar Cochba
who declared himself to be the Messiah. Jews from all
over the world flocked to him. He proclaimed himself king
(132 A.D.), and struck coins to that effect. Hadrian was
exasperated and took the field in person against him. The
resistance was desperate for a period of three and a half
years. But Hadrian won (135 A.D.). He destroyed in Palestine 50 fortresses and 985 villages, killed in battle 580,000
men, and caused untold numbers more to die of wounds and
famine. The slave markets of the East were again glutted
with Jews.

The emperor then finished the rebuilding of Jerusalem in
the classic style, with colonnaded street, forums, a basilica,
theatre and stadium, named it Ælia Capitolina, erected a
temple to Jupiter on the site of Herod's temple to Jehovah
and one to Venus where now stands the Church of the Holy
Sepulchre. He also forbade all Jews to live in it forever or
even approach near enough to see it. The detested name of
Judea was blotted from the Roman vocabulary and the land
renamed Syria Palestina. Thus definitely ended the life of

the Jews as a nation. Henceforth they have lived only as a race and a religion, scattered like dust to the four corners of the earth.

248. Israel's Troubled History. The end of the old Hebrew democracy was an appalling tragedy. Helpless in the grasp of a despotism that ruled the world with an iron hand, the nation poured out its life blood in a frantic, futile attempt to break its shackles. Throughout the world autocracy was in ascendency. But eighteen centuries must elapse before the sun of righteousness and democracy, whose first rays lighted up the hills of Palestine, was to stand in the zenith. Israel lost its national life, but the principles which its prophets and patriots had struggled to establish survived, and to-day are triumphing gloriously. The age when one powerful nation can rule the rest of the world by force of arms is forever past. At last in the councils of the nations the rights even of the small and weak races are receiving consideration. Before the sixth century the religious ideas that sprang from rocky Palestine had conquered the Roman Empire. Israel's long struggle against despotism and intrenched injustice was not in vain, for the democratic principles that Rome suppressed so relentlessly in the opening of the Christian century are to-day accepted throughout the world.

249. Israel's Priceless Gifts to the World. Israel's glory consists not in what it achieved as a nation, but in the ideals it gave to the world. Small, indeed, is our debt to the hundreds of autocratic states that have flourished in the past compared with what we owe to the little democracies of Greece and of Palestine. They are the beacon-lights that illumine the darkness of the ancient world. From Greece came art, science, philosophy, and a brilliant literature. Israel's contribution was very different but equally important. It gave the world a literature of marvellous simplicity and beauty, including lyric and elegiac poetry, epic, story and history, romances, practical maxims, stirring orations,

and letters pulsating with heroic ideals.   Through our King
James Version the ideas and picturesque idioms of the Hebrew scriptures have enriched beyond measure our English
tongue.

From Israel has come a moral code based on the Ten Commandments, which expresses, as well as mere laws can, the
fundamental duties of man to God and to his fellow man.
It sprang from an instinct for freedom and brotherhood, perhaps the earliest and certainly the most persistent mani-
festation of that instinct among the ancient peoples of the
world.   It is this code that is the basis not only of the con-
stitutions but also of the every-day life of all the great democracies of the present day.   The only improvement that
has been made on this ancient Hebrew code is to substitute
for its hundred or more separate rules of conduct, love as the
guiding motive in all action.   Emphasis on this principle of
love was Jesus' great contribution to individual and social
morality—and Jesus was a Jew.

From the Hebrew prophets, as well as from Jesus the
Prophet of Nazareth, come those principles of justice to all
men and classes, of the equality of opportunity and responsibility for every individual and nation, of good-will between
men and races, of service to the poor and needy, and of co-
operation in building a perfect society which are the essence of democracy and the watchwords of the modern world
movement.

The Hebrews, too, have led the races of the earth in the
quest for the eternal Source of all life and wisdom and goodness.   Almost from the first they recognized that he was a
God of justice and mercy as well as of might.   As they
gained deeper spiritual insight they saw that he was not
merely one of many national deities, but the one God who
rules the universe, the creator and preserver of all, the
Father in whom we live and move and have our being.   In
the Old Testament it is possible to follow each stage in the
gradual growth of this larger faith.   Above all, the Hebrew

prophets, psalmists and sages, and the greatest Prophet of them all, have taught men how to enter into living touch and personal co-operation with him, whom to know aright is life eternal.

XXXIII

THE LONG, LONG EXILE

Most histories of the Chosen People end with the destruction of the Jewish state. But Judaism did not cease in the days of Hadrian; its life has gone on to our own day. It is to bridge this long gap and relate the past to the present that this chapter is added.

250. In Roman Times. While Rome blotted out the Judaism of Judea, she fostered Jews elsewhere. Throughout the empire the Jews were allowed the same rights, the same civil and religious liberties as countless other faiths. Jews could be Roman citizens. Even down to Constantine's time (the fourth century) and after, the Jews suffered no inconveniences or persecutions except such as they brought upon themselves by their exclusiveness and their other racial peculiarities. But, as the Roman Empire gradually became Christian, popular dislike grew to hatred and frequently showed itself in acts of violence on both sides. In 429, under the emperor Honorius, the Jews were excluded from holding public office, and the religious tax formerly paid to their chief rabbi or patriarch was directed into the imperial treasury. Then learning began to die among them, the scholars emigrated from Palestine, and while Genseric the Vandal was plundering the Eternal City and taking Titus' hard-won Jewish spoils from Rome to Carthage, the last vestiges of the Jewish race were silently leaving their ancestral land, destined not to return for fifteen hundred years.

251. In the East before the Middle Ages. After the Eastern Roman Empire (the Byzantine) lost its grip in Asia (616 A.D.), the Jews in the East paid fealty to Parthian and

357

Persian kings. In Babylonia the Jews were fairly numerous, descendants of the Judean exiles who had never returned to Palestine. In the third Christian century they developed a strong intellectual life, studied the law and the traditions, and by the year 500 completed the vast work known as the Babylonian Talmud, which soon displaced the earlier Jerusalem Talmud as an authority. When Mohammed arose (c. 622 A.D.), he was at first favorable to Jews and derived much of the material of his Koran from the Old Testament. But when he found that he could not change their religion he turned against them. Many Jewish settlements were forcibly converted to Islam; others had to pay the head tax that was levied by the caliphs on all infidels. The Jews therefore began to leave the East. By the year 1100 the centre of gravity of Judaism had shifted entirely from the East to Spain.

252. **In Spain during the Middle Ages.** Trade and persecutions had long before this brought Jewish colonists into Spain. When the Western Roman Empire went to pieces and the Visigoths took southwestern Europe, they tolerated the Jews as industrious and law-abiding citizens. But Christian hatred pursued them thither. As the Catholic Church came into power, persecutions increased; so that, when Tarak and his Arab-Moorish followers crossed over from Africa in 711 and conquered the Spanish peninsula, they were welcomed by the Jews. Under the broad-minded sway of the Arab the Jew flourished. Thousands came to this oasis of Islam on the edge of the cruel Christian desert. Granada, Cordova, Toledo and other Spanish cities attracted large settlements of Jews. They had equal civil and social rights with others. A friendly rivalry grew up between Jew and Arab in intellectual matters, in philosophy, the study of language, the art of poetry, the science and practice of medicine. Many Jews rose to high office in the state. The list of noted Spanish Jews is a long and honorable one, including Maimonides (died 1204), the greatest scholar of his age.

But as the Moorish power waned and the Christians gained the upper hand again, evil times returned. The Popes framed oppressive laws and urged Christian princes to frame others. Jews were forbidden to hold office, forbidden to take interest on their loans, and made to wear a distinctive dress. In 1412 they were made to dwell only in certain quarters of each city — henceforth called the Ghetto. In 1480 the church introduced into Spain the Inquisition— that is, appointed officers and courts to hunt up heretics and punish them. As many Jews had pretended to become Christians in order to escape persecution, the Inquisition began on them, with the result that there were many imprisonments and executions, while many Jewish families fled the country. When King

Fig. 157—RELIGIOUS DISPUTATION BETWEEN JEWS AND CHRISTIANS

Public debates between Jews and non-Jews were frequently held in the Middle Ages. After the Inquisition was established under Pope Innocent III, the disputes became mock-tournaments of learning and led to relentless persecutions of the Jews. The most remarkable of all disputes was presided over by Pope Benedict XIII and lasted from Feb., 1413, to Nov., 1414. The object was to prove from the Talmud that Jesus was the Messiah. The outcome was a decree forbidding the study of the Talmud and inflicting all kinds of degradation on the Jews.

Ferdinand of Castile finally brought the Moorish power to an end and made the Christian power supreme in Spain, he made a decree (1492) banishing all Jews from the land and confiscating their property. This was a cruel edict. Hundreds of thousands of the best citizens Spain ever knew were forced into a new exile. Many went to North Africa, Italy, and even Turkey. One of the ironies of history is that Christian persecution should have driven the Jew into the merciful arms of the Turk! They went also in large numbers to neighboring Portugal. But in 1497 Portugal drove them out, and they sought refuge in England and the Netherlands. All this was a terrible blow to Judaism, for the Spanish Jews represented the highest type of culture in Europe. It was also a terrible blow to Spain and Portugal; they never recovered from this ruthless sacrifice of their best citizens, and their vast colonial empires began to shrink almost from that hour.

253. **In the Rest of Europe.** A similar fate pursued the Jews into whatever country they entered. Strangely enough, Italy was the most tolerant, for the papal power was less strong at the centre than at the extremities of its empire. In Italy the Jews became famous for learning and especially for their skill in medicine. Even the Popes, contrary to their own laws, employed Jewish physicians. After the Turks captured Constantinople in 1453 and many Greek scholars fled westward bringing their precious manuscripts of Greek philosophy and literature, none welcomed the new learning more eagerly than the Jews. They became famous humanists (teachers of the new classic culture), and by pretending to become Christians, many rose to high positions in the state and in the professions. But in 1550 the Jesuit persecutions began and gradually sealed the fate of the Italian Jew.

In the more northern countries the Jews did not reach any height of culture, but they were always strict in morals and very industrious. Charlemagne, the great Frankish emperor (c. 800), was good to them. They reached the peak of their prosperity about 1000 A.D. Then the Roman clergy began hostilities. When the Crusades were launched, the soldiers of the Cross, thinking that they could not better begin their

FIG. 158—JEWS TRANSFIXING HOSTS

Copied from the Gobelin tapestries in the cathedral of Saint Gudule, Brussels. A banker of Enghien was assassinated, and his wife and son took refuge in Brussels. The assassin spread the report that the Jews had stolen from a church the consecrated wafers of the Mass in order to pierce them with poniards and thus murder Christ afresh. This led to the burning of hundreds of Jews at Brussels, May 22, 1370, and a decree of banishment of the race from Belgium. This picture illustrates the legend that the wafers as they were pierced spouted blood. Note the consternation into which the Jews are thrown by the miracle.

FIG. 159—COSTUME OF GERMAN
JEWS OF THE THIRTEENTH
CENTURY

The Lateran Council of 1215 decreed that
all Jews should wear a badge, so that
they might not be mistaken for Christians. Usually this was some device
sewn on the garments, but sometimes
it was a hat of peculiar shape, like
those shown in this picture The
garments of Jews were usually black.
The long mantle indicates that Jews
were debarred from the handicrafts.

campaign than by mas-
sacring the murderers
of Christ, turned them-
selves loose upon the
Jews of the Rhine coun-
try and beyond. For
two months they plun-
dered and murdered
(1096), until 12,000 Jews
perished. This was the
most severe persecution
the Jews had experienced
in a thousand years. The
Second Crusade adopted
similar measures, aided
by an edict from the
Pope that no interest
need be paid by any
Christian who owed a
Jew money. The Jew
lost all political standing
and all rights before the
law. In 1242 the author-
ities began burning the
Talmud, thinking to ex-
tinguish the Jewish faith.
In Paris twenty-four
cartloads were publicly
burned. From France
the Jews were expelled in
1306; then having been
allowed to return, were
again expelled in 1394.

When the Black Death ravaged Europe in the fourteenth
century and destroyed one quarter of the population, reports
were spread that the Jews had caused it by poisoning the

wells. Chiefly in Germany the clergy and the monks invented also the
lies that the Jews were accustomed
to kidnap Christian children and eat
their flesh in connection with the
Passover, likewise to desecrate on
occasion the Sacrament of the Christians. Urged on by these holy men
the church began another horrible
persecution, to the lasting disgrace
of Christendom in general and
Germany in particular. Hosts of
German Jews now fled to Poland
and Russia. Though later princes
recognized the damage done to their
prosperity by this flight of industrious citizens, and revoked the edicts
passed against them, spasms of persecution occurred for many years.

In England the Jews were tolerated until the reign of the infamous
Richard the Lion-hearted. Then
persecutions began, incited by religious bigotry, race prejudice, and
envy of the riches of individual
Jewish merchants. Jews were finally
banished from England by Edward
I in 1290.

Thus everywhere in the Middle
Ages the Jews were politically and
socially crushed and degraded.
They had no country. Instead,
they were crowded into the ghettos
of cities, forced to wear distinctive
clothes, to pay special taxes. They
were excluded from trade, from ag-

Fig. 160—JEW OF KO-
LOMIA, IN AUSTRIAN
GALICIA

A modern costume Note
the fur on the hat, the
old-fashioned "paletot"
or coat reaching to the
ankles, and the white
socks into which the
trousers are tucked.

riculture, and from offices of state. Their only chance for a livelihood lay in petty commerce and the traffic in money. Life and property were constantly exposed to attack and seizure. Under all this abusive and cruel treatment, it is no wonder that the Jews developed a horror of Christianity that it will take centuries to dispel. Persecution, however, had one beneficial result: it brought to its highest pitch devotion to one another and to their faith. If the Jews have a united and strong religion to-day they have the Christians to thank for it.

254. **The Turn of the Tide.** Since the beginning of modern times and the development within the church of the Protestant faith and the democratic spirit, the condition of the Jew has steadily improved. In England, under Cromwell, the Jews were allowed to return, though only a few took advantage of the privilege. These came mostly from Holland —originally from Spain and Portugal. German and Polish Jews came toward the end of the seventeenth century. For a long time these were only resident aliens. They had no political nor social rights, were not allowed to attend a university, to enter a liberal profession, or hold public office. As late as 1828 only twelve Jewish brokers were allowed in London. But public sentiment grew constantly more favorable. In 1858 the last political disability was removed and Baron de Rothschild took a seat in Parliament. In 1871 the universities were opened to the Jews and their social freedom became complete. Benjamin Disraeli (Lord Beaconsfield), England's most conspicuous Jew, became prime minister under Queen Victoria (1874–1880).

After Holland was freed from the control of Catholic Spain (1581) the Jews who had come thither from Spain and Portugal in large numbers found safety and won prosperity. Amsterdam claims to-day many rich and educated Jews. In the other European states, as education and democracy have increased, the various restrictions that surrounded the Jews have been removed. Only in Russia and the Balkans, where mediæval conditions prevail, there have been occasional outbreaks against them down to our own day. Also in the despotically governed lands of Africa and Asia conditions are still mediæval. In the great modern democracies of

Fig. 161—AN ASHKENAZIM JEW OF TIBERIAS

Most Jews in Palestine belong either to the sect of the Shephardim, who speak mainly Spanish and came originally from Spain after the expulsion (Sec. 252), or the Ashkenazim, who speak Yiddish—a jargon of German and Hebrew—and consist largely of Germans, Poles, Russians and Roumanians.

Australia and America the Jews have had equal rights with citizens of other lineage. This is why the United States in particular has become the great refuge of the race, and why in the city of New York, with over five millions of people, every fifth person is a Jew. The centre of gravity of the Jewish world is now in the Western Hemisphere.

255. **The Zionist Hopes.** Throughout the long exile there have been some whose hopes have turned to the land of their

fathers.   It has seemed to them incredible that a people whose title to a country was once so clear and whose racial spirit is still unbroken should never again have a home they could call their own.   Their own sacred books give grounds for such a hope.   The Hebrew prophets spoke of a redeemed land, of peace and plenty, of a wonderful kingdom and a glorious future.

"The ransomed of Jehovah shall return and come with singing unto Zion; and everlasting joy shall be upon their heads."

"O thou afflicted, tossed with tempest and not comforted, behold, I will set thy stones in fair colors and lay thy foundations with sapphires.   And I will make thy pinnacles of rubies and thy gates of carbuncles, and all thy border of precious stones.   And all thy children shall be taught of Jehovah, and great shall be the peace of thy children."

This hope has been like a bright and morning star through the centuries, and while it has not comforted and inspired all the sons of Israel, it has beckoned many eastward.   As soon as Turkish rule was established in the Holy Land and the persecutions of Christians made Europe a long Gehenna for the Jew, pilgrims and emigrants began to return to Palestine. Especially the aged longed to spend their last days there and to be buried in its sacred soil.   Jerusalem became the seat of a large Jewish colony, enlisted chiefly from Spain.   Since the people who came were not producers of wealth, it was necessary to support them by contributions from abroad. The stream of immigrants and of money increased all through the last century, until, just before the Great War, the numbers who came rose to five thousand a year.   Agricultural colonies were started on the plain of Sharon and in the fertile valleys of Galilee—Rishon le Zion, Zammarin, Rekhoboth, Es-Sajara, and elsewhere.   In Europe and America the Zionist movement became a definite party within the Jewish fold.   Plans were outlined for the reclamation of the land by irrigation, terracing, afforestation, and the use of modern

FIG. 162—GENERAL ALLENBY ENTERING JERUSALEM

On Dec. 11, 1917, after the surrender of Jerusalem by the Turks, Gen. Allenby took formal possession of the city. Outside the Jaffa gate—the inner door of which is shown above—he was received by the military governor; then he entered on foot, without the blare of trumpets or the firing of a salute, and halted at the citadel (a hundred yards to our left), where the proclamation of military law was read in four languages to the assembled notables of the city. This act marked the passing of Palestine to Christian control after over seven hundred years of Mohammedan domination.

The blank space to the left of the tower was made by tearing down a portion of the city wall in order to facilitate the pompous entrance of Kaiser Wilhelm II in 1898! Never again! "*Sic transit gloria mundi.*"

machinery. When the Great War broke out Palestine again became the bridge by which alien armies crossed to coveted possessions beyond. Again the land was torn and drenched in blood. But the fortune of war, or the hand of Providence, seems now to have set Palestine free from the rule of tyrants and opened its gates once more to the Chosen People of old.

When General Allenby walked reverently through the Jaffa gate in December, 1917, and caused his proclamation of peace and justice to be read from the very pretorium where the Tenth Legion of Hadrian once encamped to enforce exile upon the Jewish race, a thrill of joy and of expectancy encircled the world. All are now waiting to see a new and meaningful fulfilment of the vision of the seer of old:

> "The Lord shall comfort Zion,
>   He will comfort her waste places;
> And make her like Eden,
>   Like the garden of the Lord."

No Christian will for a moment begrudge this long-suffering people their day of hope and of fulfilment. Rather will the world look on with a heart of good-will as the Jews attempt on their ancient homeland an experiment in social and economic organization in which all that is best of the teachings of their ancient priests and prophets shall conspire with the insight of the Greatest Jew and the accumulated wisdom of the Christian centuries to found a commonwealth which will at last fully represent the democratic ideals of ancient Israel.

APPENDIX

I. SUGGESTIONS TO TEACHERS

Time Required.—This book is designed for a year's work in Old Testament history. If only one recitation a week is scheduled, the text itself and the map work can be covered. If two recitations are available, the Bible sources can be added, and if three, the topics also. Community schools with shorter courses will be able to assign two chapters to a lesson. Sunday-schools can cover the text in the usual year of nine months, or if twelve months are available, the text and the more important sources.

Equipment.—It is desirable that the pupil should have in addition to this text-book a set of outline maps (these maps may be secured from Boundbrook Press, North Scituate, Mass., Mr. Richard Brown, Manager); a Bible, preferably the Old Testament volume of the Shorter Bible which gives a modern translation and a consecutive text without duplicates, or the American revised edition; a set of wax crayons (recommended: "Crayola," twelve colors, sold by the New York Sunday-school Commission, 416 Lafayette Street, New York); and a note-book (recommended: The Biflex Binder Note-book No. 21, holding sheets 8 x 10½ inches, issued by Ginn and Company, Boston). The outline maps are punched to fit this size.

Note-book Work.—The note-book should contain chapter summaries, brief story outlines from the Bible sources, biographies of leading characters, special reports on assigned topics, and maps. The immature student should be directed to make abstracts of most of the material used, in order to discover the essential points in a narrative and to help fix them in mind. It will be helpful to reserve in the note-book a separate page where the important proper names can be listed as they occur in the lessons, the teacher dictating such as in his judgment should be memorized. Place after each name a number indicating the section of the text where it first occurred. This method will facilitate review work. Pupils should be led to take pride in this work, for to keep a good note-book means training in accuracy, judgment, neatness, and artistic taste.

Map Work.—Most of the work consists in copying the printed maps or such parts of them as the teacher specifies. An historical map is a diagram of facts or events, a kind of shorthand by means of which historic processes can be made clear and definite. The act of copying also helps to fix the data.

The name of the particular outline map to be used in each case is given in parenthesis. In filling in the map, *first* use ink to write in names and other data; then use crayons for the color features. After the crayon has been applied the paper will not take ink. Put the color on heavily, then scrape the map lightly with a sharp knife. This leaves a faint tint that looks as even and delicate as a water-color wash. Where the maps in this book use one color and hatch-lines or other devices, the pupil should use two or more colors. Try to produce harmonious color effects. Instead of cumbering the maps with many names, use figures enclosed in circles as in Map No. 6, then in the margin or elsewhere write the key to the figures. Learn to print neatly; nothing is more essential to the artistic perfection of a map.

The school library should contain Smith and Bartholomew's *Atlas of the Historical Geography of the Holy Land.*

The classroom should possess the Kent and Madsen's series of historical maps and chronological chart for Bible students, on spring rollers in a case; or if the classroom is small, the corresponding abridged edition printed on paper and hung on a stand. These may be secured from any of the leading denominational publishing societies.

It is recommended also that the teacher paint on the blackboard, with white enamel paint, outline maps duplicating the Hebrew World and the Palestine sheets that the pupils use. These are invaluable for sketching in historical and geographical data while teaching, and for testing a pupil's knowledge. One should be able to identify places on a map whether the names are printed there or not.

Illustrations.—Great emphasis is placed on pictures for two reasons: they furnish an accurate idea of the physical backgrounds of the narratives, and they present definite data from which to form judgments.

The teacher who has not visited Palestine will need to study the pictures with special care and to supplement the study with careful reading. Most teachers fail in vividness and pictorial power simply because they cannot visualize the backgrounds. The stereograph will prove a great help to such. Keystone View Co., Meadville, Pa., publish a set of one hundred stereographs on Egypt, with a fascinating book of description by Professor Breasted; also one hundred on Palestine with a similar book by Hurlbut and one hundred and forty historical views with descriptions by Kent; and various other sets such as Mesopotamia, Asia Minor, and Greece, from which selections may be made. The one book of description that no teacher should fail to read is George A. Smith: *Historical Geography of the Holy Land*. Kent: *Biblical Geography and History* traces the influence of the geographical background on the life and history of the Hebrew people. After these, books on Palestine are legion, for which consult the public library. For accurate data of all kinds, see Baedeker's *Palestine* and Luke and Roach: *Handbook of Palestine and Transjordan* (1934).

Under each picture in this book are comments and questions designed to call attention to important details and to stimulate thought. Pictures must be more than glanced at, they must be studied. Teach the students to interpret details, to draw inferences, in short, to make the pictures a part of the laboratory material of the course.

Biblical Material.—Each chapter contains a list of references to the sources. Every one ought to be familiar with the Bible narratives. Unless this familiarity has already been obtained, the study of these references will demand as much time as the study of the text-book itself. Teachers must outline this work as the situation demands. Generally, however, the distinctly historical references may be omitted, for they duplicate the text, and the story references emphasized, for they supplement it. In the later chapters the sections that deal with the Psalms, Prophets, and distinctly literary portions of the Bible may well be reserved for a subsequent study, and the extra-biblical references may be ignored. As a background for effective work, each teacher should be familiar with the historical, geographical, archæological, and source material contained in the first four volumes of Kent's *Historical Bible* or with the equivalent.

Topics.—No class will have time to discuss all of the topics given in the laboratory material. The list is meant to be suggestive and to offer the brighter students a chance to make additional contributions to the interest of the recitation. If the teacher can suggest to the pupil where to look up these topics, it will save his time and no doubt prevent discouragement.

Reference Books.—Every school should have a good Bible dictionary such as Hastings' one-volume *Dictionary of the Bible*. The more extensive dictionaries and encyclopædias are likely to be too technical and voluminous for young students. See that the school library adds a few books to this department each year; and then show pupils how by the use of indexes, tables of contents, and the like they can quickly find the needed information. This mastery of the tools of scholarship is a valuable part of school training.

In addition to the books already mentioned the following should be accessible to the pupils:

HEBREW HISTORIES

Olmstead, A. T., *History of Palestine and Syria.*

Smith, H. P., *Old Testament History.*

Kent, C. F., *History of the Jewish People during the Babylonian, Persian, and Greek Periods.*

Riggs, J. H., *History of the Jewish People during the Roman Period.*

Josephus, *Antiquities* and *the Jewish War.*

ARCHÆOLOGY AND CONTEMPORARY HISTORY

Albright, W. F., *Archæology of Palestine and the Bible.*

Barton, G. A., *Archæology and the Bible.*

Price, I. M., *The Old Testament and the Monuments.*

Smith, G. A., *Jerusalem* (2 vols.).

Garstang, J., *Foundations of Bible History.*

Goodspeed, G. S., *History of the Babylonians and Assyrians.*

Breasted, J. A., *History of the Ancient World* and *History of the Ancient Egyptians.*

Hastings, J., *Dictionary of the Bible* (5 vols.).

Charles, R. H., *Old Testament Apocryphal Writings.*

De Haas, J., *Palestine the Last Two Thousand Years.*

GEOGRAPHY

Kent, C. F., *Biblical History and Geography.*

Wild, L. H., *Geographic Influences in O. T. Masterpieces.*

Smith, G. A., *The Historical Geography of the Holy Land.*

ETHICS, RELIGION, AND LITERATURE

Fowler, H. T., *Origin and Growth of the Religion of Israel.*

Smith, H. P., *The Religion of the Old Testament.*

Mitchell, H. G., *The Ethics of the Old Testament.*

Kent, C. F., *The Social Teachings of the Prophets and Jesus.*

Chamberlain, *The Hebrew Prophets.*

Willett, H. E., *The Moral Leaders of Israel.*

Moore, G. F., *History of Religions* (2 vols.).

Macdonald, D. B., *The Hebrew Literary Genius.*

Knox, R. C., *Knowing the Bible.*

The Recitation.—The recitation hour is an opportunity for discussion and teaching. There are less time-consuming ways of finding out whether a pupil has studied his lesson than the usual cross-examination method. Use summaries written outside, or a brief written quiz at the beginning of the hour. The true teacher will spend his time creating backgrounds, modernizing ancient characters and situations until they live again, inducing emotions and asking questions that test the imagination and call forth ethical judgments. The well-prepared pupil will contribute his observations and judgments, present his special topic, and ask many questions that have occurred to him during his study. The bluffer and shirker will be compelled to follow the recitation and to tell from time to time what he has just heard and what he thinks about it. Thus the recitation will be alive, every one contributing something and the master unifying and vivifying all.

Spiritual Culture.—The end of historical study is character building as well as knowledge. The material of history should be used to train the powers of observation and reflection, to establish ideals of life and standards of judgment. One of the most vital facts to keep in mind in the study of history is that ideals have a dynamic quality; they move men and mould nations quite as much as do economic considerations. The history of no people illustrates this fact better than that of the Hebrews. Show how, especially in the case of the great men of Hebrew history, ideals have controlled for good or evil, and how the whole destiny of the race has been changed by a single human will. Out of such teaching ought to emerge the great thought, especially vital for our generation, that life is not only an adjustment to environment, but oftentimes a protest against environment and a reshaping of it along ideal lines.

In studying historical material bear these topics in mind as a guide to observation and reflection:* social classes—their conflicts and adjustments; attitudes toward those who differ—tolerance and intolerance, democratic appreciation, encouragement; patriotism, including changes in the conception of loyalty; education; changing moral and religious standards. The last-named topic is of primal importance in studying the Old Testament; for everywhere in its literature are evi-

* These suggestions are adapted from Public Document No. 51 (1917), "Moral Values in Secondary Education" (Supt. of Documents, Govt. Printing Office, Washington). Valuable material will be found in Public Document No. 28, "The Social Studies in Secondary Education"; Sharp: "Moral Instruction in the High School" (Univ. of Wisconsin Bul. No. 303, High School series No. 7); Muzzey: "Ethical Values in History" (Report, Second Internat. Moral Ed. Congress, p. 109).

dences of a growth in ethical insight and a transformation in the alleged character of Jehovah that keeps pace with that growth. Try to find the moral problem in each important event. Problems are history in the making, as may easily be seen in the case of the ethical problems presented to the Peace Conference of 1919. By discovering these problems and tracing the results of their attempted solutions clear light may be shed on the individual and collective problems of to-day.

In general one may state the major ethical conceptions arising from historical study as follows:

1. Social Heredity: the acts of one generation bear fruit for good or ill in the lives of the generations that follow.
2. Social Progress: prevailing practices, in spite of their long and apparently secure intrenchment, should and can be changed for the better.
3. Social Obligation: people need to participate in common duties rather than enjoy special privileges. The undeveloped are to be respected for their potential excellence. The highest obligation of the more privileged is to give the handicapped the utmost encouragement and help to develop their own unique talents.

In studying literary material—and under this head would come the Bible stories, as well as Psalms, Prophets, and Wisdom literature—bear in mind that the essential function of literature is to clarify and enrich the understanding of life. We should help our pupils discover what objects of life are most worth-while, what are the soundest standards of success or failure, what are the personal difficulties in the way of the noblest behaviors and how these obstacles can be overcome. To become moving forces in their lives, the high behaviors with which literature deals must be genuinely admired and the low behaviors must be genuinely condemned by the pupils themselves.

All of this study and reflection should issue in a higher type of thinking, and in definite constructive and co-operative service in the home, the school, and the community.

It is the conviction of the authors of this book that Biblical History, studied and taught with these aims and methods, not only outstrips immeasurably the text-and-sermonette methods that are so often employed in teaching the Bible, but ranks among the most effective forces in forming character and ideals.

II. SUGGESTIONS FOR DETAILED WORK

CHAPTER I

MAP WORK

Copy Map No. 1. Geographical names (*Hebrew World*).
Copy Map No. 2. Fertility (*Hebrew World*).
Construct a "Comparative Area" map as follows: On an outline map of the country where you live, draw in red ink on some convenient part of it a map of the Hebrew world on the same scale, indicating only the coastlines and chief rivers. This will help you realize the actual size of the Bible lands.
Copy Map No. 3. Semitic Migrations (*Hebrew World*).

TOPICS

The Arabian Desert. The Nile. Nomads. The rôle of Syria (see G. A. Smith: *Hist. Geog. of the Holy Land,* chap. I). Our debt to the Hebrew world.

CHAPTER II

MAP WORK

On a map of the Hebrew world, indicate in red ink the places that have contributed especially to our knowledge of the past. Use any atlas, and designate on the map the places mentioned in this chapter.

TOPICS

Date of the earliest historical records. What Napoleon did for Egypt. How Sir Henry Rawlinson enriched our knowledge of ancient life. Learned societies that have excavated in Bible lands. Hieroglyphic writing. Cuneiform writing. Hebrew writing (Ras Shamra texts).

CHAPTER III

LABORATORY MATERIAL

NOTE: The proper names appearing after the following Biblical references are those that should be especially remembered. Others

found in the text may be ignored. Look up all places on a map. The
number before each reference is the section number of the text illustrated by the Biblical reference.

17a. *The Hebrew Bondage.* Ex. 1⁶⁻²². Egypt, Pithom, Raamses (Ram-
      ses and Rameses are the Egyptian and English forms of the
      same name), Joseph, Pharaoh.

17b. *The Early Life of Moses.* Ex. 2¹⁻²⁴. Pharaoh's daughter, Moses,
      Midian.

17c. *The Call of Moses.* Ex. 3¹⁻⁴²⁰. Jethro, Horeb, Jehovah, Aaron.

17d. *Demands upon Pharaoh.* Ex. 4²⁷—6¹; 7⁷⁻¹³.

17e. *The Ten Plagues.* Ex. 7¹⁴–11⁸, 12²⁹⁻³⁶. Goshen, Red Sea.
      (1) Water becomes blood, 7¹⁴⁻²⁵; (2) Frogs, 8¹⁻¹⁵; (3) Lice,
      8¹⁶⁻¹⁹; (4) Flies, 8²⁰⁻³²; (5) Murrain, 9¹⁻⁷; (6) Boils, 9⁸⁻¹²; (7)
      Hail, 9¹³⁻³⁵; (8) Locusts, 10³⁻²⁰; (9) Darkness, 10²¹⁻²⁹; (10)
      Death of first-born, 11¹⁻⁵, 12²⁹⁻³⁶.

17f. *The Passover Instituted.* Ex. 12¹⁻¹⁴, ²¹⁻²³.

17g. *The Escape.* Ex. 12³⁷⁻³⁹; 13¹⁷–15². Philistines.

TOPICS

The great rulers of the XVIIIth dynasty of Egypt. The modern
celebration of the Passover. The Land of Goshen. How many Hebrews left Egypt? Collect all possible pictures (real and ideal) on
the Egyptian sojourn of the Hebrews, beginning with the story of
Joseph, Gen. 37. What did the stay in Midian do for Moses? The
Magicians of Egypt. (See Erman, *Life in Ancient Egypt*, 353–6, 373–4,
or Budge, *Egyptian Magic*.)

Chapter IV

LABORATORY MATERIAL

24a. *The Beginnings of Organization.* Ex. 18¹⁻²⁷.

24b. *Ceremonies about Sinai-Horeb.* (1) The Blood Covenant, Ex.
      24¹⁻¹¹; (2) Giving of the Law; the Great Apostasy. Ex.
      24¹²⁻¹⁸; 31¹⁸–32³⁵; 34¹⁻⁸, ²⁸⁻³⁰; (3) The Earlest Decalogue,
      Ex. 34¹⁴⁻²⁶. Compare the Latest Decalogue, Ex. 20³⁻¹⁷.

25.   *Spies Sent to Canaan.* Num. 13¹⁻², ¹⁷⁻³³; 14¹⁻¹⁰, ²⁰⁻³⁰. Canaan,
      Hebron, Kadesh, Joshua, Caleb.

26a. *Hardships in the Wilderness.* Ex. 16¹⁻⁴, ¹²⁻²⁴, ³¹, ³⁵; 17¹⁻⁷; Num.
      21⁴⁻⁹. Elim, Sinai (Horeb), Mount Hor, Edom.

26*b*.   *Fights with Bedouin and Others.*   Ex. 17[8-16]; Num. 21[1-3].   Amalekites, Canaanites.

27*a*.   *The Advance to the East-Jordan Country.*   Num. 20[14-21]; 21[10-20]. Arnon, Pisgah (Nebo).

27*b*.   *The Conquest of the East-Jordan Country.*   Num. 21[21-35]; Deut. 2[32-35]; 3[3-11]; Num. 32[1-7, 16-19, 33, 39-42].   Sihon, Jabbok, Ammonites, Bashan, Og, Gilead, Rabbah.

27*c*.   *Balaam's Prophecy.*   Num. 22–24.   Balaam.

27*d*.   *Joshua Appointed Leader.*   Num. 27[12-23].   Joshua.

28.   *The Death of Moses; His Character.*   Deut. 34[1-12].   Abraham, Isaac, Jacob.

MAP WORK

Copy Map No. 4.   The Wilderness Wanderings (*Sinai Peninsula*).

TOPICS

From the two Decalogues alone, what do you discover about the manner of life of the Hebrews and their degree of civilization? Giants. Are the Ten Commandments still binding? What wrong acts are not forbidden by the Ten Commandments? The spirit of the Hebrews in the wilderness. The distance from Goshen to Mount Nebo. Did Moses deserve to be shut out of the Promised Land? Give reasons for your conclusion. Learn Mrs. Alexander's poem, "The Burial of Moses." How does Moses rank with Julius Cæsar, Washington, Lincoln, Napoleon?

CHAPTER V

MAP WORK

Copy Map No. 5 in colors (*Palestine*).

After studying the cross-section at the bottom of the map, make a cross-section of Palestine running north and south, including Nazareth and Hebron.

Construct a map of comparative distances (*Palestine*), as follows:

In the margin of your outline map of Palestine, write the following numbers and places, with the air-line distance between each place and Jerusalem. 1. Jerusalem; 2. Bethlehem, 6 miles; 3. Hebron, 20 miles; 4. Beersheba, 47 miles; 5. Jericho, 15 miles; 6. Mount Nebo, 32 miles; 7. Bethel, 10 miles; 8. Shechem, 30 miles; 9. Joppa, 36 miles; 10. Nazareth, 65 miles; 11. Capernaum, 80 miles; 12. Mount Hermon, (summit) 120 miles; 13. Damascus, 137 miles. On the map, with the numbers representing these places in their correct position connect the places with Jerusalem by means of straight lines.

Insert with red ink in the margin opposite No. 1. (Jerusalem), the name of the capital, or the chief city, of your state or shire; and opposite each of the other numbers write the name of the town in your state that is as far from that city as the Palestinian town is distant from Jerusalem. You have in this way superimposed your state upon Palestine.

TOPICS

Roman cities east of Jordan. Traces of volcanic action in Palestine. The plain of Esdraelon. Harbors on the Palestine coast. (See Smith, *Historical Geography of the Holy Land*, for all of these.)

CHAPTER VI

LABORATORY MATERIAL

35a. *The Summons to Conquest.* Josh. 1¹⁻¹¹. Jordan, Lebanon, Euphrates, Hittites.

35b. *Spies at Jericho.* Josh. 2¹⁻²⁴. Jericho, Rahab.

35c. *Crossing the Jordan.* Josh. 3¹, ¹⁴⁻¹⁷; 4¹⁻⁹, ¹⁷⁻²⁴, 5¹, ¹⁰⁻¹². Salt Sea, Arabah, Gilgal.

35d. *The Capture of Jericho.* Josh. 6.

36a. *The Sin of Achan.* Josh. 7. Ai, Bethel, Achan.

36b. *The Capture of Ai.* Josh. 8¹⁻²⁹.

36c. *The Stratagem of the Gibeonites.* Josh. 9³⁻²⁷. Gibeon.

36d. *The League of the Five Kings.* Josh. 10¹⁻²⁷. Jerusalem, Lachish, Beth-horon, Ajalon.

36e. *The Defeat of Jabin.* Josh. 11¹⁻¹². Chinneroth (Chinnoreth), Hermon, Dor, Waters of Merom, Sidon, Jabin.

37a. *A General Summary of Conquests.* Josh. 11¹⁶⁻²³.

37b. *Joshua's Farewell and Death.* Josh. 23¹⁻³, ¹⁴⁻¹⁵; 24¹⁹⁻³¹. Shechem.

MAP WORK

Copy Map No. 6. Final Home of Hebrew Tribes (*Palestine*). The following method will simplify the work:

1. With a blue crayon draw a line marking the limit of the Hebrew possessions. With the same crayon, put in the numbers that indicate the location of each Hebrew tribe, and make a circle round each number. Now fill in all the Hebrew space with solid color, leaving white all the spaces within the blue circles.

2. In the same manner indicate with other colors the territory of the Philistines, Canaanites, Amalekites, Edomites, Moabites, Ammonites, and Arameans.

3. In any blank space left, write with ink the key to the numbers and colors.

TOPICS

The history of Jericho. Early methods of warfare (see Hastings, *Dictionary of the Bible*, IV, 893–5). Compare Joshua with Moses, or with some other historical character. Canaan before the coming of the Hebrews (see Barton, *Archæology and the Bible*, pp. 307–8, 344–51).

CHAPTER VII

LABORATORY MATERIAL

41. *The Moabite Oppression.* Judges 3^{12-30}. Eglon, Ehud.

42. *The Canaanite Oppression.* Judges 5 (compare Judges 4). Deborah, Barak, Sisera.

43. *The Midianite Oppression.* Judges 6–8. Gideon, Baal, valley of Jezreel, spring of Harod.

The House of Gideon. Judges $8^{22}–9^{27}$. Abimelech, Jotham.

44. *The Ammonite Oppression.* Judges $10^{6, 7, 17, 18}$; $11^{1}–12^{7}$. Jephthah, Gilead.

45–46. *The Philistine Oppression.* Judges 13–16.

The Samson Stories: (1) Birth, 13^{1-25}; (2) Betrothal, $14^{1}–15^{8}$; (3) Revenge, 15^{9-20}; (4) The Gates of Gaza, 16^{1-3}; (5) Marriage to Delilah, 16^{4-22}; (6) Capture and Death, 16^{23-31}. Samson, Zorah, Delilah, Gaza.

40a. *The Sanctuary of Micah.* Judges 17. Micah.

40b. *The Migration of the Danites.* Judges 18. Danites.

40c. *The Story of Ruth.* Ruth 1–4. Ruth, Naomi, Boaz, Bethlehem.

38. *Social and Religious Conditions.*

New occupations: Judges $6^{3, 11}$; 8^{2}; 9^{27}; $9^{8, 10}$; 1^{16}; 15^{14}; 6^{4}.

New arts: Judges 17^{4}; Joshua 22^{8}; Judges 8^{24}; 6^{19}; 7^{16}; $16^{13, 14}$. The relation of the arts to success in war; Judges 1^{19}; I Sam. 13^{19-21}.

Dwellings: Joshua 22^{7b}; Judges 20^8. Contrast with Canaanite dwellings; Judges 9$^{50-52}$; 8^{17}; 1$^{27-29}$. Recall the results of the excavations at Jericho.

Intermingling of the two races: Judges 19$^{11-15}$.

Government: In Amorite towns, Judges 8^{14}; Joshua 10^3.
In Hebrew settlements, Judges 20^2; 11$^{4-11}$; 8$^{30,\,31}$; 9$^{1-4}$; 17^6.
Recall the nature of the "Judges." The judge merges into the king or national leader and counsellor (cf. Gideon).

Moral Standards: Deeds that pass uncondemned, Judges 3^{15}; 15$^{4-8,\,15}$; 16^{30}; 8^{21}; 1$^{6,\,7}$; 8^{16}; 13$^{25-27}$. Vows, 11$^{30,\,31}$; 21$^{18-21}$.

Religion: The use of old Canaanite sanctuaries, Judges 2$^{1-3}$.
Names that suggest the religious beliefs of the people, Judges 7^{1a}; II Sam. 4^{1a} (cf. I Chron. 8^{33}) II Sam. 4^4 end (cf. I Chron. 8^{34}). Jehovah and Baal confused, Hos. 2$^{16-17}$. Ritual, Joshua 18^1; 24^{26}; Judges 6$^{24-25}$; 6^{28}; 9^6; 18^{19} (cf. I Sam. 1$^{24,\,25}$); 11$^{31-39}$. Private religious shrines, Judges 17^5; 8^{27}. Ideas about God, Judges 11$^{23-24}$; 5$^{4,\,5}$; 6$^{11,\,14}$; 13^3; 5^{20}; Joshua 10^{11}; Judges 1^{19}; 2$^{11,\,12}$.

MAP WORK

Copy Map No. 7. Contour map of Galilee (Esdraelon).

Copy Map No. 8. Battle of the Kishon (Esdraelon).

The Canaanites were lowlanders. Their rallying-point is indicated by the dotted lines that centre on Harosheth. Use solid line to indicate their march. Find in Judges 5$^{13-18}$ the names of the Hebrew tribes that fought. Use dotted lines to show their assembling on Mount Tabor and a solid line to show their attack.

Copy Map No. 9. Wars of Oppression (Small Palestine).

TOPICS

The Philistines. A day in old Shechem. Are wicked nations always punished? Compare Samson and Hercules. Nazarites. Why should the book of Ruth be in the Bible? Riddles (see Hastings, Dictionary of the Bible, IV, 270–1).

Chapter VIII

LABORATORY MATERIAL

49a. *The Early Life of Samuel.* I Sam. 1–3. Hannah, Eli, Shiloh, Samuel, Ramah.

48. *Adventures of the Ark.* I Sam. 4^1–7^{2a}. Ekron, Ashdod, Gath.

49b. *Samuel Inspires Saul.* I Sam. 9¹–10¹⁶. Saul.

50.   *Saul Proves his Leadership.* I Sam. 11. Jabesh-Gilead.

51.   *The Deliverance from the Philistines.* I Sam. 13¹⁻⁷, ¹⁵ᵇ–14⁵².
       Michmash, Jonathan.

52.   *Saul's Break with Samuel.* I Sam. 10⁸; 13⁷⁻¹⁵ (*cf.* chap. 15).
       Agag, Amalekites.

53a. *Rise of David.* (*a*) I Sam. 16¹⁴⁻²³; (*b*) 17; (*c*) 16¹⁻¹⁸. Jesse,
       David, Goliath, Abner.

53b. *David's Popularity and Saul's Jealousy.* I Sam. 18¹–19¹⁷.
       Michal.

53c. *David a Fugitive.* I Sam. 19¹⁸–21⁸; 22¹⁻⁵; 23¹⁵⁻¹⁸. Nob, Adul-
       lam.

53d. *Saul's Vengeance on the Priests of Nob.* I Sam. 22⁶⁻²³.

53e. *Saul's Pursuit of David.* I Sam. 23¹⁴, ¹⁹⁻²⁹; 24; 26. Engedi.

53f. *David and Abigail.* I Sam. 25²⁻⁴². Nabal, Abigail.

53g. *David Among the Philistines.* I Sam. 21¹⁰⁻¹⁵; 27. Achish.

53h. *David and the Philistine Invasion.* I Sam. 28¹, ²; 29.

53j. *David Raids the Amalekites.* I Sam. 30.

54a. *Saul's Visit to the Medium of Endor.* I Sam. 28³⁻²⁵. Endor.

54b. *Defeat and Death of Saul and Jonathan.* I Sam. 31. Mount
       Gilboa, Bethshan.

MAP WORK

Copy Map No. 10. Saul's Kingdom (Small *Palestine*).
Copy Map No. 11. Battle of Mount Gilboa (*Esdraelon*).

TOPICS

The History of the Ark. "Seers" in the Bible. Compare David the
outlaw with Robin Hood. The harp among the Hebrews. A day
with David. Write a story (in the first person) connecting Jabesh-
Gilead and Saul. The character of Jonathan. Hebrew laws about
mediums and sorcerers.

CHAPTER IX

LABORATORY MATERIAL

56a. *David Hears of Saul's Death.* II Sam. 1.

56b. *The States Ruled by David and Ishbaal.* II Sam. 2¹⁻¹¹. Ishbaal
       (Ishbosheth), Abner, Mahanaim.

56c. *Hostilities between the States.* II Sam. 2¹²–3¹. Joab.

56d. *Abner's Disaffection and Death.* II Sam. 3⁶⁻³⁹.

56e. *The Assassination of Ishbaal.* II Sam. 4.

56f. *David Made Ruler of All Israel.* II Sam. 5$^{1-5}$.

58a. *War with the Philistines.* II Sam. 5$^{17-25}$; 8^1; 21$^{15-22}$; 23$^{13-17}$. Valley of Rephaim.

58b. *David Captures Jerusalem.* II Sam. 5$^{6-12}$. Jebusites. Zion, Hiram, Tyre.

59. *David's Wars of Conquest.* II Sam. 8$^{2-14}$; 10^{1}–11^1; 12$^{26-31}$. Syrians, Damascus.

60. *David's Mighty Men.* II Sam. 23$^{8-38}$.

61. *David's Court.* II Sam. 8$^{15-18}$; 20$^{23-25}$.

62. *David Rescues the Ark.* II Sam. 6. Uzzah.

MAP WORK

Copy Map No. 12. The Philistine Conquest (Small *Palestine*).

Copy Map No. 13. Empires, Time of David (*Hebrew World*).

Copy Map No. 14. Early Jerusalem. (*Jerusalem.*) Before copying, study carefully the contour lines in order to fix in mind the location of the hills and valleys. It may be advisable to color or shade a separate outline map in order to bring out elevations. On cross-section paper profiles may be drawn to vertical and horizontal scale with good effect.

TOPICS

Jerusalem in the Tel el-Amarna letters. David's character during his rule over Judah. Compare Abner and Joab. Learn the elegy over Saul and Jonathan.

CHAPTER X

LABORATORY MATERIAL

63. *David's Crime and Punishment.* II Sam. 11^2–12^{35}. Bathsheba, Uriah, Nathan.

64–6. *Absalom's Rebellion.* Absalom, Ahithophel, Hushai, Mount of Olives.

(1) His early crime and flight, II Sam. 13$^{23-39}$; (2) his return, 14$^{1-24}$; (3) his ambition, 14^{25}–15^6; (4) his revolt, 15$^{7-12}$; (5) David's flight, 15^{13}–16^{14}; (6) divided counsels, 16$^{15-23}$; (7) the battle, Absalom's death, 17^{24}–18^{33}; (8) David's mistakes, 19.

67a. *The Sons of Saul Executed.* II Sam. 21$^{1-14}$. Rizpah.

67b.   *The Census and Preparation for the Temple.* II Sam. 24. Beer-sheba, Gad, Araunah.

68a.   *Adonijah's Ambition.* I Kings 1. Adonijah, Solomon, Gihon.

68b.   *David's Sickness and Death.* I Kings 2^{1-11}.

TOPICS

The causes of Absalom's wickedness. Read Tennyson's "Rizpah." Why is David reckoned Israel's best ruler? David's religion.

CHAPTER XI

LABORATORY MATERIAL

70.   *Solomon Removes His Opponents.* I Kings 2^{12-46}.

72 (82.)   *The Loss of Provinces; Jeroboam's First Revolt.* I Kings 11^{14-40}. Jeroboam, Ahijah, Shishak.

73.   *The Organization and Resources of Solomon's Kingdom.* I Kings 4^{1-28}; 9^{15-25}. Gezer, Millo.

74.   *Solomon's Building Enterprises.* I Kings 5^{1}–7^{51}. Lebanon, Joppa.

76.   *The Dedication of the Temple.* I Kings 8.

77.   *High Finance.* I Kings $9^{10-14,\ 26-28}$; 10^{11-29}. Galilee, Eloth (Elath), Ophir, Tarshish.

78a.   *Solomon's Wisdom.* I Kings 3^{4-28}; 4^{29-34}.

78b.   *The Visit of the Queen of Sheba.* I Kings $10^{1-10,\ 13}$. Queen of Sheba.

79.   *Solomon's Polygamy and Idolatry.* I Kings 3^{1-3}; 11^{1-13}.

80.   *Solomon's Death.* I Kings 11^{41-43}.

TOPICS

Solomon the Magician in Hebrew and Arabic story. The arts of Phœnicia. Queen of Sheba stories in Hebrew and Arabic. The proverbs of Solomon. Early ships. How much of the world was known in Solomon's day?

CHAPTER XII

LABORATORY MATERIAL

81.   *The Rebellion of the Northern Tribes.* I Kings 12^{1-25}. Rehoboam, Shechem.

84.   *Rehoboam's Reign; the Invasion of Shishak.* I Kings 14^{21-31}.

85a.   *Jeroboam's Sanctuaries.* I Kings 12^{26-33}.

85b.   *Jeroboam's Death.*   I Kings 14[19, 20].

86.   *The Attitude of the Prophets Toward Jeroboam.*   I Kings 13[1]–14[18].

MAP WORK

Copy Map No. 15.   The Divided Kingdom (Small *Palestine*).

TOPICS

Animal-worship among the Hebrews.   Was Jeroboam an idolater? Compare the results of the division in Israel with those in the United States in 1861.

CHAPTER XIII

LABORATORY MATERIAL

87.   *The Petty Kings of Israel and Judah.*   I Kings 15[1]–16[20].   Baasha,   Zimri, Asa, Benhadad I.

88.   *The Reign of Omri.*   I Kings 16[21-28].   Omri, Samaria.

91.   *The Reign of Ahab.*   I Kings 16[29-34].   Ahab, Jezebel, Ethbaal.

92.   *Jehoshaphat of Judah.*   I Kings 22[41-50].   Jehoshaphat.

93.   *Ahab's Wars.*   I Kings 20.

94.   *Ahab's Death.*   I Kings 22[1-40].   Ramoth Gilead.

MAP WORK

Copy Map No. 16.   The Kingdom of Omri and Ahab (*Palestine*).

TOPICS

The capitals of Israel.   Ahab as a statesman.   The inscription on the Moabite Stone (see Barton, *Archæology and the Bible*, pp. 363–5). What light does the following inscription of Shalmaneser II, in reference to the battle of Karkar (854 B.C.), throw on Ahab's position in western Asia?

"One thousand two hundred chariots, 1,200 horsemen, 20,000 men of Dad'idri (Benhadad II) of Damascus; 700 chariots, 700 horsemen, 10,000 soldiers of Irhulini of Hamath; 2,000 chariots, 10,000 soldiers of Ahab of Israel; 500 soldiers of Guai; 10,000 soldiers of the land of Muçri; 10 chariots, 10,000 soldiers of the land of Irkanat; 200 soldiers of Mattan-baal of Arrad; 200 soldiers of the land of Usanata; 30 chariots, 10,000 soldiers of Adoni-baal of Shiana; 1,000 camels of Gindibu of Arba . . . 1,000 soldiers of the Ammonite, Basa, son of Rehob; these twelve kings he (Irkanat) took to help him. For battle and combat they advanced against me. . . . From Karkar to Gilzan I effected their defeat. Fourteen thousand of their troops with weapons I slew; like Adar (the storm-god) I rained down a flood upon them; I scattered their corpses; . . . I took possession of the river Orontes." This is the earliest mention of Israel in the annals of Assyria.

CHAPTER XIV

LABORATORY MATERIAL

97a. *Elijah Announces a Drought.* I Kings 17. Cherith, Zarephath.
97b. *Elijah's Victory at Mount Carmel.* I Kings 18. Mount Carmel.
97c. *Elijah's Flight and Wilderness Experience.* I Kings 19$^{1-18}$.
97d. *The Call of Elisha.* I Kings 19$^{19-21}$. Elisha.
98. *Naboth's Vineyard.* I Kings 21. Naboth, Jezreel.
99a. *Attempts to Capture Elijah.* II Kings 1. Ahaziah.
99b. *Elijah's Translation.* II Kings 2.

MAP WORK

Copy Map No. 16. Elijah's Journeys (*Palestine*).

TOPICS

Compare Jezebel and Lady Macbeth. Phœnician colonies.

CHAPTER XV

LABORATORY MATERIAL

100a. *The Reign of Ahaziah.* I Kings 22$^{51-53}$.
100b. *The Reign of Jehoram.* II Kings 3$^{1-3}$. Jehoram.
100c. *The Reign of Joram.* II Kings 8$^{16-24}$. Joram (Jehoram).
100d. *The Reign of Ahaziah of Judah.* II Kings 8$^{25-29}$; 9$^{27-29}$. Ahaziah.
101a. *Elisha as Wonder-Worker.*

> (1) The widow's oil, II Kings 4$^{1-7}$. (2) Miraculous food, II Kings 4$^{38-44}$. Gilgal. (3) The recovery of lost axe, II Kings 6$^{1-7}$. (4) The restoration of Shunammite's son, II Kings 4$^{8-37}$. Shunem, Gehazi. (5) The restoration of Shunammite's land, II Kings 8$^{1-6}$. (6) The healing of Naaman the leper, II Kings 5. Naaman.

101b. *Elisha as Counsellor.*

> (1) The war with Moab, II Kings 3$^{4-27}$. Mesha. (2) The deception of Arameans, II Kings 6$^{8-23}$. Dothan. (3) The siege and deliverance of Samaria, II Kings 6^{24}–7^{20}.

102.   *Elisha as Revolutionist.*
        (1) Elisha and Hazael, II Kings 8⁷⁻¹⁵.   Hazael.   (2) **Elisha**
        and Jehu, II Kings 9¹⁻³.   Jehu.
103.   *The Revolution of Jehu.*   II Kings 9.
105.   *The Usurpation of Athaliah.*   II Kings 11¹⁻³.   Athaliah.
106.   *Jehu's Bloody Slaughter.*   II Kings 10¹⁻³¹.
108.   *The Revolution in Judah.*   II Kings 11⁴⁻²⁰.   Jehoiada.
109a.   *Jehu's Reign.*   II Kings 10³²⁻³⁶.
109b.   *Elisha's Farewell and Death.*   II Kings 13¹⁴⁻²¹.   Joash.

TOPICS

The "Schools of the Prophets."   Contrast Elijah and Elisha.   Was
Jehu justified in his revolution?   The Black Obelisk of Shalmaneser
III.

Chapter XVI

LABORATORY MATERIAL

110.   *The Reign of Joash (Jehoash).*   II Kings 11²¹–12²¹.   Joash.
111a.   *The Reign of Jehoahaz.*   II Kings 13¹⁻⁹.   Jehoahaz, Benhadad III.
111b.   *The Reign of Jehoash.*   II Kings 13¹⁰⁻¹³, ²²⁻²⁵; 14⁸⁻¹⁶.   Jehoash,
        Amaziah.
111c.   *The Reign of Amaziah.*   II Kings 14¹⁻¹⁴, ¹⁷⁻²¹.   Azariah.
112.   *The Reign of Uzziah (Azariah).*   II Kings 14²²; 15¹⁻⁷.   Uzziah,
        Jotham.
113.   *The Reign of Jeroboam II.*   II Kings 14²³⁻²⁹.   Jeroboam II.
115a.   *Amos.*   2⁶⁻¹⁶; 5⁴⁻¹⁵, ²¹⁻²⁴; 6¹⁻⁸.
115b.   *Hosea.*   4¹⁻¹⁴.

MAP WORK

Copy Map No. 17.   The Syrian Domination (Small *Palestine*).
Copy Map No. 18.   Assyrian Advance, Waves I to III (*Hebrew World*).
Copy Map No. 19.   Israel's Indian Summer (*Hebrew World*).

TOPICS

Damascus past and present.   A day with Amos at Bethel.   Lepers.
Tekoa (see G. A. Smith, *Book of the Twelve Prophets*, I, 74–81).

Chapter XVII

LABORATORY MATERIAL

116*a.*   *The Reign of Zechariah.*   II Kings 15⁸⁻¹².   Zechariah, Shallum.
116*b.*   *The Reign of Shallum.*   II Kings 15¹³⁻¹⁶.   Menahem.
117*a.*   *The Reign of Menahem.*   II Kings 15¹⁷⁻²².   Pul (Tiglath-pileser IV).
117*b.*   *The Reign of Pekahiah.*   II Kings 15²³⁻²⁶.   Pekah.
118*a.*   *The Reign of Jotham.*   II Kings 15³²⁻³⁸.   Rezin.
118*b.*   *The Reign of Ahaz.*   II Kings 16; Isaiah 7¹⁻¹⁷.   Ahaz, Isaiah.
119*a.*   *The Reign of Pekah.*   II Kings 15²⁷⁻³¹.   Hoshea.
119*b.*   *The Reign of Hoshea.*   II Kings 17¹⁻⁶.   Shalmaneser III, Sargon.
120.   *The Explanation of Israel's Downfall.*   II Kings 17⁷⁻¹⁸.

MAP WORK

Copy Map No. 20.   Assyrian Advance, Waves IV–VI (*Hebrew World*).

TOPICS

Compare the fate of Israel with that of Belgium or Serbia in the Great War.   Human sacrifice among the Hebrews.

Chapter XVIII

LABORATORY MATERIAL

121.   *The Reign of Hezekiah.*   II Kings 18¹⁻⁸; 20²⁰⁻²¹.   Hezekiah.
123.   *Isaiah's Warnings Against Egypt.*   Isaiah 31¹⁻³.
124.   *Hezekiah's Sickness and the Embassy from Babylon.*   II Kings 20¹⁻¹⁹.   Merodach-baladan.
125.   *Sennacherib's First Invasion.*   II Kings 18¹³⁻¹⁶.   Sennacherib.

TOPICS

Isaiah's methods of publicity.   How the Assyrians made war.   From the inscription on Sennacherib's cylinder (see Barton, *Archæology and the Bible,* pp. 372–3), construct a map of his conquests (*Hebrew World*). Compare Isaiah's call with that of Moses and Joan of Arc.

Chapter XIX

LABORATORY MATERIAL

129–130.   *The Great Reformation.*   II Kings 18$^{1-6}$; Micah, Isaiah.
131.   *Sennacherib's Second Invasion.*   II Kings 18^{17}–19^{37}.
131b.   *A Psalm of Deliverance.*   Psalm 46.

TOPICS

Compare Isaiah with any of the earlier prophets.   Micah as a "Red."
The overthrow of Sennacherib's army.   (See the account of Herodotus
as given in Barton, *Archæology and the Bible*, p. 376, and compare the
last sentence with section 48 of this book.)

Chapter XX

LABORATORY MATERIAL

133.   *The Reign of Manasseh.*   II Kings 21$^{1-18}$.   Manasseh.

TOPICS

Assyrian religion.   The Library of Ashurbanipal.   Ishtar and her
equivalents in other religions.

Chapter XXI

LABORATORY MATERIAL

139.   *The Reign of Amon.*   II Kings 21$^{19-26}$.   Amon, Josiah.
141.   *The Reign of Josiah.*   II Kings 22^{1}–23^{27}.   Tophet, Valley of
          Hinnom.
143.   *Selections from Deuteronomy.*   Deut. 12$^{1-4,\ 13,\ 14,\ 27}$; 17$^{2-7}$; 10$^{18-19}$;
          15$^{7-15}$; 23$^{15-16,\ 19-20}$; 22^{8}; 24$^{6,\ 10-22}$; 25^{4}.
147a.   *The Death of Josiah.*   II Kings 23$^{28-30}$.   Pharaoh-Necho.
147b.   *The Everlasting Arms.*   Psalm 90.

MAP WORK

Copy Map No. 21.   The Break-up of Assyria (*Hebrew World*).

TOPICS

Deuteronomy: its authorship and literary form.   Slavery in Deuteronomy.   Relations of rich and poor in Deuteronomy.

Chapter XXII

LABORATORY MATERIAL

148a.   *The Reign of Jehoahaz.* II Kings 23³¹⁻³⁵. Jehoahaz, Jehoiakim.
148b.   *The Reign of Jehoiakim.* II Kings 23³⁶⁻24⁷. Nebuchadrezzar.
149.   *The Fall of Nineveh.* Nahum 3.
151a.   *Jeremiah's Preaching and Trial.* Jer. 26. Jeremiah.
151b.   *Jeremiah's Roll and its Reception.* Jer. 36. Baruch.
152.   *The Reign of Jehoiachin: The First Deportation.* II Kings 24⁸⁻¹⁷.
         Jehoiachin.
154.   *The Reign of Zedekiah: his Rebellion.* II Kings 24¹⁸⁻25². Ezek.
         19. Zedekiah, Chaldeans.
155a.   *The Perfidy of the Hebrews During the Siege.* Jer. 34.
155b.   *Jeremiah's Arrest and Deliverance.* Jer. 37–38; 39¹⁵⁻¹⁸.
156.   *The Second Capture of Jerusalem.* II Kings 25³⁻²¹.
157a.   *The Treatment of Jeremiah by the Babylonians.* Jer. 39¹¹⁻40⁶.
157b.   *The Governorship of Gedaliah.* II Kings 25²²⁻²⁶. Jer. 40⁷⁻41¹⁸.
         Gedaliah, Mizpah.

MAP WORK

Copy Map No. 22. The Babylonian Conquest (*Hebrew World*).

TOPICS

Nineveh. The Scythians. Modern excavations at Nineveh. The
sieges and destructions of Jerusalem. (See G. A. Smith, *Jerusalem*,
vol. II, appendix.) The art of writing among the Hebrews.

Chapter XXIII

LABORATORY MATERIAL

160.   *The Flight to Egypt.* Jer. 43, 44. Tahpanhes.
164a.   *Ezekiel's Messages to the Scattered Exiles.* Ezek. 25, 27, 28,
         37¹⁻¹⁴. Edom.
164b.   *Poems of the Exile.* Lam. 1–2; Psalms 130, 137; Isaiah 21¹⁻¹⁰.

TOPICS

The Book of Lamentations. Ezekiel's strange methods as preacher.
(See Ezek. 4¹⁻¹¹, 5¹⁻⁴, 6¹¹⁻¹², 12¹⁻¹², ¹⁷⁻²⁰, 17¹⁻¹ .) Synagogues. The
Papyrus from Elephantine (see Barton, *Archæology and the Bible*, pp.
387–391).

Chapter XXIV

LABORATORY MATERIAL

170. *The Decree of Cyrus.* Ezra 1$^{1-4}$, 6$^{3-5}$. Cyrus, Darius.
171. *The First Return.* Ezra 1$^{5-11}$, 5$^{14,\ 15}$.
172. *Worship Re-established.* Ezra 3. Zerubbabel.
173. *Opposition to Rebuilding the Temple.* Ezra 4.
174a. *The Second Attempt to Rebuild.* Ezra 5^{1}-6^{15}; Hag. 1. Haggai, Zechariah.
174b. *The Dedication of the Temple.* Ezra 6$^{16-22}$.
176. *Poems of the Second Temple.* Psalms 84, 85, 87, 93, 95–100.

MAP WORK

Copy Map No. 23. The Persian Empire (*Hebrew World*).

TOPICS

The character of Cyrus (see Xenophon's *Cyropædia* and Herodotus' *History*). The Second Temple.

Chapter XXV

LABORATORY MATERIAL

178. *Nehemiah to the Rescue.* Neh. 1^{1}-2^{20}. Nehemiah, Artaxerxes.
179a. *Rebuilding the Walls.* Neh. 3–4. Sanballat.
179b. *Unsuccessful Plots against Nehemiah.* Neh. 6; Ezra 4$^{7-23}$. Tobiah.
179c. *Dedication of the Walls.* Neh. 12$^{27-43}$.
180a. *Nehemiah's Social Reforms.* Neh. 5.
180b. *Nehemiah's Religious Reforms.* Neh. 12^{44}-13^{31}.
182. *Psalms of the Persian Period.* Psalms 22, 60, 130, 51, 71, 120, 27, 107, 116.
183. *The Second Isaiah.* Isaiah 40$^{1-11}$, 41$^{8-16}$, 42$^{1-13}$, 43$^{1-7}$, 52^{13}-53^{12}.

MAP WORK

Copy Map No. 24. Time of Nehemiah (Small *Palestine*).
On an outline map of modern Jerusalem, draw a line in red ink showing the position of the city walls in Nehemiah's time (*Jerusalem*).

TOPICS

Susa. "The Suffering Servant of Jehovah" (Is. 52^{13}-53^{12}).

CHAPTER XXVI

LABORATORY MATERIAL

189. *The Patriot-Queen.* Esther. Ahasuerus. Mardecai. Hamon.
190a. *Joel's Interpretation of a Public Calamity.* Joel 1^1–2^{27}.
190b. *The Coming "Day of Jehovah."* Joel 2^{28}–3^{21}.
190c. *The Mystery of Suffering.* Job (selected portions, *e. g.*, chaps. 1–2, 8–9, 19, 29, 38–42).
190d. *A Runaway Prophet.* Jonah.
191. *The Samaritan Schism.* Josephus: *Antiquities,* XI, 7, 2; 8, 2. Sanballat II.

TOPICS

Music among the Hebrews. Musical hints in the titles of Psalms (*e. g.*, Ps. 4, 5, 6, 22, 53, 56). Alphabetical Psalms (*e. g.*, Ps. 42–43, 107, 136). Is the book of Esther worthy of a place in the Bible? The moral and religious teachings of the book of Jonah. Nature in the book of Job. Compare the spirit of the book of Psalms with that of other ancient hymns. (See Barton, *Archæology and the Bible,* pp. 398–406.)

CHAPTER XXVII

LABORATORY MATERIAL

195a. *The Jews under Greek Rulers.* I Mac. 1^{1-15}; Josephus: *Antiquities,* XII, 1, 1–4. Alexander the Great, Antiochus Epiphanes. II Mac. 3–4.
195b. *The Wise and Their Works.* Prov. 1^{1-6}, 8^1–9, 30, 31.
195c. *Experiments in Wisdom.* Ecclesiastes 1–2, 11^{9-12}.
195d. *The Wisdom of Jesus the Son of Sirach.* Ecclesiasticus 1^{1-10}, 2^{1-9}, 3^{17}–4, 6. Ben Sira.
195e. *Psalms of the Greek Period.* Psalms 19, 68, 72, 73, 86–89.

MAP WORK

Copy Map No. 25. The Syrian Conquest (*Hebrew World*).

TOPICS

Josephus and his writings. Alexandria. Simon the Just. Antioch. Hebrew wise men. The structure of the book of Proverbs. (See Kent, *Makers and Teachers of Judaism,* pp. 159–167.) The plan of a Greek city. A day in a Greek stadium. The chief features of Greek architecture. The Septuagint. The Apocrypha.

Compare the Biblical proverbs with the Babylonian, Assyrian, and Egyptian. (See Barton, *Archæology and the Bible*, pp. 407–412.)

Chapter XXVIII

LABORATORY MATERIAL

206. *The Outrages of Antiochus.* I Mac. 1¹⁶⁻⁶⁴; II Mac. 5–7.

209a. *Psalms of Despair.* Psalms 74, 79, 83.

209b. *Encouragement for a Persecuted Nation.* Daniel (selected stories).

210. *The Uprising of Mattathias.* I Mac. 2; II Mac. 8¹⁻⁷. Mattathias, Judas, Modin.

212. *Judah's Victories.* I Mac. 3¹⁻⁴³⁵; II Mac. 8⁸⁻³⁶, 11¹⁻12¹. Apollonius, Beth-horon, Emmaus.

213. *The Temple Restored.* I Mac. 4³⁶⁻⁶¹; II Mac. 10¹⁻⁹. Lysias.

215. *Psalms of Victory.* Psalms 110, 115, 118.

TOPICS

An apocalypse. Judas Maccabæus as a general.

Chapter XXIX

LABORATORY MATERIAL

216. *Further Campaigns of Judas.* I Mac. 5¹⁻⁶⁶³; II Mac. 9¹⁻²⁹, 10⁹⁻³⁸, 12–13. Idumea, Galilee.

217. *Later Struggles: Death of Judas.* I Mac. 7¹⁻9²²; II Mac. 14¹⁻15³⁶. Nicanor.

218a. *Jonathan's Contests and Victory.* I Mac. 9²³⁻⁷³. Jonathan.

218b. *Jonathan's Later Wars.* I Mac. 10¹⁻12³⁸.

218c. *The Death of Jonathan.* I Mac. 12³⁹⁻13³⁰.

219. *Simon's Prosperous Reign.* I Mac. 13³¹⁻16²⁴. Simon.

221. *Hyrcanus.* Josephus: *War*, I, 2, 3–7; *Antiquities*, XIII, 9, 1; 10, 5–7. John Hyrcanus.

222. *The Sects.* Josephus: *Antiquities*, XVIII, 1, 2–4; *War*, II, 8, 2–14. Pharisees, Sadducees.

223a. *Aristobulus.* Josephus: *Antiquities*, XIII, 11, 1–3. Aristobulus.

223b. *Alexandra and her Sons.* Josephus: *War*, I, 4, 5. **Alexander,**

Janneus, Alexandra, Aristobulus, Hyrcanus.
Copy Map No. 26. The Maccabean Kingdom (Small *Palestine*).

TOPICS

The Jewish Sabbath. Petra. The Messianic Hope.

CHAPTER XXX

LABORATORY MATERIAL

225. *The Entrance of Rome.* Josephus: *War*, I, 6. Antipater, Pompey.
226. *Pompey Takes Jerusalem.* Josephus: *War*, I, 7.
228. *The Schemes of Antipater.* Josephus: *War*, I, 9, 10. Julius Cæsar, Herod.
229. *Herod Favored by Rome.* Josephus: *War*, I, 11–18. Mark Antony, Cleopatra, Octavius (Augustus).

TOPICS

Pompey in Syria. The Decapolis. Julius Cæsar and the Jews.
The Psalms of Solomon.

CHAPTER XXXI

LABORATORY MATERIAL

232. *Herod's Personal Qualities.* Josephus: *War*, I, 21.
233. *Herod's Family Troubles.* Josephus: *War*, I, 22–24, 27–29.
        Mariamne, Salome.
234. *Herod's Political Shrewdness.* Josephus: *War*, I, 19–20.
235. *Herod's Building Enterprises.* Josephus: *War*, I, 21. Cæsarea.
237. *The Temple of Herod.* Josephus: *Antiquities*, XV, 11, 1–6.
238. *Herod's Last Years.* Josephus: *War*, I, 30–33.

MAP WORK

Copy Map No. 27. Kingdom of Herod I (Small *Palestine*).

TOPICS

Herod's Palaces. Mariamne (see Stephen Phillips, *Herod*). Herod
and Jesus. Why is Herod called Great? The book of Enoch. The
Sibylline Oracles.

Chapter XXXII

LABORATORY MATERIAL

240. *Herod's Successors*. Josephus: *War*, II, 1, 2, 6. Archelaus, Herod Antipas.

242. *Paul's Contacts with Roman Rulers*. Acts 23³¹–24²⁷, 26. Herod Agrippa II.

244. *The Siege of Jerusalem*. Josephus: *War*, V, 2–9. Vespasian, Titus.

MAP WORK

Copy Map No. 28. Palestine under Hadrian (Small *Palestine*).

TOPICS

Roman methods of besieging a city. The Jerusalem of Hadrian.

Chapter XXXIII

TOPICS

Jews in Scott's novels. Is Shylock a caricature? The Jews in Russia. Zionism. The status of the Jew in the treaty between the Allies and Poland, June, 1919. The Jew under Nazi rule in Germany, 1933–1935.

III. THE MOUND OF BETH-SHAN

The finest possible view of the successive waves of conquest, settlement and political control that have inundated Palestine is afforded by the excavations at Beisan, ancient Beth-shan. The work on this mound has been done by the University of Pennsylvania, beginning 1921. It has exposed the history of six thousand years with the clarity of a diagram. Because the mound touches our present story at so many points, it has seemed best to place here a digest of the findings, compiled from various issues of the *Museum Journal* of the University of Pennsylvania, from Alan's Rowe's volume, *The Topography and History of Beth-shan* (Univ. of Penn. Press, 1930), and subsequent Bulletins of the American Schools of Archæology.

(For the location of Beth-shan, see Map No. 11.)

Beisan was settled in remote antiquity because of its strategic position. It commands one of the few fords of the river Jordan, the north and south trade lines along the Jordan valley, and the exit westward up the vale of Jezreel to the sea. It lies on one of the oldest caravan routes from Mesopotamia to Egypt. The isolated mound rises on the south bank of the river Jalud and must have been in its day a formidable fortress.

Courtesy of the University of Pennsylvania Museum.

FIG. 163—THE MOUND OF BETH-SHAN. FROM THE SOUTH

Forty-five feet of debris excavated between First Egyptian Period and the present

Thirty-three feet of debris excavated between earliest level and the First Egyptian

— 1921	A.D.	Date when excavation began
— 1918		Conquest of Palestine by British
— 1900		
— 1800		
— 1700		
— 1600		
— 1500		Period N. SECOND ARAB AND TURKISH
— 1400		
— 1300		
— 1200		
— 1100	1187 / 1099	Period M. CRUSADERS
— 1000		
— 900		Period L. FIRST ARAB
— 800		
— 700	636	
— 600		
— 500		Period K. BYZANTINE
— 400		
— 300	330	
— 200		
— 100	A.D.	
— 1		Period J. GRÆCO-ROMAN
— 100	B.C.	
— 200		
— 300		
— 400	302	Period H. SCYTHIAN, BABYLONIAN, PERSIAN, GREEK (Early Iron III)
— 500		
— 600	627	
— 700		Period G. HEBREW, ASSYRIAN (Early Iron II)
— 800		
— 900		
— 1000		
— 1100	1167	Period F. PHILISTINE (Early Iron I)
— 1200		Period E. SECOND EGYPTIAN, HEBREW JUDGES
— 1300	1313	
— 1400	1447	Period D. EXODUS, CONQUEST (Late Bronze)
— 1500	1501	Period C. FIRST EGYPTIAN
— 1600		
— 1700		
— 1800		Period B. HYKSOS (Middle Bronze)
— 1900		
— 2000		
— 2100		
— 2200		
— 2300		
— 2400		Period A. EARLY BRONZE
— 2500		
— 2600		
— 2700		
— 2800		
— 2900		
— 3000		
— 3100		
— 3200		Period A. CHALCOLITHIC
— 3300		
— 3400		
— 3500		
— 3600		
— 3700		
— 3800		Period A. NEOLITHIC
— 3900		
— 4000	B.C.	

NOTE.—The last three cultural periods are all grouped under Period A because separately they are not in this case historically significant. The date of the lowest excavated stratum is purely conjectural and may be a thousand years later than is here suggested.

Reading the records of the mound from the bottom upwards, in the order in which the deposits were laid down, the results are as follows:

PRE–HISTORIC.   25,000(?)–4000(?)

The excavators have found nothing that falls within this period, and therefore are not responsible for the statements in this paragraph. But from discoveries of human remains in a Galilee cave twenty-eight miles north of Beth-shan and of others in a cave near Athlit thirty-two miles west, it seems probable that if Beth-shan were wholly excavated to bed rock evidences of extremely early human occupation would be found. The nine Athlit skeletons, all solidly embedded in limestone breccia, have been definitely classified as a variety of Neanderthal man, in the Middle Paleolithic or Mousterian culture, which geologists date at 25,000 B.C. or higher. Later cultures have also been unearthed not far away, reaching down to historic times. But confirmation of this conjectural earliest occupation of Beth-shan awaits further excavation.

PERIOD A.   4000(?)–2000 B.C.

Grouped in this period are eight separate levels of occupation. The lowest settlement numbered XIX by the excavators was found on a level platform of red earth falling abruptly away at the edges. This floor contained pits about ten feet across and from five to ten feet deep, evidently once roofed over with matting and used for shelter. Flint implements and rough pottery were also found.

At the lowest building level, XVIII, perhaps about 3500 B.C., traces of walls of plano-convex brick appear.

At level XVI, approximately 3000 B.C., copper first occurs, and the earliest example of a habitable building.

Levels XV to XIII, covering a thousand years of occupation, are rich in flint implements. Buildings are small and insignificant. The data point to the transition from the Early Bronze period to Middle Bronze and warrant the terminal date of about 2000 B.C.

PERIOD B.   HYKSOS, 1900–1570

In the two levels XI and X, unmistakable Hyksos pottery appears and characteristic Hyksos burials beneath the house floors. Interments were in jars, some showing the bones of infants but most showing adults, two or three together, with alabaster vases, copper daggers and occasionally scarabs. This period corresponds with that of the Hebrew Patriarchs beginning with Abraham.

PERIOD C. FIRST EGYPTIAN, 1501–1447 B.C.

The excavators have uncovered two temples of this period: (1) a southern temple built of brick on stone foundations and dedicated to "Mekal, the Lord of Beth-shan." A stela of this god was found with an inscription in Egyptian hieroglyphics. (2) A northern temple dedicated to his female counterpart, a serpent deity. The southern temple, remodeled after 1479 B.C. by Thutmose III, probable Pharaoh of the Oppression, is a combination of a Canaanite "high place," in the standing stones of which the Baal resided, and an Egyptian temple with altars and a human image of the god. The citadel was provided with a double wall and at least three great towers.

PERIOD D. EXODUS–CONQUEST PERIOD, 1447–1313 B.C.

This period, so important in Israelitish history, comprises the reigns of Amenhotep II (1447–1420), probable Pharaoh of the Exodus; Thutmose IV (1420–1411); Amenhotep III (1411–1375), and Akhnaton (1375–1358), in whose reigns the Tel el-Amarna tablets were written and the conquest of Canaan was begun by Joshua; the little Pharaohs at the end of the eighteenth dynasty and the first two of dynasty nineteenth, Horemheb and Ramses I.

The excavations have uncovered a fine temple of Amenhotep III dedicated to Ashtoreth of the Two Horns and to the god Mekal. In the city the Pharaoh maintained a garrison of Sardinian mercenaries from the Carmel region to protect it against the Khabiri (Hebrews), Hittites, and others. Mention of this garrison is made in a Tel el-Amarna tablet from the king of Jerusalem, but no letter has been found from the "king" of Beth-shan.

During the weakening of Egypt's foreign policy under Akhnaton, the old fortress of Thutmose III passed out of Egyptian control, and remained out till the reign of Seti I.

PERIOD E. SECOND EGYPTIAN—HEBREW, JUDGES, 1313–1167 B.C.

Seti I (1313–1292) reconquered Palestine in the first year of his reign and erected a fort and a temple in Beth-shan. His stela found here tells of repelling an invasion from east of Jordan. He was making a drive against the Hittites of the north but turned aside to secure this important fortress on his flank. Ramses II (1292–1225), his son, continued campaigns against the Hittites. In Beth-shán he renewed the citadel and built two temples which continued in use till the times of the Philistines. He also set up a stela beside his father's in the ninth year of his reign (1283 B.C.), boasting of his military prowess. The stela does not mention Israelites.

Ramses III (1198–1167 B.C.) is represented by a statue of himself. With the aid of mercenaries he repulsed an invasion of Ægean peoples in 1193 B.C. in Egypt, and again when they overran Syria and Palestine he defeated them not far from Beth-shan. In 1187 B.C. his soldiers set up this statue in the temple of Beth-shan. A group of dated records found in situ shows that the town remained in Egyptian hands practically from 1313 to 1167 B.C.

PERIOD F.   PHILISTINE DOMINATION, 1167–1000 B.C.

At the death of Ramses III (1167 B.C.) the Mediterranean mercenaries took over the Beth-shan fortress for themselves. Egyptian power

From Olmstead: History of Palestine and Syria.

FIG. 164—TEMPLE OF ANATH BUILT BY RAMSES II AT
BETH-SHAN

Restoration. The view is to southeast. The Pylon and Corridor are to the
right.

now wanes and the Hittites are giving way before a new invasion of the Ægean peoples from Crete and southern Anatolia. These peoples are now called Philistines. About 1080 B.C. the garrison at Beth-shan amalgamated with the incoming hordes of their fellow countrymen. These Philistines were therefore in firm possession of the fortress when they defeated Saul and Jonathan at the battle of Mt. Gilboa about 1020 B.C. It was on the walls of this town that the bodies of the Hebrew king and his son were hung.

In this level have been found statues and various cult objects of the goddess Ashtoreth. Her temple has been unearthed, a rectangular building about 75 by 60 feet, erected by Ramses II and used continuously through this period. This is undoubtedly the "house of the Ashtoreth" mentioned in I Sam. 31[10] within which was hung Saul's armor. The second of the temples built by Ramses II was dedicated to the corresponding male deity whom the Philistines called Dagon. According to I Chron. 10[10] they fastened up in this temple the head of Saul. The wooden roofs of these temples were supported on two stone columns with palm tree capitals, as was often the case in Egypt. The local Syrians probably regarded them as Mazzebahs or sacred standing stones, and worshiped them accordingly. It was the worship of these posts, whether stone or wood (Asherah) that seduced the Israelites as so often recounted in the Bible.

PERIOD G. HEBREW, ASSYRIAN, 1000–627 B.C.

About 1000 B.C. David conquered the Philistines and destroyed Beth-shan. The remains show that the entire Egyptian-Philistine building was destroyed by a great conflagration. Everywhere the mud-brick walls were baked red in the terrific heat, especially in the northern portion where the oil and grain were stored. Here the debris had filled corridors and rooms to a depth of over three feet. Following the Hebrew rebuilding, the city was captured by Shishak, of Egypt, in 926 B.C.

PERIOD H. SCYTHIAN, BABYLONIAN, PERSIAN, GREEK, 627–302 B.C.

No special evidence has been obtained of settlements during the later periods of Hebrew history. The fortress shared no doubt the general fortunes of Palestine. The Scythians swept through the country and conquered Beth-shan in 627 B.C. In and over the ruined fortress walls were found the ruins of their occupation, a group of small houses crowded together without system. The presence of the descendants of these settlers nearly three hundred years later probably suggested to the Greeks the name Scythopolis, which they gave to the place. The curtian had been rung down on the glories of the old Semitic Beth-shan.

PERIOD J. GRÆCO-ROMAN, 302 B.C.–330 A.D.

After Alexander's conquest of Palestine, Ptolemy, son of Lagos, rebuilt this town. The earliest evidences are two fragments of columns belonging to a great temple on the summit, and a hoard of silver coins all of Ptolemy Soter I, 323–285 B.C. For some reason this building was not completed till Roman times. The columns were fifty-one inches in diameter with Corinthian capitals, all in coarse white marble on basalt foundations. A garlanded head of Bacchus from the frieze suggests that the temple was dedicated to that divinity. In or in front of the temple stood a gigantic white marble statue of Bacchus or some Roman emperor; it must have been at least twenty-five feet high. only two toes and a finger joint have been found. No doubt the figure was broken up to make lime.

By 198 B.C. Palestine passed to the control of Antiochus III of Syria. In 108 B.C. Beth-shan was betrayed to John Hyrcanus and the Jews held it till Pompey came in 64 B.C. In 57 B.C. it was rebuilt by the Roman proconsul, Gabinius, who probably also erected the theatre and hippodrome to the south of the mound. Beth-shan now became very prosperous, the chief of the ten independent cities of the Decapolis. Irrigation made possible the wide cultivation of flax, renowned throughout the Roman world. Its population was at this time greater than Jerusalem. Jesus and his disciples must frequently have passed through its streets, especially on their journeys to and from Jerusalem via Perea. During the Jewish revolt, Vespasian stationed in Bethshan the V and X legions.

Beth-shan was one of the last Palestinian cities to give a home to Christianity, which it did at the end of the second century. The faithful suffered severely in the persecutions under Diocletian (245–313 A.D.). The martyrdoms took place probably in the hippodrome. At the end of the persecutions the new religion spread rapidly. In 325 the city was of sufficient importance to send its bishop, Patrophilus, to the famous council at Nicæa.

PERIOD K. ⸆ BYZANTINE, 330–636 A.D.

This period marks the height of Byzantine splendor in Beth-shan. St. Eusebius was exiled to Scythopolis in 365 A.D. for refusing to take part in the condemnation of Athanasius. Under his influence the city became a great monastic centre and produced from time to time men famous in the annals of the Church. The Christians now built a magnificent church on the summit of the hill, using the material of the old pagan temple. The great drums of the columns and their huge Corinthian capitals were used as filling material for the platform. The church was a regular Roman basilica with central nave and aisles; across the western façade, a narthex; at the east end a small semi-circular apse containing a high altar. The nave was paved with white marble squares, the side aisles with elaborate colored mosaics, and the walls were covered with colored glass mosaics. The interior was embellished with rose, green, and white marble columns. The roof was of wood with terra-cotta tiles. The entire top of the acropolis was reserved for ecclesiastical buildings.

In 361, when the emperor Julian instituted persecutions, a mob looted and burned the church, scattered the bones of Bishop Patrophilus and used his skull as a lamp. Portions of the walls may have been overthrown by the earthquake of 362, but the city recovered. The old church was superseded by another built on a circular plan. The narthex and apse of the old church were preserved and the rotunda was laid out between the two. This was one of the largest and finest of its era. The eight columns of the colonnade were of verde antique with Corinthian capitals of white marble. A dome open at the top surmounted the whole, one hundred feet in diameter. This building remained intact until 636 A.D., when the Arabs overthrew the Byzantine power.

PERIOD L.   FIRST ARAB OCCUPATION, 636–1099 A.D.

The Byzantine church was used as a mosque until earthquakes overthrew it. By the year 784 the plan of the church was wholly obliterated by the regularly laid out streets and walls of an Arab town. This new town utilized the old Egyptian gate at the northwest corner as the sole entrance. The ancient name of the town had survived among the natives and now came again into universal use under the form Beisan.

During the siege by the Arabs in 636 the inhabitants as an additional measure of defense cut the irrigation ditches on the plain west of the town, thus permitting the water to spread over the fields. After the conquest the Arabs made no effort to repair the damage, and gradually a vast pestilential swamp took the place of the rich lands. Thus a new enemy was introduced, the malarial mosquito, which played a more fatal and decisive part in its subsequent history than any human element. For this reason the town never again grew to any importance.

Period M. Crusaders, 1099–1187 a.d.

The Crusaders, recognizing the importance of the hill for defensive purposes, projected a great fortress here and laid the foundation of the northwest corner. This was done in the early years of the twelfth century. The knight in charge was Adam, Lord of Bethune in France, an ancestor of King George V. He took the title "Lord of Beisan." His buildings included fortifications, living quarters, refectory, kitchens and bakery. Cooking utensils have been found. But malaria drove the Crusaders out. They went to the summit of the hill some miles to the north and built their fortress "Belvoir." The small garrison left at Beisan surrendered to Saladin in 1183. While the abandonment of Beisan was a great tactical mistake since it left the main gate open, the mistake was caused not by stupidity but by mosquitoes.

Period N. Second Arab and Turkish, 1187–1918 a.d.

In 1192 Saladin restored the city. In 1265–8 the Crusaders destroyed Beth-shan during the invasion by Beibars, Mameluke Sultan of Egypt. All through the middle ages and into the nineteenth century malaria desolated its population until the town became a mere group of tiny hovels about forty in number, inhabited by an enervated people, a mixture of every race, without skill or incentive to cultivate their crops and forced to turn for a living to nefarious practices.*

In 1918 Palestine was wrested from the Turks and Beth-shan was captured by British cavalry on September 20. With the new government, prosperity began to increase. The population in 1930 was about 2000. At the present time scientific projects are under way to drain the marshes and restore a vast area to the cultivation of grain, flax, and fruits. The caravan routes still cross the Jordan by the fords and pass through the town. With peace, health, energy, and good government Beth-shan will once more find itself as a great city.

* Reports by Seetzen, German explorer, 1806; Burckhardt, Swiss traveller and orientalist, 1912; De Bertou, French surveyor, 1839; Robinson, American orientalist, 1850, who reported a population of about 500.

IV. THE PATRIARCHAL PERIOD

For two or three generations past, the literary critics of the Bible have felt that the Hebrew patriarchs were not historic persons but rather idealized portraits of mythical ancestors created by the prophets as vehicles of religious teaching. But in these days archæology has forced us to admit that the older scholars were wrong. We are beginning to discover that Genesis 12–50 is full of historical material. These narratives now appear to stand to the later history of the Hebrews much as the Aegean culture stood to the Hellenic. Just as Troy, Mycenæ and Knossos were thought by the mid-nineteenth century to have been created by the imagination of Homer but now are proved to be actual cities with a history that fits into the demands of the Iliad and the Odyssey, so the alleged mythical character of Abraham suddenly takes on reality as the spade reveals Palestinian and Mesopotamian civilizations that are accurately reflected in the Bible stories and are a necessary preliminary to the history that follows. Among the evidences are the following:

1. Practically all the towns of Palestine mentioned in the narratives of the patriarchs were in existence in the patriarchal age, and there is no mention of cities that we know were founded later. This could not be so if the stories were invented in the ninth or eighth centuries before Christ.

2. The life of the patriarchs, nomadic yet attached to fixed bases, could not have been guessed by late writers. But an examination of mounds shows that the hill country was sparsely settled and that population was concentrated on the costal plains, Esdraelon and the Jordan valley. The patriarchs are said to have ranged just this highland section where there are almost no towns or town cemeteries but many solitary burials of a nomadic people of the patriarchal period. These conditions were not true when the alleged late inventor of the stories wrote.

3. The report that the Jordan valley was well watered and fruitful when Abraham first came, and that a great catastrophe caused a departure of population is corroborated by the evidence. The period of densest population there proves to have been in the Early Bronze age. This could not have been guessed by a late writer but was contemporary fact for the early saga maker.

4. Sodom and Gomorrah situated at the south end of the Dead Sea and now covered by its waters must have been destroyed not later than 1800 B.C. This is proved by the great fortified site of Bab ed-Dra high above the plain—evidently a shrine and festival place for a large sedentary population. The occupation ended abruptly. This matches the Bible story of the destruction of these cities by some cataclysm and fixes the date of Abraham in the nineteenth century before Christ.

5. Some names of the ancestors of Abraham as given in Genesis 10: 21 ff., have been found to be the names of places in the vicinity of Haran in Assyrian times. Those place names were probably derived from more ancient clan names and therefore testify to the historicity of the Biblical personages.

6. The Joseph story, which in its present form is a romantic tale, is witness to the close relation between the Israelites and Egypt in the Hyksos period. The name of a Hyksos ruler was Yakob-har, and of a chancellor, Hur—both recognized as Hebrew.

Such are some of the considerations that show the stories of the patriarchs to be based on historic fact. The sagas themselves were originally transmitted in poetical form and were much later rendered in the prose form given in Genesis. A parallel is the story of Deborah, where the poetical version (Judges 5) and the prose transcription (Judges 4) have both been preserved.

The above is based on Albright: *Archæology of Palestine and the Bible,* pages 129–151.

V. THE CHRONOLOGY OF THE CONQUEST AND PERIOD OF THE JUDGES

The chronology adopted in this book is that of Professor John Garstang and other British scholars, based principally on excavations at Jericho. Garstang's conclusions are very enticing, particularly to those of the general public who would like to see the statements of the Old Testament corroborated. It is easy to feel the enthusiasm with which Sir Charles Marston, for example, has adopted and amplified them in his book, *New Bible Evidence*, Revell, 1934. But the reader should be on his guard. All scholars do not agree with Garstang. Dr. W. F. Albright, Director of the American School of Oriental Research at Jerusalem, and acknowledged to be one of the most brilliant scholars in the field, decides from the evidence found at Bethel that that town was destroyed by the Hebrews somewhere in the thirteenth century before Christ, and consequently decides against the date of 1407 for the destruction of Jericho. (Bulletin of the Amer. Sch., No. 56, Dec., 1934, pp. 9–10.) But it should be added that Albright is heretical also in the matter of Egyptian chronology since he puts the date of the first dynasty in the 29th–28th centuries instead of the 35th of Breasted, and the 52nd of Petrie!

When authorities disagree who shall decide? Nevertheless it seems to the writer that the earlier dates fit the Egyptian history better than the later ones, and do not put too great a tax on the archæological findings in Palestine. Accordingly the following summary of the chronology of the period of the judges is given, condensed from Garstang's book, *The Foundations of Bible History* (Richard Smith, N. Y., 1931).

THE CONQUEST

Joshua's dates as judge may be set at 1407–1377 B.C. This period of thirty years corresponds to the Egyptian apathy under Amenhotep III. The chief opposition to Joshua came from the coalitions headed by Jerusalem in the south and by Hazor in the north as Egyptian vassal cities responsible for peace in their districts. Egypt sent them no help.

The Elders ruled after Joshua's death for a period of ten years, 1377–1367. This coincides with the first part of the reign of the pacifist Akhnaton when, according to the Amarna tablets, the country fell away to the Khabiri.

THE OPPRESSIONS

1. *The Oppression by Cushan, eight years*, 1367–1359 B.C.   This was a Hittite conquest from the north during the latter part of the reign of the pacifist Akhnaton of Egypt.   The period of "rest" that ensued under Othniel, lasting for forty years, 1359–1319, represents the years when Egypt reasserted its ascendency over Palestine in the reigns of Tutankhamen and Horemheb.   Israel was safe from foreign invasion and from chaos, though subject to Egyptian overlordship.

2. *The Moabite Oppression, eighteen years*, 1319–1301 B.C.   The monuments confirm the fact of raids from the east on western Palestine.   In the first year of his reign we know that Seti I (1313–1292) sent an expedition to repel and punish these invaders.   The success of it is recorded on a stela set up by him at Beth-shan and there found. The period of rest that ensued after Ehud's exploit lasted eighty years, 1301–1221 B.C.   This fills the latter part of the reign of Seti I and all of Ramses II (d. 1225 B.C.).   Egypt was strong in Palestine all this time, Ramses II having delivered a crushing blow on the Hittites in 1288 B.C. and prevented further trouble from the north, while from Beth-shan he held the Bedouins in check.   His stela also was found in Beth-shan.   See Appendix III.   It was during this period of peace that the northern tribes of Israel made good their foothold in central Palestine and Galilee.

3. *The Canaanite Oppression, twenty years*, 1221–1201 B.C.   Merneptah was now Pharaoh of Egypt.   He claimed on a boastful monument (Figs. 14 and 21) that he had plundered Canaan and devastated Israel.   The context shows that this part of Israel must have been in the central and northern parts of Palestine.   Shortly after that date, 1223 B.C., Merneptah withdrew to fight sea raiders in Lybia and came not again to Palestine.   Groups of these raiders were already active in Syria.   Sisera was one of these raiders who allied himself with Jabin, king of Canaanite Hazor.   The withdrawal of Egypt and the subsequent anarchy in that land were the occasion of the "oppression." The period of rest after Deborah's victory lasted forty years, 1201–1161 B.C.   Egyptian overlordship was again enforced by the first king of the nineteenth dynasty, Set-Nekht (1200–1198), and preserved by Ramses III (1198–1167), the last of the great Pharaohs.   Even the formidable sea invasion by the Philistines and their defeat by Ramses in Phœnician waters did not affect the peace of the Hebrew hinterland.   But after the death of Ramses III, Egypt was no longer suzerain of Palestine.

4. *The Midianite Oppression, seven years*, 1161–1154 B.C. The Midianite raids were made possible by the decay of Egyptian authority and the impoverished condition of Palestine. The "rest" under Gideon, lasting forty years from 1154 to 1114 B.C., was in this instance not due to a reassertion of Egyptian authority, but to the organizing ability of Gideon. Thus for the first time the Hebrew tribes are able unaided to dominate the whole central plateau.

5. *The Ammonite Oppression, one year*, 1111 B.C. After his victory Jephthah maintained his leadership during the years 1110–1105 B.C.

6. *The Philistine Oppression, forty years*, 1105–1065 B.C. This period, ending with the rise of Eli, includes the so-called judgeship of Samson lasting twenty years. The Philistines doubtless kept up the fiction of loyalty to Egypt, but to all intents they were independent until David subdued them.

TRANSITION TO THE MONARCHY

According to the Septuagint, Eli was judge at Shiloh for twenty years, which, according to our theory, would fall at 1065–1045 B.C. Samuel ruled not less than twenty years, 1045–1025; and Saul's reign is estimated at fifteen years, 1025–1010 B.C.

All these Hebrew dates are subject to a possible variation of not more than six years either way; the Egyptian dates may be regarded as fixed.

VI. MAP INDEX OF IMPORTANT GEOGRAPHIC NAMES

References consisting of a letter and a figure are to squares on the large inserted map of Palestine. A simple number refers to the small maps in the map section of the book immediately following.

INDEX

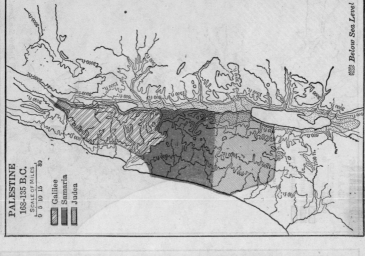

PALESTINE
168-135 B.C.
SCALE OF MILES
0 5 10 15   30

Galilee
Samaria
Judea

Below Sea Level

MAP No. 26—THE MACCABEAN KINGDOM

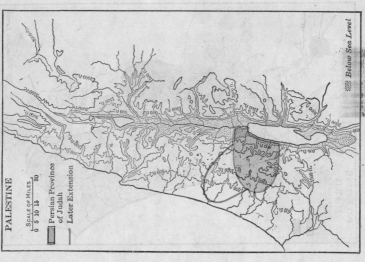

PALESTINE

SCALE OF MILES
0 5 10 15   30

Persian Province
of Judah
Later Extension

Below Sea Level

MAP No. 24—THE TIME OF NEHEMIAH.
445-432 B.C.

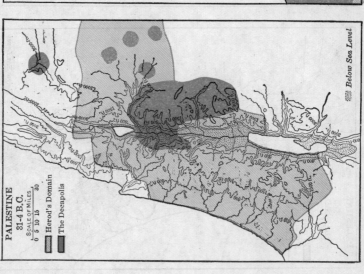

PALESTINE
31–4 B.C.
SCALE OF MILES
0 5 10 15   30

Herod's Domain
The Decapolis

Below Sea Level.

PALESTINE
135 A.D.
SCALE OF MILES
0 5 10 15   30

Phœnicia
Palestina
Arabia Petræa

Below Sea Level.

Map No. 27—THE KINGDOM OF HEROD I   Map No. 28—PALESTINE UNDER HADRIAN

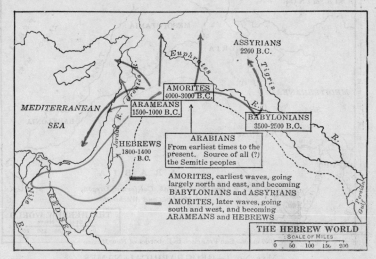

MAP No. 3—SEMITIC MIGRATIONS

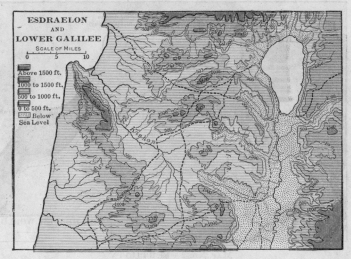

MAP No. 7—CONTOUR MAP OF GALILEE

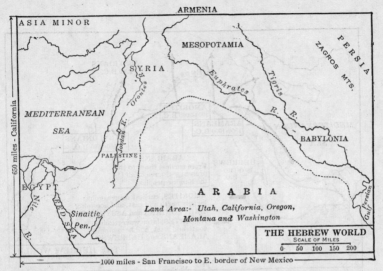

ARMENIA

ASIA MINOR

MESOPOTAMIA

P E R S I A

SYRIA

ZAGROS MTS.

Euphrates

Tigris

650 miles - California

MEDITERRANEAN

SEA

BABYLONIA

PALESTINE

EGYPT

A R A B I A

Land Area:- *Utah, California, Oregon,*
Montana and Washington

Sinaitic
Pen.

RED SEA

Gulf Persian

THE HEBREW WORLD
SCALE OF MILES
0   50   100   150   200

1000 miles - San Francisco to E. border of New Mexico

MAP No. 1—GEOGRAPHICAL NAMES

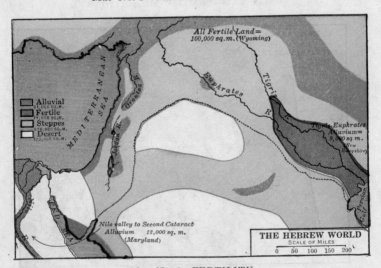

All Fertile Land=
100,000 sq.m.(Wyoming)

MEDITERRANEAN SEA

Euphrates

Tigris

Alluvial
21,000 sq.m.
Fertile
79,000 sq.m.
Steppes
28,000 sq.m.
Desert
173,000 sq.m.

Tigris-Euphrates
Alluvium=
9,000 sq.m.
(New Hampshire)

RED SEA

Nile valley to Second Cataract
Alluvium   12,000 sq. m.
(Maryland)

THE HEBREW WORLD
SCALE OF MILES
0   50   100   150   200

MAP No. 2—FERTILITY

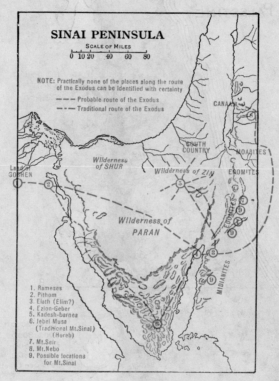

SINAI PENINSULA

SCALE OF MILES

0 10 20 40 60 80

NOTE: Practically none of the places along the route of the Exodus can be identified with certainty

‒ ‒ ‒ Probable route of the Exodus

‒ · ‒ · Traditional route of the Exodus

CANAAN

SOUTH COUNTRY

MOABITES

Wilderness of SHUR

Wilderness of ZIN

EDOMITES

Land of GOSHEN

Wilderness of PARAN

EDOM

MIDIANITES

1. Rameses
2. Pithom
3. Elath (Elim?)
4. Ezion-Geber
5. Kadesh-barnea
6. Jebel Musa
   (Traditional Mt.Sinai)
   (Horeb)
7. Mt.Seir
8. Mt.Nebo
9. Possible locations
   for Mt.Sinai

MAP No. 4—WILDERNESS WANDERINGS

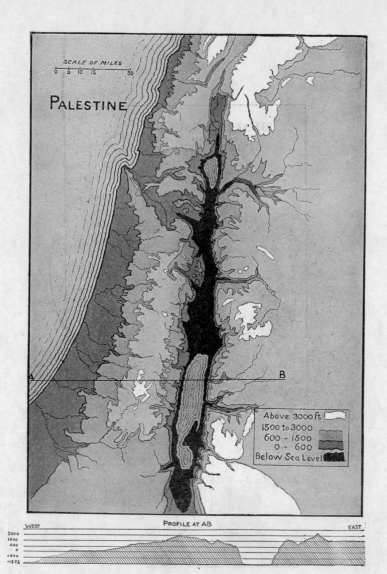

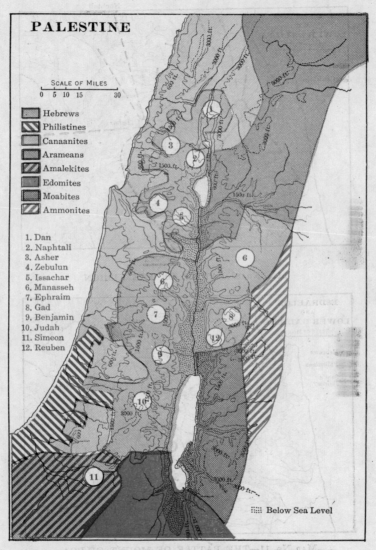

PALESTINE

SCALE OF MILES
0 5 10 15   30

- Hebrews
- Philistines
- Canaanites
- Arameans
- Amalekites
- Edomites
- Moabites
- Ammonites

1. Dan
2. Naphtali
3. Asher
4. Zebulun
5. Issachar
6. Manasseh
7. Ephraim
8. Gad
9. Benjamin
10. Judah
11. Simeon
12. Reuben

::::: Below Sea Level

MAP No. 6—FINAL LOCATION OF THE TRIBES, 1100 B.C.

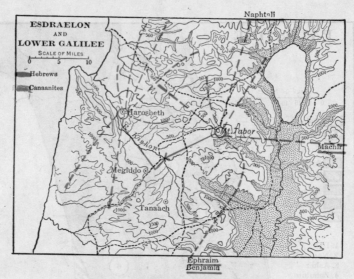

MAP No. 8—BATTLE OF THE KISHON

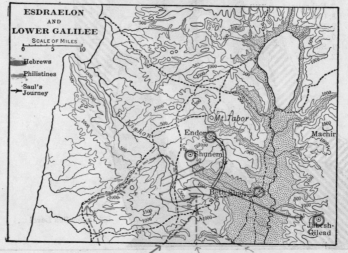

MAP No. 11—THE BATTLE OF MOUNT GILBOA

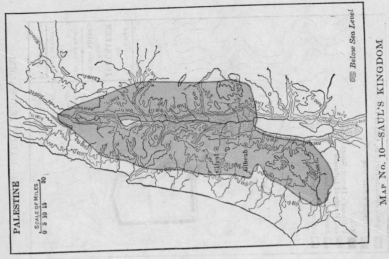

PALESTINE

Scale of Miles
0 5 10 15   30

MAP No. 10—SAUL'S KINGDOM

░░░ Below Sea Level

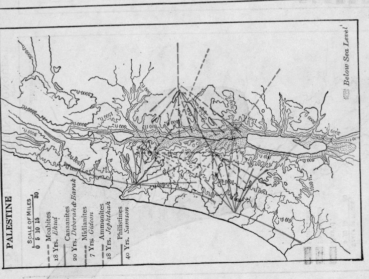

PALESTINE

Scale of Miles
0 5 10 15   30

———— Moabites
      18 Yrs. *Ehud*
- - - - Canannites
      20 Yrs. *Deborah & Barak*
———— Midianites
      7 Yrs. *Gideon*
- - - - Ammonites
      18 Yrs. *Jephthah*
———— Philistines
      40 Yrs. *Samson*

MAP No. 9—WARS OF OPPRESSION

░░░ Below Sea Level

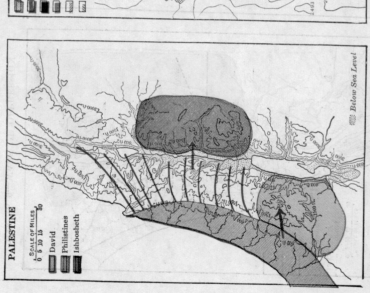

Ophel; Jebusite Fortress, City of David

Solomon's Additions

Millo?

Solomon's Throne-Room and House of Lebanon

Solomon's Palace

Solomon's Temple

Upper City

Lower City

Millo

Mt. Moriah

★ Gihon

En Rogel

CONTOUR MAP
OF
JERUSALEM
AND
SURROUNDINGS

INTERVALS
IN
FEET

SCALE OF FEET
0   500 1000 1500

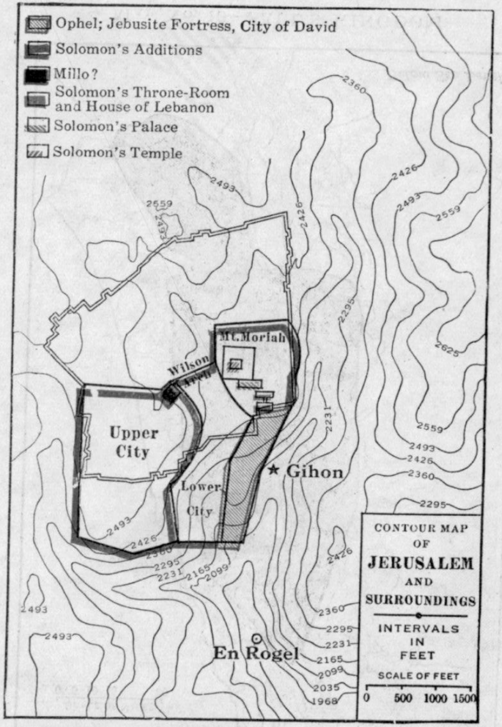

Map No. 14—EARLY JERUSALEM

PALESTINE

SCALE OF MILES
0 5 10 15   30

David

Philistines

Ishbosheth

Below Sea Level

Map No. 12—THE PHILISTINE CONQUEST

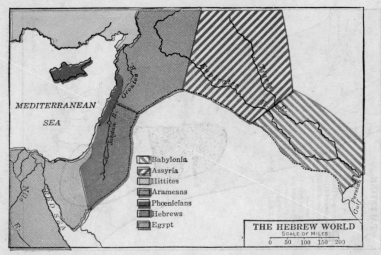

MAP No. 13—EMPIRES, TIME OF DAVID, 1000 B.C.

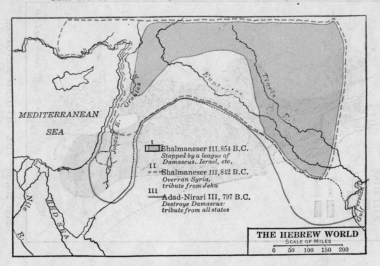

MAP No. 18—ASSYRIAN ADVANCE: WAVES I TO III

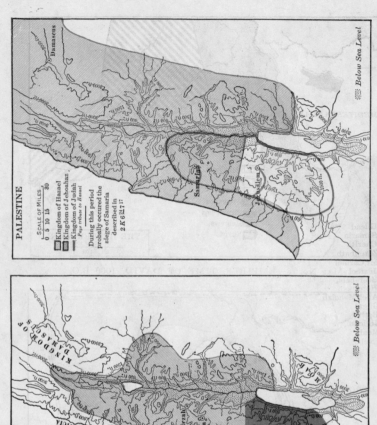

PALESTINE

SCALE OF MILES
0 5 10 15   80

▢ Kingdom of Hazael
▢ Kingdom of Jehoahaz
▢ Kingdom of Judah
Pays tribute to Hazael

During this period
probally occured the
siege of Samaria
described in
2 K 6:14:17

Damascus

Samaria

Jerusalem

Below Sea Level

MAP No. 17.—THE SYRIAN DOMINATION,
810 B.C.

PALESTINE
937 B.C.

SCALE OF MILES
0 5 10 15   80

▢ Israel
▢ Judah

PHOENICIA

KINGDOM OF DAMASCUS

Tirzah
Shechem

PHILISTIA

Below Sea Level

MAP No. 15.—THE DIVIDED KINGDOM

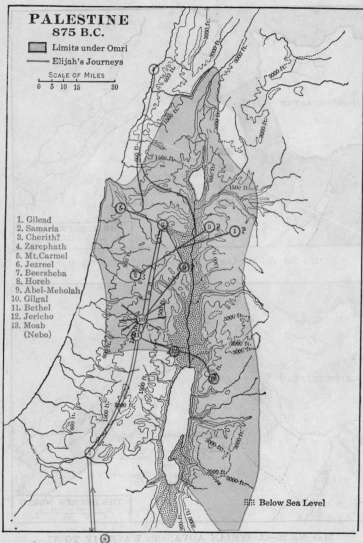

PALESTINE
875 B.C.

▨ Limits under Omri
— Elijah's Journeys

SCALE OF MILES
0   5 10 15   30

1. Gilead
2. Samaria
3. Cherith?
4. Zarephath
5. Mt. Carmel
6. Jezreel
7. Beersheba
8. Horeb
9. Abel-Meholah
10. Gilgal
11. Bethel
12. Jericho
13. Moab
    (Nebo)

⁙ Below Sea Level

Map No. 16—THE KINGDOM OF OMRI AND AHAB

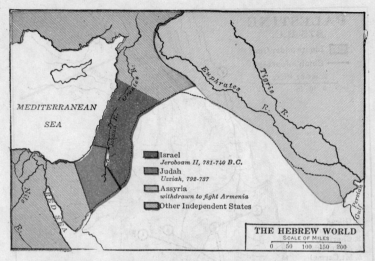

MAP No. 19—ISRAEL'S INDIAN SUMMER, 745 B.C.

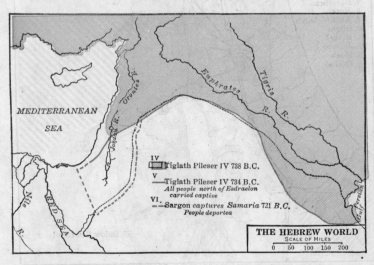

MAP No. 20—ASSYRIAN ADVANCE: WAVES IV TO VI

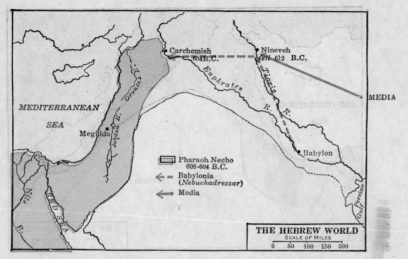

MAP No. 21—THE BREAK-UP OF ASSYRIA, 612-604 B.C.

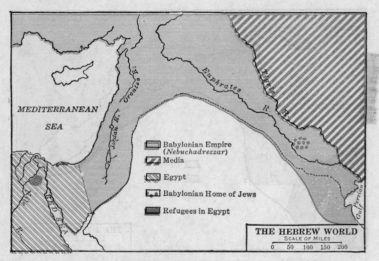

MAP No. 22—THE BABYLONIAN CONQUEST, 586 B.C.

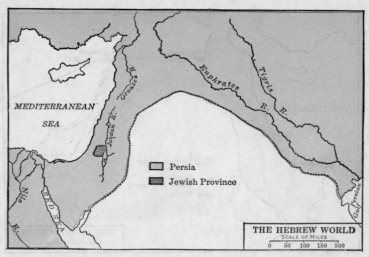

MAP No. 23—THE PERSIAN EMPIRE, 525 B.C.

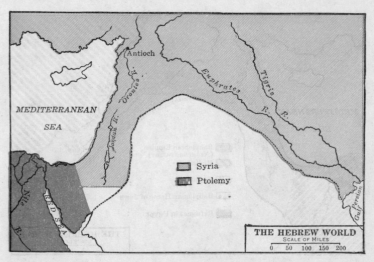

MAP No. 25—THE SYRIAN CONQUEST, 198 B.C.